A Behavioural Theory of Economic Development

A Behavioural Theory of Economic Development

The Uneven Evolution of Cities and Regions

Robert Huggins and Piers Thompson

Great Clarendon Street, Oxford, OX2 6DP,
United Kingdom

Oxford University Press is a department of the University of Oxford.
It furthers the University's objective of excellence in research, scholarship,
and education by publishing worldwide. Oxford is a registered trade mark of
Oxford University Press in the UK and in certain other countries

First Edition published in 2021

Published in the United States of America by Oxford University Press
198 Madison Avenue, New York, NY 10016, United States of America

British Library Cataloguing in Publication Data
Data available

Library of Congress Control Number: 2020944368

ISBN 978–0–19–883234–8

DOI : 10.1093/oso/9780198832348.001.0001

Printed and bound by
CPI Group (UK) Ltd, Croydon, CR0 4YY

To Angela, from Rob
and
To Wenyu, from Piers

Contents

List of Figures

List of Tables

1
Introduction

Behaviour and the Development Problem

1.1 The Motivation and Rationale for the Book

This book is motivated by a belief that theories of economic development can move beyond the generally known factors and mechanisms of such development, with the aim being to analyse deeper and more fundamental causes of uneven development. In particular, influences such as innovation, entrepreneurship, knowledge, and human capital are widely acknowledged as key levers of development and are essentially some of the major components underlying Schumpeter's (1934) enduringly influential book on 'The Theory of Economic Development'. However, what are the sources of these factors, and why do they differ in their endowment across places? Principally, this book seeks to theoretically argue and to empirically illustrate that differences in human behaviour across cities and regions are a significant deep-rooted cause of uneven development. Fusing a range of concepts relating to *culture, psychology, human agency, institutions*, and *power*, it proposes that the uneven economic development and evolution of cities and regions within and across nations are strongly connected with the underlying forms of behaviour enacted by humans both individually and collectively.

Integrating theoretical and empirical analysis, this study addresses a clear intellectual gap in terms of making sense of the components and elements that lead to long-term differentials in economic development, particularly at the city and regional level. Following Nelson and Winter's (1982) landmark publication *An Evolutionary Theory of Economic Change*, the process and dynamics of economic development are widely acknowledged to pursue evolutionary pathways resulting from particular forms of individual and organizational behaviour. However, both 'traditional' and so-called 'alternative' theories of economic development continue to pay little attention to the role of human behaviour in shaping economic evolution and change, particularly within a spatial context (Reinert et al., 2016). This is surprising given that human behaviour and the urban and regional economies in which

A Behavioural Theory of Economic Development: The Uneven Evolution of Cities and Regions. Robert Huggins and Piers Thompson, Oxford University Press (2021). © Robert Huggins and Piers Thompson.
DOI: 10.1093/oso/9780198832348.003.0001

individuals are situated are fundamentally intertwined. The problem for scholars and policy analysts is that such behaviour does not easily fit into existing economic frameworks (Granovetter, 2017).

Urban and regional development theory is largely rooted in explanations based on the location, agglomeration and organization of firms, industries, and capital. While the field of economics has begun to embrace behaviourism, economic geography appears to have largely adhered to Sauer's (1941: 7) contention that 'Human geography…, unlike psychology and history, is a science that has nothing to do with individuals but only with human institutions or culture'. As Pred (1967) pointed out some years later, divorcing culture or institutions at the spatial level from the behaviour of individuals is logically a contradiction, since individual behaviour necessarily contributes to the formation and differences in these cultures and institutions. Indeed, the formation and subsequent outcomes of individual or collective behavioural action, or what can be termed human agency, are a central feature of our thesis, and one of the intellectual contributions it seeks to make is to provide a greater and more systematic understanding of the role of individual and collective behaviour in determining urban and regional development outcomes.

Given a world of finite and limited resources, coupled with a rapidly growing population—especially in cities and urban regions—human behaviour, and the expectations and preferences upon which it is based, would appear to be central for understanding how notions of development may change in coming years. In other words, the 'prosperity' associated with 'development' may come in different forms as values evolve, challenges change, and new opportunities emerge (Jackson, 2017). New economic and social frameworks are likely to form to address this evolution, especially frameworks based on understanding micro-level behaviour, and a key argument within this book is that the city or region in which individuals are situated will be deeply connected with their economic behaviour. Essentially, cities and regions shape behaviour, which itself subsequently impacts upon the economic development fortunes of these places, especially over the long term.

An underlying rationale of this approach is to address the fact that uneven development across cities and regions is a global phenomenon (Prager and Thisse, 2012), with the world now witnessing what Myrdal (1957) presciently described as the 'drift toward regional economic inequalities'. In general, the historical evolution of cities and regions tends to be a story of gradually growing economic divergence across territorial boundaries, and the emergence of a limited number of urban and regional superpowers. In the Britain of 1891, for example, the region of Wales generated economic output per capita that equated to 96.2 per cent of the national average; similarly, in the

East Midlands output per capita was equal to 96.4 per cent of the British average (Crafts, 2004). By 2017, output per capita in Wales was only 72.2 per cent of the average, and 79.3 per cent of the average in the East Midlands. By contrast, London's output per capita increased from 150.4 per cent in 1891 to 177.3 per cent in 2017, with regions in close proximity to the capital seeing similar rates of economic development.

Such evolutionary trends can also be observed elsewhere, and in some cases the speed of divergence has become ever more rapid. For example, in the United States the rise of an elite band of superstar cities, including New York, San Francisco, and Los Angeles, is fast becoming economically decoupled from cities and regions elsewhere in the nation, resulting in significantly widening development gaps (Florida, 2017). However, is the economic pre-eminence of these superstar cities assured in the long term? As Jane Jacobs (1961) describes and analyses with such real-world eloquence, when the distribution of power in a city or region becomes restricted to a relatively small number of human agents, the chances are that their long-term economic evolution and development prospects will be harmed. Jacobs (1961) argued that the narrow power base existing in cities such as New York in the 1950s and 1960s was a cause of urban and regional decline, and it is likely that the broadened distribution of power across wider networks of agency within such cities has led to their rejuvenation and heightened rates of economic development.

More generally, we propose that the rise in importance given to cultural values has led to the emergence of a 'new sociology of development' entwining the role of geography with factors relating to individual and collective behaviour (Sachs, 2000). Essentially, human behaviour is fundamental to the social sciences in terms of understanding what people do, where and why they do it, and the costs and benefits of this behaviour. In order to understand 'aggregate' differences in socio-economic activity and performance, it is informative to explore how these differences stem from the experiences and actions of individual and group actors.

Theoretically, we seek to build on conceptualizations relating to the geographical political economy of a city or region in terms of the role of agency and bounded determinacy (Pike et al., 2009). Nevertheless, the book argues that, although the geographical political economy approach seeks to understand how human agency may be incorporated into an understanding of urban and regional development, it has had less to say about the causes of differing behaviours within often similar spatial environments, which is a gap we seek to address. As Amin and Thrift (2017) argue, human behaviour comes from a meeting of the minds and bodies of individuals and the machines and matter that form the 'daily sociality' provided and formed by the urban and regional environment. It is precisely this relationship between such human behaviour and the spatial environment that we aim to explore and analyse.

1.2 Behaviour and the Development Problem

Although growing inequalities can be observed across cities and regions within and across many nations (Florida, 2017), the search for equality is likely to be elusive and in many ways futile. Instead, the quest should be for 'equity' within and between cities and regions, which comes in the form of fairness in terms of access to opportunities and the capability and capacity for individual development, self-efficacy, and enhancement regardless of location. In order to consider issues of equity and equality, economic development theory—in particular urban and regional development theory—has been largely dominated by downstream perceptions based on explanatory factors relating to resources and capital and their allocation, as well as patterns of economic structure and the configuration of economic systems (Capello and Nijkamp, 2009). However, variations in economic performance are often not possible to explain through differences in traditional inputs such as labour and capital, even when accounting for human capital and knowledge production (Obschonka et al., 2015). Furthermore, economic growth does not necessarily result in 'good development', with low-quality growth manifesting itself through increased economic and social inequality (Stiglitz, 2013). More generally, while there has been some recent recognition that behavioural and cultural influences have a role to play in development processes, they have not been systematically considered, despite these influences potentially having a profound effect on the type of development sought and attained.

In terms of existing scholarly recognition, the role of institutions in fostering or constraining development is increasingly acknowledged (Rodríguez-Pose, 2013), as well as three key interrelated concepts—culture, psychology, and agency—that provide a basis for establishing a framework facilitating an explanation of how behavioural factors interact and result in development differentials across cities and regions (Huggins and Thompson, 2019). In essence, behavioural theories of development are rooted in the relationship and interplay between cultural and psychological factors, with institutions acting as a moderator between intended and actualized behaviour. Such actualized behaviour comes in the form of the human agency impacting upon urban and regional development outcomes. Furthermore, the nature of agency and institutions in a city or region will be dependent upon the role and forms of existing power and the extent to which this is distributed through particular networks that influence evolutionary patterns of development (Huggins and Thompson, 2019).

Given these scholarly advances, in recent years there have been moves toward a (re)turn to addressing the role of human behaviour in determining urban and regional development outcomes. In particular, psychocultural behavioural patterns may provide a basis for understanding the type and nature of human agency within cities and regions (Huggins et al., 2018). Furthermore, such agency is based on a rationality that is likely to be spatially bounded and intrinsically linked to the nature, source, and evolution of institutions and power. Given this, an integration of human behavioural aspects into urban and regional development theory offers significant potential for exploring and explaining long-term evolutionary patterns of development.

1.3 The Fundamentals of Behaviour and Development

As a way of sketching the fundamental issues and concepts relating to the role of human behaviour in fostering or hindering development, the rest of this chapter summarizes some of the arguments and findings in the remainder of this volume. Initially, Chapter 2 illustrates that the roots of behavioural differences across cities and regions are co-determined by two key factors, namely, socio-spatial culture and personality psychology. It is the interaction of these two factors that forms the behavioural intentions of individuals. Socio-spatial culture refers to the broader societal traits and relations that underpin places in terms of prevailing mindsets and the overall way of life within these places (Huggins and Thompson, 2015a). Personality psychology refers to one of the predominant paradigms in behavioural psychology for understanding and measuring differences in personality traits across individuals (McCrae and Terracciano, 2005). It is proposed that there is a relationship between socio-spatial culture and the aggregate personality psychology within cities and regions that is interactive and interdependent.

The interaction between psychological and cultural elements forms the basis of the spatially bounded psychocultural behavioural footprint of a city or region. However, this does not immediately lead to certain forms of behaviour or agency, but more to the 'intentions' of individuals to behave in a particular way. Therefore, it is argued that the combination of personality psychology at the individual level and the socio-spatial culture of a city or region in which an individual is located co-determines the intention to behave in a particular manner. Institutions, however, may constrain or incentivize particular intentions, but also mould and enable habits, preferences, values, and actions. In essence, people create social systems, and these systems then organize and influence people's lives (Bandura, 2006). Within a city or region, therefore, the translation of behavioural intentions to actual behaviour will be moderated by an institutional filter based on the underlying incentives and constraints to act in certain ways.

Actual behaviour is expressed through human agency, which can be defined as 'acts done intentionally' to achieve change or to deliberately reproduce previous actions. Therefore, the behaviour of individuals and collectives within cities and regions that is actualized will establish the types of human agency impacting upon the systems and trajectory of development. Furthermore, the level of development across cities and regions will depend on the nature of this human agency.

Existing studies have recognized the influence of institutions in constraining or enabling differing forms of behaviour (Van den Bergh and Stagl, 2003), while accepting the ability of individuals to take intentional, purposive, and meaningful actions (Hodgson, 2006). What is missing, however, is an understanding of how power affects the ability to deploy agency and achieve change, and it is important, therefore, to consider the nature and role of power with regard to agency that influences long-term development. This leads to the proposition that the possession and exercising of power determine the way in which agency influences the evolution and the form of urban and regional institutional filters.

Given the above, a long-term perspective on development should acknowledge that the genetic—encompassing personality psychology—evolution of humans and their cultural evolution are ultimately interactive, that is positive and negative interactions between cultural and biological evolution may occur and give rise to cultural-genetic co-evolution (Van den Bergh and Stagl, 2003). In Chapter 3, we shall see that the interaction between culture and psychology forms part of the complex adaptive systems that shape economic and social outcomes (Martin and Sunley, 2015a). Furthermore, as genetic and cultural factors can be considered co-evolutionary, in the context of urban and regional development outcomes existing theories may have greater explanatory power if more emphasis is given to spatio-temporal dimensions in terms of the relationship between current behaviour and behaviour in the middle or distant future. Drawing on data from the UK and the US, the 'psychocultural life' of cities and regions is examined to understand differing types of behaviour and their relationship with development outcomes. An empirical analysis of cities and regions in the UK identifies and explores three underlying forms of geographic psychocultural behaviour—*Diverse Extraversion, Inclusive Amenability*, and *Individual Commitment*—that are found to be associated with rates of urban and regional development.

As discussed in Chapter 4, urban and regional histories concerning the formation and endurance of local cultures and institutions are central factors mediating the relationship between behavioural intentions and actualized human agency within a city or region. Institutions come in a multiplicity of forms through both formal rules and laws and, perhaps more importantly, informal conventions that either incentivize individuals to seek, or constrain them from seeking, to act out and actualize their initial behavioural intentions. Therefore, these institutions can be conceptualized as a filter through which intentions either flow into behavioural actions or become blocked or at least diluted. Indeed, institutions not only moderate human agency but are also themselves formed by such agency, something that is often neglected in some branches of economic geography, particularly that stemming from an evolutionary perspective (MacKinnon et al., 2009). Studies have highlighted the dangers of path dependence and institutional lock-in, but this does not take into account the endogenous activities that can lead to path creation (Martin and Sunley, 2006). In this sense, to be an agent is to intentionally make things happen by one's actions (Bandura, 2001), and in order to unpack and delineate the forms of agency that potentially impact on urban and regional development outcomes, the field of psychology provides some useful pointers. In particular, the social cognitive theory proposed by Bandura (2001) distinguishes three modes of agency: personal agency in the form of the power to originate actions for given purposes; proxy agency that relies on others to act on one's behest to secure desired outcomes; and collective agency exercised through socially coordinative and interdependent effort.

Bandura's (2001) three forms of agency necessarily occur through a host of differing forms of agent within a city or region, but from the perspective of urban and regional development theory it is useful to identify with more precision the types of agent, agency, and action that are likely to achieve desired (or undesired) results and outcomes. Although a wide range of overlapping forms of agency at differing scalar levels can be considered, Chapter 4 argues that three meta-forms of localized agency are particularly likely to impact on urban and regional development outcomes, namely, entrepreneurial agency, political agency, and labour agency. These forms of agency and agent in a city or region are likely to be a key factor determining the level and types of development occurring. From the perspective of economic development, agents will shape the structure, organization, and dynamics of industry within a city or region. In particular, they will determine: the types of capital—human, physical, knowledge, entrepreneurial, and the like—that are sought and invested in; the form of industrial structure and the range and rate of innovative economic activity; and the nature of industrial organization and dynamics, especially that concerning the governance and clustering of market and non-market economic activity, that is the economic systems of cities and regions, and their evolution. Taking a historic perspective, Chapter 4 indicates how the persistence of local cultures shapes the contemporary systems and dynamics of urban and regional economies.

If the human behaviour found in a city or region shapes its evolutionary development, it is necessary to explore how these behavioural elements interface and interact with more transparent and acknowledged developmental factors in the form of the structure, nature, and organization of firms within an economy, and more broadly the institutions and governance of the political economy (see Chapter 5). Fundamentally, within any city or region the interpersonal social networks formed by key agents establish the framework for the distribution of power, particularly power that impacts upon the evolution and development of the economy. To this end, Chapter 5 is structured around the proposition that the distribution of wealth and welfare creating power within a city or region is a function of the scale and nature of the social networks through which economically and socially beneficial knowledge flows.

Cities and regions that have more inclusive networks of this type are likely to be more advanced and developed, and will also be more equitable in terms of their access to opportunity and ability to partake in a fair urban and regional community. We argue that, across nations, leading urban regions often possess the most inclusive power networks and are also the most equitable. This is quite a controversial suggestion given that such places are usually considered to have the highest levels of inequality, but existing measures of inequality, such as income-based Gini coefficients, mask an understanding of the deeper behavioural considerations of prosperity differences within cities and regions.

Social network theory and analysis indicate that many of the most advanced cities and regions around the globe have relatively flat and open (equal) social networks with regard to developmental factors, while lagging cities and regions tend to be more hierarchical (unequal) and be populated by a relatively limited number of agents operating within elite 'small world' networks (Watts, 1999). Furthermore, engagement in these networks tends to be linked to the underlying personality traits of agents (Burt, 2012), which means that, since more developed regions usually have more agents possessing an 'openness' to their behaviour, they are more likely to have flatter, more inclusive, and equitable networks.

Based on this line of reasoning, there has been a tendency to ignore the probability that not all agency is likely to have the same level of power, with some agents hindered by their position in terms of existing social networks, which may allow elites to capture urban and regional development agendas (Gregson, 2005). In effect, power can be viewed as an instrumental force, which reflects the ability to mobilize others to undertake activities they would not normally consider (Dahl, 1957). However, it can also be viewed in the softer sense of individuals coming together to achieve intended shared goals. It is important, therefore, to consider both perspectives, given that collaborative relations are themselves rarely completely harmonious and equal (Cumbers and MacKinnon, 2011).

As an outcome of these behavioural factors, cities and regions with the most equitable power networks are more likely to evolve as talent centres fuelled by 'brain attraction', with a rich base of knowledge workers, technology, and expertise, and dense and flexible labour markets. Such places will also have a higher propensity for public- and private-sector engagement in innovation, and higher rates of entrepreneurship and associated venture finance. As well as flat social networks, business network formation will be prevalent, coupled with a relatively plentiful opportunity to access entrepreneurial support mechanisms. There is also likely to be strong industrial clustering, especially among firms operating in highly tradable markets. Unfortunately, in cities and regions with inequitable and hierarchical social-power networks the reverse is likely to be true, with the following being manifest: a stagnant and relatively low skills base, compounded by 'brain drain'; weak labour markets; a low density of public- and private-sector engagement in innovation; below-average (national) rates of entrepreneurship and venture finance; and a lack of strong industry clusters. Given that economic-development theory largely points to these factors as being the key drivers of such development, such drivers are themselves shaped by the nature of power networks within and across cities and regions.

1.4 Empirically Testing the Theory

In order to fully examine the association between the nature of concepts such as personality psychology, culture, human agency, and institutions, as well as the causal impact on various factors relating to the economic development of cities and regions, it is necessary to establish an empirical evidence base that assesses the theoretical connections discussed above. To achieve this, Chapters 6–8 quantitatively analyse the nature, source, and co-evolution of behavioural factors within cities and regions and their development capabilities. Chapter 6 empirically investigates the relationship between culture, personality psychology, and institutions at the city and regional level. It recognizes that any relationship between these constructs are likely to be bidirectional, with it being inappropriate to assume that one can be regarded as an independent factor that drives the other (Rentfrow et al., 2009, 2013). Therefore, the analysis examines the particular relationships between each of the three constructs in order to capture evidence on the existence of their intertwined nature.

Chapter 6 tackles issues relating to the requirements for examining culture, psychology, and institutions more broadly. This is achieved through a discussion of each of the constructs in terms of how they have been captured in previous work, for example Beugelsdijk and Maseland (2011) in terms of culture in economics, and Rodríguez-Pose's (2013) discussion of institutions for economic development. The focus here is on the theoretical differences between the three constructs, and having outlined the broad issues that need to be resolved when measuring the three constructs, the chapter further examines existing empirical studies of culture (for example Tabellini, 2010; Huggins and Thompson, 2016), personality psychology (Rentfrow et al., 2015), and institutions (Charron et al., 2014) to critically examine the different available measures of each. The analysis is undertaken both at an urban and regional level using the UK as a case study, but also across nations where formal institutions are likely to play a stronger role. It draws upon data covering regions in Europe for international analysis, while focusing on cultural measures developed at the urban and regional level by Huggins and Thompson (2016) and personal psychology variables from the BBC psychology lab dataset (Rentfrow et al., 2015). Mechanisms such as selective migration are examined to provide evidence of their role in the generation of particular personality psychological profiles, cultures, and formal institutions.

Whereas Chapter 6 seeks to understand the interactions between culture, psychology, and institutional factors, Chapter 7 focuses on explaining how these interactions impact on the agency of individuals in cities and regions. This is accomplished through a focus on measuring agency in its different forms and examining the influence of this agency. Sen's (1985) perspective of agency as a situation whereby individuals are free to undertake activities and pursue particular goals of importance to them is instructive in understanding how agency relates to participation in various activities concerning economic development. There are a number of different measures of agency (Alkire, 2005), which according to Sen (1999) can be distinguished through four dimensions: global or multidimensional; direct control or effective power; well-being and freedom; and autonomy or ability. Such dimensions include components relating to mobility, decision-making, and a sense of self-worth (Jejeebhoy et al., 2010), and power is an important part of the analysis, with many definitions of agency referring to it as the ability to make choices either individually or collectively (Ozer and Bandura, 1990; Bandura, 2000; Alsop et al., 2006).

To address these issues, the analysis undertaken here utilizes measures from the European Social Survey (Kaasa et al., 2010), as well as considering measures such as those associated with self-efficacy, that is the perception of individuals in terms of their capability to pursue particular goals (Bandura, 1997), and the autonomy element of self-determination theory (Ryan and Deci, 2000). These are discussed in terms of understanding some of the fundamental building blocks of agency such as the nature of Human Agency Potential (HAP) and Human Agency Actualization (HAA), and the analysis focuses on the role of cultural values, as well as forms of political, labour, entrepreneurial, and environmental agency (Lee and Peterson, 2000). This facilitates a broader range of urban and regional development measures to be considered, with Chapter 8 focusing more particularly on an analysis of the relationship between agency and the presence of entrepreneurial and innovative activities within cities and regions.

Although entrepreneurial activity is often proxied by new venture creation data, Chapter 8 recognizes broader measures of entrepreneurial activity. This is intended to reflect the fact that entrepreneurial activity is not restricted to small business ownership and new venture creation but may also encompass entrepreneurial agency within larger established businesses and the public sector (Rae, 2010). To account for this broader interpretation of entrepreneurship, data is drawn not only from traditional sources but also from alternatives such as measures based on entrepreneurial orientation (Khandwalla, 1977; Knight, 1997; Miller and Friesen, 1978), In summary, the chapter empirically determines the extent to which agency actually results in economically beneficial entrepreneurship and innovation across cities and regions.

1.5 Modelling and Addressing Behaviour and Uneven Development

Building upon both the theoretical and empirical analysis, in Chapter 9 we establish an extended Behavioural Model of Economic Development encompassing the key elements and relationships that link them in order to provide a more complete understanding of economic development. This is accomplished by considering how constructs can be captured in a compatible manner and exploring the design of an empirical estimation strategy to account for personality psychology, culture, institutions, and agency within an urban and regional economic development model. First, consideration is given as to how economic development may be best captured. This includes assessing measures that have been traditionally utilized such as Gross Domestic Product (GDP) growth (McCann and Ortega-Argilés, 2015), employment (Fratesi and Rodríguez-Pose, 2016), and average income (Rattsø and Stokke, 2014). It also takes into consideration the argument that development needs to account for the needs of the residents of a city or region itself (Pike et al., 2007). This means expanding the discussion to incorporate concepts such as competitiveness (Huggins and Thompson, 2017a) and resilience (Martin, 2012; Martin and Sunley, 2015b), as well as acknowledging that different measures may affect the patterns observed across regions and cities (Cellini et al., 2017). Also, there is a requirement to consider broader measures of development, such as those associated with wider notions of well-being (Frey and Stutzer, 2000; Huggins and Thompson, 2012; Puntscher et al., 2015).

Chapter 9 discusses future developments that are required to extend knowledge concerning the development role played by personality psychology, culture, agency, and institutions from an empirical standpoint. This is achieved through critically examining the empirical analysis undertaken in the chapter, as well as the three preceding chapters, and the measures included within them. In particular, attention is paid to limitations with regard to available data at different levels of spatial aggregation and the timeliness of variables. Methodological issues and potential solutions are discussed in relation to the empirical tools available.

In bringing the book to a conclusion, Chapter 10 seeks to focus on policy and the levers for change, highlighting that uneven economic development across cities and regions is the result of historic long-term evolutionary behavioural processes whereby the psychological, cultural, and economic dimensions of cities and regions continually reinforce each other, for better or worse. In particular, psychocultural behaviour has the potential to be persistent and deeply rooted in previously dominant economic activities, so that its influence is felt many decades later. For example, historically high levels of mining are found to be associated with lower levels of entrepreneurial activity (Glaeser et al., 2015), positive attitudes to collective behaviour in the form of unionism (Holmes, 2006), and preferences against redistribution (Couttenier and Sangier, 2015).

In the context of mature cities and regional economies in advanced nations, there are strong reasons to suggest that the concentration of large-scale traditional industries in these regions has left a lasting psychological imprint on local culture, with selective outmigration resulting in more optimistic and resilient individuals with relatively positive and agentic mindsets seeking new environments that offer new economic opportunities, leaving an indigenous population in the home region that is often lacking in 'entrepreneurial spirit' (Stuetzer et. al. 2016; Obschonka et al., 2017).

As a means of addressing the unevenness resulting from the differing 'spirit'—in other words, psychocultural behaviour—across cities and regions, the mix of political, worker, and entrepreneurial agency will determine the development fates of these places. In particular, entrepreneurs represent key catalysts of change, and throughout history urban and regional transformation has been catalysed by a core group of entrepreneurial agents that have taken a lead in positively evolving the economies in which they are physically situated, with new generations of agent often producing innovations that further push forward the technological frontier set by their predecessors. In mature and less developed urban and regional economies it is all too often the case that these types of agents have migrated to other regions with stronger ecosystems and greater opportunities, or that the underlying psychocultural traits of the region have meant that such agency has not been nurtured in the first instance. This leaves these cities and regions in an economic situation in which they lack a critical mass in the types of industries and sectors through which value and competitiveness can be best achieved.

It is concluded that while the above points to the role of policy in attracting, retaining, and supporting existing agents, the key to renewal and transformation is likely to lie with the nurturing of new indigenous agents. One route, which is necessarily a long-term one, to achieving this is through changes to urban and regional education systems, especially those that seek to provide individuals with the mindsets resembling the 'extrovert' entrepreneurial agents that are considered to be central to resilient urban and regional ecosystems (Martin and Sunley, 2011).

2
Human Behaviour and the Development of Cities and Regions

2.1 Introduction

Theories of urban and regional development are predominately based on explanations concerning the location and structural organization of firms, the types of industries in which these firms operate, and the rates and forms of capital they employ (Gordon and McCann, 2005). However, contemporary economic geography theory has begun to address the role of human behaviour in determining rates of urban and regional development (Huggins and Thompson, 2016, 2019; Lee, 2017; Garretsen et al., 2019). As a result, it is relevant to consider the range of agents that are recognized as important to urban and regional development processes and mechanisms beyond a focus on firms (Pike et al., 2009). Incorporating these multiple elements into a single holistic approach is clearly not without challenges, which arise in terms of integrating different levels of analysis, as well as addressing the differing ontological approaches used to examine systems as complex as urban and regional economies (Pike et al., 2009, 2015; Martin and Sunley, 2015a).

Research examining the association between economic development and behavioural concepts such as culture further highlights the difficulties of separating out the causal impacts of human behaviour at the group level on economic activity (Alesina and Giuliano, 2015). This work takes the approach of linking culture, through changes in preferences, to outcomes. However, to successfully achieve this there is a need not only to identify the relationships that generate and reproduce particular cultural traits but also to isolate the mechanisms behind these relationships. This is consistent with research on the notion of geographical political economy, which emphasizes the importance of plural and interdependent methodological approaches of both a quantitative and qualitative nature (Pike et al., 2009). Nevertheless, while the geographical political economy framework attempts to delve into the role of human agency in urban and regional development processes, it has not unpacked the nature of differing behaviours across spatial environments.

A Behavioural Theory of Economic Development: The Uneven Evolution of Cities and Regions. Robert Huggins and Piers Thompson, Oxford University Press (2021). © Robert Huggins and Piers Thompson.
DOI: 10.1093/oso/9780198832348.003.0002

A behavioural approach to examining development is not, however, strictly 'new' in either comparative economics or what we now term economic geography. Myrdal (1968), for example, takes a behavioural and cultural approach to understanding economic development across Asian economies, in particular the role of religious and social (caste) systems. From the 1960s, there was also an emerging school of behavioural geography largely concerned with identifying the cognitive processes that lead to individuals and communities codifying, reacting to, and recreating their environments (Boal and Livingstone, 1989). Pred (1967), in particular, argued that economic geography and locational distribution patterns are a consequence of the aggregate manifestation of decisional acts made at the individual, group, and/or firm level. This provoked a significant behavioural 'turn' in the field of location studies and economic geography (Philo, 1989). However, subsequent cultural turns in the wider field of human geography triggered the demise of behavioural geography (Strauss, 2008).

Somewhat in contrast, within the field of economics there has been an emergence and resurgence of behavioural and psychological studies and theories that seek to capture and explain the decision-making processes of individuals. In particular, behavioural economists have sought to integrate psychological theories of behaviour as a means of explaining economic action (Camerer and Loewenstein, 2004). Such theories have shown the limits of rational choice theories in explaining economic, as well as social, action and the underlying decision-making processes of individuals in determining such action (Hodgson, 2013). Drawing on Simon's (1982) notion of 'bounded rationality', behavioural economics suggests that the minds of individuals are required to be understood in terms of the environmental context in they have evolved, resulting in restrictions on human information processing due to limits in knowledge and computational capacity (Kahneman, 2003).

Within urban and regional development theory, the rise in prominence concerning the role of cultural values has led to new advances relating to socio-spatial culture and the spatial nature of personality psychology that have sought to address knowledge gaps relating to the role of context and environment in shaping behaviour (Obschonka et al., 2013a; Huggins and Thompson, 2016). From the psychological perspective, Obschonka et al. (2015), for example, draw on the Five-Factor Theory of Personality—the Big Five traits—which is the predominant personality model in contemporary psychological science utilized to explain differences in behaviour across places. Furthermore, scholars have increasingly highlighted the role of agency and associated institutions in fostering urban and regional development, particularly though the welfare effects it generates within and through communities (Bristow and Healy, 2014). As Mokyr (2015) suggests, once institutions are accepted as an important factor in explaining development differences, cultural explanations—in the form of the beliefs and values on which institutions are founded—are unlikely to be far behind.

In this context, the notion of urban and regional development should not be confined to material aspects that are principally related to economic growth and the 'productionist' view of development, but should also incorporate more 'humanistic' aspects, in particular conceptions of well-being (Chang, 2013). Explanations of place-based development at the urban or regional level, therefore, should encompass broader notions concerning how places improve and 'get better' in relation to a wider variety of socio-economic elements (Pike et al., 2007). In other words, urban and regional development should be conceptualized as representing a change for the better for those living and working in particular cities and regions. There is no unique perfect form and such urban and regional development may come in a range of differing forms.

This chapter argues that the roots of behavioural theories of development relate to the interplay between cultural and psychological factors, with institutions playing a moderating role between intended and actualized human behaviour. It proposes that the forms of human agency associated with such behaviour are likely to impact upon urban and regional development outcomes. It introduces the role of power, and how this underpins the means by which agency facilitates institutional change. To connect the arguments made in the preceding sections, it sketches an emergent conceptual behavioural model of urban and regional development, and concludes that urban and regional development theories should seek to engage further with behavioural explanations as a means of understanding long-term evolutionary patterns.

2.2 Psychocultural Behaviour: Socio-Spatial Culture and Personality Psychology

Within strands of the economic geography literature there have been calls to better understand the role of 'microprocesses' on 'macrostructures' within cities and regions, as well as the impact of macrostructures on these microprocesses (MacKinnon et al., 2009). The aim of this section, therefore, is to argue that the sources of behaviour across cities and regions are co-determined by factors that combine microprocesses and macrostructure in the shape of socio-spatial culture and personality psychology. It is further argued that psychocultural evolution is at the heart of changing development outcomes.

The concept of culture generally refers to the way in which people behave, often as a result of their background and group affiliation. Guiso et al. (2006: 23) define it as 'those customary beliefs and values that ethnic, religious and social groups transmit fairly unchanged from generation to generation'. Rather than concerning individual behaviour, it relates to shared systems of meaning within and across ascribed and acquired social groups (Hofstede, 1980). Van Maanen and Schein (1979) suggest that culture can be defined by the values, beliefs, and expectations that members of specific social groups come to share, while Hofstede (1980) refers to it as the collective programming of the mind, which distinguishes one group or category of people from another. As indicated in Chapter 1, socio-spatial culture relates to the broad societal traits and relations that underpin cities and regions through prevailing mindsets and the overall way of life within these locations (Huggins and Thompson, 2015a). It principally constitutes the social structure and features of group life within cities and regions that can generally be considered to be beyond the economic life of such places (Huggins and Thompson, 2016). Fundamentally, therefore, the socio-spatial culture of cities and regions consists of the ways and means by which individuals and groups within place-based communities interact and shape their environment.

Huggins and Thompson (2015a, 2016) establish a model of socio-spatial (or what they also term 'community') culture whereby five component factors are argued to be of principal importance: (i) engagement with education and work—partly drawing on Weber's (1930) enduring notion of the work ethic and attitudes to economic participation; (ii) social cohesion—relating to Durkheim's (1893) notion of mechanical and organic solidarity social cohesion, whereby trait similarities and interdependence among individuals result in a perceived unity, togetherness, and less likelihood of exclusion; (iii) femininity and caring attitudes—relating to Hofstede's (1980) typology of national cultures and the notion of the femininity or masculinity of these cultures, with masculine cultures considered to be more competitive and materialistic than their feminine counterparts, which are more caring and harmonious in their outlook; (iv) adherence to social rules—referring to the acknowledged role of such adherence for coordination purposes (Rodríguez -Pose and Storper, 2006), but also noting that it may constrain creative and innovative behavioural intentions; and (v) collective action—referring to the extent to which cities and regions adopt equity-driven, cooperative action approaches as opposed to more individualistic action approaches (Johnstone and Lionais, 2004).

As indicated above, work on socio-spatial culture has begun to address knowledge gaps relating to the role of context and environment in shaping behaviour (Huggins and Thompson, 2015a, 2016). In related studies it has been found that more open tolerant societies grow faster (Rodríguez-Pose and Hardy, 2015). This openness allows access to more ideas but can also help exploit the knowledge held and developed within cities and regions as more diverse sets of skills become available (Jacobs, 1969; Glaeser, 2002). This suggests that one explanation for persistent differences in the development trajectory of cities and regions is the role that socio-spatial community culture plays. Studies such as Tabellini (2010) have found a connection between culture and institutions and the economic development of regions. Other studies have found a link between community culture and the types of entrepreneurial activity that may be responsible for differing local or regional economic growth rates (Freytag and Thurik, 2007; Huggins and Thompson, 2015a, 2016). Overall, the existing literature suggests the influence of different aspects of culture on behavioural intentions, although this group-level impact ignores the influence of the individual in the formation of these behavioural intentions.

Alongside socio-spatial culture, personality psychology refers to one of the predominant paradigms in behavioural psychology that seeks to understand and measure differences in personality traits across individuals (McCrae and Terracciano, 2005). Within studies of geographical personality the measures normally considered are those associated with the so-called Big Five framework of personality traits, consisting of (i) openness—the tendency to be open to new aesthetic, cultural, or intellectual experiences; (ii) conscientiousness—the tendency to be organized, responsible, and hard-working; (iii) extraversion—an orientation of one's interests and energies towards the outer world of people and things rather than the inner world of subjective experience, characterized by positive affect and sociability; (iv) agreeableness—the tendency to act in a cooperative, unselfish manner; and (v) neuroticism (cf. emotional stability)—a chronic level of emotional instability and proneness to psychological distress, while emotional stability is largely the opposite and concerns predictability and stability in emotional reactions, with an absence of rapid mood changes (Goldberg, 1992).

In parallel with scholarly work in the field of socio-spatial culture, researchers of personality psychology have found that in terms of economic prosperity there is a positive link with openness and extraversion (Rentfrow et al., 2015). Lee (2017) further finds that conscientiousness in England and Wales is positively associated with innovation as captured by patenting activity, while Obschonka et al. (2015) include conscientiousness in their entrepreneurial index, which they find is positively linked to actual entrepreneurial activity.

Although the majority of work on personality psychology has examined the impact of individual personality traits on a variety of outcomes, the idiographic perspective suggests that a more holistic view should be taken (Rentfrow et al., 2013). This idiographic perspective refers to understanding behaviour through a configuration of differing traits, which at a geographical level facilitates an investigation of the extent to which particular configurations of traits occur with some regularity in specific regions (Rentfrow et al., 2013). Certain configurations of traits have been found to be good predictors of developmental outcomes such as achievement at school (Hart et al., 2003); the development of social support networks, and the likelihood of having spells in unemployment (Caspi, 2000); and older-age health outcomes such as the prevalence of strokes and heart disease (Chapman and Goldberg, 2011).

Rentfrow et al. (2013) use a cluster analysis approach to identify three psychological profiles of regions covering the forty-eight contiguous US states: friendly and conventional; relaxed and creative; and temperamental and uninhibited. The friendly and conventional profile is low on neuroticism and openness but high on extraversion, agreeableness, and conscientiousness. The relaxed and creative states have low extraversion, agreeableness, and neuroticism, but are high on openness. The final set of states described as temperamental and uninhibited are low on agreeableness and conscientiousness, and high on neuroticism. These places display strong differences in terms of a variety of political, economic, social, and health outcomes. Economically, the friendly and conventional states are those which are the least successful. More generally, personality psychology traits are found to play an important role not only independently, but in terms of the combinations formed.

Although personality psychology represents a potentially powerful means of explaining the uneven development of cities and regions, it is important to highlight that personality traits in the form of the Big Five are defined without reference to context, that is situation or socio-spatial culture (Almlund et al., 2011). Indeed, in the long term any perspective on development should acknowledge that the genetic evolution of humans, including personality, and their cultural evolution are interactive, with the interaction of cultural and biological evolution giving rise to cultural-genetic co-evolution (Van den Bergh and Stagl, 2003). Such co-evolutionary forces can be related to theories of 'generation' and 'collective memory', or what Lippmann and Aldrich (2016) refer to as 'generational units' in the form of meaningful collectives that move through time with high degrees of self-awareness.

Rentfrow et al. (2015) highlight three routes that may result in personality traits differing across or within regions. These mechanisms act through traditions and social norms; selective migration; and physical environment. In the first of these, the traditions and customs associated with socio-spatial culture generate particular social norms, and in due course these social norms impact upon individuals' attitudes and behaviours (Hofstede and McCrae, 2004). McCrae (1996), for example, indicates that attendance at college has a positive effect on individual openness. Exposure to a more diverse population is also found to be positively associated with greater acceptance and openness (Pettigrew and Tropp, 2006). For instance, it might be expected that urban and regional socio-spatial cultures displaying higher levels of femininity and caring activities may generate social norms focused on looking after and out for others in society. This may alter behaviours and expectations in such a manner that individuals within a city or region become more agreeable.

The second mechanism, selective migration, is also linked to socio-spatial culture, with Jokela (2009), for example, illustrating how creative individuals are more likely to migrate and shape culture in their new locations. In the USA, Rentfrow et al. (2013) suggest that those with greater openness seek out novelty, with states classed as relaxed and creative being settled by self-selecting individuals who are more adventurous. The third mechanism, physical environment, impacts upon individual personality traits in the form of a person's feelings and levels of belonging to a place, which in the long term shape the values and beliefs associated with socio-spatial culture (Van de Vliert, 2009; Huggins and Thompson, 2016). More generally, although particular local cultural traits may attract or deter the inward migration of individuals with certain personality traits, once located within a particular city or region such personality traits will cause cultures to evolve and to potentially reproduce themselves in ways that are likely to have either positive or negative connotations for development. This may be a slow process, but where, for example, cities and regions with more diverse socio-spatial cultures attract individuals of a more extravert nature, this is likely to lead to a greater willingness to try out new ideas and form more extended networks (Glaeser, 2002).

In summary, urban and regional development outcomes can be said to be contingent upon two key behavioural traits, namely, socio-spatial culture and personality psychology. Socio-spatial culture refers to behaviour conditioned by place-based group affiliation, while personality psychology consists of the innately determined nature of individuals that conditions behavioural intentions and outcomes. At the level of the city or region, the relationship between the two can be considered bidirectional, with the underlying personality traits of individuals influencing overall socio-spatial cultural traits, and vice versa. Therefore, it is proposed that:

Proposition 2.1
There is an interactive and interdependent relationship between the socio-spatial culture of a city or region and the aggregate personality psychology of the individuals located in these cities and regions.

The interaction between psychological and cultural factors underpins the spatially bounded psychocultural behavioural footprint of any city or region. However, this footprint does not immediately lead to a particular form of behaviour or agency but to the 'intentions' of individuals to behave in a particular way. In this sense, the behavioural intentions of individuals in a city or region are determined by the existing psychocultural footprint of the place in which they are situated. Such intentions concern behaviour that is planned but is not always actioned due to a range of intervening and mediating factors. Given this, the following is proposed:

Proposition 2.2
The combination of an individual's personality psychology and the socio-spatial culture of the city or region in which they are located determine their intention to behave in a particular manner.

2.3   Behavioural Intentions and the Institutional Filter

Behavioural intentions refer to behaviour that is planned but not necessarily actioned, and are indications of how hard people are willing to try, and how much of an effort they are planning to exert, in order to behave in a certain way (Ajzen, 1991). In general, the stronger the intention to engage in a particular form of behaviour, the more likely should be its performance (Ajzen, 1991). However, this does not make clear the mechanisms through which the strength of intention or ability to perform such behaviour are regulated. One possible explanation is the role of institutions in either promoting or restricting individual behavioural intentions, which subsequently impacts on the nature of actualized behaviour. Institutions are 'the rules of the game' in the form of humanly devised constraints on (or enablers of) certain forms of behaviour (North, 2005). In this section it is proposed that the relationship between behavioural intentions and actualized behaviour is moderated by an institutional filter, which refers to the set of 'rules' that determines behaviour at the urban and regional level. As MacKinnon et al. (2009) highlight, institutions are likely to constrain or incentivize intentions, and also to mould and enable behaviour in the form of habits, preferences, values, and actions. In other words, social systems are created by people, with these systems acting as an organizing and influencing factor on people's lives (Bandura, 2006). In one sense, if culture is the mother, children are the institutions (Harrison and Huntington, 2000), with such institutions having two broad faces: one that incentivizes or constrains behaviour and action; and another that is itself the product of human agency (Lowndes and Roberts, 2013).

If individuals are given a sufficient degree of actual control over their behaviour, they can be expected to carry out their intentions when the opportunity arises, and intentions can be assumed to be the antecedent to actual behaviour (Ajzen, 2002). The institutional filter, therefore, is a determining factor of the level of available control. Van den Bergh and Stagl (2003) outline a number of mechanisms through which institutions impact on the behaviour of individuals (and groups of individuals). As well as including the enabling or constraining of particular forms of behaviour, institutions may select among the diversity of individual behavioural intentions and preferences, with alternative institutions often competing and enforcing norms through rewarding or punishing individuals that do (or do not) follow these norms. These institutions are of particular importance given the acceptance of bounded rather than perfect rationality, since when faced with limited ability and uncertainty, routines and rules guide actors through the mechanisms and processes that lead from intentions to actions and agency (MacKinnon et al., 2009). Given this, the institutional filter can be defined as the humanly devised constraints that structure interaction, covering both formal (de jure)—rules, laws, constitutions—and informal (de facto)—conventions—constraints and their enforcement, which then define the incentive structure of societies and their economies (North, 2005).

Within the literature on institutions two core streams have emerged: that associated with economic and political science (North, 1990); and that drawing on sociology and organizational theory (DiMaggio and Powell, 1983). The former stream concerns institutions shaped by rules, procedures, and agreements, while the latter focuses on the role of individuals as decision-making agents, whereby such decisions are based on heuristics associated with conventions linked to shared cultures. Although some institutions are necessarily fixed across nations, such as law, regulation, and property rights, others may be subject to urban and regional differentiation. Urban and regional institutions can be considered to consist of the underlying rules of the game relating to factors such as the incentive to save and invest; embrace competition, innovation, and technological development; engage in education, learning, or entrepreneurship; and participate in networks. They will also be reflected in the presence and structure of property ownership; and provision of public services (Huggins, 2016). Enabling institutions will take account of urban and regional contextual factors, with complementary institutions developing through repeated interactions. Constraining institutions may limit the directions in which a city or regional economy can develop in the future. Therefore, choices that push places towards the development of a particular set of institutions over another may influence the nature of long-term development.

Rodríguez-Pose and his collaborators (Rodríguez-Pose and Storper, 2006; Farole et al., 2011; Rodríguez-Pose, 2013) have developed a framework of community (which represents a spatially localized notion of institutions) and society (which represents spatially broader institutions) in order to place institutionalist approaches more centrally within urban and regional development theory. In the process, this framework highlights the importance of geographical context when examining institutional models of development. Both community and society are considered to influence development through the expectations and incentives provided to agents (Farole et al., 2011). However, how these effects vary across cities and regions remains little understood but are likely to differ as a result of psychoculturally determined behavioural intentions.

Contributions from new institutional economics have recognized the temporal nature of institutions, with embedded informal institutions considered to be more enduring than those associated with more formal governance mechanisms (Williamson, 2000; Rafiqui, 2009). In general, institutions introduced indigenously, and which evolve endogenously, are the most likely to persist over time and to be relatively 'sticky', as they will have evolved from pre-existing institutions and beliefs (Boettke et al., 2008). Institutions emerging exogenously from, for example, national government are likely to be less sticky, even less so in the case of institutions and institutional change emerging from supranational governments. This emphasizes the need to consider not only the notion of institutional 'thickness' but also institutional 'stickiness'. In particular, such stickiness may accentuate the role of urban and regional institutional filters in compounding economic and social inequalities within contemporary development systems, such as through the incentivization of rent-seeking behaviour (Stiglitz, 2013; Piketty, 2014). As Stiglitz (2013) argues, this can occur when certain people are able to set the rules and choose the referee. Therefore, institutional filters play a central role in determining behaviour within the urban and regional context, and subsequently the action of particular agents within cities and regions:

Proposition 2.3
The translation of the behavioural intentions of individuals and their actual behaviour will be moderated by an institutional filter in the form of the underlying incentives and constraints to behaving in certain ways within a particular city or region.

2.4 Human Agency

The contribution of institutionalism in economic geography has helped provide an understanding of the constraints and promotion of particular forms of behaviour, but such contributions have been criticized for failing to account for the agency that is central to the formation and evolution of institutions (Cumbers et al., 2003). In the structuration theory proposed by Giddens (1984), structure in the form of social and economic systems provides the underlying conditions that bound, yet do not determine, the activities of particular agents (Moos and Dear, 1986). Through this theoretical approach, Giddens (1984) has sought to reconcile part of the ongoing tension within both cultural and institutional analysis in relation to the connection between the impact of economic and social structure and the agency of individuals operating within these structures. Within this framework, agents are considered to be active, knowledgeable, reasoning persons and are vital components of any analysis of subsequent outcomes (Moos and Dear, 1986). Therefore, opening the black box of place-based structure to encompass psychocultural behaviour alongside institutional factors potentially facilitates a fuller explanation of the determinants of outcomes in the context of urban and regional development.

As Storper (2013) indicates, it is vital to shed further light on the role of agency in fostering urban and regional development, particularly through the welfare effects it generates within and through communities, and it is important to recognize that institutions moderate, but are also formed by, human agency. One approach to understanding this translation is methodological individualism, whereby macro-level outcomes are retraceable to individual decision-making agents (Hodgson, 2007). Such approaches stem from the work of McClelland (1967), which suggests that the level of motivation embodied in individual agents to achieve particular outcomes will be linked to the ensuing rates of development of the societies in which these individuals operate. Within Bandura's (2006) social cognitive theory primacy is given to the role of 'personal efficacy', which he considers relates to the level of belief that individuals have in their capability to achieve desired results from their actions. However, it should be noted that such expectations are not necessarily perfectly rational but bounded by their psychological, cultural, and institutional setting. Without such personal efficacy, which Bandura (2006) considers to be the cornerstone for understanding human agency, individuals are unlikely to have the incentive to act in a particular manner.

Fundamentally, agency refers to acts done intentionally, which is in line with the concept of behavioural intentions outlined above. For example, in the case of workers agency will require that they be an autonomous force (Bandura, 2001). Therefore, agency relates to intentional actions taken to produce change or to deliberately reproduce previous actions, which avoids Castree's (2007) criticism of the tendency for the term agency to be used to refer to any form of action. Bandura's (2001) social cognitive theory distinguishes three modes of agency: personal agency based on forms of power to originate actions for given purposes; proxy agency based on a reliance of others to act at one's behest and on one's behalf to secure desired outcomes; and collective agency based on exercising action through socially coordinative and interdependent effort.

In most fields, research on agency has tended to focus on the role of personal agency, even though many individuals do not necessarily have direct control over ensuing conditions that affect them. In these circumstances, socially mediated proxy agency may better facilitate well-being due to the lack of the necessary competencies or the perceived capability by some individuals to undertake particular responsibilities (Bandura, 2006). While the upside of proxy agency is that it can promote development outcomes at multiple levels, it can also stifle the nurturing of competencies and breed vulnerability due to power resting elsewhere (Bandura, 2001). Alongside personal and proxy agency, the interdependency between individuals and their aggregate power to achieve particular outcomes through sharing information, knowledge, and skills can be considered to be the result of a collective agency based on the interactive dynamics existing across individual agents (Bandura, 2006).

Some Marxist-influenced scholars deny individual or personal agency (Mokyr, 2015), and within the field of urban and regional development theory an increased emphasis has been given to the role of collective agency through networks of individual agents and actors (Bristow and Healy, 2014; Cumbers et al., 2016). However, the balance of particular forms of agency is likely to vary across cities and regions precisely due to differing psychocultural behavioural conditions. Indeed, Bandura (2006) suggests that 'successful functioning' requires an agentic blend of the three forms, and while he is mainly referring to the functioning of individuals, it is likely that such a blend is also necessary for the successful functioning of cities and regions.

Behavioural action will clearly result in a myriad of activities, and from the perspective of urban and regional development it is important to pinpoint actions in the form of human agency that may impact on the development outcomes of a city or region. In this case, such agency refers to intentional action initiated through personal, proxy, or collective means that may either positively or negatively determine subsequent urban and regional development outcomes. Therefore, it is proposed that:

Proposition 2.4
The actualized behaviour of individuals and collectives of individuals within cities and regions will result in particular forms of human agency that underpin the development systems and trajectories of these cities and regions.

Bandura's (2001) agency forms are useful for considering urban and regional development in terms of highlighting the general types of action that may or may not take place. However, it is also possible to give consideration to the forms of agency that can impact upon development within cities and regions. These are explored in more depth in Chapter 4, but are summarized here as entrepreneurial agency, political agency, and labour agency. Aligning these more specific forms of agency with Bandura's (2001) generic forms, it is possible to conceptualize them as a matrix of behavioural agency for urban and regional development. This Behavioural Agency Matrix, presented in Figure 2.1, examines the extent to which these specific forms of agency related to urban and regional development intersect with the types of agency stemming from the field of psychology, especially Bandura's (2001) threefold taxonomy.

Proposition 2.5
The rate and forms of development across cities and regions will depend on the nature of the human agency employed within these cities and regions.

	Personal Agency	Proxy Agency	Collective Agency
Entrepreneurial Agency	Individual Entrepreneurs	Investors	Entrepreneurial Networks
Political Agency	Political Leaders	Funders and Supporters of Political Leaders	Political Parties/Groups
Labour Agency	Worker and Community Leaders	Workers and Community Members	Worker and Community Groups

Figure 2.1 Behavioural agency matrix.

2.5 The Nature and Source of Power

Coupled with agency, the role of power—especially the ability to deploy and exercise agency—is vital if changes resulting in improved economic development are activated. Initial institutional work in economic geography tended to concentrate heavily on factors relating to interaction and collaboration between firms, somewhat ignoring interactions with the potential for conflict between societal groups within regions (Cumbers et al., 2003). In this sense, Allen (2003) highlights the importance of distinguishing between the possession of power and the exercise of power, as only the latter is likely to be the basis for achieving material effects. Power might be held by an agent, but it can only be fully exercised through the fluid social relations established with others. Nevertheless, where agents hold power they are in a position to influence the direction of development. Therefore, it is necessary to examine the power relations and mechanisms that allow these agents to capture value (Cumbers and MacKinnon, 2011). For example, within their analysis of an oil refinery on the east coast of England, Ince et al. (2015) highlight the particular role of the 'spatialized power relations' generated by labour agency, with such agency taking the form of not only localized actions but also transnational forms of agency. Such power is exercised through a number of possible modes: domination; expertise; coercion; manipulation; seduction; and negotiation and persuasion (Allen, 2003).

Although power is often examined from the perspective of labour and capital relations, issues of unequal power can affect the agency of other groups. For example, within innovation and production collaborations, small and medium-sized enterprises (SMEs) are often dominated by larger firms (Tödtling and Kaufman, 2001). Other groups within cities and regions that may experience power conflicts include local elites such as business leaders and state managers; the private and public sectors; and the owners of foreign capital and domestic enterprises (Cumbers et al., 2003). Power divisions can also exist between regions, such as the relationship between dominant core regions and more peripheral locations (Massey, 2001). Overall, the importance of power from social relations can be clearly perceived, but a further consideration is the source of this power.

To explore the source of power it is useful to draw further on some of the analyses undertaken within the labour geography literature. For example, Coe and Jordhus-Lier (2011) highlight four sets of wider relations within which the power of labour agency can be considered: global production networks; the state; the community; and labour market intermediaries. The development of interconnected global production networks has a potentially considerable impact on the power of workers, such as reducing their agency in cases where competition is high, leading to the growing presence of precarious employment (Coe, 2013). Labour market intermediaries have an impact on the relationship between labour, capital, state, and community. Employment may become more fragmented in terms of: employers (administratively); employee contracts (contractually); and shift patterns (temporally) (Lier, 2009). From a cultural and behavioural perspective, such employment is often filled by migrants, and this fragmentation may hinder collective action, thereby reducing power and making existing employer power harder to navigate (Datta et al., 2007).

On the other hand, workers with scarce skills may enjoy a privileged position within global production networks, providing them with considerable power (Silvey, 2003). This reflects the assets and resources utilized by actors to support adaptation, which include land; social capital; ethnic symbolic capital; political capital; cash inflows; and human capital (MacKinnon, 2017). Such asset utilization reflects Allen's (2003) notion of exercising power through the accumulation of expertise, as long as effective modes of negotiation and persuasion are also in place. In general, the contextual influences on power can be both temporal and spatial in nature, with differing labour–capital relations across groups of workers often leading to considerable disparities in power (Castree et al., 2004; Rutherford and Holmes, 2007).

Interestingly, the state has often been overlooked in labour geography studies (Castree, 2007), but it clearly has a key role for the development of institutions based on the regulatory framework it provides (Peck, 2001), with one outcome being that it can weaken the power of labour (Coe and Kelly, 2002). This may lead to workers having quite different power positions according to the institutional and regulatory frameworks present (Coe et al., 2009). However, decisions of the state can influence labour agency well beyond the labour market, in terms of other services it provides and supports (McDowell, 2009). It is also an employer itself, and workers can obtain 'symbolic power' if their cause gathers support from the electorate (Webster et al., 2008). Changes in state regulations that previously protected workers, and greater outsourcing, along with the rise of global production networks, have often left workers looking for alternative sources of support to facilitate collective and individual agency (Pike, 2007; Coe and Jordhus-Lier, 2011). Also, the state is not a cohesive whole but is assembled from a large number of actors with a combination of competing priorities, with often no clear boundary between society and state (Jones, 2012). Therefore, institutional change may come from groups in society based on their power and status, legitimized by underlying institutions (Cumbers et al., 2003).

Jones et al. (2013) analyse developments in behavioural change policies to illustrate how particular agents within and outside government develop power through social relations that allow them to push particular agendas and policies through a combination of dominance, coercion, and negotiation. Such policies have been seen by some as the state using power through a mode of manipulation to achieve the government's own objectives (Whitehead et al., 2011; Pykett, 2013). Given concerns as to how behavioural-change policies may be wielded by those with power, it is argued that there should be openness and transparency with regard to their formulation and implementation (Thaler and Sunstein, 2008).

The above arguments make clear that human agency is responsible for the creation of the very institutions that underpin the development systems of regions and cities. However, the extent to which this agency is effective in generating institutional or even wider cultural change is dependent on the power of individuals and groups. Such power is itself determined by social relations, context (development), and institutions. As power is based on social relations, it is not constant but temporal in nature. The following can therefore be proposed:

Proposition 2.6
The power possessed and exercised by individuals or groups will determine the extent to which agency can influence the type and evolution of institutional filters within cities and regions.

2.6 Towards a Behavioural Theory of Urban and Regional Development

Both evolutionary and institutional economic geography have attempted to provide an understanding of the factors that determine the development of urban and regional places. However, such thinking has often taken a somewhat narrow view of the concept of development (Pike et al., 2009), and furthermore has not fully accommodated the different levels and layers of interaction required to incorporate agentic influences (Pike et al., 2015). In response, it is argued here that the economic and social fortunes of cities and regions are partly determined by the behaviour and human agency of the individuals and collectives of individuals located in these places. Also, such behaviour and agency are proposed to be based on a rationality that is spatially bounded. In particular, through the prevailing forms of culture, personality psychology, and institutions, cities and regions themselves produce a spatially bounded rationality. Such spatially bounded rationality determines the forms and types of human agency apparent in a given city or region, and subsequently the nature and rate of development. Clearly, such development will be an outcome of factors related to the structure of industry, nature of governance, resource allocation, and so on. However, a behavioural insight into the determinants of urban and regional development suggests that these factors are themselves linked to the human agency resulting from the psychocultural behavioural dimensions manifest in any city or region.

Throughout this chapter various streams of literature have been used to generate a set of propositions that can be configured to produce a behavioural framework for analysing urban and regional development, which is illustrated by Figure 2.2. This framework recognizes that urban and regional sociospatial culture and personality psychology are interrelated (Proposition 2.1). Furthermore, the combination of these factors has an important role in determining the nature of the spatially bounded rationality of places, which leads to particular behavioural intentions (Proposition 2.2). However, the extent to which these behavioural intentions are translated into actual behaviour is influenced by the institutional filters associated with rules, regulations, and their enforcement within a city or region (Proposition 2.3). Behaviour that is actualized and purposive will result in human agency that produces actions, or reproduces actions, by individuals or groups (Proposition 2.4).

This agency will be manifest through particular forms with the potential to impact on development trajectories (Proposition 2.5). In order to realize this potential, individuals or groups must have access to power through their

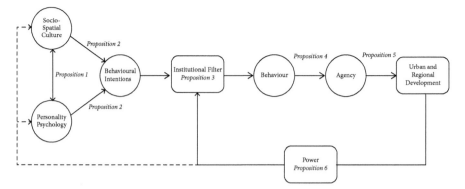

Figure 2.2 A behavioural framework for analysing urban and regional development.

social positions and network relations (Proposition 2.6). The framework, therefore, recognizes the role of institutions and agency, and that both are influenced by one another, as shown by the feedback loop in Figure 2.2. Similarly, it may be possible to influence the types of intended behaviour that enter the system via policies and interventions that interact with psychocultural factors. This means that in the long term this feedback loop is likely to extend further, slowly reshaping the cultural and personality traits of a city or region. As such, interventions are themselves dependent on institutional change, which is itself a function of agency and power.

In conclusion, this chapter has sought to respond to two limitations within existing theories of urban and regional development. First, theorizing has traditionally focused on downstream explanations relating to resources and capital, their allocation and accumulation, alongside the structure, systems, organization, and dynamics of urban and regional economies. While providing significant insights, the embedded and human sources of these relationalities and resources have not been integrated into such theorizing to any great extent. Second, although scholarly work on the impact of culture and institutions has shown the importance of identifying the mechanisms that link these influences to economic and other outcomes (Guiso et al., 2006), this work has not always accounted for the behavioural aspects behind these mechanisms. As a result, it can be argued that there is considerable potential for urban and regional theory to engage further with more upstream behavioural explanations of long-term evolutionary patterns of development. Psychocultural behavioural patterns, and their evolution, provide a basis for understanding the type and nature of human agency that exists within cities and regions. Such agency, along with the power that allows its application, is likely to be one of the key rooted drivers associated with more traditional downstream explanatory causes underlying uneven urban and regional development outcomes. However, the primacy of behavioural explanations of urban and regional development, and the extent to which any related policymaking can be configured, require a research agenda that provides robust empirical validation of some of the key propositions put forward here.

Although there is a range of emerging evidence that shows a significant association between psychocultural behavioural patterns and urban and regional development factors and outcomes, there is a clear need to analyse in more depth the causal mechanisms and the dynamic interplay and interrelationships of the key components within these mechanisms. Paramount, perhaps, in the quest to determine the nature of the spatially bounded rationality of cities and regions is the requirement to develop a more detailed framework for understanding human agency and agentic behaviour in the context of urban and regional development. An interesting avenue for research in this field would be to identify key agents operating at different layers within a city or region, and to examine how and why they enact this agency and seek to shape and impact upon development outcomes. Some agents, such as political and business leaders, are likely to be highly visible, while others may operate away from the mainstream but still exert influential power in shaping the development trajectory of cities and regions. Importantly, such agency should not necessarily be seen as normative, given its potential to take the form of rent-seeking, rather than wealth- or welfare-creating, behaviour. Furthermore, a behavioural approach allows the identification of agents that are either relatively core or peripheral in terms of the extent to which they are able to influence particular spheres of urban and regional development. In summary, the continued and more detailed exploration of these factors suggests an exciting and potentially highly informative interdisciplinary research agenda, which the following chapters of this volume continue to explore.

3
The Psychocultural Life of Cities and Regions

3.1 Introduction

A new emphasis on psychocultural behaviour has entered the equation in terms of efforts that seek to explain regional and urban differences in performance and development. As part of these equations it is argued that socio-spatial community culture will influence how resources such as physical capital, labour, and human capital are utilized (Rauch et al., 2013). Even when traditional and some non-traditional inputs, such as knowledge flows, are held constant, there are still considerable differences in economic growth rates across places (Davidsson and Wiklund, 1997). As such, it is important to consider these urban, local, and regional differences when determining policy, and whether a place-based policy is likely to be more appropriate than place-neutral policies (Barca et al., 2012).

This chapter initially seeks to explore the role of culture in relation to economic development in a place-based context, and secondly to examine the adoption of a more holistic perspective of behaviour at the regional and local level that considers specific configurations of human behaviour, which in combination influence the outputs attained (Rentfrow et al., 2013). In particular, it combines theories of socio-spatial community culture and personality psychology into a holistic spatially oriented perspective in order to identify distinct psychocultural behavioural profiles, drawing on an empirical example of regions and localities across Great Britain. This psychocultural behavioural approach is based on the interaction between the community culture apparent in these localities, which generates the social norms that influence the behaviour of individuals (Scott, 2007), and the personality traits of individuals located in these places.

As outlined previously, the inclusion of personality traits within the rubric of geographic psychocultural behaviour is a recognition of the growing research stream in psychology that utilizes large personality sets in order to show the distinctiveness and meaningfulness of regional and local

A Behavioural Theory of Economic Development: The Uneven Evolution of Cities and Regions. Robert Huggins and Piers Thompson, Oxford University Press (2021). © Robert Huggins and Piers Thompson.
DOI: 10.1093/oso/9780198832348.003.0003

personality differences (Rentfrow et al., 2013, 2015; Obschonka et al., 2015, 2016). However, an outstanding gap in our knowledge is the extent to which the clustering of community culture and personality traits influences factors such as economic growth. In essence, this chapter seeks to identify the typical pattern of personality traits and culture that together builds the functional psychocultural character of a locality, and to test the extent to which this is associated with economic outcomes. The chapter suggests that there is a process of co-evolution between community culture and personality traits within localities, cities, and regions, and that certain combinations of each impact upon the economic performance of these places.

3.2 Culture and Development

The greater focus on growth and development at the subnational level is impacting on the way that factors such as 'culture' and 'identity' are conceptualized within the political economy of places, especially cities and regions (Thrift, 2000; Biscoe, 2001; Keating et al., 2003; Syssner, 2009). This has led to calls for further analyses of regional and urban culture, identity, and mentality that capture concepts such as the 'regional self' (Syssner, 2009). Such analysis is considered to require a more detailed understanding of the nature of culture and cultural change at both regional and local levels, especially their significance for the development of these places (Jackson, 1991; Kockel, 2002). Due to their relative intangibility, cultural factors are often absent from analyses of economic change and development, divorcing the nature of social places from the economic spaces within which they are situated. The rationale for place-based analyses of development is now fairly well rehearsed, with subnational spatial levels becoming increasingly important—at least relative to nations as a whole—as the locus of development in the 'age of globalization' (Storper, 1997; Scott and Storper, 2003; Krugman, 2005; Radcliffe, 2006; Hassink and Klaerding, 2012). However, the reason why some places develop more than others, and why some once successful cities and regions have failed to change in step with apparently similar places, remains a matter of keen debate (Westlund and Bolton, 2003; Kitson et al., 2004).

The focus on defining and conceptualizing place-based culture is a reaction to the fact that, although some research suggests that culture does have a causal effect on development (Guiso et al., 2006; Tabellini, 2010; Farole et al., 2011), most of the extant literature seeking to make the link between the cultural traits and economic performance of places has generally drawn solely on the concept of either social capital or institutions. Due to the adoption of these terms in many different ways, social capital cannot be said to be a concept that robustly captures the cultural traits of places in a systematic and comparable manner (Putnam et al., 1993; Fukuyama, 1995; Putnam, 2000; Schneider et al., 2000; Beugelsdijk and van Schaik, 2005). Similarly, the concept of institutions, which captures the economic and political 'rules of the games' (Farole et al., 2011; and see Chapter 4), principally across nations (North, 1990, 2005; Acemoglu and Robinson, 2012), does not fully address the extent to which cultural factors impinge on the adoption of these rules or influence the establishment of such rules within particular places. Furthermore, while some studies have addressed cultural aspects that can be considered to relate to either the economic systems of places or their more societal, community-based systems (Shane, 1993; Hauser et al., 2007), few studies have sought to examine both in tandem or to examine their interrelationship.

As others have indicated, the notion of 'community' is a slippery concept and can relate to societal groupings that may, or may not, be place-based (Miller, 1992; Storper, 2008). Such communities may also be strongly tied or rooted to prevailing economic culture or activity, for example communities of practice (Storper, 2008). This is not to imply that one community culture is necessarily 'better' or 'superior' to another—in the sense that Bourdieu (1986) views some communities as having greater endowments of 'cultural capital'—but that they may be differently configured. For example, a key area of contention in regional and urban policy circles is the need for either social diversity or cohesion (see also Section 3.4), with diversity considered almost simultaneously to be both a positive and negative factor in ensuring safety within particular communities (Raco, 2007; Robinson, 2007).

In his seminal contribution, Tylor (1871: 1) defines culture as 'that complex whole which includes knowledge, belief, art, morals, law, custom, and any other capabilities and habits acquired by man as a member of society'. Similarly, according to Hofstede (1980) culture consists of the collective programming of individual minds that may include various facets and traits, such as language, social organization and stratification, education and training, the law, political economy, material culture, values and attitudes, and religion (Tönnies, 1957; Peet, 2000; Licht et al., 2007; Rutten and Gelissen, 2010). In their examination of the role of culture in economic thinking, Beugelsdijk and Maseland (2011) consider culture to be the collective identity of communities, suggesting that cultural analysis is traceable back to anthropological work such as Mauss's (1925/1990) cross-cultural study of economic processes in *The Gift*. Anthropological approaches have often taken the perspective of highlighting how the culture of underdeveloped societies itself constrains this development.

More economic approaches, such as the work of Hirschman (1965), criticize the cultural constraint approach as being ethnocentrically biased, suggesting the question: can communities and societies have the 'wrong culture'? Others, such as Williamson (2000), view culture as the ultimate source of constraints. From a spatial perspective, therefore, culture can be considered as an element of the bounded rationality of places. As Fayolle et al. (2010) note, at the national level the connection between culture and development can be traced back to the work of Landes (1953). Others trace it to the work of Weber (1930), which suggests an endogenous relationship between culture and development (Frederking, 2002; Tabellini, 2010). Along with antecedent routes such as the work of Weber (1930), Beugelsdijk and Maseland (2011) argue that the strong influence of Marxist approaches to the examination of culture has necessarily led to its politicization.

In the context of regional and urban development, the work of Doreen Massey is important in drawing attention to the link between the geography of industry and work and the wider and underlying structures of society across regions and localities (Massey, 1984). Clearly couched in the Marxist tradition, Massey (1984) seeks to understand the connections between economic structure and class relations through a lens rich in the use of Marxist terminology. Although the structure of industry and work in the case of the UK has changed quite rapidly since Massey's original analysis, it remains an important analytical account of the importance of the reproduction of places as socio-economic and socio-cultural spaces and the resulting socio-spatial nature of uneven development. Although Massey does not engage with cultural or institutional theory in the explicit sense that is known today, her work implicitly connects with these themes through her examination of the reproduction of inequality. Nevertheless, there is need to move beyond a view of place-based culture framed largely by class relations.

The link and intersection between economic life and social cultural relations at the place-based level have been increasingly discussed, but again without significant empirical analysis (Amin and Thrift, 1994; Gertler, 1997; Hassink and Klaerding, 2012). However, and as indicated above, from the perspective of place-based development the role of culture is central to emerging debates concerning the extent to which intervention should be either place-based or place-neutral (Garcilazo, 2011; Barca et al., 2012). While place-neutral advocates promote the role of aspatial 'people-based' policies (Gill, 2010), place-based approaches highlight the importance of the interactions between place-based communities, institutions, and geography for development and development policies, requiring researchers 'to explicitly consider the specifics of the local and wider regional context' (Barca et al., 2012: 140). Advocates of place-based policy approaches argue that a spatially decentralized political base can allow for differentiation in regional economic policies, including entrepreneurship, and in a normative sense policy should seek to encourage diversity and experimentation across regions (Morgan, 1997; James, 2011). In an idealistic sense, the most appropriate response of policy would be the development of regional institutional systems that fit with an underlying set of cultural values, norms, and preferences (Rutten and Gelissen, 2010; Beugelsdijk and Maseland, 2011).

3.3 The Place-Based Context

As with the economic arguments concerning the continued and reinforced importance of places as economic 'actors' within a globalizing environment, similar arguments can also be applied to the cultural sphere. As Hall (1993: 354) suggests, 'paradoxically, globalization seems also to have led to a strengthening of "local" allegiances and identities within nation-states; though this may be deceptive, since the strengthening of "the local" is probably less the revival of the stable identities of "locally settled communities" of the past, and more that tricky version of "the local" which operates within, and has been thoroughly reshaped by, "the global" and operates largely within its logic.' Speculating on the role of culture in promoting regional economic growth, Syssner (2009) views it as a concept that is continually evolving, as well as something rooted, fixed, and place-bound. There is, however, little underlying research that seeks to integrate both community and economic perspectives in order to provide a cohesive framework for understanding how the social condition of particular communities relates to the economic development trajectories of the places within which communities are situated.

When discussing culture, Harvey (2001) notes that the maintenance of a sense of value depends crucially upon the type of interpersonal relationships occurring in particular places, which alludes to the notion of social capital and more especially the role of trust. Most discussions of social capital proclaim it an unqualified 'good', that is something to be maximized (Putnam, 1995; Kearns and Forrest, 2000; Adler and Kwon, 2002; Durlauf and Fafchamps, 2003). However, social capital may also have a downside in that strong, long-standing civic groups may stifle development by securing a disproportionate share of resources or inhibiting individual economic advancement by placing heavy personal obligations on members that prevent them from participating in broader social networks (Olson, 1965; Portes and Landolt, 1996; Woolcock, 1998). As Woolcock (1998) states, the challenge for development theorists and policymakers alike is to identify the mechanisms that create, nurture, and sustain the types and combinations of social relationships conducive to building dynamic participatory societies, sustainable equitable economies, and accountable states. While acknowledging the importance of social capital and trust to development, it is equally important to understand the mechanisms that facilitate its creation, which would seem to be firmly rooted in the cultural characteristics of place.

Clearly, the economy interacts with a broad array of socio-cultural forces and is itself a set of material and cultural practices involved in the reproduction of existence (Peet, 1997, 2000). Historically, the apparent divide between the 'cultural' and the 'economic' stems from an outdated European model of civil society dating back to the nineteenth century (Shields, 1999). However, as Peet (2000) notes, following Weber (1947), there is an understanding that economic rationalism consists not only of those factors that are quantitatively calculable but also of those oriented to more ultimate ends, such as ethical values. Also, the cultural traits of places are increasingly considered to be related to the norms and values underlying the economic systems of these places, especially with regard to the values associated with activities related to entrepreneurship (Casson, 1993; Mueller and Thomas, 2001; Fayolle et al., 2010; Rutten and Gelissen, 2010; Huggins and Williams, 2012). These traits may consist of the economic or business culture of these places, with there being an increasing emphasis on the socio-cultural aspects of the differing performance of regional and urban economies, particularly in terms of their growth and innovation capabilities, with studies drawing on a range of interdisciplinary work from economics, geography, and sociology (James, 2005, 2011).

Culture shapes what individuals perceive as opportunities, and therefore factors such as entrepreneurial alertness are linked to judgement, creativity, and interpretation (Hofstede, 1991; Lavoie, 1991; Hampden-Turner and Trompenaars, 1994; Sautet and Kirzner, 2006; Hechaverria and Reynolds, 2009). Given this, a culture supportive of entrepreneurship may make it possible for economic actors to take advantage of perceived opportunities (Carree et al., 2002; Sautet and Kirzner, 2006; Farole et al., 2011; Huggins and Williams, 2012). Places with an entrepreneurially conducive culture may increase their economic advantage by attracting investment, skills, and talent (Turok, 2004). In particular, places with strong entrepreneurial traditions may reproduce these advantages if they are able to perpetuate them over time and generations (Audretsch and Fritsch, 2002; Beugelsdijk and Noorderhaven, 2004; Parker, 2004; Mueller, 2006). Flora and Flora (1993) suggest that, with local places facing increasing responsibilities to provide for their own well-being and development, 'entrepreneurial social infrastructure' is a necessary ingredient for successfully linking local business communities, particularly as people often appear to learn more from like-minded individuals.

With regard to the concept of socio-spatial community culture, it is important not to conflate the conception of 'community' and that of 'place', which are analytically distinct—although strong communities are often embedded in specific places (Miller, 1992; Storper, 2008). Like culture, the meaning of the term community is ambiguous, often referring to either a morally valued way of life or social relations in a discrete geographical setting (Agnew, 1989; Miller, 1992). In essence, community culture refers to the overarching or dominant mindsets that underlie the way in which places function in a broader societal sense. Places consist of what is termed 'the location of culture' and 'the space of the people' (Bhabha, 1994). Massey (2004) refers to a 'global sense of place' within which localities are formed in part as a product of relations which spread out beyond it.

Hudson (2001) suggests that space refers to the economic evaluation of a location, principally its capacity for profit, with place referring to the social evaluation of location based on meaning. To this extent, therefore, community culture can be considered a place-bound phenomenon, whereas economic culture refers to behaviour and systems within an economic space that may have a mix of both place-bound and more business-bound characteristics. These business-bound characteristics will generally relate to the wider networks within which economic actors operate and function. Florida (2002) has suggested that the particular community culture traits of cities influence their performance as economic spaces. This suggests a synergistic relationship between space and place (Johnstone and Lionais, 2004). However, while deprived communities may have lost much of their economic rationale as space, they may retain the social relations of place (Fischer, 1977; Lee, 1989; Johnstone and Lionais, 2004).

Moulaert and Nussbaumer (2005) refer to the term 'community' to define the nature of human interactions within groups that can be defined according to geographic, sociological, political, or economic considerations, whereby 'local communities' are viewed as an appropriate level for practices related to improvement through social innovation. In this sense, cultural concepts such as collective action can be conceptualized as a continuum of forms of action coordination, with specific actions deriving much of their impetus from the characteristics of community and place (Habermas, 1989; Miller, 1992). The notion of community is associated with the nature of social ties and interaction, as well as the nature of the morality and behavioural norms present and practised within localities (Gerson et al., 1977; Smith, 1999). In theorizing the concept of community culture, it is useful to consider that key concepts, such as the 'structure of feeling' and 'knowable communities', stem from the groundbreaking work of the Welsh cultural scholar Raymond Williams, who famously stated that 'culture is ordinary' (Williams, 1958; Longhurst, 1991). Adding culture to the attributes of places has the impact of making rather commonsensical notions of locality and community quite complex concepts (Gupta and Ferguson, 1997). Interestingly, Williams (1989) argued that the culture he encountered during his time at Cambridge University was sadly wanting compared with that of the Welsh 'Border Country' in which he was brought up (Hall, 1993).

Both economic and community culture may directly impact upon economic and societal well-being outcomes (Beugelsdijk and Noorderhaven, 2004). Well-being, for example, may be positively associated with the business community, where satisfaction is obtained directly from work-related activities, as opposed to the payment received for these activities. Community culture may improve economic outcomes in that collective action helps overcome coordination failures (Hall and Soskice, 2001). In this sense, community culture may complement, and in some situations substitute for, formal institutions in promoting economic development (North, 1990; Rodríguez-Pose and Storper, 2006; Farole et al., 2011). It may also allow the generation of social capital and trust (Putnam, 2000; Fukuyama, 2001; Bowles and Gintis, 2002; Beugelsdijk et al., 2004), leading to a reduction in transaction costs (Storper, 1997); alleviate the dangers of opportunistic behaviour and moral hazard (Streeck, 1992; Putnam, 2000); help overcome informational asymmetries (Granovetter, 1985; Wade, 1987); and match individual and aggregate interests (Rodríguez-Pose, 2001). Bowles and Gintis (2002), for instance, refer to the notion of community governance as consisting of small-group social interactions that, along with the more traditional and acknowledged roles of the market and state, determine economic outcomes.

When referring to the work of Raymond Williams, Harvey (2001: 171) notes how he embodies the 'local place-bound internalization of capitalistic values'. To a large extent, this is undoubtedly true, and moving beyond analyses of place-based differences in class structure to ones which acknowledge cultural variety within the socio-economic systems underlying regions and localities is partly akin to the recognition that most nations can be analysed in terms of regional, urban, and local 'varieties of capitalism' (Hall and

Soskice, 2001). Most work in this area has been framed within the bounds of institutional, rather than emerging cultural, theories (Crouch et al., 2009; Peck and Zhang, 2013; Rodríguez-Pose, 2013). However, institutional and cultural explanations are clearly interrelated, with concepts and measures for each often overlapping. As discussed in following chapters, institutional change potentially represents a relatively dynamic means for facilitating development compared with cultural change. Culture is often inherently reproduced over time, with it being possible, for example, to trace the origins of the individualism found in certain regions of England back to the thirteenth century (Macfarlane, 1978; North, 2005).

A 'stronger' community culture, however, may in itself not always lead to a stronger economy. An overreliance on community, rather than on formal institutions, can open a community up to the dangers of rent-seeking by individuals at the expense of the group as a whole, as well as the existence of insider–outsider problems whereby the existing community benefits at the expense of those who are not members (Trigilia, 1992; Farole et al., 2011). Also, while trust may be developed within communities, it may not be the type of generalized trust required for economic development (Rodríguez-Pose and Storper, 2006). As such, not all close-knit communities will have positive effects on economic development (Rodríguez-Pose, 2001; Martin and Sunley, 2003; Storper, 2005). Therefore, it is the nature of and interaction between community culture and institutions which are likely to be of greatest importance, with both potentially able to offset the weaknesses of the other (North, 1990; Rodríguez-Pose and Storper, 2006; Farole et al., 2011). Also, communities may have to fit with the physical environment within which they are based, while cultures may also drive the development of the physical and built environment, either positively or negatively.

Culture, be it community or economic, forms part of the place-based development systems linking economic performance with societal well-being (Tönnies, 1957; Easterlin, 1974; Beugelsdijk et al., 2004; Johnstone and Lionais, 2004). It is the cultural attributes of places that act as the glue forming the interdependency between the economic logic and societal logic of places (Moulaert and Nussbaumer, 2005; Storper, 2005). In some regions and cities this cultural glue is a facilitating force enabling economic development and relatively enhanced levels of well-being, while in others it is a factor impeding the development of places in an economic sense, as well as pushing down relative levels of well-being. However, as already indicated, no particular prevailing community culture across places should necessarily be seen as superior (Miller, 1992; Syssner, 2009). It is not necessarily clear that the success of a city or region should be entirely based upon economic measures of success, and while some place-based cultures may not encourage the development of a complementary thriving business and enterprise culture, they may provide lifestyle benefits captured only in broader well-being measures (Layard, 2005). Similarly, when considering the economic outcomes of a place's combined culture, only a snapshot is being considered. Although a cohesive community may encourage the development of positive attitudes towards entrepreneurship, for example, a too strongly bonded community may lack openness to new ideas, stifling innovation and preventing long-term success.

3.4   Cultural Analyses of Economic Development

There has been considerable work examining different types of economic systems, but less that specifically examines the impact of community culture on the economic culture of places. This is not to say that business and economy has been seen as completely divorced from the cultural environment, with Hofstede's (1980) seminal work developing dimensions of culture that led to the establishment of a stream of literature examining this issue in considerable depth. While Hofstede's work was based around a specific survey of individuals within one large international organization, IBM, the findings from his work have been adapted and applied to a variety of settings, especially at the national level (for a review, see Klyver and Foley, 2012).

Fundamentally, culture in these cases consists of the overarching or dominant mindsets that underlie the way in which cities and regions function; that is, the ways and means by which individuals and groups within communities interact and shape their environment. The decisions of individuals within these cultures, therefore, may have an arbitrary coherence as individuals try to ensure they are consistent with personal and collective cultures as well as past decisions (Ariely, 2008; Knott et al., 2008). At a national level, the World Values Survey (WVS) has allowed researchers to investigate differences in culture based on scales such as traditional versus secular-rational, and survival versus self-expression (Inglehart and Welzel, 2010). Prior to the WVS, many studies frequently looked for evidence of the key constructs of culture identified by Hofstede (1980), in particular: (1) power distance—indicating the extent to which a society expects and accepts inequalities between its people, and an unequal distribution of power and responsibility within its institutions and organizations; (2) uncertainty avoidance—related to the extent to which nations and their institutions establish formal rules and fixed patterns of operation as a means of enhancing security and avoiding ambiguity and doubt; (3) individualism–collectivism—related to the degree to which people in a nation prefer to act as individuals rather than members of groups; (4) masculinity–femininity—the more 'masculine' a society, the more it values assertiveness and materialism (promoting competition, meritocracy, decisiveness, and strong leadership), with 'feminine' societies promoting harmonious relations in the workplace; and (5) long-term/short-term orientation—with the 'long-term' relating to factors such as thrift and perseverance, and the 'short-term' to values concerning respect for personal tradition and social obligations.

The difficulty with transferring Hofstede's findings from an organizational to a place-based setting is that there is often greater within-group (community, nation) variation than between-group variation, and, outside the like-for-like comparison of individuals undertaking the same roles within the same organization in different nations, contextual elements are likely to have a substantial effect. This will be further influenced by any self-selecting elements of the occupational and non-occupational roles that individuals choose. Nevertheless, these cultural dimensions have been found to relate to a wide variety of measures of development (Guiso et al., 2006), both narrowly economically defined as well as in terms of broader development measures (Pike et al., 2007).

As previously mentioned, in order to examine the relationship between development and community culture Huggins and Thompson (2016) establish a framework of five dimensions of socio-spatial community culture capturing: engagement with work and education; social cohesion; feminine and caring activities; adherence to social rules; and collective actions. Each of these is discussed below.

Engagement with work and education draws upon Weber's (1930) consideration of the impact of 'work ethic' on economic outcomes and the importance of education as a cultural feature of places (Tabellini, 2010). Both of these may be associated with self-sufficiency and making an appropriate contribution to society (Brennan et al., 2000; Becker and Woessmann, 2009). However, in order to accomplish this, the correct investments in human capital must be made, and this requires a long-term orientation. This means that much of this measure is closely associated with Hofstede's (1980) long-term/short-term orientation measure.

Hofstede (1980) defines national cultures as more *masculine* or *feminine* in nature based on measures of greater or lesser competition and individuality, a pattern that others have shown is still present in advanced societies (Shneor et al. 2013). Although individualist and competitive societies may achieve greater economic success, this is not necessarily the case if competition is too great. Conflict and violence can result, with fractures appearing within the community. The market offers an opportunity for this competition to be used in a less destructive manner than could be the case. However, there is still potential for resources to be wasted, for example in the desire to possess certain goods without regard for the generation of negative externalities on others (Hirsch, 1977), or where higher income levels do not necessarily lead to greater well-being (Easterlin, 1974). This means that although many of the traits associated with business activities are often thought to be masculine in nature (Bennett and Dann, 2000; Bruni et al., 2004), in order to achieve higher levels of well-being and greater work–life balance, lower working hours and greater flexibility may be beneficial (Hundley, 2001).

Social norms and expectations may result in contrasting effects on male and female welfare, as differing domains take precedence for each gender. Female involvement in economic activities could be highly influential given that men and women prioritize outcomes of different kinds (Parasuraman et al., 1996). Where roles regarding employment and household production are more traditionally split, as captured by the economic activity of women, a more masculine approach to the economic activity might be expected to dominate. Also, activities including entrepreneurship and new venture creation are frequently identified with masculine competitive and individualistic cultures (Bennett and Dann, 2000; Bruni et al., 2004). However, such approaches do not necessarily yield the highest levels of broader well-being, in part because of upwardly adjusting reference points (Layard, 2006)—although some empirical studies have found positive relationships between economic competitiveness and broader well-being (Huggins and Thompson, 2012).

Social conventions are important in helping to coordinate activities that boost efficiency (Rodríguez-Pose and Storper, 2006; Lorenzen, 2007). Where *adherence to* such *conventions and rules* is relatively low, delinquent behaviours can become the norm (Kearns and Forrest, 2000), hindering economic activities. A knock-on effect is that where places become associated with such behaviours, residents can suffer from a stigma effect, hindering their ability to participate in wider economic and social activities (Atkinson and Kintrea, 2001). However, some studies have suggested that particular activities, such as entrepreneurship, can be born of frustration (Noorderhaven et al., 2004), and are positively associated with rule-breaking at a younger age (Obschonka et al., 2013b). In general, there is a danger that, if unchecked, subversive activities could become the new social norm and be seen as acceptable forms of behaviour (Kearns and Forrest, 2000). Where this is the case, the level of trust within the community is likely to fall, plus it will be harder to form bridging ties to other communities due to the stigma effect (Atkinson and Kintrea, 2001).

There is some debate as to whether more individualist cultures or those that facilitate *collective activities and action* best promote economic development (Thomas and Mueller, 2000; Kirkman et al., 2006; Hayton and Cacciotti, 2013; Wennberg et al., 2013). As discussed in relation to masculinity–femininity, competitiveness may be associated with individualistic behaviour, but collective approaches may still be successful when directed outwards towards competition with other groups (Greif, 1994; Casson, 1995; Ettlinger, 2003). In more individualistic systems, although less trust may be built up within the community, it may possess a greater propensity toward market activities. More collective systems can create greater trust within groups, but any 'aggressive' tendencies must usually be directed outward at other groups. Closely associated with collective action is a desire for equality or greater equity, and where this is the case the rewards achieved by successful businessmen and businesswomen, or other successful agents, may be viewed less positively by the remainder of the community.

The notion of *social cohesion* draws on the literature that has highlighted the importance of social capital in achieving various economic development facilitators (Putnam et al., 1993), such as entrepreneurship (Davidsson and Honig, 2003; Williams et al., 2017), and innovation (Camps and Marques, 2014; Murphy et al., 2016). Social cohesion may be strongly influenced by the extent to which there is a cohesive and uniform group that makes up the majority of the community population. Some evidence has suggested that group membership symbolizing this is correlated with stronger economic growth (Knack and Keefer, 1997; Zak and Knack, 2001; Beugelsdijk et al., 2004; Guiso et al., 2004). Equally, if groups within a community are deeply divided, this can hold back economic growth, as generalized trust is reduced (Easterly and Levine, 1997; Aghion et al., 2004). Development may be achieved through aiding knowledge transmission, reducing economic profiteering, and encouraging collective action (Callois and Aubert, 2007). However, as Olson (1982) suggests, it should also be noted that social associations linked with the promotion of particular interests may have a detrimental effect and raise inequality. Other studies show that it is often the distinction between bridging and bonding social capital that is important, with the former boosting income and the latter having a neutral effect (Hoyman et al., 2016). Bonding social capital may increase trust and informational flow within a group, but also isolate the group from outside ideas (Granovetter, 1973). It has also been suggested that less socially cohesive and diverse communities may benefit from access to new ideas and inward flows of human capital, resulting in novel ways of deploying available resources (Portes and Landolt, 2000; Florida, 2002; Levie, 2007).

From the perspective of socio-spatial community culture and development, the most commonly analysed of the five cultural dimensions outlined above is the last discussed, social cohesion, which reflects the complexity of the cultural-economic growth relationship. Studies such as Easterly et al. (2006) have found social cohesion, as captured by the lack of ethnic fractionalization, to be positively associated with economic growth, with greater social cohesion reducing transaction costs and improving cooperation and information flows (Beugelsdijk and van Schaik, 2005; Kwon and Adler, 2014). These increased levels of cooperation and information flows are achieved through the generation of greater trust from the development of social capital (Dasgupta, 2011). In this case, institutions associated with publicly funded education may have a key role in developing the common social norms that benefit society (Gradstein and Justman, 2000). Such cooperation and collaboration are considered to be important components of the innovative activities required to achieve lasting economic growth (Rutten and Boekema, 2007). It is no surprise, therefore, that where deep divisions exist within communities these are often associated with poorer economic performance (Aghion et al., 2004). However, as already argued, social cohesion may also have a downside when it leads to rent-seeking behaviour by dominant groups and produces insider–outsider problems (Rodríguez-Pose and Storper, 2006).

Alongside the role of social cohesion, another group of studies inspired by Florida (2002) found that open, tolerant societies grow faster, reflecting the attraction of both conventional human capital and a greater presence of the so-called creative class (Florida et al., 2008). Other studies suggest that migrants may be better placed to see the opportunities available by providing a fresh pair of eyes and drawing on international and extra-local networks (Levie, 2007). For example, Rodríguez-Pose and Hardy (2015) examine the link between diversity and entrepreneurial activity and find that place-of-birth diversity, rather than ethnic background, has the strongest relationship with entrepreneurship. Nevertheless, empirical studies have provided mixed evidence, with some finding stronger rates of economic growth in cases where the membership of community groups reflects a greater level of cohesion (Guiso et al., 2004), while others find little connection between stronger, more closely bonded, societies and greater economic success (Rodríguez-Pose, 2001).

A related stream of research finds evidence of a relationship between social capital and improved performance at the level of individual firms, but there is less indication of this when considering a region or locality as a whole (Cooke et al., 2005). A potential explanation for the mixed results found by existing studies is that it is not always appropriate to study cultural dimensions purely in terms of one aspect, but rather through specific combinations. Social capital is often explored as a unidimensional construct, but in reality it has different components that should be considered from a holistic perspective. Seminal work by Coleman (1988) and Putnam et al. (1993) on conceptualizing social capital recognizes three components in the form of social trust, social norms, and associational activity, but much empirical work analyses only one single measure of overall social capital (Bjørnskov, 2006). The argument is often made that repeated interactions through associational activity lead to greater social trust, which is termed the relational approach (Rutten and Boekema, 2012), but others suggest that at best this is only weakly related to generalized trust (Knack and Keefer, 1997). In a similar vein, Bjørnskov (2006) finds that only social trust is related to outcomes such as improved governance and life satisfaction. On the other hand, some studies find that associational activity, and the weak ties this generates, are of particular importance for economic activity related to innovation (Hauser et al., 2007). Furthermore, the form of social capital and associated policy interventions may vary depending on the type of innovation sought, for example traditional, hidden, or social innovation (Murphy et al., 2016). The complexities of the association between cultural measures and economic performance measures are further compounded by studies that find links between economic growth and individualism or a lack of collectivism and more 'masculine' cultures (Huggins and Thompson, 2016; Gorodnichenko and Roland, 2017).

3.5   Psychocultural Life and Development

As outlined in Chapter 2, in parallel with theoretical and empirical developments concerning the influence of culture on economic growth, another stream of literature has considered how individual behaviour may have an impact at the aggregate and spatial level (Obschonka et al., 2013a; Stuetzer et al., 2016). There have long been studies within psychology and personality science with regard to the different personality traits possessed by individuals (Cattell, 1943). To recap, one of the most commonly utilized approaches is that associated with the Big Five framework, which consists of the identification and measurement of the following concepts: extraversion; agreeableness; conscientiousness; neuroticism; and openness (Costa and

McCrae, 1992). Studies have found that more extravert individuals tend to exhibit higher levels of sociability and energy, while prosocial behaviour as captured by the notion of agreeableness is found to be linked to factors such as social capital and reduced crime (Rentfrow et al., 2008; Rentfrow, 2010). Conscientiousness is found to be associated with individual levels of organization and self-discipline, with neuroticism reflecting differences in anxiety and depression. The concept of openness is associated with individual differences in curiosity and liberal values.

While these psychological measures have traditionally been used to examine how particular personalities may lead to particular behaviours and outcomes at the individual level (Judge et al., 1999), the use of large surveys has allowed much bigger databases that compare personality traits across nations to be established (Schmitt et al., 2007). The size of these surveys has facilitated an examination of the distribution of personality traits across different areas of countries such as the United States (Rentfrow et al., 2009; Rentfrow, 2010) and the United Kingdom (Rentfrow et al., 2015). Unlike cultural norms, which are formed at the group level, these personality traits are necessarily based on the individual, but where a place has a relatively larger proportion of individuals with particular types of personality, this may affect local or regional factors such as economic or other quality-of-life outcomes (Obschonka et al., 2013a). For example, Rentfrow et al. (2015) find a positive link between economic prosperity and openness and extraversion, while conscientiousness displays a negative association. More generally there is a recognition that activities such as innovation and entrepreneurship are likely to be promoted by certain cultural characteristics or the presence of particular personality traits (Wyrwich, 2015). As with community culture, the majority of psychological research has examined the impact of particular individual personality traits on a variety of outcomes in isolation.

When examining the culture and personality traits present within a city, locality, or region, studies have frequently noted that the two are likely to be closely linked, without explicitly examining this link. For example, in their study of voting patterns Rentfrow et al. (2009) suggest a bidirectional relationship between culture and the presence of particular personality traits. As indicated in Chapter 2, this is understandable given research suggesting that in the long term the genetic and cultural evolution of humans is interactive through cultural-genetic co-evolution (Van den Bergh and Stagl, 2003). Given this, it can be proposed that it is this interactive and co-evolving psychocultural behaviour, rather than an individual trait or aspect of community culture, that is most likely to be important for economic growth. In order to understand this co-evolution it is necessary to examine the mechanisms that have been suggested by previous studies linking the development of one to the other.

Initially, it should be recognized that personality traits are usually found to be stable or slowly evolving at the individual level (Cobb-Clark and Schurer, 2012). As shown in Chapter 2, Rentfrow et al. (2015) highlight a number of routes that may result in differences in personality developing within countries or regions. Three highlighted mechanisms act through traditions and social norms, physical environment, and selective migration, with the prevalence of certain cultural features helping to shape personality traits via the influence of social norms, rules, and customs (Hofstede and McCrae, 2004).

As well as community culture influencing the personalities of those residing in these communities, it is just as plausible that personality at an individual level will affect the development of community culture through its influence on social norms and attitudes. This may be a slow process, but where, for example, a less socially cohesive community culture attracts individuals of a more extravert and less agreeable nature, such individuals are likely to reinforce the reproduction of existing social norms associated with such a local community culture. The potential for a reinforcing pattern to behavioural development is captured by studies such as Florida (2002), which suggests that the presence of bohemians attracts other high-skilled individuals. This presumably operates through those pursuing a bohemian lifestyle that helps to generate a tolerant community culture and does not exclude outsiders, particularly more extravert individuals who are willing to explore new ideas.

At the other end of the spectrum, where agreeableness is higher it is suggested that outward migration is reduced (Boneva et al., 1998; Jokela et al., 2008). This helps to generate a more socially cohesive society, potentially to such an extent that outsiders are excluded (Rodrıguez-Pose and Storper, 2006). Societies with more bonding social capital have been found to place greater weight on non-materialistic outcomes and a higher value on family life (Beugelsdijk and Smulders, 2003), which may become engrained in the social norms of the community culture present. To complete the analysis of the relationships between personality and community culture, it is important to reiterate the role played by institutions. It has been recognized that collective community culture at an informal level is an influence on endogenously formed formal institutions (Easterly et al., 2006), as well as potentially compensating for cases where formal institutions in particular places are weaker (Gorodnichenko and Roland, 2017).

In terms of the mechanisms and processes through which the psychological and cultural profile of a place may impact upon development outcomes, establishing a composite psychocultural profile may better facilitate an understanding of the factors that lead to economic development (Hauser et al., 2007; Wyrwich, 2015; Stuetzer et al., 2016). The key point to stress here is that the combined and holistic psychological and cultural profile of cities, localities, and regions is likely to shape development mechanisms and processes, as well as subsequent outcomes. Furthermore, the influence of the psychocultural profile of a place on economic outcomes may have a temporal variance, particularly with regard to macroeconomic cycles. In times of widespread rates of high economic growth, some local profiles may be better suited and positioned to capitalize on these positive economic conditions. Conversely, in times of recession and austerity, other types of local psychocultural profiles may be better placed to foster resilience within a local economy (Martin and Sunley, 2017).

In a study to determine psychocultural profiles across the UK, Huggins et al. (2018) find the existence of three key psychocultural profile types based on principal components analysis. The first component describes a psychocultural behavioural profile that can be termed *Inclusive Amenability*, as it has high levels of agreeableness, conscientiousness, social cohesion, femininity and caring activities, and adherence to social rules, but low levels of openness. Behaviour related to the 'sticking to rules' may attract to a locality those individuals who are conscientious or promote such behaviours within the existing population (Bourgeois and Bowen, 2001). This psychocultural behaviour is least evident in more developed cities and regions such as Greater London and more prevalent in the less developed north of England, Scotland, and south Wales—see Figure 3.1. Higher levels tend to be found in more rural localities, with larger urban areas displaying less evidence, which could again reflect the selective migration of more ambitious individuals to more dynamic economies (Boneva et al., 1998), or conditioning by the economic climate (Steel et al., 2008; Jokela et al., 2015).

The second component displays low openness, high social cohesion, and little evidence of extraversion or collective activities. It also has a large positive loading from engagement with education and employment, and while having a degree of agreeable and conscientious traits, this psychocultural profile places an emphasis on individualism, with less evidence of caring socially for others. Given this, the second component is termed *Individual Commitment*, with its characteristics likely to be manifest through relatively low levels of altruistic behaviour or consideration for wider well-being (Huggins and Thompson, 2012). High levels of individual commitment are

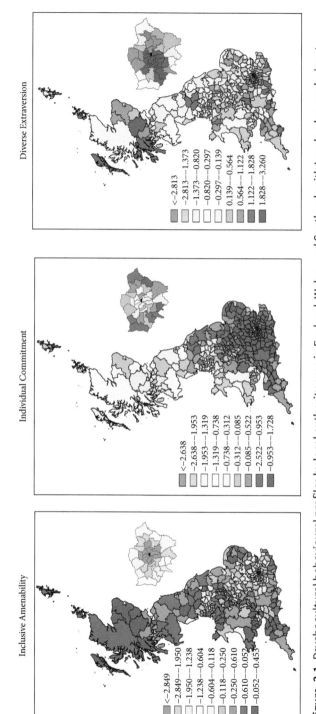

Figure. 3.1 Psychocultural behavioural profiles by local authority area in England, Wales, and Scotland, with London boroughs inset.
(Note: localities shaded black represent missing data; PCA creates measures with an average value of zero, so those with positive values represent those areas displaying an above average value of the psychocultural behaviour.)

found around London, diminishing towards more peripheral regions such as Scotland, Wales, and the region of the North East of England.

The third component is termed *Diverse Extraversion* and is positively associated with extraversion and openness, and displays low social cohesion. Conscientiousness and adherence to social rules are less evident than in the other two components. Neuroticism is also low. This psychocultural profile might be seen as linked to creativity and innovation, with greater bridging social capital formed (Putnam, 2000; Hauser et al., 2007), and an openness to new ideas and people (Levie, 2007; Florida et al., 2008). The highest levels found for this psychocultural behaviour are in parts of London and the main transport corridors stemming from London. Not all of London has uniformly high levels of this psychocultural behaviour, with the traditionally less developed parts of east London displaying lower levels. There are, however, surprisingly higher levels found in some rural areas, which may reflect commuter belts for cities such as Edinburgh and Leeds.

Given the economic development success of the dominant regions of London, the South East, and East of England, it is to be expected that their cities and localities display higher levels of individual commitment and diverse extraversion. Individually committed psychocultural characteristics may promote activities associated with economic growth as they incorporate the higher conscientiousness that Lee (2017) associates with innovation. However, adherence to social rules is high, which some suggest does not benefit entrepreneurial activities (Obschonka et al., 2013a, 2015; Rentfrow et al., 2015; Huggins and Thompson, 2016). On the other hand, diverse extraversion is high in extraversion and openness, and low in neuroticism, which are characteristics linked with entrepreneurial cultures (Obschonka et al., 2013a, 2015). Although possibly lowering transaction costs (Beugelsdijk and van Schaik, 2005), inclusive amenable psychocultural behaviour may support broader measures of well-being rather than economic growth (Beugelsdijk and Smulders, 2003). It is also important to recognize that localities with this particular psychocultural profile may enjoy better access to factors such as social capital.

Huggins et al. (2018) undertake a range of analyses, and initially find that inclusive amenable behaviour has a significant negative association with economic growth. Given the nature of this psychocultural profile, it may reflect localities that tend to place greater importance on broader non-economic development outcomes. This confirms the need to consider the constitution of development from the perspective of those experiencing it (Pike et al., 2007). It may also be the case that psychocultural behavioural profiles develop to cope with more challenging environments (Steel et al., 2008; Jokela et al.,

2015). Interestingly, individually committed behaviour shows a positive relationship with measures of economic resilience, particularly when places are having to overcome the effects of recession. This may reflect a behavioural profile promoting hard work and tenacious tendencies, which are likely to be particularly important when trying to make the most of opportunities in periods of uncertainty (Lee, 2017). It is also consistent with the finding that conscientiousness is positively linked to the long-term survival of businesses (Ciavarella et al., 2004). Diverse extravert behaviour shows a positive relationship with growth, which is consistent with those studies that note the importance of being open to other individuals and ideas (Florida, 2002; Levie, 2007). Such a relationship during recessionary periods may reflect the benefits of openness with respect to managing uncertainty (Hodson and Sorrentino, 1999). Alongside explanations of urban and regional development associated with agglomeration, specialization, and increasing returns (Storper, 2010), the coping mechanisms associated with inclusive amenable behaviour may boost well-being in those localities with lower wealth (Steel et al., 2008; Jokela et al., 2015). However, they may also become part of the problem in terms of preventing growth in subsequent periods.

Other findings stemming from the Huggins et al. (2018) study indicate that, with regard to community culture as measured by engagement with education and employment, cities and regions in the most developed parts of the UK show the greatest engagement. There is a particularly marked north–south divide with regard to a community culture that is collective in its nature. Localities in Wales, Scotland, North East, and North West are the most culturally collective. Conversely, localities in the South West, East, and South East of England are the least collectively oriented communities. Alongside collective activities, another measure of the cultural bonding within local communities is the rate of social cohesion. Social cohesion is highest in the localities of North East England, followed by Scotland, Wales, and North West England. The relationship between social cohesion and economic competitiveness across local authority districts shows a significant negative relationship, which suggests that localities with more diverse community cultures tend to be more economically competitive. Similarly, a negative correlation is found for feminine and caring activities, adherence to social rules, and collective actions. This would appear to indicate that competitiveness is greater in those areas that follow the typical masculine (Bruni et al. 2004), employment-orientated (Weber, 1930), atomistic (Kirkman et al., 2006), unconstrained-by-rules (Noorderhaven et al., 2004), but networked (Huggins and Thompson, 2015b) culture.

In terms of personality psychology, as measured by conscientiousness, cities and regions in the more prosperous south of the nation have a strong density of individuals reporting conscientiousness behaviour. Also, individuals with the most extravert personalities tend to be clustered in and around London. With the exception of a small number of localities, the most extravert places are again all situated in the south of the nation, with the London boroughs of Hammersmith and Fulham, Richmond upon Thames, Wandsworth, Kensington and Chelsea, and Lambeth being particular hotspots.

In general, there is a very strong and significant positive relationship between levels of extravert behaviour and economic competitiveness across cities and regions. This indicates that the geography of personality traits with regard to rates of extravert–introvert behaviour is strongly associated with economic performance. Similar to extraversion, high densities of individuals with behaviour that can be regarded as open tend to be found in urban areas of the south of Britain. London boroughs account for sixteen of the top twenty localities in terms of openness, led by Hackney, Islington, Kensington and Chelsea, Camden, and Southwark. As with extravert behaviour, an open personality psychology is positively associated with economic behaviour at the local level. Overall economic competitiveness is also associated with greater extraversion, openness, emotional stability (low neuroticism), and lower agreeableness and conscientiousness. This begins to suggest that having people with the 'right' personality in your city or region may be an important influence on long-term competitiveness and economic development. Cosmopolitanism and outwardly facing behaviour tends to foster greater economic strength and competitiveness, and suggests the possibility that some regions and localities possess the 'wrong' type of behaviour—if not, the wrong culture—when it comes to catalysing economic development.

Complementary studies, particularly at the individual level, have suggested that the combination of, rather than specific, personality traits may be important for outcomes such as success in education (Asendorpf and van Aken, 1999; Hart et al., 2003) and the development of social networks (Caspi, 2000). For example, although the US states classed by Rentfrow et al. (2013) as friendly and conventional are high in extraversion and emotional stability, they also tend to be low in openness, high in agreeableness, and exhibit poorer economic performance. The combined psychocultural behaviour measures used by Huggins et al. (2018) find a positive relationship with individual commitment and diverse extraversion, and a negative relationship with inclusive amenability. This suggests that inclusive amenable psychocultural behaviour—which is high with regard to more tightly bonded, friendly, and caring characteristics—is less likely to promote competitiveness. Diverse extraversion, on the other hand, is the form of behaviour which appears to have the strongest positive relationship with competitiveness due to its extravert, emotionally stable, and more open profile. Based on previous studies this might be expected, as such an environment, with higher levels of these characteristics, generates individuals suited to artistic and investigative occupations that may promote innovative activities.

3.6 Conclusion

In conclusion, the available analysis clearly points to a confirmation of the proposition that the underlying socio-spatial community culture and aggregate personality psychology found in particular localities, cities, and regions are determining factors of the level of economic development found in these places. Given this, the interplay between culture and psychology in the form of the psychocultural behaviour of cities and regions appears to shape their long-term development trajectories. Cities and regions that have relatively atomized behavioural environments with high levels of individual commitment tend to enjoy development benefits. Similarly, places with high rates of cultural diversity and extravert individuals have relatively high levels of economic development. On the other hand, cities and regions that are more socially inclusive, with a significant number of people with amenable and agreeable personality traits, experience relatively low rates of economic development.

To a large extent, the findings make intuitive sense, with, for example, the individual commitment found in competitive regions being a manifestation of a 'personal competitiveness' that subsequently becomes visible at an aggregated spatial level. However, the relationship between psychocultural human behaviour and urban and regional competitiveness is unlikely to be a direct one. It is more likely that behaviour initially impacts upon on other sources of development, such as the form and efficiency of local institutions, as well as the capability and capacity to generate and mobilize the types of agency and capital required for high rates of economic development, which form the subject of the following chapters.

Finally, rather than study aspects of socio-spatial community culture and personality psychology independently, this chapter has considered the means by which the socio-spatial community culture and personality traits of cities, regions, and localities holistically combine in the form of local psychocultural profiles that influence the economic growth they experience. Complementary community cultures and personality traits tend to reinforce one another to create quite distinct psychocultural behavioural profiles

(Boneva et al., 1998; Hofstede and McCrae, 2004; Rentfrow et al., 2013). In the case of the example illustrated here, three forms of psychocultural behavioural profile are identified. While one, diverse extraversion, displays lower levels of social cohesion and neuroticism and higher levels of extraversion and openness, the other psychocultural profiles display higher levels of agreeableness, social cohesion, and collective traits—defined as inclusive amenability—or independent and self-sufficient characteristics, defined as individual commitment. Although individual aspects of community culture and personality psychology traits have been linked to local economic activities and growth (Huggins and Thompson, 2015a; Obschonka et al., 2015; Stuetzer et al., 2016), it can be concluded that they may be even more strongly influenced by combinations that generate specific forms of a holistic psychocultural behavioural profile (Rentfrow et al., 2013).

4
Agency, Economic Evolution, and History

4.1 Introduction

A host of factors relating to the availability of capital in the form of investment and resources, the skills of the workforce, the availability and capability of entrepreneurs, and other agents of innovation, as well as the cooperation and collaboration achieved through ecosystems, are all offered as explanatory factors for the economic development of regions and cities (Capello and Nijkamp, 2009; Cooke et al., 2011; Stimson et al., 2011; Shearmur et al., 2016; Spigel, 2017). In general, these approaches echo the notion of regions as 'Schumpeterian hubs' for recombining human capital in order to generate innovation (Wolfe, 2017). In particular, notions relating to ecosystems and agency suggest that merely investing in capital may not be enough to secure entrepreneurship leading to greater innovation and higher rates of economic growth, especially the type of transformative renewal and development required in many cities and regions, particularly industrially mature and economically lagging areas.

This chapter argues that the type and nature of human agency existing within cities and regions at particular points in their development are significant factors explaining the capacity of these places to achieve economic transformation and renewal. In particular, it seeks to set notions of entrepreneurial human agency within wider and emerging theories of regional economic renewal and transformation. It is suggested that, while the configuration and capability of economic ecosystems—which are conceptualized through notions such as clusters, innovation systems, and industrial districts—determine regional development outcomes, at the micro level it is the role played by certain key human agents within regions that actually shapes the nature and evolution of these ecosystems.

In other words, human agency is considered to be a primary driver associated with economic development and transformation, and should be viewed seriously when addressing the routes available to economically mature and

A Behavioural Theory of Economic Development: The Uneven Evolution of Cities and Regions. Robert Huggins and Piers Thompson, Oxford University Press (2021). © Robert Huggins and Piers Thompson.
DOI: 10.1093/oso/9780198832348.003.0004

underdeveloped cities and regions in their bid to foster renewal and transformation. For example, it is argued that entrepreneurship, innovation, and creativity are social processes that involve groups of people who build off one another historically, and are the products of cities and regions that act as the key organizing unit for these activities, bringing together the firms, talent, and other regional institutions necessary to support entrepreneurship (Florida et al., 2017). Similarly, the symbiotic relationship between key agents and their location is found in research relating to the role of a limited number of 'star' scientists in promoting the innovation performance of certain cities and regions (Zucker et al., 1998; Moretti, 2012).

One of the key arguments put forward in this chapter is that, during periods of economic and innovative transformation, in particular cities and regions there will be a relatively small number of key human agents that are the core, but not necessarily sole, drivers of such development. Through such agency, regions can become 'incubators of new ideas' and provide opportunities for entrepreneurship to take place, as well as for discovering valuable new knowledge (Huggins and Williams, 2011; Hülsbeck and Pickavé, 2014). Successful urban and regional economic transformation may emerge from forms of agency that promote institutional and cultural change, especially through the introduction of economically efficient institutions and cultural change and diversity across time. Regions and cities that are unable to effectively transform economically and industrially may be marked by agents that promote institutional and cultural persistence, in particular through rent-seeking institutions, and cultural reproduction and homophily across time. In the second part of this chapter, it is argued that contemporary community cultures in underdeveloped cities and regions are often a legacy of past industrialization and the social scars and 'haunting' that may linger for many years in these places.

4.2 Theories of Urban and Regional Economic Evolution

This section considers the evolution and development of regions and cities and the institutions within them. One example of a general regional evolutionary framework has described a process of genesis, development, growth, renewal/demise (Huggins, 2008). A genesis phase is usually the result of an institutional trigger that acts as an initial magnet for attracting talented agents, particularly entrepreneurial individuals, and although there may not necessarily be a single institution responsible for their attraction, there is a high degree of correlation between rates of development and the existence of specific universities and research institutes within a regional 'cluster' (Harrison et al., 2004; Moretti, 2012). The development phase of a region is based on forces that spin off knowledge from the institutional trigger, which remains localized, while the growth phase occurs when a region successfully develops a critical mass, acting as a centripetal magnet for new capital inputs and agents (Ter Wal and Boschma, 2011). The renewal or demise stage of regional development is largely dependent on the technological trajectory or path of its product and process base (Boschma and Martin, 2010). Regions that are able to adapt to disruptive knowledge shifts, through the creative destruction associated with new product and market development, will survive and grow, whereas those regions that have become overly path-dependent will enter the demise stage (Peterson, 2000).

Perhaps the most important feature of economic renewal is the requirement for the continual development and mobilization of human capital. This is strongly related to the capacity to renew networks and create new modes of interaction, often with actors who are one step removed and have only indirect ties with existing associations, (Martin and Sunley, 2011). If one examines perhaps the most resilient and self-transformative of all regional economies in the modern era, Silicon Valley, it is found that firms of all sizes interact in the ecosystem, in which superior technology trumps business size, with innovation occurring in a highly decentralized environment, with the benefits of proximity—dense social and professional networks, informal information exchange, cross-firm collaboration, and serendipity—outweighing the high and rising costs of being in the ecosystem (Saxenian, 1994; Saxenian and Sabel, 2008; Spigel, 2017).

A fundamental thrust of urban and regional evolutionary theory is that innovation no longer occurs in isolated laboratories, but through collaborative co-development networks between increasingly specialist producers, that is connected and collective agency. At all stages of the production process, innovation is a highly iterative and non-linear process. Learning happens through continuing interactions facilitated by social networks and open labour markets, which allow know-how and information to circulate freely (MacKinnon et al., 2002). It is possible to contribute to the formation of such an ecosystem, but it cannot be easily planned from the top down, and once it begins to emerge, the strength of such a system is that it fosters unanticipated recombinations of skill and technology, and multiple, often parallel, experiments with technology, organization, markets, and so forth (Saxenian and Sabel, 2008). In essence, the emergence of Silicon Valley perhaps best represents an empirical example of the agency-system paradigm presented by some evolutionary economists (Dopfer et al., 2004; Dopfer and Potts, 2004).

In older industrial regions where there has been a process of demise rather than renewal, deindustrialization results in capital flight. As Harvey (2003: 116) notes, 'if capital does move out, then it leaves behind a trail of devastation and devaluation; the deindustrializations experienced in the heartlands of capitalism…in the 1970s and 1980s are cases in point', giving rise to the many problems associated with old industrial regions. Martin and Sunley (2011) argue that the evolution of regional economies can be best analysed by considering them to be manifestations of complex adaptive systems consisting of numerous components with functions and interrelationships that provide the system with a particular identity and a degree of connectedness, and with the adaptive perspective highlighting the importance of recombination and reuse of resources. Renewal, they argue, depends on reworking the legacies from preceding economic cycles, particularly through the engagement of 'extrovert' entrepreneurs. Martin and Sunley (2011) further suggest that the micro-behaviours—or agency—of individual system components (individuals and firms) are the most significant factor for evolutionary courses during periods of change and transition.

As a general schematic, urban and regional evolutionary frameworks are at pains to highlight the importance and focus on the 'collective' nature of regional development. Although certain examples confirm this, more generally across many regions these frameworks may lack a realism as coordination mechanisms do not provide such 'harmonious' development. This is further accentuated if such coordination does not stem from the form of the culture and informal institutions that guide, promote, and constrain particular activities. However, such cultures and institutions are not fixed and may be shaped by human agents within regions in the form—for example—of entrepreneurs and policymakers, in particular, into a cultural and institutional environment that is more conducive to innovative transformation, renewal, and economic development. This sounds intuitively plausible and suggests that theories of regional evolution need to better incorporate the role of the coordinating and constraining influence of culture and institutions, alongside the mechanisms by which entrepreneurs and other agents are influenced by, and influence, these cultures and institutions.

4.3 Human Agency and Economic Development

This section seeks to consider in some depth the notion of human agency and how it may relate to processes of urban and regional development. It addresses how the activities of different forms of agent and agency may translate into different forms of regional development. To begin with, a compelling analysis of the role of human agency in propelling economic transformation is provided by Mokyr (2017), who argues that from 1500 to 1700 parts of European society—largely the educated elite—developed a set of cultural traits and accompanying institutions that were highly attuned to fostering the forms of intellectual innovation and knowledge that ultimately propelled the Industrial Revolution. Specifically, Mokyr (2017) suggests that key cultural changes relating to the increased value placed on innovation and ideas occurred during this period, and, through the formation of a market for ideas, a relatively small number of cultural entrepreneurs across Europe were responsible for driving this cultural change. Mokyr (2017) describes how these entrepreneurs stimulated directly and indirectly economic evolution on an unprecedented scale, with the interaction of cultural evolution and evolutionary biology resulting in the emergence of adaptive agents who chose whether to adopt new ideas from a series of cultural menus that led to intellectual innovation.

Returning to the urban and regional scale, the literature points to three forms of agency that may act as catalysts of transformation: *entrepreneurial agency* (Drakopoulou Dodd and Anderson, 2007), *political agency* (Ayres, 2014), and *labour agency* (Coe and Jordhus-Lier, 2011). In the case of *entrepreneurial agency*, entrepreneurs are increasingly depicted as agents of economic and social change, often enacting a collective identity that facilitates and shapes development (Lippmann and Aldrich, 2016). From both a spatial and a temporal perspective, entrepreneurs are further conceived as 'generational units' in the sense that they are agents who mould collective memories through space and time (Lippmann and Aldrich, 2016). Crucially, they are often highly heterogeneous agents and possess a wide range of personality traits including extraversion, openness to experience, conscientiousness, and the ability to bear risk (Fritsch and Wyrwich, 2015).

Entrepreneurship is generally considered to form a part of endogenous modes of economic development consisting of activities, investment, and systems arising and nurtured within a city or region, as opposed to being attracted from elsewhere (Audretsch and Keilbach, 2004). As part of these modes, the capability of entrepreneurs to influence economic growth is related to their capacity to access and exploit knowledge and generate innovation. Entrepreneurship, therefore, is increasingly recognized as a crucial element in fostering economic development (Audretsch et al., 2006).

Entrepreneurs can be said to take the role of a mediator between culture and development, which corresponds with the aggregate psychological-traits perspective of development (Beugelsdijk and Maseland, 2011).

Alongside economic development, growing evidence suggests that entrepreneurship may provide considerable value in terms of social development and well-being beyond that achieved indirectly through higher rates of economic growth (Schjoedt, 2009). Studies have repeatedly found that autonomy and independence, rather than pecuniary reasons, are cited as motivations for engaging in entrepreneurial activities (Hundley, 2001). Furthermore, the opportunity to use the creative side of our personalities also features in the motivations for business ownership (Huggins and Thompson, 2016).

The notion of the entrepreneur and the contribution of entrepreneurship to development have been widely interpreted. Entrepreneurship has been used to define types of individuals (Say, 1880), types of decisions (Knight, 1921), and forms of behaviour (Schumpeter, 1934). As a discrete concept, entrepreneurship has its origin in the work of Cantillon (1931), and has since developed beyond the neoclassical school's emphasis on equilibrium, which found no place for the entrepreneur as a cause of economic activity, to the Austrian school's argument that entrepreneurship is crucial for understanding economic growth, leading to Schumpeter's statement that 'The carrying out of new combinations (of means of production) we call "enterprise"; and the individuals whose function it is to carry them out we call "entrepreneurs"' (1934: 74).

The Austrian school can be considered to consist of two broad theoretical views, both of which contest the neoclassical rational market perspective of entrepreneurship. The 'efficiency' approach highlights the role of entrepreneurs as human agents driving the market forward towards efficient outcomes by exploiting profit opportunities and moving economies towards equilibrium (Kirzner, 1973). The 'innovation' or 'Schumpeterian' approach suggests that markets tend towards disequilibrium as entrepreneurs contribute to the market's process of 'creative destruction', with new innovations replacing old technologies (Schumpeter, 1934). Both approaches suggest that entrepreneurship involves the nexus of entrepreneurial opportunities and enterprising individuals, with the ability to identify opportunities being a key part of the entrepreneurial process.

Enterprise and entrepreneurship are now commonly viewed as the process of establishing and growing a business. However, this can be seen as a narrow perspective and disregards Schumpeter's (1934) contention that entrepreneurship is a function of changes in society and occurs in a variety of circumstances. While the creation of a new business is an accurate description of one of the many outcomes of entrepreneurial activity, entrepreneurship encompasses far more than business start-ups. It derives from the creative power of the human mind (Sautet and Kirzner, 2006) and is characterized as a behavioural characteristic of individuals expressed through innovative attributes, flexibility, and adaptability to change (Wennekers and Thurik, 1999).

At the urban and regional level, rates of entrepreneurship often vary greatly, with some cities and regions becoming the test beds for new ideas that provide opportunities for entrepreneurship to take place, and for discovering valuable new knowledge (Glaeser, 2002; Huggins and Williams, 2011). In more 'entrepreneurial regions', network mechanisms are formed through the evolutionary interdependency emerging between entrepreneurs and other economic agents as a result of the recognition and necessity for knowledge and innovation-based interactions beyond the market (Cooke, 2004). Given this, entrepreneurial agency can be considered to operate across the personal–proxy–collective continuum. Most prominently, there is the personal agency of individual entrepreneurs, but the networks and collaborations they form with each other conform to a collective agency that will impact on urban and regional development outcomes. Furthermore, their connections with other economic agents, such as investors in the form of venture capitalists and the like, take the form of a proxy agency whereby entrepreneurs are empowered to achieve the outcomes of this wider group of stakeholders.

Alongside entrepreneurial agency, the agency of those associated with the political economy of cities and regions—*political agency*—represents another form of active behaviour that determines the future of these places. Leading commentators such as Chang (2013) and Piketty (2014) highlight the role of political leadership in determining economic outcomes. Arguments to increase the global democratic power apportioned to city- and regional-level governments, as opposed to national government, are examples of the perceived role of urban and regional-level political agency in shaping not only development at a subnational level but also on the international stage (Beer and Clower, 2014). Indeed, a growing literature suggests that the economic performance of cities and regions is linked to the quality of leadership within these places (Stimson et al., 2009). Others note the role of political agency and behaviour in facilitating or hindering urban and regional development, with rent-seeking behaviour being an example of how negative development outcomes can result from political agency (Storper, 2013).

Localized political agency, and the leadership it potentially offers through politicians, local authority professionals, as well as numerous other state and non-state agents, can act as a key facilitator of change and innovation (Ayres, 2014). Some consider local political agency to be a means of filling the innovation and leadership gap stemming from national governments, and while the behavioural changes they are capable of effecting may be small and incremental, in the long term they may have a significant cumulative development impact on local communities (Lowndes and McCaughie, 2013). Within this context, political agency may be apparent in the form of the personal agency of individual political leaders and professionals or the proxy agency activated via the supporters and funders of these leaders. However, perhaps the most potent forms of political agency at the local level concern collectives of agents promoting policy and societal changes. Chapter 7 will look in more detail at how this collective and proxy agency might be captured.

A lack of local collective political agency in the form, for example, of political schisms may result in unstable or incoherent responses to particular development needs, as well as promoting the type of rent-seeking behaviour that results in negative development outcomes (Beer and Clower, 2014). Political rent-seeking in this instance can be considered to consist of resources allocated by politicians and public officials, principally in terms of the time they give to certain activities (Vasilev, 2013), to compete for control of larger shares of public funds. Such rent-seeking is manifest in the form of resources that are used to maintain or further develop existing interests, to engage in policy and political turf wars, and, more generally, to enhance political capital.

In general, the bigger the size of the public sector within an urban or regional economy, the more scope there is for rent-seeking activity that results in economic inefficiencies (Gelb et al., 1991; Persson and Tabellini, 2000). This can be especially harmful to innovation-related activities, which in turn hampers development (Murphy et al., 1993). Urban and regional economies with a significant public-sector wage premium and high public-sector employment are consistently more likely to be engaged in government rent-seeking that results in inefficiencies through non-productive activities occurring within public administration (Vasilev, 2013).

Finally, an important yet often overlooked form of agency that impacts on urban and regional development outcomes concerns the agency of labour and workers—*labour agency*. As Coe and Jordhus-Lier (2011) discuss, from the 1970s through to the 1980s labour agency was implicitly a key concept within the Marxist-inspired economic geography of the time (e.g. Massey, 1984; Smith, 1984), in particular the role of capital–labour relations and the changing nature of the agency of labour and the outcomes it was capable of achieving.

The debates and issues raised by Massey (1984) and discussed in Chapter 3 in relation to labour agency have figured less in accounts of urban and regional development since the 1990s, instead 'capital' itself has become the predominate source of critique, discussion, and analysis. As a result, it has been suggested that there is a need to re-embed the notion of labour agency within the discourse of economic geography, particularly in light of debates concerning the requirement for individuals, groups, and cities and regions to establish developmental paths that are as resilient as possible to external shocks (Coe and Jordhus-Lier, 2011; Martin and Sunley, 2015b). Such re-embeddedness can be conceptualized in the form of three broad forms of labour agency (Coe and Jordhus- Lier, 2011): resilience—small actions related to workers 'getting by'; reworking—actions to materially improve social and economic conditions; and resistance—challenges to existing social relations to (re)gain control of worker time and its use. This last category consists of more 'game-changing' actions, which are generally less likely to be prevalent in contemporary capitalist eras than either resistance or reworking forms of labour agency. However, this is not to say that resistance labour agency is totally absent, and Ince et al. (2015) present a vivid account of how workers at an oil refinery complex on the east coast of England sought to resist the changes proposed by the refinery's employers to wage and working conditions. Such agency is transnational, but not necessarily in the sense of the international ownership of the refinery itself, rather in the sense of the high international mobility of its highly qualified workforce, and therefore highlights the role of migration as a form of labour agency.

When examining the concept of labour branching by redundant workers, MacKinnon (2017) subdivides the actions associated with labour responses in terms of the relatedness of activities undertaken and the location of such activities. Within these responses three dimensions can be identified: iteration—which is habitual in nature and informed by the past; projectivity—whereby there is a focus on future possibilities; and practical evaluation—which strives to consider past habits and future opportunities in the present context (Emirbayer and Mische, 1998). The last two are fundamental in allowing labour to adapt to shocks that may lead to the loss of employment or weakened employment positions.

Research in the field of labour agency has sought to articulate further its spatial and temporal dimensions as well as its key forms, with worker (union) relations increasingly considered to sit alongside more community-driven forms of agency (Coe and Jordhus- Lier, 2011). Furthermore, the intersection of worker and community organizations is considered to shape the overall nature of urban and regional labour agency (Pike, 2007). Clearly, therefore, labour agency is largely a collective endeavour, with the most effective forms of such agency likely to stem from a collective efficacy

(Cumbers et al., 2016). However, it is also possible to conceptualize it as a form of proxy agency whereby organized bodies represent the views and wishes of workers. Also, there are aspects of personal agency in the form of the actions of worker and community leaders, as well as the action of particular workers, such as the highly mobile workers described by Ince et al. (2015). Allied with this, there is a need to acknowledge that labour agency by one group of workers may impact on others, and therefore there is a requirement to gain an understanding of the views on justice, rights, responsibilities, and entitlements that workers apply to themselves and others (Castree, 2007).

4.4 Agency and Urban and Regional Ecosystems

Building on notions of bounded rationality, scholars such as Porter (1981) argued that there is a need for a more agentic position for understanding economic development, whereby agents in the form of entrepreneurs and managers are able to exercise power in their choice of markets and other options that are not predetermined by the underlying structure of the industry in which they are positioned. In due course, Porter (1990) developed his thinking further through his examination of the concept of regional systems of 'clusters', which he considered help capture important linkages, complementarities, and spillovers of technology, skills, and information that cut across firms and industries. In this sense, Porter is discussing an ecosystem that connects economic agents to provide value—in the form of productivity gains, innovation, and entrepreneurial opportunities—for each (Huggins and Izushi, 2011).

Following in the footsteps of Mokyr (2017), it is of interest to examine whether his key agent thesis of development at a pan-European level holds up when regional and city territories are analysed. Although a full analysis would require extensive new data collection, one useful and bounded source of information is Peter Hall's (1998) *Cities in Civilization*. In this book, Hall describes the evolution of eighteen cities and regions at the height of their innovative and transformative prowess on a chapter-by-chapter basis, that is, as fully functional urban or regional ecosystems. Although Hall's own analysis may be partial in terms of its coverage, it does give a good indication of the protagonists at the heart of the regional transformation process. Therefore, it is of value to undertake a content analysis of Hall's text in order to identify whether the role proposed for agents can be identified.

As part of the results of the content analysis, Table 4.1 presents a summary of the key agents and the time of their most important agentic activity highlighted by Hall (1998) in nine of the leading cities and regions he describes, ranging from the emergence of Silicon Valley and the Bay Area of San Francisco between 1950 and 1990 to as far back as the Roman Empire from 50 BC to AD 100. What is marked is that in the majority of cases approximately twenty to thirty agents are considered to have been the major catalysts that fuelled urban and regional innovation and development. Within these, there are examples of entrepreneurs who through their innovations

Table 4.1 Agents of innovation, transformation, and development for a cross section of cities and regions at key points in their evolution

City (time period)	Key agents
Silicon Valley/ Bay Area (1950–90)	Alexander M. Poniatoff (1944–56); Bill Gates (1981); Charles Litton (1932); Cy Elwell (1909); Ed Roberts, Leslie Solomon, and Roger Melen (1974); Frederick Terman (1951); Gary Kildall (1973); Harold Lindsay (1947–56); Lee De Forest (1906); Robert Noyce (1956); Stephen Wozniak and Steven Jobs (1976); William Weber, Sigurd Varian, and Russell Varian (1939).
Los Angeles (1910–45)	Adolph Zukor (1903–6); Alexander Black (1893–1994); Thomas Armat and Charles Francis Jenkins (1895–6); Carl Laemmle (1912); David W. Griffith (1915); Harry Cohn (1920); Horace Henderson Wilcox (1883); John P. Harris and Harry Davis (1905); Louis B. Mayer (1924); Thomas Alva Edison (1887–9); Harry, Albert, Sam, and Jack Warner (1918); William Fox (1903).
New York (1880–1940)	Alexander Graham Bell (1876); Clifford M. Holland (1919–27); John B. Dunlop (1888); Thomas Alva Edison (1879); Frank Julian (1887); John Augustus (1844); John Francis Hylan (Red Mike) (1920s); Fiorello La Guardia (1934–40); Ottmar Mergenthaler (1885); Othmar Hermann Ammann (1931); Robert Fulton (1807); George Westinghouse (1868); William J. Wilgus (1903–13).
Berlin (1840–1930)	Emil Rathenau (1889–90); Frank J. Sprague (late 1880s); Friedrich Wilhelm Anton von Heynitz (1778–99); Sir Humphry Davy (1808); John Gibbs and Lucien Gaulard (1880); Nikola Tesla (1887); Samuel Morse (1837); Werner von Siemens (1879).
Detroit (1890–1915)	Charles E. Duryea and J. Frank Duryea (1893); Gottlieb Daimler and Karl Benz (1885); Etienne Lenoir (1860); Henry Ford, Ransom E. Olds, and Charles B. King (1870s–1890s); Oliver Evans (1875); Nikolaus A. Otto (1876); Ransom E. Olds (1899); Alfred P. Sloan (1918 onwards); Wilhelm Maybach (1893).
London (1825–1900)	Jeremy Bentham (1784); Sir Edwin Chadwick (1839–42); Dr John Snow (1849); Henry Fielding (1750); John Howard, Sir William Blackstone, and William Eden (1778); John Nash (1820s); Lord John S. Eldon (1819); Lord Charles Grey (1830); Lord John Russell (1839); Messrs Haden of Trowbridge (1842); Prince of Wales (1865); Colonel Sir Charles Rowan and Sir Richard Mayne (1829); William Allen (1817); William Farr (1841).
Glasgow (1770–1890)	James Beaumont (1828); Henry Bell (1812); William Denny (1818); John Elder and Alexander C. Kirk (1854); John Golborne (1775); Samuel Hall (1834); Patrick Miller and William Symington (1788); David Mushet (1801); David Napier (1819 and 1822); James Napier (1830); J. C. Perier (1775); John Robertson (1812); John Roebuck (1760); Sir John Biles (1880); William Symington (1801); Tod and MacGregor (1836 and 1850); James Watt (1769); John Wilkinson (1787); Thomas Wingate (1838).

Continued

Table 4.1 *Continued*

City (time period)	Key agents
Manchester (1760–1830)	John Aikin (1795); Richard Arkwright (1771); Edmund Cartwright (1786); Peter Clare (1778); Samuel Crompton (1779); Abraham Darby (1709); Edward III (1331); William Galloway (1790); Grimshaw of Gorton (1790); James Hargreaves (1765); John Kay (1733); William Lee (1589); Thomas Lombe (1721); **Robert Peel**; Richard Roberts (1825); **Andrew Ure** (1835); John Wyatt and Lewis Paul (1741).
Rome (50 BC–AD 100)	**Augustus Caesar** (22 BC); **Julius Caesar** (1st and 2nd century and 7th BC); **Claudius** (AD 52); **Domitian; Sextus Julius Frontinus** (AD 96); **Marcus Vipsanius Agrippa** (20 and 12 BC); Gaius Sergius Orata (95 BC); **Marcus Vitruvius Pollio** (30–15 BC).

Source: Based on the authors' analysis of Hall (1998) and other materials. Underlined names are those founding businesses as entrepreneurs; those in bold are stakeholders with key responsibility for developing the institutions and infrastructure that allowed entrepreneurship to flourish; others are largely inventors and innovators working for others when they made their main contribution.

changed the direction of the region or city, for example Stephen Wozniak and Steven Jobs (Silicon Valley), Thomas Alva Edison (Los Angeles), Werner von Siemens (Berlin), and Richard Arkwright (Manchester). There are also those civil engineers such as John Augustus Roebling (New York) and Frederick Terman (Silicon Valley) who helped create the infrastructure such as transport links and science parks that are vital in allowing commerce and entrepreneurship to flourish and to promote a form of culture and effective institutions required to stimulate development. This begins to suggest that, much like Mokyr's (2017) arguments regarding the role of an elite group of entrepreneurial agents in triggering the role of the Industrial Revolution, as well as research on the role of star scientists in underpinning regional innovation success (Zucker et al., 1998; Moretti, 2012), a more historical analysis of urban and regional transformation is likely to pinpoint a relatively small number of agents as being central catalysing forces propelling the evolution of their respective urban and regional ecosystems.

It is interesting that the US examples largely constitute private-sector entrepreneurs, who brought new innovations to the market that have radically reshaped the regional economy and also society. By contrast, in the earlier examples of Berlin and, in particular, London there is a much more prominent role played by those creating the conditions for entrepreneurs to prosper through public-health improvements (for example John Snow's influence on improvements in the sewer system) and the enforcement of laws (Henry Fielding's work in early police forces).

In order to consider the process of transformative regional evolution a little more closely, Tables 4.2 and 4.3 present more detailed findings from the

Table 4.2 Agents of innovation, transformation, and development in Manchester 1760–1830

Agent	Occupation:	Year (time):	Key contribution to economic development
Edward III	Monarch	1400	Brought Flemish weavers to settle in various places in the north of England including Manchester, Rossendale, and Pendle in the 14th century (later, the Weavers' Act of 1555 freed the weaving industry from medieval regulations, and thus Lancashire enjoyed a rare degree of economic freedom)
William Lee	Clergyman	1589	Invented the stocking frame, creating complex domestic production
Abraham Darby	Ironmaster and Quaker	1709	Smelted iron with coal
Thomas Lombe	Silk thrower	1721	Built the first recognizable factory
John Kay	Innovator and industrialist	1733	Invented the flying shuttle, which increased the efficiency of weaving twofold. This eventually created pressure on the supply of weft needed for weave
John Wyatt and Lewis Paul	Carpenter and innovator	1741	Innovated and applied the system of spinning cotton by rollers
James Hargreaves	Weaver, carpenter	1765	Invented the spinning jenny, which reduced the labour required to produce yarn
Richard Arkwright	Economist, industrialist	1771	Did the most to make the spinning machine useful for production
Peter Clare	Clockmaker	1778	Proposed to establish a philosophical school emphasizing mechanics and similar subjects
Samuel Crompton	Biographer, industrialist	1779	Invented the mule machine, which was cheap, compact, light, and could be hand-operated in an ordinary house
Edmund Cartwright	Professor of poetry	1786	Improved a weaving machine model which stopped if the thread was accidentally broken
Robert Peel	Industrialist	1787	Improved the factory system and built an integrated spinning, weaving, and printing factory
William Galloway	Mining engineer, professor, and industrialist	1790	Established firms to make waterwheels
Grimshaw of Gorton	Industrialist	1790	Developed the power loom
Richard Roberts	Millwright	1825	Developed the self-acting mule at the request of manufacturers affectedby the strikes of spinners

Source: Based on the authors' analysis of Hall (1998).

Table 4.3 Agents of innovation, transformation, and development in Glasgow 1770–1890

Agent	Occupation:	Year (time):	Key contribution to economic development
John Roebuck	Inventor and industrialist	1760	Established the first Scottish blast furnaces
James Watt	Instrument maker	1769	Invented the Watt steam engine
John Golborne	Contractor, navigation engineer	1775	Deepened the Clyde Channel
Robert Wilson	Founder of blast furnaces	1780	Set up a foundry with the first furnace
John Wilkinson	Ironmaster	1787	Used iron in part construction of a barrage called 'Trial'
Patrick Miller and William Symington	Banker (Miller) and engineer/inventor (Symington)	1788	Sailed a steamboat on Dalswinton Loch; the speed of the boat was about 5 mph
Sir John Biles	Professor	1880	Devised new means of turbine efficiency
David Mushet	Engineer	1801	Found that materials mined in the district abandoned as 'wild coal' contained at least 30–50 per cent iron when raw and up to 70 per cent when calcined
William Symington	Engineer and inventor	1801	Fitted a steamboat with a Watt engine
Henry Bell	Steamboat developer	1812	Started the first commercial steamship services
John Robertson	Engineer	1812	Developed the original 'Comet' engine, used mainly for land travel
William Denny	Shipbuilder	1818	Built 30-horsepower engines
David Napier	Marine engineer	1819 and 1822	Built the boiler for the *Comet* and engines for the *Talbot*; also established the first commercial steamship line between Liverpool, Greenock, and Glasgow
James Beaumont	Manager	1828	Discovered how to use hot instead of cold air in furnace blast
James Napier	Engineer and inventor	1830	Invented the horizontal tubular boiler, giving 25–30 per cent fuel saving
Samuel Hall	Engineer	1834	Patented a condenser
David Tod and John MacGregor	Engineers and shipbuilders	1836 and 1850	Opened the first Clyde iron shipyard; regular transatlantic passenger traffic by iron steamship
Thomas Wingate	Engineer	1838	Made the first Glasgow-based transatlantic steam voyage in 1838, the *Sirius*
John Elder and Alexander C. Kirk	Engineers	1854	Elder's compound engine of 1854 and Kirk's triple-expansion engine of 1886 offered price and speed advantages

Source: Based on the authors' analysis of Hall (1998).

content analysis of Hall (1998) for the cases of the growth of the textile industry in Manchester between 1760 and 1830 and the shipping industry in Glasgow between 1770 and 1890. In both cases it is clear that a series of entrepreneurs, industrialists, and intellectuals built on the success of their predecessors in each city through a process of knowledge accumulation and both radical and incremental innovation that typifies the regional evolutionary framework discussed above. Both cities eventually hit a period of decline with a slower rate of transformation that is still ongoing with regard to more service-driven cities. Given the important role played by political agents in many regional efforts, it is interesting to consider whether regions and cities such as Silicon Valley have been better able to adapt—for example from hardware to design and software creation—due to agency being driven by market or political intervention. This has contemporary ramifications in terms of state-driven transformations such as those experienced by, for example, fast-changing cities such as Dubai (Alfaki and Ahmed, 2017), whereby the private sector has played a lesser role in furthering the development of an entrepreneurial culture and associated institutions.

Clearly, the source of long-term regional economic success and renewal is to create a behavioural environment that fosters positive lock-in allowing entrepreneurship and innovation to become culturally embedded. As illustrated by Figure 4.1, this would seem to require agents within regional economic systems that promote institutional and cultural change. In particular, such agents will be responsible for creating local economic institutions that are wealth creating in the sense that they incentivize innovation and help remove barriers to change.

4.5 Entrepreneurial Agency, Innovation, and Development

The prevailing discourse on regional development is largely positioned within structural explanations based on varieties of analysis concerning the spatial organization of industry, with little consideration paid to the role of

	Positive Lock-In Regions	Negative Lock-in Regions
Agents	Agents Promoting Institutional and Cultural Change	Agents Promoting Institutional and Cultural Persistence
Culture	Cultural Change and Diversity Across Time	Cultural Reproduction and Homophily Across Time
Institutions	Wealth Creating Institutions	Rent Seeking Institutions

Figure 4.1 Behavioural sources of positive and negative regional lock-in.

agents within particular regional structures and systems. However, the analysis presented above indicates that the role of human agency plays a fundamental factor in facilitating development at the urban and regional level, specifically in terms of innovative transformation and evolutionary renewal. This role concerns three key factors: (1) in the lineage of structuration theory, it is the case that the configuration, efficiency, and sustainability of the regional ecosystems that push or hinder economic development are a primary result of the actions and agency of a particular cadre of individuals within a specific location; (2) the regional ecosystems of development are contingent on the underlying culture and institutional environment within a specific region, with the nature and type of human agency moderating the relationship between this environment and the more tangible economic systems operating within the region; and (3) the mix and interaction of different forms of human agents and agency within a region will determine the nature of the form of economic system—for example cluster, innovation system, or milieu—within this region and subsequently its development trajectory and capacity for innovative transformation and economic renewal.

Building on these propositions, especially the third, there is a strong indication that across many regions at different points in time the role of entrepreneurship has been a pivotal source of agency in fostering development, transformation, and renewal. Furthermore, the interaction of entrepreneurial agency with other forms, such as political and labour agency, has resulted in particular types of regional economic evolution. Therefore, the absence of significant entrepreneurial agency will result in a city or region being unable to achieve sustainable and long-term development, and it is necessary to consider how human agency in regions becomes manifest in the form of entrepreneurship.

The analysis outlined above suggests the following: (1) the confluence of group-level culture within a city or region and the personality psychology of individuals within this city or region produce a psychocultural environment that creates certain forms of human agency that may or may not have a propensity toward entrepreneurial traits, especially in the form, for example, of legitimation and moral approval; (2) once again following structuration arguments, the propensity to action upon entrepreneurial traits—that is, agency—will at least be partly determined by the nature of the underlying regional economic ecosystems, especially with regard to apparent opportunity and economic returns; and (3) the nature of personal, proxy, and collective forms of human agency in a city or region will result in a specific variant of entrepreneurial form within this city or region.

In general, in economically successful regions entrepreneurship is harnessed, distributed, and capitalized upon through ecosystems of connected agents who create networks, knowledge, and institutions that positively and openly evolve to sustain innovation and economic development. Alongside this, economic renewal, transformation, and the formation of effective and efficient regional ecosystems will at least be partly determined by the behavioural life of cities and regions in terms of the underlying and dominant cultural and psychological traits of individuals within these places. As argued above, these traits determine the forms of human agency to be found in particular regions, and this agency itself is a determinant of the economic (eco) systems within them.

Human agency necessarily comes in many forms and varieties, but a key form of agency necessary for innovation-led renewal and transformation concerns entrepreneurial agency. Supported by, for example, political and worker agency, entrepreneurs represent key catalysts of change at the urban and regional level. It appears that throughout history urban and regional transformation has been led by a core group of entrepreneurial agents that have taken a lead in positively evolving the economies in which they are physically situated. Through evolutionary processes new generations of agent often produce innovations that push further forward the technological frontier set by their predecessors. In mature and lagging regional economies it is all too often the case that these types of agents have migrated to other regions with stronger ecosystems and greater opportunities, or that such agents have not been nurtured in the first instance due to the underlying psychocultural traits of the region (Rentfrow et al., 2015). This leaves these regions in an economic situation in which they lack a critical mass of the types of industries and sectors through which value and competitiveness can be best achieved. In other words, it is the capability to facilitate institutional and cultural change—which is likely to be generational—that is the centrepiece of urban and regional economic transformation. Therefore, the persistence and reproduction of a cultural and institutional environment that often actively works against an evolutionary trajectory embedded in creating economic systems steeped in entrepreneurship remain, perhaps, the greatest challenges for these regions. Given this, psychocultural behaviour is often persistent and deeply rooted in cities and regions, with lagging post-industrial places enduring a form of 'social haunting' or 'ghosted' affective atmosphere that has lingered for many decades (Gordon, 1997; Bright, 2016).

4.6 Urban and Regional Economic Histories and Culture

In order to consider more fully these forms of 'social haunting' and 'ghosted' atmosphere, this section examines how the types of urban and regional culture established during the Industrial Revolution tend to persist today. The Industrial Revolution was clearly a major watershed in socio-economic history, transforming production, work, class structures, lifestyles, urbanization, and income arguably more than any other event since the domestication of animals and plants during the Neolithic Revolution. While the Industrial Revolution was certainly not a singular event but a process, this process was rather quick compared to change in medieval times. However, in the case of countries such as Britain, the Netherlands, and the United States, the Industrial Revolution was uneven across their subnational territories (Zijdeman, 2009; Glaeser et al., 2015). This was more than partly driven by the emergence of large-scale industries such as iron and later steel and textiles that largely depended on the availability of cheap coal as an energy source (e.g. Glaeser et al., 2015; Stuetzer et al., 2016).

Some studies indicate that culture can be split into fast-moving and slow-moving components (Guiso et al., 2006). Peer group effects constitute fast-moving elements (Manksi, 2000), while Guiso et al. (2006: 23), on the other hand, describe culture as being fairly unchanged from generation to generation. These cultural dimensions are passed on from parents to children across each generation without being fully questioned in terms of their optimality (Bisin and Verdier, 2000; Fernández et al., 2004). In cases where parents pass on particular cultural traits, this can be reinforced through the experiences of children. For example, children whose parents encourage trust are more likely to trade with others and learn more trustworthy behaviour (Guiso et al., 2008). Therefore, culture may both determine and be determined by economic activity.

Other studies have used the attitudes and actions of second-generation immigrants to examine the persistence of culture (Alesina and Giuliano, 2010; Luttmer and Singhal, 2011). Evidence of persistence occurs where second-generation immigrants, although exposed, like all youngsters in a country, to the context and institutions of their country of birth, they still exhibit the culture of their parents' home country, even though they have not been brought up there (Alesina and Giuliano, 2015). However, beyond the second generation there is evidence that not all cultural traits persist (Giavazzi et al., 2014). In terms of the community element, this refers to societal groupings. In reality, these groupings may, or may not, be place-based (Miller 1992; Storper 2008), but we define community culture as being those social values and norms held by groups that are largely place-based. Community culture is group-based and an outcome of social interaction, which is determined by the spatial proximity of the community members and the facilitation of knowledge flows (e.g. Jaffe et al., 1993), the development of shared world views, beliefs, and attitudes (e.g. Wyrwich et al., 2018). Such flows and interaction connect with issues grounded in relational economic geography (e.g. Bathelt and Glückler, 2003) and evolutionary economic geography (e.g. Boschma and Frenken, 2006), especially the role of networks, as discussed in Chapter 5.

Connecting culture with industrialization further relates to evolutionary economic geography and the emergence of large-scale industries such as textiles, steel, and mining, which led to the development of specific organizational routines in these industries (Nelson and Winter 1982; Boschma and Frenken, 2006). Organizational routines in large-scale industries, especially regarding the coordination of a large number of low-skilled employees, directly speak to mechanisms such as unionization and preferences for redistribution that shape shared meaning, world view, and attitudes. In other words, localized institutions are related to the formation and evolution of particular localized community cultures. Culture, therefore, is not fixed across a country but instead features local differences due to the path-dependent nature of socio-economic development In the following, we theorize on how industrialization—which affected different parts of the UK in different ways in the eighteenth and nineteenth centuries—has left an imprint on contemporary community culture.

Modernization theories and changing culture. The Industrial Revolution resulted in many important changes that ultimately led to the modern era. There are theories that suggest that, as regions and cities become more modern, universal patterns are present in cultural development, so that cultures become more tolerant, open, and less obedient to authority, with a greater emphasis placed on self-expression (Inglehart, 1971; Inglehart and Baker, 2000). Inglehart (1971) argues that changes in values reflect changing priorities associated with Maslow's (1970) hierarchy of needs. The most important values are those associated with the lowest unfulfilled level on the hierarchy of needs. As societies develop and become more prosperous, they may move their focus from food, shelter, and security towards self-expression and self-actualization, leading to a shift in values from acquisitive to 'postbourgeois'. However, Flanagan (1982) proposes a different perspective based around functional constraints, whereby society chooses behaviours that are most appropriate and rewarded given the socio-economic context.

For example, in agrarian communities uncertainty requires austerity; piety (to appease the gods); conformity (to aid cooperation); and deference to authority (to ensure community support).

Development enables a reduction in the need to obey, and society may move from an authoritarian set of values to a more libertarian environment that allows for more self-expression. Changes in these values are likely to be determined through new generations due to childhood and early adolescence socialization (Inglehart, 1971; Milkis and Baldino, 1978). It has been suggested that these changes may lead to a convergence of values across modernized societies (Parsons, 1977).

Developing these theories of cultural change, Eisenstadt (2004) introduces the theory of 'multiple modernities', whereby global influences are adjusted according to the local traditions present, so that there is a degree of path dependency and persistence in cultures (Inglehart and Baker, 2000). In particular, the form that industrial development takes may have a key and lasting impact on the current values that are possessed within societies. This means that despite suggestions that rising GDP per capita leads to societies becoming more secular-rational (rather than traditional) and displaying values of self-expression (rather than survival) (Inglehart and Baker, 2000), there are still groupings of economies based on factors such as their religious histories, the socio-economic participation of women, or conflict resolution.

Fundamentally, culture may be long-lasting but it is not fixed and, as noted above, development does lead to change, with Inglehart and Baker (2000) suggesting that the rate of economic activity in different industrial sectors influences the social values held. While industrialization, in terms of increasing employment in industry (rather than agriculture), is associated with a move from traditional to secular-rational values, it has less impact on survival-self-expression, which is found to show a stronger relationship with employment in the services sector, with a move to post-industrial economies. Potentially, this may mean that cities and regions with a traditionally higher level of reliance on large-scale industry may find it hard to reorientate after their decline (Power et al., 2010), as they still retain a survivalist perspective.

Historical industrialization and culture. Having noted how industrial development may lead to changes in community culture, there is a requirement to examine the particular mechanisms associated with the historical industrialization that has occurred in many nations. Starting in the eighteenth century in England, but prominent in the nineteenth century within many countries, this industrialization was particularly associated with the development of large-scale industry, which was unshackled from the countryside and a reliance on water power through the development of reliable steam power. As this industrialization occurred, community cultures were also evolving, and care needs to be taken when examining the drivers and determinants of change due to potential issues of endogeneity (Nunn, 2008; Huggins and Thompson, 2016). In particular, it is important to consider specifically how historical industrialization may influence community culture. Below we discuss four potential mechanisms through which industrialization affected culture: (1) working conditions; (2) unionization; (3) mineral wealth and preferences for redistribution; and (4) self-selecting migration.

Working conditions. Scholars from various disciplines such as sociology, economics, and psychology have long acknowledged the socialization effects of everyday working conditions and experiences. Based on observations during the Industrial Revolution, Karl Marx (1859) developed the 'being determines consciousness' principle, which refers to the effect of working conditions on the thinking and identity of the workforce. Adam Smith (1776: 850) noted that the division of labour comes with detrimental psychosocial effects for workers, such as ignorance, inability in judging, and the expense of virtues. The increasing division of labour was driven by technological change and the availability of coal-based energy in emerging industrial centres, and this greatly influenced the organizational routines of firms. Instead of many smaller producers relying on specialized artisans, the new mode of production in larger-scale factories relied on low-skilled and labour-intensive work (Acemoglu, 2002). The assembly line dictated the rhythm of the work. The working conditions in these industrial centres was often highly repetitive, dangerous, and physically taxing.

Scholars from different disciplines have reported on the lasting effects of harsh working conditions. Psychology research reports that repetitive work with low personal control, which was standard at the assembly line, is associated with stress and reduced well-being (Lundberg, et al., 1989; Humphrey et al., 2007). Sociologists view socialization through work conditions and experiences as an important determining factor for the persistence of societal stratification (Kohn and Schooler, 1983). The so-called 'long arm of the job' shapes personality factors and attitudes (Roberts et al., 2003). Moreover, a parent's working conditions and experiences can also affect the raising of offspring (Crouter et al., 1999), mainly through transmitting values in children's early formative years (Luster et al., 1989).

Unionization—Holmes (2006) suggests that unions are one mechanism through which large-scale industry may affect the wider economy, and in turn the socio-cultural nature of a city or region. As discussed above, the living and working conditions where large-scale industry is dominant may lead to a negative impact from the stress associated with economic hardship and low socio-economic status (Lynch et al., 1997; Gallo and Matthews, 2003; Matthews and Gallo, 2011; Obschonka et al., 2017). Trade union development, therefore, may be one coping mechanism to counter these effects (Hopkins, 2000), although traditional unionism may not be restricted to the industries that encourage their initial formation.

Trade unions, however, may be restricted to workers in one trade (for example, mining), and a number of possible mechanisms exist that allow unionization to be transmitted to other sectors. Union members, with their pro-union attitudes, can move to other sectors (Freeman and Medoff, 1984; Fullagar et al., 1995; Hester and Fuller, 2001). They may also promote unionization through their children who work in other sectors but develop the same pro-union attitudes from their parents (Deshpande and Fiorito, 1989). If union membership is regarded as an experience good with uncertain benefits, the risk of joining will be reduced where there are more members locally to learn from through social contact (Erdem and Keane, 1996). Practically, unions may function better where there are more members locally to support, for example, strike action (Marshall, 1967). Equally, unions may actively look to spread their influence to other localities and regions (Holmes, 2006).

Holmes's (2006) study uses the distribution of mining and steel-making activity in the US South, which is almost 100 per cent unionized (Douty, 1960; Lewis, 1963), and examines the prevalence of unionized activities in the healthcare and grocery sectors, which are not normally unionized. It is found that unionization is much higher in these traditionally non-union sectors when there is also a history of mining and steel-making. Holmes (2006) examines whether or not this reflects the actions of the mining and steel unions expanding their activities, or whether other mechanisms are at play. It is found that mining and steel unions expand into the healthcare sector, although not all the spillover is explained by concentrating on activities organized by these traditional unions. It is also found that service union presence is greater when there is a history of mining and steel-making. Therefore, development in one industry may lead to types of labour organization that are not only restricted to the industry in question but spill over into other industries that are geographically proximate, resulting in wider cultural change.

Preferences for redistribution—Mineral resources and industrial employment may further be associated with wider spatial identity, especially beliefs relating to the organization of economic activities (Diamond, 2006). In particular, there is a lively debate on whether or not the presence of mineral resources increases or decreases the populace's preferences for redistribution (e.g. Couttenier and Sangier, 2015; Di Tella et al., 2010), which can influence, for example, voting behaviour. The case for decreasing preferences for redistribution comes from Couttenier and Sangier (2015), who find that US states with an above-median number of mineral mines are more likely to be against redistribution of wealth. This may reflect mineral resources resulting in income increases that reduce the willingness to redistribute (Romer, 1975; Piketty, 1995). Workers may also believe that their effort in a labour-intensive industry such as mining matters for their pay, with any higher taxation disincentivizing their effort (Piketty, 1995; Couttenier and Sangier, 2015). The case for higher preferences for redistribution is presented by Di Tella et al. (2010), who find that if income from oil resources depends more on luck (for example, rising oil prices) than effort, people in the US prefer more redistribution and government action.

Beyond luck versus effort in mining, two more general theoretical models may explain regional differences in redistribution preferences applicable to industrialization. First, there are voting models in the tradition of Meltzer and Richard (1981). This literature argues that taxing the rich and subsequent redistribution pays off for the median voter if income is distributed unequally. Unequal distribution of income and wealth was very present in the United Kingdom of the eighteenth- and nineteenth-century (Piketty, 2014), particularly in the industrialized regions (Justman and Gradstein, 1999). The second model explaining preferences for redistribution builds on fairness arguments. In situations where income and wealth are considered to be received 'unfairly' and not based on effort or talent, people have higher preferences for redistribution (Alesina and Angletos, 2005).

The fairness model is also applicable to industrialization as capital accumulation in the form of machines and equipment is a key driver of such industrialization. Such capital represents wealth and is inherited by one generation from another (Galor and Moav, 2004). This inherited wealth may be interpreted as 'unfair' and leads to redistribution preferences. The strong connection between mining and manufacturing trade unions and the Labour Party in the UK is indirect evidence of greater preferences for redistribution in certain communities.

Self-selecting migration—Finally, while conditions associated with historical industrialization may affect individuals in a city or region at a time of adolescence and early adulthood, there is a possibility that it may also attract particular types of personality from outside. It has been shown that historical factors can lead to self-selecting migration patterns whereby particular personality traits are reinforced on an ongoing basis (Obschonka et al., 2017). In the case of the indirect link between industrial development and community culture, large-scale industry can clearly play a role. Obschonka et al. (2017) show how those attracted to industrializing areas often came from rural and other peripheral regions out of necessity rather than choice (Redford and Chaloner, 1976). When the industrial regions began to decline, the less resilient, proactive, and optimistic individuals were more likely to remain, resulting in a less geographically mobile population (Jokela et al., 2008; Obschonka et al., 2017).

4.7 Industrial Development and Culture

This section draws on the mechanisms covered in the previous section linking historical industrialization to community culture to develop a thesis relating to the evolution of specific cultural dimensions. The cultural dimensions are those taken from the five aspects of socio-spatial community culture indicated in previous chapters, namely, engagement with employment and education; social cohesion; feminine and caring activities; adherence to social rules; and collective activities.

Engagement with employment and education—In terms of the ability to engage with employment and education, industrialization has been suggested by some to provide opportunities for greater social mobility compared to previous feudal systems and agriculturally based economies (Fukumoto and Grusky, 1993). However, historical studies have generally not found large increases in social mobility compared to prior periods (van Leeuwen and Maas, 2010). In particular, countries such as England have seen relatively little change in social mobility over the past 200 years (Erikson and Goldthorpe, 1992; Clark and Cummins, 2014). One explanation is that large-scale production may increase power distance (Hofstede, 2001), with upper and working classes becoming more segregated (Heberle, 1948). Nevertheless, if opportunities for upward mobility remains restricted, or is perceived to be restricted, this could mean that large-scale industry has a lasting effect.

The restricted development towards knowledge-based economies in many cases could further influence this element in a fashion similar to Sanderson's (1972) analysis of literacy's limited effect in industrializing Lancashire, with higher educational achievement having restricted benefits for localities with a greater industrial heritage. Zijdeman (2009), who explores localized data within the Dutch province of Zeeland, finds that social mobility is restricted by greater urbanization and industrialization. In such situations engagement with education and employment associated with higher levels of work ethic are likely to fall (Lipset, 1992).

Although much has changed in these communities since they were dominated by large industry, and many have lost their manufacturing employment, it is possible that a form of learned helplessness has been created (Kolvin et al., 1990). As noted by studies such as Lynch et al. (1997), Matthews and Gallo (2011), and Obschonka et al. (2017), poor economic conditions and limited socio-economic positions may impact on cognitive, psychological, and social functioning and the ability to deal with their restricted position. Individuals' own problems are likely to be attributed to external factors, and solutions to these problems, naturally come from the outside too. Within this line of thought, there is a clear link with preferences for redistribution and government action. This may mean that, although opportunities are available for social advancement, culture may have turned away from following these alternative paths, even resulting in an anti-education culture developing (Brennan et al., 2000) and weakening educational performance (Ananat et al., 2017).

An alternative theory that may be relevant for localities 'blessed' with access to coal is that of the resource curse (Auty, 1993). Communities dominated by industries such as steel and other large-scale industry experienced a relatively large supply of employment opportunities requiring lower levels of education and fewer positions rewarding the possession of education. Therefore, there was little incentive for the workforce to invest in their own education or that of their offspring. This may even result in reduced investments in education as returns to human capital are restricted due to the relative expansion of the natural-resources sector and those industries associated with it (Gylfason, 2001). Stuetzer et al.'s (2016) finding that (entrepreneurial) human capital and activity remain repressed in places with a greater history of large-scale industry development is consistent with this theory. Regardless of which mechanism is most pertinent, they collectively suggest a negative relationship between the historic presence of large-scale industry and engagement with education and employment.

Social cohesion—The development of large-scale industry may potentially influence the social cohesion of a locality in a number of ways. First, working conditions may strengthen social cohesion in communities. Work in the factories and mines of industrializing regions was physically demanding and potentially dangerous, which may have created a sense of togetherness. Sometimes paternalistic firm owners even helped to create this togetherness as an element of social control by providing social benefits (such as housing or medical care) (Thompson, 2008). Working men's clubs (Price, 1971) and sport activities like rowing (Tranter, 1988) also shaped togetherness and cohesion among the working class in the industrialized regions.

Second, trade unions are likely to have strengthened social cohesion in these communities. Trade unions promote collective bargaining with employers concerning working conditions and wages, and this fosters cohesion and togetherness, especially when collective bargaining produced tangible results for the union members starting from the mid-nineteenth century in the UK. The growing political influence through the emerging Labour Party should also not be undervalued (Laybourn, 1992), with trade unions in the eighteenth and nineteenth century being predominantly formed by skilled workers in certain crafts. It was not until the new unions in the 1880s that they became more inclusive (Laybourn, 1992).

Third, preferences for redistribution can strengthen social cohesion in communities. In particular, the standard of living for the dominant blue-collar workforce did not improve substantially until 1850, as documented by real-wage time series and the height time series of British soldiers (Feinstein, 1998; Komlos, 1998). If many people in communities have the same low standard of living and little prospect of upward mobility, it can create an atmosphere of 'us' against 'them' (cf. Perdue et al., 1990). This suggests that in cities and regions where large-scale industry was more important, contemporary community culture will be more socially cohesive.

Feminine and caring activities—Although earlier modernization theory suggests that there will be a move towards particular values promoting, amongst others, more equal gender values (Lerner, 1958; Weiner, 1966), Inglehart and Baker (2000) suggest a more complex pattern of evolution. Self-expression is more closely associated with a move to post-industrialism and employment in the services sector. Therefore, industrialization in developed economies may be associated with more masculine orientations (Spence and Helmreich, 1978). Such gendered roles can be persistent (Spence and Helmreich, 1978). Interestingly, this may mean that feminine and caring activities are higher in localities that impose a home-based and family-orientated role on women. In relation to the working and living conditions associated with industrialization, greater caring and feminine activities may emerge as a coping mechanism to alleviate the community challenges associated with industrialization. Taken together, this leads to the thesis that in places where large-scale industry was more important, contemporary community culture places a greater importance on feminine and caring activities.

Adherence to social rules—working and living conditions during the Industrial Revolution may have resulted in a lower adherence to social rules, and some of Marx and Engel's arguments suggest that industrialization led to greater criminal activity, reflecting the subservient position of labour in places where large-scale industry develops. Declines in appropriate behaviour and standards are linked by some to the dissolution of previous methods of social control through family, patronage, deference, and the Church, prior to the development of new formalized institutions such as the police and local authorities, as well as those developed by the working classes themselves (Thompson, 1981). Any decline in traditional industries may lead to economic deprivation, which is associated with criminal activity (Shihadeh and Ousey, 1998; Power et al., 2010) and decreasing trust (Alesina and La Ferrara, 2000). As time progresses, this may also be associated with Obschonka et al.'s (2017) finding that the collapse of large-scale industry results in higher levels of neuroticism in the population. At the individual level, Kohn and Schooler (1982) find evidence that the nature of the work itself can promote or limit the degree of self-direction exhibited by individuals in their lives as a whole. Where work is more routine and closely monitored, workers exhibit lower self-directed orientations, which can lead to less adherence to social rules.

Migration may also lead to less adherence to social rules. As people with different backgrounds, values, and attitudes flock together, pre-existing social rules are challenged and shared mental models about what is right or wrong are challenged. Empirical evidence for this relationship comes from many studies showing that racial and ethnical diversity lowers trust in communities (e.g. Alesina and La Ferrara, 2000; Sturgis et al., 2014). Obschonka et al. (2017) outline how those attracted to industrializing areas often came from rural and other peripheral regions (for example, Ireland and Scotland) out of necessity rather than choice (Redford and Chaloner, 1976). This indicates that where large-scale industry was more important, contemporary community culture will display lower rates of adherence to the social rules accepted by wider society.

Collective action—collective activities are an important cultural feature of urban, regional, and local communities and may be associated with a desire for equality and greater equity. Historically, Inglehart (1971) considered how these values may develop as affluence increases and security becomes less important, suggesting that those raised after World War II are more likely to exhibit postbourgeois values. These values are also found to be strongly correlated with political preferences, with the postbourgeois more likely to vote for left-of-centre parties even after controlling for their parents' voting preferences. Inglehart's (1971) study, however, was at the national level and does not account for differences in voting patterns within countries, and it largely relates to absolute levels of affluence, whereas relative affluence may be more important between localities.

Working conditions, redistribution preferences, and unions can contribute to more collective action. Regarding working and living conditions and unions, those areas of the UK associated with the development of large-scale industry have typically suffered higher levels of deprivation, poorer environmental conditions (both in terms of pollution and living standards), and frequently poorer working conditions (Power et al., 2010). Whereas Inglehart (1971) argued that there would be a shift from acquisitive to postbourgeois values and a greater allegiance to the new-left political parties, within countries this need not be the case. Where greater inequality develops it is possible that, while becoming more affluent, in absolute terms those localities with histories of large-scale industry may experience rising relative poverty. If such communities consider that they lack power, they may favour collective action, as advocated by left-wing parties and trade unions (Holmes, 2006).

Redistribution preferences, because of either perceived 'unfair' inherited income distribution or luck in the deposits of mineral resources, can be channelled into collective action because individual action is unlikely to significantly impact upon income distribution. Instead, collective action can overthrow seemingly enduring socio-economic disparities. Occasional strikes, widespread labour unrest, the forming of political parties, and lasting revolutions and revolts are different points on the spectrum of collective action (Laybourn, 1992). This suggests that in places where large-scale industry was more important, contemporary community culture will continue to favour collective activities.

4.8 Conclusion

Innovation is a prerequisite component of the urban and regional development process. In economically successful regions, innovation is harnessed, distributed, and capitalized upon through ecosystems of connected agents who create networks, knowledge, and institutions that positively and openly evolve to sustain innovation and economic development. In mature and lagging regions the requirement for innovation is paramount if they are to renew and transform their economies and shift away from economic systems that are steeped in processes of negative, rather than positive, lock-in. This chapter has principally argued that economic renewal, transformation, and the formation of effective and efficient urban and regional ecosystems will at least be partly determined by the forms of human agency to be found in particular cities and regions, with this agency itself being a determinant of the economic (eco)systems within them.

In relation to the link between historical urban and regional industry, it is clear that economic actions are embedded and based not only in structures of social relations (Bathelt and Glückler, 2003) but also in urban and regional economic histories that shape the structure of these social relations, such as towards more social cohesion and collective action. Regarding evolutionary economic geography (Boschma and Frenken, 2006), it is likely that organizational routines in large-scale industries shape urban and regional culture. Also, to the extent that there are feedback effects from culture on organizational routines, regional and urban cultures are likely to be the means by which specific organizational routines can be transferred over time within particular spaces—even if they hinder, rather than facilitate, economic performance and development. Similarly, informal institutions can persist over a significant period of time even when the initial determinant of these institutions has long since passed (Martin, 2000), and the nature of these institutions, both informal and formal, are the focus of the following chapter.

5

Institutions, Capital, and Network Behaviour

5.1 Introduction

A perennial question in the field of urban and regional studies is why some regions, cities, and territories are better able to foster innovation—broadly defined as the introduction of new products, services, and ways of doing business and working—and economic growth than others. As indicated in Chapter 4, as well as the availability of capital, a range of additional factors including the availability and capability of entrepreneurs through urban and regional ecosystems are important determinants (Capello and Nijkamp, 2009; Cooke et al., 2011; Stimson et al., 2011; Shearmur et al., 2016). Undoubtedly, each factor is likely to matter, but there is little understanding of how these factors are related or connected. As a means of seeking to better understand these connections and consider the deeper and less transparent drivers of urban and regional development, this chapter examines the institutional determinants of the innovation and growth capability and capacity of cities and regions. From the institutional perspective, cities and regions are portrayed as growth systems in which the availability of a range of capital and institutional forms play a key role in promoting innovation and growth. Having established the means by which the types of institutions and associated capital within a city or region impact upon its evolutionary development, the second part of the chapter argues that within any city or region the institutions concerning the networks formed by key agents will establish the framework for the distribution of power, particularly power that impacts upon the evolution and development of the economy.

5.2 Institutions, Innovation, and Growth

Theoretical perspectives on urban and regional development are predominately focused on the function of innovation and economic growth in fostering this

A Behavioural Theory of Economic Development: The Uneven Evolution of Cities and Regions. Robert Huggins and Piers Thompson, Oxford University Press (2021). © Robert Huggins and Piers Thompson.
DOI: 10.1093/oso/9780198832348.003.0005

development, as well as understanding the sources of this innovation and growth, leading to two related forms of analysis (Huggins and Thompson, 2014). First, those analyses and theories that seek to understand the processes and organizational factors relating to the innovation process within regions, that is regional (which can also be taken as encapsulating the urban and city dimension) innovation theories. Second, a theoretical strand focused on understanding the role of innovation in facilitating regional economic growth, that is innovation-based theories of regional growth. As shown by Figure 5.1, the conceptual frameworks employed by both theoretical approaches largely consist of either a resource-based view or an interaction-based view. The resource-based view concerns the assets and endowments within a region, and from the perspective of regional innovation theories this relates to the types of industries, the industrial mix, and the capacity of these industries to foster regional innovation.

From the innovation-based growth perspective, scholarly concern is very much focused on the notion of endogenous growth and the accumulation of the forms of intangible capital associated with triggering and sustaining long-term growth. The interaction-based view is complementary to the resource-based view, focusing on the nature of the relationships, linkages, and networks that exist between regional actors engaged in innovation. Most prominently conceptualized as regional innovation systems, innovation milieu, clusters, and more recently entrepreneurial ecosystems, the interaction-based view considers these modes of connectivity to provide diffusion channels allowing the knowledge required for innovation to flow within and across regions (Cooke et al., 2011).

	Regional Innovation Theories	Innovation-Based Theories of Regional Growth
Resource-Based Frameworks	Industrial structure, (smart) specialization, diversity, relatedness, path dependency, absorptive capacity, knowledge economy, entrepreneurship	Endogenous growth, agglomeration, human capital, creative class, entrepreneurship capital, knowledge capital and research capital
Interaction-Based Frameworks	Regional innovation systems, entrepreneurial ecosystems, innovative milieu, technopoles, industrial districts, local production systems, networks, buzz, knowledge pipelines, learning regions, clusters and open innovation	Network-based view of regional growth, knowledge accessibility, network capital, social capital and spillovers

Figure 5.1 Theoretical perspectives on regional innovation and growth.

With regard to innovation-based growth theories, there is a growing discourse that conceptualizes these channels and flow mechanisms as a form of capital—for example, network capital and social capital—that are part of the mix of 'capitals' that can be accumulated as part of endogenous growth processes (Huggins and Thompson, 2014). Similarly, these growth processes are a component of a wider theoretical canvas that focuses on the 'success' of regions, mainly related to their economic development trajectories (Huggins, 2016). Urban and regional economic development principally concerns the capacity and capability to achieve economic growth, and understanding how and why such growth occurs is central to a number of research streams beyond innovation-based theories. For instance, research in spatial economics seeks to understand the role of agglomeration effects, trade costs, and other regionalization and urbanization factors (Storper, 2013). More generally, contributions from economic geography and spatial economics have become increasingly concerned with understanding and demonstrating the regional micro-foundations of macroeconomic growth models.

Alongside the endogenous model of growth, an emerging field of study has sought to cut into the growth debate at a different level by placing the concepts of institutions as the central source for understanding growth differentials (Farole et al., 2011; Rodríguez-Pose, 2013; Tomaney, 2014). Somewhat contrary to the capital accumulation model of regional growth, institutional theorists argue that differences in growth and prosperity across regions are more fundamentally related to the type, stage of development, and efficiency of the economic and political institutions that underpin economic systems (Acemoglu and Robinson, 2012; Rodríguez-Pose, 2013; Tomaney, 2014). Institutions, therefore, relate to the incentives and constraints concerning the organization of production. Within this institutional paradigm, the prevailing view is that differences in 'the rules of the game' across economic systems are considered to be a key driver of growth differentials, with more efficient institutions facilitating the development of the conditions that allow the forms of capital accumulation associated with innovation-led growth to flourish (Huggins, 2016). As indicated in Chapter 2, institutions are defined as the humanly devised constraints that structure interaction covering both formal (de jure—rules, laws, constitutions) and informal (de facto—norms, behaviour, conventions) constraints and their enforcement, which then define the incentive structure of societies and their economies (North, 2005). Scott's (2007) three categories of institutional forces recognize a similar division, with the *regulative pillar* capturing rules of the game, monitoring, and enforcement; the *normative pillar* drawing on socially accepted norms within professional and organizational interaction;

and the third being a more culturally orientated *cognitive pillar*. The first pillar can be seen to be related to more formal institutions, with the second and third pillars associated more with the concept of informal institutions.

The influential 'varieties of capitalism' approach to institutional evolution argues that differing institutions develop to match the activities undertaken in an economy (Hall and Soskice, 2001). In other words, institutions that dominate an area are partly created by the activities undertaken within the area. For example, this literature normally regards most continental European economies as coordinated market economies (CMEs), in which strategic interaction between firms and other actors such as trade unions is used to coordinate activities. The United Kingdom and other Anglo-Saxon nations are perceived to possess more liberal market economies (LMEs), in which markets coordinate the activities of firms and other actors. In their review, Acemoglu and Robinson (2012) advocate that the institutions of democratic capitalism are the principal means of achieving prosperity, which could be perceived as a perspective that is ethnocentrically skewed toward the cultural values of nations with a system of relatively strong democratic capitalism. However, it is not necessarily the case that capitalist economic systems are fixed within a nation, with some scholars suggesting the existence of regional varieties of capitalism within nation states (Crouch et al., 2009).

Institutions, especially those of a more formal nature, can be further categorized as (1) economic institutions, such as individual property rights, contracts, patent laws, and the like; or (2) political institutions, which generally refer to the extent to which democratic political rules underlie the nature of territorial governance. Institutions can also be categorized according to whether they are innately 'extractive' or 'inclusive', with extractive institutions tending to be those which result in rent-seeking behaviour (Acemoglu and Robinson, 2012). In effect, institutions, in the shape of both the tangible and intangible characteristics constituting the political economy of regions are either enablers of, or constrainers on, growth. Institutional enablers are the conditions and factors that facilitate growth by creating an environment conducive to firms operating at their highest level.

Enablers principally encompass institutions that support economic actors in taking advantage of perceived opportunities. Although some of these institutions are fixed across nations—such as law, regulation, and property rights—others may be subject to regional-level differentiation. National-level constrainers may take the form of some type of 'Big Brother' dampening, for instance, the aspirations of entrepreneurs in particular places. As Storper et al. (2007: 320) state:

there is clear existence of a problem of society versus community: regional entrepreneurs have low ambitions, not because they lack creativity or knowledge, but because of rational fear of the risks that come from the national (societal) environment, and this lack of generalized confidence is not counterbalanced by the alternative of solid communities that could facilitate coordination.

As outlined in Chapter 2, regional-level institutions consist of factors such as the incentives to save and invest; embrace competition, innovate and pursue technological development; engage in education, learning, and entrepreneurship; participate in networks. They are also reflected in the presence and structure of property ownership and the provision of public services. Cities and regions with institutions conducive to enabling economic development are likely to increase their growth by attracting investment, skills, and talent. Some examples include local business regulations that allow commercial activity to be efficient; the ease of doing business; local government initiatives; and ultimately, the perceptions of businesses and individuals in a city or region (Huggins, 2016). In general, institutional theories analyse urban and regional growth from quite a different perspective to capital accumulation approaches, but as the following section argues, this does not prevent the theoretical streams from complementing one another.

5.3 Urban and Regional Growth Systems

Regional endogenous growth theory argues that long-term differentials in growth across cities and regions will emerge as a result of differences in the structure of their economic systems, especially their endowment of assets and the preferences of economic actors (Capello and Nijkamp, 2009; Stimson et al., 2011). While endogenous capital accumulation theories of growth are based on preferences, endowment, resource allocation, and intentional investment decisions (Romer, 1990), institutional theories of growth are based on constraints, incentives, and organizational arrangements (North, 2005; Acemoglu and Robinson, 2012).

Although these two theoretical positions are usually considered as distinct explanations of economic growth differences, it is interesting to consider the extent to which they may overlap and have implications for one another, given that both theories can be considered to be endogenous in nature (Farole et al., 2011). For example, preferences and investment decisions may be shaped by prevailing institutions, while the availability and accumulation of capital may shape incentive structures and organizational arrangements. Furthermore, an institutional approach facilitates a consideration of the ownership structure of stocks of capital. Recent work on regional and urban development has sought to develop a more transparent link between institutional and capital accumulation theories of growth, whereby regional economies are conceptualized as growth systems through which different forms of institution are associated with different forms of capital accumulation (Huggins, 2016).

In this model, the capital drivers of growth are not merely the result of preferences and existing capital endowments but are mediated by a set of institutional factors. As shown by Figure 5.2, such a model builds on the existing acknowledgement that both capital and institutional factors influence the nature, quality, and performance of (1) firm-level growth dynamics—which concerns the role of human capital and knowledge capital, and the learning and innovation institutions that constrain or incentivize the accumulation of these forms of capital; (2) inter-firm-level growth dynamics—which concerns the transactions and interactions between firms through the markets and networks they form, and the role of entrepreneurship capital and entrepreneurial institutions in market processes, as well as network

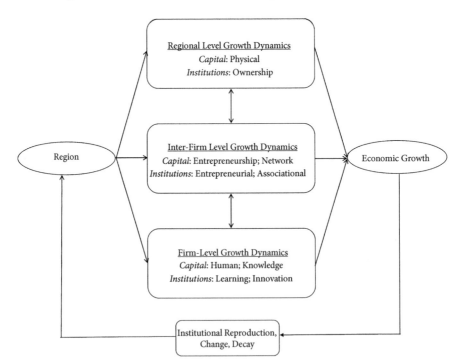

Figure 5.2 Regional growth systems—key components.
Source: adapted from Huggins (2016).

capital and associational institutions in network formation; and (3) regional-level growth dynamics—which relates to the overall governance of regional political economies, especially with regard to the institutions of ownership and physical capital (Huggins, 2016). Although each growth dynamic will help shape and determine rates of economic growth, the firm level is clearly central with regard to the dynamics of knowledge creation. Firms are dependent on the role of human capital and knowledge capital and, therefore, the learning and innovation institutions that constrain or incentivize the accumulation of these forms of capital (Glaeser, 2011).

In the case of human capital, learning institutions, such as intraregional and interregional labour markets, create incentives and constraints as to the type of skills formed in a particular region, as well as conventions in relation to workforce development and regional education systems. Institutions in the form of labour markets enable human capital to take advantage of the benefits of specialization, encouraging economic growth. Therefore, there is likely to be a recursive relationship between the nature of firms in a region, as typified by patterns of economic specialization and the institutions and human capital available. Similarly, institutions influence firm behaviour and subsequently patterns of industrial specialization, with the relationship being bidirectional in nature, that is, firm behaviour also impacts upon relevant institutions. Conversely, regions may have a more diversified portfolio of firms that are either related or unrelated in their 'variety', with institutions again playing a role in determining these patterns (Boschma and Capone, 2015).

With regard to knowledge capital, there is a need to consider innovation institutions in the form of the incentives and constraints to creating and/or embracing new technology, as well as conventions in relation to the financing of innovation and norms regarding the 'restriction' or 'freedom' of ideas (Storper, 2013). For example, where innovative opportunity exploitation is encouraged through greater rewards (for example, lower effective tax rates) or at the very least are not discouraged (as might be the case where high administrative burdens are present), the marginal latent innovator is more likely to pursue innovation opportunities. Although conventions in relation to the financing of innovation, and incentives and constraints with regard to undertaking differing forms of innovation, are likely to stem from national and supranational level institutions, more localized formal and informal institutions also play a role. Less formal institutions in the shape of the nature of competition are also likely to be a factor in shaping the knowledge capital capacity of a region. Furthermore, the competition conditions under which firms in a region operate are likely to shape the rate and character of innovation, with those firms operating in the most sophisticated and demanding markets tending to be those that are most likely to possess the highest levels of innovation.

Alongside firm-level dynamics, it is increasingly argued that the inter-firm level has grown in importance, as it is the flow and diffusion of created knowledge that determines long-run rates of innovation. Both the concepts of 'open' and 'interactive' innovation acknowledge that innovation processes are rarely linear or independent activities but rely on the markets and networks that firms operate through in order to connect themselves to the most important sources of knowledge. Inter-firm-level growth dynamics concern the transactions and interactions across economic agents, with the effectiveness of firms to enter and successfully compete in their respective markets being likely to rely on the accumulation of entrepreneurship capital. Such capital refers to the capacity of a region to generate entrepreneurial activity, whereby entrepreneurs are alert to market opportunities and subsequently contribute to economic growth (Audretsch and Keilbach, 2004). Entrepreneurship capital encompasses not only the available entrepreneurial talent that allows firms to operate in high value and tradable markets but also the capability to access the finance entrepreneurs may require to invest in the resources necessary to engage in these markets. Entrepreneurial institutions come in the form of incentives and constraints to engaging in entrepreneurial activity, including property rights, tax codes, social-insurance systems, labour market legislation, competition policy, trade policies, capital market regulation, and the enforcement of contracts and law and order (Henrekson and Sanandaji, 2011).

As well as markets, research has identified the role of both interregional and intraregional networks as a type of capital shaping regional growth processes—that is, network capital—in the form of the investments firms make in cooperative and collaborative relationships with other firms and organizations in order to gain access to economically beneficial knowledge (Huggins and Thompson, 2014). In this case, the capital value of networks within and across regions is likely to be regulated by a series of 'associational institutions' in the form of conventions with regard to interorganizational collaboration and cooperation, especially associational business behaviour and the norms of trust and collective action. Cities and urban regions, in particular, are considered to be key locations for high rates of network formation due to the high density of actors and high frequency of human interactions (Glaeser, 2011; Florida et al., 2017). An institutional perspective on these networks and flows suggests that firms are incentivized to engage in networked activity through the availability of formal associational institutions, such as chambers of commerce, business and trade associations, as well as more informal institutions in the form of the geographic clustering of firms within which networked cooperation and collaboration are fostered through embedded institutional norms and customs. The significance of network behaviour on development trajectories is explored in more detail in the following section.

5.4 Network Behaviour and (Un)equitable Development

In the second part of this chapter it is argued that wealth and welfare distribution within a city or region is a function of the power structure resulting from the scale and nature of institutions, and the behaviour stemming from interpersonal and interorganizational networks through which economically and socially beneficial knowledge flows. If cities and regions have more inclusive networks, they are more likely to be economically advanced and developed, and provide access to opportunity and the ability to partake in a fair urban and regional community within which power is relatively equitably distributed. Leading urban regions are found to possess the most inclusive networks and therefore can be considered to be the most equitable.

In the context of network behaviour, the emergence of the network paradigm has led to a growing interest and recognition in understanding the influence of network structures in the context of spatial analyses (Boschma et al., 2014), in particular understanding network structures pertaining to knowledge flows and patterns of innovation (Capello and Camilla, 2013; Sebestyén and Varga, 2013). Social network analysis, as developed by sociologists, maintains a key behavioural assumption that any actor typically participates in a network system involving other actors who are significant reference points in decision-making (Knoke and Kuklinski, 1982). The nature of the relationships a given actor has with other system members may, therefore, affect the focal actor's actions. Social network analysis has been increasingly applied to examinations of the flow of knowledge to facilitate innovation (Fleming et al., 2007; Schilling and Phelps, 2007; Sammarra and Biggiero, 2008; Zaheer et al., 2010). More specifically, there is a growing school of research focused on analysing the impact of network structures on innovation outcomes (Powell et al., 1996; Schilling and Phelps, 2007; Whittington et al., 2009).

Research has drawn on network structure conceptions such as 'small worlds', whereby dense clusters of network actors are linked to other clusters via a relatively small number of bridging links (Watts and Strogatz, 1998; Watts, 1999; Uzzi and Spiro, 2005; Gulati et al., 2012). Similarly, research drawing on Burt's (2005) notion of structural holes, whereby actors who link previously unconnected actors within a network are considered to occupy privileged and powerful central positions, has been applied to innovation studies (Ahuja, 2000; Zaheer and Bell, 2005; Zaheer and Soda, 2009). These studies all tend to identify network actor centrality as a determinant of innovation outcomes, as well as the extent to which actors are embedded within either closed or open network structures (Fleming and Waguespack, 2007; Belussi et al., 2010; Cassi and Plunket, 2015). The vast majority of research, however, has focused on innovation returns for particular firms and organizations, rather than the regions in which they are located. The notable exception here is Fleming et al.'s (2007) study that found some evidence of an association between network structure and regional innovation productivity.

Some scholarly research suggests that the nature of networks is related to underlying patterns of knowledge flow (Giuliani, 2007; van Wijik et al., 2008). The position of an actor within networks is found to be correlated with relative power, which refers to a set of resources that an actor (could) mobilize through its existing set of relationships, in this case knowledge (Mizruchi and Galaskiewicz, 1994; Ahuja et al., 2012). At the individual level, these resources are usually considered to take the form of social capital, consisting of the benefits accruing from interpersonal networks (Coleman, 1988; Putnam, 2000). At the organizational level, however, such resources are considered to be a form of network capital—as discussed above—consisting of the benefits accruing from interorganizational networks (Huggins and Johnston, 2010, 2014; Kramer et al., 2011; Kramer and Revilla Diez, 2012; Lawton Smith et al., 2012). In general, social network research finds that higher rates of return are obtained by actors based on their 'structural holes', which refers to the degree to which an actor is constrained from accessing contacts who possess non-redundant information (Zaheer and Bell, 2005; Crespo et al., 2014).

Alongside the importance of the structural position of an actor within a network, its spatial and geographic position clearly remains of considerable relevance in terms of understanding patterns of regional innovation and subsequently development. Indeed, within debates concerning network systems, the roles of space are recognized as increasingly important features of network structure and operation (Ter Wal and Boschma, 2011; Doran et al., 2012). A study by Huggins and Prokop (2017) seeks to test the relationship between centrality in a social network configuration and the association with returns on innovation at the regional level. Based upon a network analysis of empirical data of links between agents in industry and universities for regions across the UK, it is found that the most innovative and economically developed regions are more likely to be the location for actors holding highly central and influential positions within network architectures.

Within the Huggins and Prokop (2017) study, the UK's regions are grouped to represent their regional innovation ranking based on the European Union's Regional Innovation Index (Hollanders et al., 2014). Figure 5.3(a) illustrates the networks of the four highest-ranked regions, termed here as 'leading regions', with Figure 5.3(b) showing the four middle-ranked regions, termed 'moderate regions', and Figure 5.3(c) the bottom four regions, termed 'lagging regions'. In each of the illustrations, the light-grey nodes represent firms and organizations located in the regions, the dark-grey nodes universities located outside the region, and the black nodes university actors located within the region. Among the four leading regions, the network structure of firms and organizations located in the South East region is the thickest, possessing the most aggregate links overall, as well as significant links with universities across regions. It is quite tightly clustered, with the edge of the network having few connections with other clusters. The network created in London is similarly tightly clustered, but in this case a number of bridging connections with other subclusters are more noticeable involving both local and non-local agents. In the South West the network is largely polycentric in its formation, possessing a number of clusters largely anchored around local agents. Importantly, in all cases there are agents that bridge connections across these clusters.

In overall terms, Huggins and Prokop (2017) find that the four innovation-leading regions have by far the highest proportion of ties outside their respective region, which indicates that they tend to be more strongly engaged within boundary-spanning networks. As can be seen in Figure 5.3(b), agents in regions ranked as moderate in terms of innovation tend to be relatively less concentrated than those in leading innovation regions. Also, although there are a significant number of linked agents in both the North West and Scotland, these linkages tend to be more with other local agents than is the case for the networks in the leading innovation regions. In the case of the North West, the network is clearly highly fragmented, lacking a concentration of actors or connectivity across them. Interestingly, while the networks in Wales and Northern Ireland are as similarly fragmented as those found in the North East, the networks in the West Midlands and Yorkshire and the Humber appear to possess traits that belie their lowly innovation ranking (Figure 5.3(c)). In general, however, agents in the moderate and lagging regions tend be more biased toward intraregional ties, as opposed to the high proportion of interregional ties held by agents in leading regions, indicating more spatially closed network structures in lower performing networks.

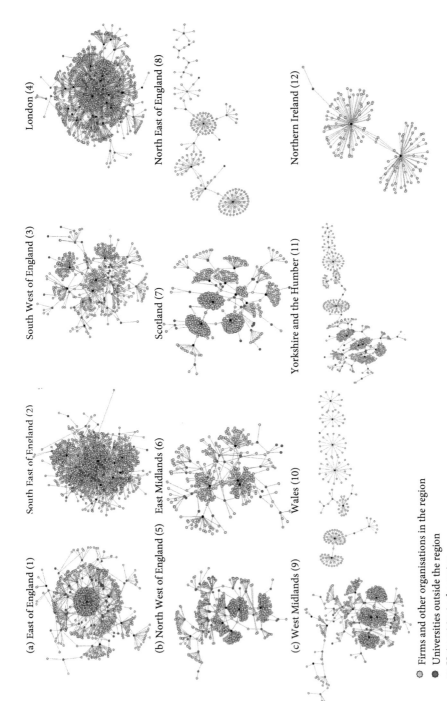

Figure 5.3 Networks of firms and organizations by UK region (ranked by Regional Innovation Scoreboard data).
Source: Huggins and Prokop (2017).

(a) East of England (1)

South East of England (2)

South West of England (3)

London (4)

(b) North West of England (5)

East Midlands (6)

Scotland (7)

North East of England (8)

(c) West Midlands (9)

Wales (10)

Yorkshire and the Humber (11)

Northern Ireland (12)

◯ Firms and other organisations in the region
◉ Universities outside the region
● Universities in the region

On average, agents in London possess the most influential positions within the network, with an average centrality that it is more than twice that of all firms in the network. With the South West, South East, and East of England ranking second, third, and fourth respectively, there appears to be a degree of correspondence with regional innovation rates. Unsurprisingly, agents in Wales, the North East and Northern Ireland have the lowest rates of centrality. In conclusion, Huggins and Prokop (2017) find a positive relationship between innovation rates across regions and the centrality of agents within these regions, with the relationship generating a Spearman's correlation coefficient of 0.68 (p-value = 0.02).

Similarly, there is a positive relationship between average centrality across regions and regional GVA per capita. Indeed, the relationship is rather stronger in this case, with a Spearman's correlation coefficient of 0.76 (p-value = 0.004). The analysis strongly suggests that more innovative and economically developed regions are more likely to have a higher proportion of agents holding highly central and influential positions within the network architecture. This indicates that the structures formed from network behaviour are an important indicator of regional innovation capacity and capability, as well as regional economic development more generally. This link between network structure and regional innovation supports the work of others (Broekel and Hartog, 2013; Fleming et al., 2007; Sebestyén and Varga, 2013), as well as indicating that the structural tie component of networks may be as important as the tie strength component (Capaldo, 2007; Borgatti and Halgin, 2011; Huggins and Thompson, 2014).

It is likely that factors related to the economic structure of regions and their network structure will co-evolve in a pattern of cumulative causation, with one reinforcing the other. Huggins and Prokop (2017) find that while local intraregional interactions account for a significant proportion of links, it is the extent of non-local interregional ties that allows some actors to occupy more central positions than others. In general, agents with more interregional ties tend to be more centrally positioned. These agents often act as bridges between clusters within the network and are well positioned to manage and influence knowledge flows, and presumably to maintain high rates of innovation within their organization. This echoes the findings of studies that have found a significant association between network structure and organization-level rates of innovation (Schilling and Phelps, 2007; Whittington et al., 2009). Furthermore, network behaviour with a high capacity to establish interactions with actors in other regions is more likely to be centrally positioned within a network, with agents occupying highly central positions within a network being more likely to experience higher rates of innovation.

From the perspective of cities and regions and their performance, it appears to be the case that those regions with a high proportion of agents engaged in interregional interactions are likely to be significantly more innovative and economically developed than those with a bias toward local-level ties. This indicates the importance of these actors as boundary-spanning and bridging agents (Fleming and Waguespack, 2007; Cassi and Plunket, 2015), with them being at the heart of a wide spatially configured network architecture. Therefore, those regions with open and porous regional innovation ecosystems are significantly more likely to experience higher rates of innovation capability and capacity. This is an important insight to the extent that it adds weight to the argument that spatially unbounded networks and ecosystems are an increasingly important element of routes to achieving regional competitive advantage (Torre, 2008; Huggins and Thompson, 2014). More generally, understanding network behaviour adds to explanations of patterns of uneven urban and regional development. Clearly, the determinants of urban and regional development are multidimensional, but the adoption of a relational behaviour approach to understanding differing economic geographies indicates that network systems are a key component of the development mix.

5.5 Institutions, Capital, and Networks

In order to better understand the nature of regional economic systems and their growth performance, it appears useful to add institutional factors to such system frameworks. More specifically, it would seem appropriate to address the institutions that facilitate or impede the extent to which the capital inputs of regional economic systems are effectively transferred into high-value outcomes. Similarly, there is a need to consider how institutions enable the transfer of economic outputs into high-grade outcomes. There are clearly different routes to achieving growth and prosperity (Kitson et al., 2004; Malecki, 2007), and some of these routes are likely to be more attractive for certain regions than others. However, whether or not regions are truly free to choose their economic development paths, or whether past history dictates the future potential of an economy, is another question. The evolutionary school of economic geography suggests that regional development and associated institutions are likely to be determined, at least to some extent, by past histories, as discussed in Chapter 4 (Boschma and Frenken, 2006; Martin and Sunley, 2006; Boschma and Martin, 2010).

Regions that are tightly bound in their structures and networks may not be able to easily move to alternative development paths, so when hit by exogenous shocks, they are unable to escape from a declining growth spiral (Martin and Sunley, 2006; Huggins and Izushi, 2007). These factors have ramifications for regions, especially in the long term, as activities taken to increase growth may have hidden costs in terms of the welfare of the population, which may compromise future growth, particularly if key workers cannot be retained (Florida et al., 2011; Mellander et al., 2011). The evolutionary nature of regional economic development may further limit a region's ability to move away from industries associated with providing a low contribution to growth. As already indicated, institutional theorists suggest that a key means of escaping a downward evolutionary economic trajectory is through the development of institutions that facilitate effective economic development (North, 1990, 2005; Acemoglu et al., 2005; Acemoglu and Robinson, 2012).

Regional institutions may be those that are spatially either inward- or outward-looking—such as the networks discussed above—with such institutions sometimes being in conflict with formal national-level institutions, resulting in unintended consequences (Thornton, 1999). Where there is conflict between formal and informal institutions, North (1990) suggests that informal institutions determine underlying behaviour to the greatest extent. One perspective is that informal and formal institutions may be substitutes for one another, and strong urban and regional community cultures may develop to fulfil the role of weak ineffective formal institutions (Durlauf and Fafchamps, 2003). This means that, where formal institutions no longer support existing activities within a region, it is not beyond the realms of possibility that the prevailing informal institutions may actually strengthen to fill this gap (Huggins and Thompson, 2015c).

As argued above, social network analysis indicates that the most developed cities and regions tend to have relatively flat, open, and equal social networks, with underdeveloped cities and regions having more hierarchical (unequal) networks due to these consisting of a relatively limited number of agents operating within elite 'small world' networks (Watts, 1999). Furthermore, network actors are likely to vary in terms of the power they possess, which determines their capability to exercise their human agency potential, especially where elites capture urban- and regional-development agendas (Gregson, 2005). As power can operate as an instrumental force to mobilize the activities of others or a means to pursue intended shared goals, the equitability of the power networks within and across cities and regions plays an important role in their evolution and development.

An analysis of the contemporary growth patterns of cities and urban areas in the UK by Martin et al. (2014) finds that, with only a few exceptions, high growth almost exclusively occurs in the south of England, especially the cities and regions in and around London and the greater South East. On the other hand, those cities and urban regions with the lowest recorded economic growth are exclusively situated in the more northern quarters of the UK. This suggests significant differences in the economic growth systems across each type of city and region. As a means of beginning to consider these differences, Table 5.1 summarizes some of the key capital and institutional features that distinguish high- from low-growth cities and urban regions. These are differentiated into three levels depending on the scale that these growth dynamics occur: firm; inter-firm; or urban/regional. In the south, urban growth systems are relatively high in terms of capital accumulation and institutional quality across the three growth levels, being rich in terms of the availability of human capital, knowledge capital, and enabling institutions. Similarly, they possess high-quality institutions and rates of capital in relation to organizational arrangements concerning markets, networks, and political governance. Based on this, these cities and regions can be said to typify urban and regional growth systems that are far more likely to result in relatively high rates of long-term economic growth. Unfortunately, the relative paucity of capital and high-quality institutions across cities and regions in the north leads to them being categorized as possessing low-growth systems. In a comparative study of two cities in the UK—Cambridge ('south') and Swansea ('north')—Simmie and Martin (2010) identify a number of similar differences in growth system traits to those found more broadly across high- and low-growth cities.

In terms of the measurement of urban- and regional-level growth dynamics, Charron et al. (2014) develop regional measures of the quality of government for EU regions based on the World Bank's Governance Indicators national measures (Kaufmann et al., 2009) and a citizen survey gathered at the regional level (Charron et al., 2011). The citizen survey captured ratings for three public services—education, healthcare, and law enforcement—in terms of their quality, impartiality, and corruption. It is not possible to utilize social surveys at the local level in Great Britain. Therefore, in order to extend Charron et al.'s (2011) approach, we use here a number of complementary sources to identify differences in the quality of government across the localities, cities, and regions of Great Britain, including satisfaction surveys of the police (Home Office Statistics and Scottish Policing Performance

Table 5.1 General features of economic growth systems in high- and low-growth cities of the UK

	High-growth cities	Low-growth cities
Firm-level growth dynamics		
Human capital	Evolving global talent centre, fuelled by 'brain attraction'	Stagnant and relatively low skills base, compounded by 'brain drain'
Knowledge capital	Rich base of knowledge workers, technology, and expertise	Lack of knowledge workers and associated technology and expertise
Learning institutions	Dense and flexible labour markets	Weak labour markets
Innovation institutions	High density of public- and private-sector engagement in innovation	Low density of public- and private-sector engagement in innovation
Inter-firm-level growth dynamics		
Entrepreneurship capital	High rates of entrepreneurship and associated venture finance	Below-average (national) rates of entrepreneurship and venture finance
Network capital	High incidence of business network formation and knowledge flows	Relatively low rates of business network formation and knowledge flows
Entrepreneurial institutions	Plentiful opportunity to access entrepreneurial support mechanisms	Lack of opportunity to access entrepreneurial support mechanisms
Associational institutions	Strong industrial clustering, especially among firms operating in highly tradable markets	Lack of strong industry clusters
Urban and regional-level growth dynamics		
Physical capital	Strong infrastructure, transport systems, and built environment	Weak and dated infrastructure
Institutions of ownership	History of inclusive institutions—centre of public ownership, especially since the 1970s; key location for the headquarters of large domestic and international firms	History of extractive institutions—extractive industries, dependency on the branch plant activity of international firms

Framework), General Practitioners (NHS England, National Survey for Wales, Health experience of General Practitioner services, and Scottish Health and Care Experience Survey), measures of the quality of institutions such as complaints against the police (Her Majesty's Inspectorate of Constabulary and Scottish Policing Performance Framework), average primary-school class size (Department for Education, Schools Census results and Summary Statistics for Schools in Scotland), and the proportion of

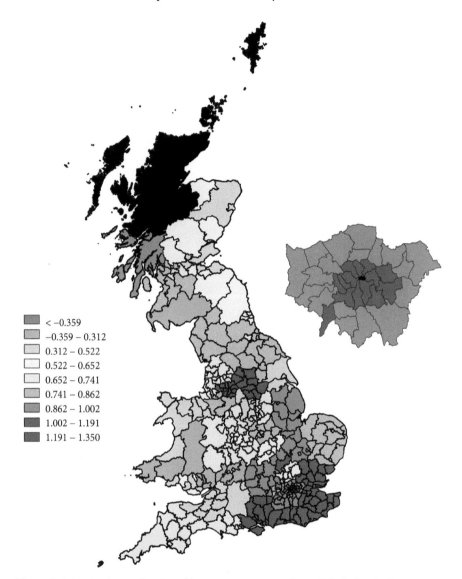

Figure 5.4 Institutions—Quality of Government across Great Britain (excluding northern parts of Scotland).

schools rated as good or above (Office for Standards in Education, Children's Services and Skills (Ofsted), Estyn and School Estate Statistics).

As shown by Figure 5.4, the highest local quality of government is largely found in London and South East England. Localities in Wales, South West England and Scotland have, on average, the least effective local governments (Table 5.2), which in any age of austerity is likely to become further accentuated. Indeed, for some places the mix of poor institutions and forms of psychocultural behaviour that do not appear to promote economic growth and

Table 5.2 Index of Quality of Government by region of
Great Britain

Rank	Region	Institutions
1	South East	1.06
2	London	1.00
3	Yorkshire and Humber	0.93
4	East of England	0.91
5	North West	0.85
6	North East	0.70
7	East Midlands	0.69
8	West Midlands	0.66
9	Scotland	0.59
10	South West	0.52
11	Wales	0.39

competitiveness continue to make them highly vulnerable over both the short and long term.

Beyond the UK, China offers one of the best spatial laboratories for examining the differing nature of urban growth systems, with evidence suggesting that growth models across its leading urban regions are clearly linked to their pre-existing capital and institutions (Huggins et al., 2014a). In the case of the leading city of Shanghai and its wider Yangtze River Delta city region, it has advantages in terms of its embedded industrialization and urbanization, which predate the period of Chinese reform. Since reform, however, the region has rapidly evolved its economic structure, such that it is clearly the most innovative and technology-driven region in China, partly due its more pronounced shift toward a capitalist and market-oriented economy. By contrast, while Beijing and the surrounding Bohai Gulf region possesses capital resource advantages, it is limited by the prevailing institutional structure. At the outset of reform, the city region may have appeared to be best positioned in terms of the capital available for use within the knowledge economy, but it has not moved as swiftly towards a market-oriented system as Shanghai, mainly due to historical factors and the continuing momentum of a planned-economy approach.

In Beijing, capital has proved less appropriate when the institutions are examined, with policies placing a rigid hold on these resources. Any convergence in growth systems across cities and regions will be dependent on the extent to which central and regional policymakers seek to, and are able effectively to, transfer policy lessons from across and within regions, particularly policies aimed at increased marketization, or policies focused on indigenous innovation (Zhao and Tong, 2001; Wei and Ye, 2009; Huggins et al., 2014a). Zhang and Peck (2016) have similarly noted the differences in the economic systems underpinning Chinese regions, finding significant heterogeneity and sub-models of China's variegated capitalism.

Although the key takeaway from this analysis is the need for cities and regions to ensure the quality of their institutions, in reality the means by which institutions and their quality can be measured is a matter that continues to challenge institutional economists, with no clear methodology emerging beyond trying to identify relevant and robust proxies (Robinson, 2013; Voigt, 2013). Perhaps the most promising route forward is to relate behavioural changes among a particular community, in this case a city or region, to institutions and institutional arrangements that are more likely to promote or constrain particular types of behaviour, in this case that associated with the facilitation of economic development. Where significant positive behavioural changes occur, and no significant external 'noise' is identified, it could be argued that institutions are of a relatively 'high' quality.

The intangibility of institutions, however, makes appropriate measurement of quality a complex undertaking. Institutional theorists tend to argue that it is the difference in the efficiency of institutions that underpins growth and prosperity (Acemoglu et al., 2005; Acemoglu and Robinson, 2012). At first sight this seems a more than plausible means of measuring institutional success that is neoclassical in its approach by suggesting some form of optimal input–output ratio between institutions. In reality, however, this is unlikely to exist, especially within an urban context, as one of the innate features of 'good' institutions will be their inefficiency. This feature was noted by Jacobs (1969) when she discusses the valuable inefficiencies of cities:

> Cities are indeed inefficient…the largest and most rapidly growing at any given time are apt to be the least efficient. But I propose to argue that these grave and real deficiencies are necessary to economic development and thus are exactly what make cities uniquely valuable to economic life. By this, I do not mean that cities are economically valuable in spite of their inefficiency and impracticality but rather because they are inefficient.   (Jacobs, 1969: 85–6)

A contemporary example of Jacobs's inefficiencies is Silicon Valley, the most prosperous and growth-oriented urban region in the world (Huggins et al., 2014b). Despite this position, however, an efficiency approach to understanding its growth system would suggest that its relative levels of productivity and growth should be considerably higher than they are compared with a number of 'competitor' regions. Its institutional behaviour in terms of innovation, as measured by metrics such as patenting, entrepreneurship (as measured by access to venture finance) and associational activity (as measured by collaborative and cooperative network activity), would suggest that it should economically outperform other regions far more than it actually does

(Saxenian, 1994; Huggins et al., 2014b). However, this ignores the embedded institutional inefficiency required to gain these returns in the first instance. Tenner (2018) refers to this as 'the Efficiency Paradox', whereby a seemingly inefficient institutional framework allows agents to productively learn from the random and the unexpected.

Within Silicon Valley, many firms are investing large amounts in innovations resulting in patents and the like that accrue little or no economic returns, with only a relatively smaller number of firms investing in innovations resulting in economically blockbusting products and services. Similarly, much of the venture finance available in the region will not result in sustainable entrepreneurship, and many business networks will result in knowledge exchange that does not facilitate commercializable innovation. Nevertheless, the few make up for the many and, within the evolutionary innovation-driven context of urban and regional economics, it is the natural inefficiency of institutions that provides the most fertile framework for economic growth, but at the same time can result in the crises of capitalism, which Schumpeter (1934) clearly recognized. In summary, efficient institutions and systems may not always be the most economically equitable for a city or region (Storper, 2013).

5.6 Conclusion: Integrating Theories of Development

This chapter has sought to provide an introduction to some contemporary theoretical perspectives on regional innovation and growth, in particular the concepts of regional growth systems and institutions, as well as behavioural theories concerning both cultural and psychological explanations. This suggests that both behavioural and institutional-based conceptual frameworks can usefully complement existing theories of urban and regional innovation and growth. For example, although existing conceptual frameworks such as the regional innovation systems literature note the importance of entrepreneurship as a feature of such systems, it is not formally incorporated into these models. Indeed, even though the legacy and prevalence of Schumpeterian discourse have led to 'entrepreneurship' and 'innovation' more often than not being uttered in the same breath, the connection between the two is usually implicitly, rather than explicitly, formulated. This indicates the need for further theoretical integration, particularly through the deployment of a behavioural conceptual lens.

As outlined by Figure 5.5, behavioural-based frameworks incorporating cultural and psychological aspects help us understand why particular agents

	Regional Innovation Theories	Innovation-Based Theories of Regional Growth
Behavioural-Based Frameworks	Socio-spatial culture, personality psychology, and entrepreneurial agency	Regional behavioural systems, psychocultural behaviour, and agency
Institution-Based Frameworks	Rules of the game, constraints/incentives, and the institution-capital interface	Regional growth systems, growth dynamics, and innovation institutions

Figure 5.5 New theoretical perspectives on regional innovation and growth.

within a region, especially entrepreneurial agents, may possess a proclivity towards fostering innovation, as well as how the interaction between cultural and psychological factors result in urban and regional behavioural systems with a higher or lower tendency to sustain long-term economic growth. As we have argued, psychocultural behavioural patterns, and their evolution, provide a basis for understanding the type and nature of human agency that exist within cities and regions. In addition to this, institutional-based frameworks allow us to consider how both informal and formal institutions are likely to moderate the behaviour of urban and regional actors, with institutions forming part of the broader systems and dynamics that ultimately determine urban and regional economic growth. By identifying the connection between types of institutions and forms of 'growth capital', it is possible to consider distinct varieties of economic growth systems at play across regions.

Positive urban and regional growth and development require high-quality institutions, in the form of growth-enabling rules and incentives, alongside the types of capital suggested by regional competitiveness theory (Huggins et al., 2014b). Therefore, a means of explaining economic development is to conceptualize cities and regions as growth systems within which the interaction between available capital assets and the institutional infrastructure is a major determinant. Such a systems-based approach to connecting endogenous capital accumulation and institutional theories of regional growth and development potentially offers a means of delineating a framework to better understand how investment in capital assets, especially intangible assets, is related to the institutions underlying the economic functioning of cities and regions. Within a systems-based approach, network behaviour can be conceptualized and analysed from both a capitalization (ties and pipelines) and an institutional (governance and coordination) perspective (Sunley, 2008; Glückler, 2013), with such behaviour offering a fruitful means of understanding the growth and development systems of cities and regions from a more theoretically integrated standpoint. Indeed, it has been argued that networks are key explanatory factors underlying the reasons why cities and regions often grow and flourish (Glaeser et al., 1992; Gordon, 2013).

In the past, both capital accumulation and institutional theories of growth and development have been criticized by some scholars for their lack of explanatory power (Glaeser et al., 2004; Chang, 2011), which is perhaps a result of each theory being viewed somewhat in isolation. A meshing of theoretical approaches, however, indicates that urban and regional growth is a highly endogenous, recursive, and evolutionary process whereby the interaction between capital and institutions at a number of different, yet interdependent, levels of organizational arrangement may offer more explanatory power. Finally, Storper (2010) argues that it is difficult to propose 'varieties of city capitalism' in a similar manner to that employed by those analysing institutions in a comparative manner across nations (Hall and Soskice, 2001). Nevertheless, by identifying the connection between types of institutions and forms of 'growth capital', it is possible to consider distinct varieties in the economic growth systems and models at play across cities and regions.

6

The Co-evolution of Culture, Psychology, and Institutions

6.1 Introduction

The preceding chapters have illustrated the theoretical importance of factors relating to individual behaviour and collective decisions on urban and regional economic and social development (Huggins and Thompson, 2019). This chapter starts to consider how the role of these behavioural factors might be measured and the relationships between them. It acknowledges the lack of agreement that exists not only in terms of what are the key constructs to examine, but also how these may be operationalized (Rentfrow et al., 2008). In this chapter and those that follow we also try to overcome some of the issues that have developed, especially in behavioural sciences that often focus on one group of constructs but ignore related studies by others (Parks-Leduc et al., 2015).

Fundamentally, we empirically investigate the relationships that hold between culture, personality psychology, and institutions. The analysis recognizes that any relationships between these constructs are likely to be bidirectional, and therefore it is inappropriate to assume that one can be regarded as an independent factor that drives the others (Rentfrow et al., 2009, 2013). Therefore, the analysis examines those specific relationships between each of the three constructs to capture evidence for the existence of their intertwined nature. In particular, we focus on how selective migration due to particular psychological traits can be associated not only with the psychological profiles of 'exporting' and 'receiving' areas (Boneva et al., 1998; Jokela, 2009, 2013; Rentfrow et al., 2015), but also how these patterns relate to the culture of the receiving areas and how they develop over time (Rentfrow et al., 2013). This is accomplished through six sections: (Section 6.2) measurement issues for culture, personality psychology, and institutions; (Section 6.3) existing measures of key constructs; (Section 6.4) relationships between personality psychology, culture, and institutions; (Section 6.5) the distribution of values formed by the psychocultural profile of places; (Section 6.6) an empirical

A Behavioural Theory of Economic Development: The Uneven Evolution of Cities and Regions. Robert Huggins and Piers Thompson, Oxford University Press (2021). © Robert Huggins and Piers Thompson.
DOI: 10.1093/oso/9780198832348.003.0006

examination of the connections between psychocultural profiles and values; and (Section 6.7) an investigation of migration patterns between psychocultural profiles. Section 6.8 will summarize the chapter in terms of the insights it provides in relation to the earlier theoretical chapters and how this links to later empirical chapters.

6.2 Measurement Issues for Culture, Personality Psychology, and Institutions

As has been outlined in preceding chapters, one of the main difficulties within the literature is that personality, culture, and institutions are concepts that are difficult to place hard boundaries around. This leads to there being a blurring of the constructs, so that studies may discuss the same concepts while classifying them differently. For example, there is a degree of overlap between some definitions of culture and institutions (Rodriguez-Pose, 2013; Huggins and Thompson, 2015a). This overlap is often reflected when institutions have been categorized by type, such as Scott's (2007) typology of institutional forces discussed earlier: regulatory pillar—rules of the game, encapsulating monitoring and enforcement through rules, laws, and sanctions; normative pillar—socially accepted norms in professional and organizational interaction empowered through certifications and accreditations; and a culturally orientated pillar—common beliefs and shared logics of action which are taken for granted.

In the case of the first pillar there is a clear distinction from culture, while both the third and to some extent the second pillars have clear commonalities with the concept of culture as captured by others. Similarly, work on institutions drawn from economic and political science views institutions operating through rules, procedures, and agreements (North, 1990). Others drawing on sociology and organizational theory assume individuals make decisions based on heuristics associated with conventions linked to shared cultures (DiMaggio and Powell, 1983, 1991). Consistent with this approach, Beugelsdijk and Maseland (2011: 13) describe culture as being 'a subset of institutions related to societal collective identity'. However, they also note the difficulties in determining who should be considered to be a member of different communities. A further difficulty with this blurring is that each of the constructs has a different level at which it ought to be empirically measured and captured. Whereas personality psychology should be measured at the individual level (Cattell, 1943), community culture is a group-held construct (Van Maanen and Schein, 1979; Beugelsdijk and Maseland, 2011), and institutions, although also group-held, are usually presumed to be held at higher levels and more formally (North, 1990, 2005).

As will be discussed below in more depth, there are individual measures or proxies for personality, culture, and institutions that frequently encompass a number of items that are combined to produce these measures. Those taking this approach argue that this provides a more robust measure that is less likely to be influenced by outliers for a single item (Welzel, 2013). In many cases the approach adopted is to use principal component analysis or factor analysis of one type or another to find variables that group together in order to capture a single measure (Hofstede, 2001; Tabellini, 2010). One division in the development of cultural, personality, and institutional measures is whether or not a data-driven empirical approach is taken, such as that adopted by Hofstede (2001). Here no preconceptions are made about the form that culture should take. Methods such as factor analysis (Hofstede, 2001) or cluster analysis (Steenkamp, 2001) are used to identify the common patterns in the individual items, and cultural components or dimensions are named from the resulting groupings. The advantage is that cross-country measures can be developed without the fear of imposing values or norms from one perspective.

The alternative is to use a more theoretically driven approach (Kaasa et al., 2014). Here the benefit is that, whereas empirical approaches could technically produce meaningless cultural measures, there is a good philosophical reasoning behind the measures developed by this approach. Later studies have often drawn from both approaches, where items may be chosen to measure particular constructs, and these may be both theoretically justified and/or those regularly found by more empirical approaches (Tabellini, 2010; Kaasa et al., 2014; Huggins and Thompson, 2016). As noted above, in most cases studies have sought to develop measures that are created using approaches isolating the common element. This means that the approach used is a dimensional logic. However, Welzel (2013) argues against such an approach, instead suggesting a more formative or compository logic whereby items are included based on their theoretical alignment with the measure being sought. It is argued that there is no requirement for any correlation between the measures, as each provides a more rounded perspective of the underlying dimension. This contrasts with the traditional approach whereby any differences from the main component are discarded. Welzel (2013) also argues that the standardization process used in factor analysis reduces the impact of variables with greater variance, which may not be appropriate. The value of any mean is also lost due to the standardization processes of factor analysis.

6.3   Existing Measures of Key Constructs

Throughout this chapter and those that follow the relationships between personality and culture with economic development are explored, alongside the relationships that these have with one another. For each of these constructs there are no official figures and measures published either nationally or internationally. Much of the data generated is either from academic surveys or utilizes data originally intended for other purposes to act as a proxy. Each of the measures available tends, therefore, to come with its own strengths and weaknesses. This is further compounded when examining institutions, community culture, or personality traits at the regional level where sub-samples limit the extent to which intranational differences can be reliably captured. As a result, this book does not draw upon a single data source or operationalization of the constructs, but rather utilizes those measures that provide the greatest insight into the particular relationship being examined. As such, it is necessary for each of the empirical chapters to start by considering the different measures of relevant constructs that can be identified in the literature to isolate those which are most appropriate. The remainder of this section explores in turn the measures present in the existing literature for each of the three primary constructs considered in this chapter.

Personality traits. A large number of different instruments have been developed to capture personality. This partly reflects a lack of theoretical clarity and methodological rigour (Inkeles and Levinson, 1969; Le Vine, 2001). Some of the approaches used in earlier studies, in particular, might be perceived to have more in common with capturing culture or institutions such as those examining the customs of nations (Benedict, 1946; Mead, 1951) or distinguishing between national stereotypes (Peabody, 1988). As we have discussed, more recent studies have tended to find more common ground through being based around the Big Five personality dimensions of extraversion, agreeableness, conscientiousness, neuroticism (emotional stability), and openness (John et al., 2008). The five dimensions can be described as follows (John et al., 2008: 138): *extraversion* implies an energetic approach toward the social and material world and includes traits such as sociability, activity, assertiveness, and positive emotionality; *agreeableness* contrasts a prosocial and communal orientation toward others with antagonism and includes traits such as altruism, tender-mindedness, trust, and modesty; *conscientiousness* describes socially prescribed impulse control that facilitates task- and goal-orientated behaviour; *neuroticism* contrasts emotional stability and even-temperedness with negative emotionality, such as feeling anxious, nervous, sad, and tense; and *openness* to experience describes the breadth, depth, originality, and complexity of an individual's mental and experimental life.

The Big Five personality traits were developed from an analysis of natural language terms people use to describe themselves, building on the early work of Cattell (1943). Tupes and Christal (1961) used a variety of samples to examine the relationships between those traits identified by earlier work and concluded that they could be captured within five factors. As such, the Big Five allow previously developed measures of personality to be integrated within them to provide a set of clear and easy to interpret measures (John and Srivastava 1999). Wide usage has ensured that considerable work has been undertaken in developing and testing instruments to capture personality traits of this kind (Credé et al., 2012). However, studies such as Leutner et al. (2014) find that the Big Five do not necessarily perform as well when attempting to predict certain behaviours and attitudes when compared to those measures that are specifically designed to examine them. They find that extraversion is related to entrepreneurial activity, and extraversion and agreeableness are both negatively linked to invention entrepreneurship. However, the Measure of Entrepreneurial Tendencies and Abilities (META) developed by Ahmetoglu et al. (2011) to specifically capture tendencies to engage in opportunity recognition, opportunity exploitation, innovation, and value creation, has a stronger association with entrepreneurial activity (see Table 6.1).

Other studies have suggested that certain personality traits can reverse their relationship with some behaviours when present at extreme levels (Miller, 2014). This would imply that simple linear measures and analysis are not appropriate. Klotz and Neubaum (2016) criticize approaches that consider such traits in this manner, arguing that in many cases positive and negative aspects are related to different traits. Achievement and control come from conscientiousness, while ambition, dominance, energy, and optimism are facets of extraversion. Their point is that, rather than being extremes of these positive traits, factors like overconfidence and mistrust are actually facets of neuroticism, while aggression is low agreeableness.

Another area of contention is that traits' influences on outcomes do not act independently of one another but are found by many studies to interact with one another (DiNisi, 2015), and/or contextual factors (Bee and Neubaum, 2014). For example, while conscientiousness is strongly associated with overall job and entrepreneurial performance (Hurtz and Donovan, 2000; Zhao et al., 2010), this relationship disappears for those with low levels of agreeableness (Witt et al., 2002). In terms of context, moods may influence work performance (Rothbard and Wilk, 2011), but not when

Table 6.1 Personality trait measures

Scheme	Measure	Description	Combination	Sources
Big Five	Extraversion	Traits such as sociability, activity, assertiveness, and positive emotionality	Principal component analysis	Tupes and Christal (1961); Goldberg (1992); Leutner et al. (2014)
	Agreeableness	Traits such as altruism, tender-mindedness, trust, and modesty	Principal component analysis	
	Conscientiousness	Socially prescribed impulse control that facilitates task- and goal-orientated behaviour	Principal component analysis	
	Neuroticism	Contrasts emotional stability and even-temperedness with negative emotionality	Principal component analysis	
	Openness	Describes the breadth, depth, originality, and complexity of an individual's mental and experimental life	Principal component analysis	
Measure of entrepreneurial tendencies and abilities	Entrepreneurial vision	I want to make a difference in the world	Principal component analysis	Ahmetoglu et al. (2011); Leutner et al. (2014)
	Entrepreneurial proactivity	I am quick to spot profitable opportunities	Principal component analysis	
	Entrepreneurial creativity	In groups, I usually have the most innovative ideas	Principal component analysis	
	Entrepreneurial opportunism	I try to take advantage of every profitable opportunity	Principal component analysis	

considering those with high levels of agreeableness (Ilies et al., 2006). This would imply that overall profiles rather than individual measures need capturing, but should this be at the individual level, as argued above, or group level?

As noted above, personality is perceived to be present at the individual rather than group level. However, there is a growing body of literature considering the geography of personality (Rentfrow et al., 2008). This reflects a belief that a greater presence of particular personality traits can influence various economic and social outcomes ranging from innovation (Lee, 2017) and entrepreneurship (Obschonka et al., 2013a) to voting patterns (Rentfrow et al., 2009). The mechanisms behind these have been discussed in Chapters 2 and 3. In the vast majority of cases the approach taken to produce regional personality measures has been to capture the mean of the individual residents' personalities (Rentfrow et al., 2008). However, others have recognized that within groups, even for a single personality trait, the mix of personalities can be important (Prewett et al., 2018), with extreme values having more impact on group decisions than the average (Mathieu et al., 2014), such as the 'bad apple effect' (Felps et al., 2006). Equally, as introduced above, Rentfrow et al. (2013) suggest that personality traits should not be considered in isolation, but the combination of personality traits may be more important.

Community culture measures. Although many studies recognize the importance of culture or informal institutions for economic development, particularly in assisting regional learning, there are disagreements concerning what culture or informal institutions consist of and how it is possible to capture them (Rodríguez-Pose, 2013). As indicated in Chapter 3, probably the most influential attempt to measure culture was undertaken by Hofstede (1980) at the national level. Using survey data from the IBM Corporation across a large number of countries, he used factor analysis to identify four dimensions of culture: individualism–collectivism, masculinity–femininity, uncertainty avoidance, and power distance. The factor analysis was conducted using group means rather than the individual data to avoid issues of outliers and missing data. Later a fifth dimension was added after work with Michael Bond identified a Western bias in the items used to collect the data that ignored a dimension initially described as the 'Confucian work dimension' and relabelled 'long-term orientation' (Hofstede and Bond, 1988; Hofstede, 2001).

Hofstede's (1980, 2001) cultural dimensions are not without criticism. Kaasa et al. (2014) argue that Hofstede's (1980, 2001) dimensions are based on work-related values and do not explore wider experiences across society. It is also true that Hofstede's (1980) original measures are captured only at the national level, while in reality there is evidence that there is considerable variation in culture within countries (Hofstede, 2001; Dolan et al., 2004; Hofstede et al., 2010). In particular, studies have found that regions either side of national borders often have more in common culturally than with other regions in their countries (Lenartowicz et al., 2003). Kaasa et al. (2014) find that countries do differ in their degree of the regional variation of culture. They also find that regions of a particular country often display cultural differences on one dimension but not others, while another country may show regional variation across a completely different dimension with no clear pattern evident (Kaasa et al., 2014).

In order to overcome the limitations of Hofstede's (1980) measures in terms of unit of analysis and attitudes covered, Kaasa et al. (2013) and Kaasa et al. (2014) utilize different data sources available for Europe. Kaasa et al. (2013) use the European Social Survey (ESS), which has been repeated every two years since 2002. A limitation is that, while many items relating to culture are collected in each wave, some of the items were only captured in the first wave. Items were selected to correspond to Hofstede's (1980) four cultural dimensions. These are measured at the NUTS0, NUTS1, NUTS2 levels of aggregation, with weights supplied in the dataset used to ensure representativeness with the underlying population. The mean weighted values are then used in factor analysis to produce the overall cultural dimensions. For power distance, uncertainty avoidance, and masculinity a single factor was extracted. However, for individualism–collectivism two factors were extracted. The first is reflective of individualistic values, so was referred to as overall individualism. The second factor distinguishes between family-related collectivism, and that with friends and wider society. It is therefore described as family-related collectivism.

Kaasa et al. (2014) try to overcome the problem of Kaasa et al.'s (2013) measures in terms of them not being possible to update due to having to rely on items only collected in the first wave (2002) of the ESS. In order to achieve this, they use data from the fourth wave of the ESS and combine it with the 2010 fourth wave of the European Values Survey (EVS). The EVS is collected every nine years starting from 1981. Replacing some of the ESS measures of Kaasa et al.'s (2013) study with EVS data from 2010, Kaasa et al. (2014) are able to produce regional measures for Hofstede's (1980) four dimensions. As with the ESS, the EVS provides weights to ensure representativeness, and the mean values of the items in regions are employed in the factor analysis. As both the ESS and EVS are focused on individual attitudes more broadly, rather than just relating to work attitudes, it is argued that these measures, while being correlated with Hofstede's (1980) estimates, are better able to capture the impact of culture across a wider range of society behaviours.

Considering the evolution of values across time with respect to development, as discussed in Chapter 4, Inglehart (1971) develops a scale for 'acquisitives' and 'post-bourgeois', also described as a measure of post-materialism. The theory is that values having the most importance are those that have the lowest unfulfilled ranking on Maslow's (1970) hierarchy of needs. As economies develop, society fulfils its food and shelter needs and places less importance on these, becoming more focused on self-actualization. The categorizations were originally based on a question that required respondents to choose two of the four items listed as being the most desirable: (i) maintaining order in the nation; (ii) giving the people more say in important political decisions; (iii) fighting rising prices; and (iv) protecting freedom of speech.

Those choosing items (i) and (iii) were classed as acquisitives, while those choosing (ii) and (iv) were regarded as postbourgeois. Roughly half the sample were classed as a mix, picking neither combination above. Flanagan (1982) criticizes Inglehart's (1971) measures on a number of grounds, arguing that 'maintaining order' is not an economic issue, so does not necessarily reflect prioritizing such issues. Materialism can also be a life cycle rather than intergenerational issue, with concern over the economy rising in middle age before falling back (Milkis and Baldino, 1978). There is also an issue of distinguishing between value preferences and value priorities (Flanagan, 1982). The former relates to particular preferences over how society is organized, while the latter relates to a number of desirable outcomes and how they are prioritized. Flanagan (1982) argues that Inglehart's (1971) scale is a combination of these. Various versions of Inglehart's measure have been used by others, and their relationship to a variety of political, social, and economic measures are examined. For example, Uhlaner and Thurik (2007) use data from the World Values Survey to examine links between post-materialism and entrepreneurship. Gerhards (2010) uses the index within a study of non-discrimination towards homosexuality, which could have important ramifications for economic development given those studies linking tolerance to the presence of the creative classes (Florida, 2002).

Somewhat contrary to Inglehart (1971), Flanagan (1982) suggests that a scale of authoritarian to libertarian is more appropriate. This uses items that describe authoritarians as being more conformist, deferential, and stressing social order, so that they have more austere hierarchical lives. This assumes that development affects values by influencing the socio-economic environment. Individuals have to choose the best way to act in order to survive within this socio-economic environment. Flanagan (1982) uses data from two Japanese national-election surveys (1967 and 1976) to capture this scale. The 1967 items include 'Would you say you are the type of person who tends to save money or the type of person who tends to spend it so as to have a good time?'—*austerity*; 'Do you believe in god (gods)?'—*piety*; 'When you deal with such problems as education, occupation, marriage and so on, how do you make a decision? Do you decide in terms of your own interests, largely in terms of your own interests, largely in terms of your family's interests, or do you decide in terms of your family's interests?'—*conformity*; 'Do you feel that young people today need more discipline or not?'—*deference to authority*; 'Do you feel that young people today should respect their parents' opinion more or not?'—*deference to authority*; and 'Would you say you are more or less a new type of person or an old type of person?'—*multidimensional*.

In 1976 these items were updated to consist of 'If community members actively come around to collect contributions, it is better to donate without complaint in order to preserve neighbourhood harmony even if you do not necessarily agree with the purpose'—*conformity*; 'At meetings in your neighbourhood, place of work, PTA or the like, when opinions are sharply divided, it is better to cut the discussion short in order to avoid bad feelings afterward'—*conformity and deference*; 'The moral principles of filial piety and respect for one's seniors, which were much discussed in the old days, have gone out of fashion in the postwar period. These time-honoured Japanese morals must be strongly supported'—*deference*; 'Since those who have attained positions of leadership over others are outstanding people, it is proper to respect their opinions'—*deference*; 'For the sake of improving the country, if outstanding political leaders came forward, it would be best to entrust things to them rather than have the people hotly debate matters among themselves'—*deference*; and 'Since Diet representatives and governors are the representatives of the people, it is proper for them to command respect'—*deference*. Even though piety and austerity were not included in the 1976 dimensions, the strong intercorrelation means this has little effect on the outcomes.

Like Inglehart and Abramson (1999), Welzel (2013) draws upon the World Values Survey (WVS) and European Values Survey (EVS) to create two dimensions of culture based on emancipative and secular values. In the case of the former, this relates to measures of self-expression (Galassi et al., 1974), but strips out the happiness, trust, and signing petitions, which are argued not to be values, but emotional well-being, assessments of others' trustworthiness, and an action respectively. This leaves a liberating orientation and egalitarian perspective. Instead, secularization relates to the distance from power sources of different types: religious, patrimonial, state, and confirmatory norms.

Hirschle and Kleiner (2014) draw upon Schwartz's (2006) Human Value Scale, which was developed to capture how cultural value orientations evolve to confront particular problems and established four measures of culture: hedonism, individualism, social harmony, and traditionalism. Hedonism reflects a propensity to socially connect with friends and the importance placed on seeking pleasure. Individualism reflects the value placed on being able to try things out and experiment without constraint. Social harmony is reflective of the importance of being loyal and caring for others in a fair fashion. Traditionalism is related to the obedience of rules, traditions, and authority. Data for this can be drawn from the European Social Survey between 2002 and 2010, allowing the evolution of such cultural traits to be examined. However, when breaking down such measures to the regional level, the sample sizes frequently require years of data to be combined to provide robust values.

The GLOBE study surveys middle managers from three industrial sectors to generate nine cultural practice dimensions: performance orientation; future orientation; gender egalitarianism; assertiveness; institutional collectivism; in-group collectivism; power distance; humane orientation; uncertainty avoidance (House et al., 2004). Stephan et al. (2015) examine the impact of culture on social entrepreneurship using the GLOBE study to generate a measure of a socially supportive culture based around a humane orientation and the inverse of assertiveness to capture cultural norms providing experiences of friendliness, supportiveness, cooperation, and helpfulness to encourage cooperation (Stephan and Uhlaner, 2010). This measure is regarded as a normative informal institution (Scott, 2005, 2007). However, they acknowledge that the GLOBE study has been criticized in the way it captures culture values (Brewer and Venaik, 2010; Maseland and van Hoorn, 2010).

What becomes apparent from the different measures of culture summarized in Table 6.2 is that, although there is some overlap in schemes, they often cover particular facets of human behaviour more strongly than others. Data-driven approaches do not necessarily produce identical schemes to those with a more theoretical basis. It is also notable that most schemes, with the odd exception (Inglehart, 1971), have tended to claim that there are different elements, dimensions, or facets to culture, so culture cannot be captured on a single scale. It should be noted that, where single scales are the focus, it is not necessarily the intention of the authors to reflect culture as a whole.

Table 6.2 Culture measures

Scheme	Measure	Description	Combination	Sources
Local community culture	Engagement with employment and education	Activities including male economic activity, proportion with no formal education, primary- and secondary-school absenteeism	First factor from principal component analysis	Huggins and Thompson (2016)
	Social cohesion	Ethnic similarity, religious similarity, gross migration, proportion UK-born, host-country nationality	First factor from principal component analysis	
	Feminine and caring activities	Female economic activity; female part-time employment; unpaid care provision	First factor from principal component analysis	
	Adherence to social rules	Age-standardized alcohol deaths; adolescent conceptions; non-sexual violent crimes; crimes by deception	First factor from principal component analysis	
	Preference for collective action	Trade union membership; voting for left-of-centre parties	First factor from principal component analysis	
Hofstede's cultural dimensions from work-related attitudes	Power distance	Non-managerial employees afraid to disagree with managers; bosses perceived to take decisions in autocratic or paternalistic ways; subordinates' preference for non-consultative style of decision-making	Standardization and summation of three components	Hofstede (2001)
	Uncertainty avoidance	Rule orientation (company rules should not be broken even if there is disagreement); employment stability (intention of staff to stay with company more than five years); stress (how often feeling nervous or tense at work)	Standardization and summation of three components	
	Individualism–collectivism	Importance of jobs that provide personal time; have training opportunities to improve skills; challenging work giving a sense of accomplishment; use of skills; good physical working conditions; freedom to adapt approach	First factor extracted from factor analysis of 14 work goals.	
	Masculinity–femininity	Importance of jobs that provide opportunity for good relationships with manager; working with people who cooperate; live in desirable area; employment security; challenging work giving a sense of accomplishment; advancement to high-level jobs; recognition when do a good job; high earnings	Second factor extracted from factor analysis of 14 work goals	
	Long-term orientation–short-term orientation	Importance in private life of thrift, respect for tradition	Standardization and summation of 2 components	

Dimension	Items	Method	Reference
Power distance	ESS: politicians care what people think; politicians interested in votes not opinions; trust parliament; satisfied with democracy; able to organize daily work; allowed to influence work directions; able to organize daily work; change work tasks	First factor of principal component analysis	Kaasa et al. (2013)
Uncertainty avoidance	ESS: Important to live in a safe area; important strong government ensures safety; importance of job security; most people can be trusted; important to behave properly; better if everyone shares customs; immigrants make a country a better place to live	First factor of principal component analysis	
Overall individualism–collectivism	ESS: important to think of new ideas; important to make own decisions; important to have a good time; important to seek fun and pleasure	First factor of principal component analysis using 7 measures of important things in life	
Family-related collectivism	ESS: family ought to be main priority; membership of voluntary organizations; importance of friends	Second factor of principal component analysis using 7 measures of important things in life	
Masculinity–femininity	ESS: important to get respect; importance of showing abilities and being admired; importance of success; importance in life of work; importance in life of religion; giving men priority when jobs are scarce; gays and lesbians should be free to live	First factor of principal component analysis	
Power distance	Confidence in parliament (ESS); satisfaction with democracy (EVS); allowed to decide daily work organization (ESS); free to make decisions on the job (EVS); government should reduce inequality (ESS); children should learn obedience (EVS)	First factor of principal component analysis	Kaasa et al. (2014)
Uncertainty avoidance	Important to live in a safe area (ESS); important strong government ensures safety (ESS); importance of job security (EVS); people can be trusted (EVS); immigrants make a country a better place to live (ESS); important to follow traditions and customs (ESS)	First factor of principal component analysis	
Individualism–collectivism	Important to make own decisions (ESS); important children learn independence (EVS); importance of fun and pleasure (ESS); importance to have a good time (ESS); importance of leisure time (EVS)	First factor of principal component analysis	
Masculinity–femininity	Importance of showing abilities and being admired (ESS); importance of success (ESS); importance of a responsible job (EVS); importance of being rich and having expensive things (ESS); giving men priority when jobs are scarce (ESS); importance of religion (EVS)	First factor of principal component analysis	

Another common theme is that culture itself appears impossible to measure directly. Measures developed are often based on the outcomes of the culture being present. In the case of some studies these are the values expressed by those interviewed (Welzel, 2013; Hirschle and Kleiner, 2014). In others they are activities associated with a particular underlying culture, as with Huggins and Thompson's (2016) measures (discussed in detail in Chapter 2). As discussed in Chapter 9, this is reflective of the data limitations and costs of acquiring data directly. Observation might provide a more direct and accurate measure of culture itself but would not be practical for achieving a database of regional measures in a timely and cost-effective manner. Measures based on values are better able to provide coverage but may still suffer from small regional samples and, as discussed in Chapter 3 and further expanded on in Section 6.4 below, assume that values are only formed on the basis of culture, which is unlikely to be true. Those measures based on outcomes and activities further extend the problem of proxying rather than directly measuring culture, but allow more spatially disaggregated data collection, replication, and updating. As culture is presumed to be a group-held construct, even regional-level data may hide important differences, and local or even neighbourhood-based measures would be more appropriate. Chapter 9 returns to these compromises in more detail.

Measures of institutions As discussed above, there is considerable overlap between institutions and culture in the literature (Huggins and Thompson, 2015a). This reflects the fact that institutions can vary from formal regulatory institutions and laws through to informal norms and values (Scott, 2007). At the regional level, it is the latter, more informal institutions where greater differences are likely to exist within countries. With the exception of nations with significant regional autonomy, such as the Germany and Spain (Börzel, 1999; Keating, 2003; Hooghe et al., 2010), more formal institutions are likely to show less variation. This means that differences based on national institutions are identified, but there are also effects from relative distance to other regions where similar behaviours are adopted (Arbia et al., 2010). Equally, national formal institutions may show some spatial spillovers across borders (Hall and Ahmad, 2012). Some have argued that, although laws and regulations may not vary within a country, their interpretation and implementation can (Scott, 2007; Miörner et al., 2018). On the whole, however, this means that for the analysis in later chapters institutions will not be formally measured and modelled, but the impact of these institutions will be evident in the relationships found between other constructs.

Frequently it is difficult to obtain objective measures of institutions, and instead it is more common for measures to take the form of survey responses that reflect the perceptions of stakeholders or experts with regard to the functioning of institutions. At the national level, there are a wide range of academic, private, and non-profit organizations producing such subjective measures both on a commercial and non-commercial basis. Examples of studies seeking stakeholder opinions for at least some their items include the World Economic Forum's Executive Opinion Survey (Schwab, 2018) and the World Bank's Worldwide Governance Indicators (WGI) (Kaufmann et al., 2009). Those measures based on expert opinions include indices such as the International Country Risk Guide (ICRG) (PRS Group, 2013) and the Freedom in the World Index (Freedom House, 2019). Some measures are available at the national level based on more objective approaches, such as the Political Constraint Index (Henisz and Zelner, 2017) and Checks (Beck et al., 2001). Each of these originates by attempting to count the number of vetoes present and then making further adjustments.

Reflective of work such as that of Miörner et al. (2018), at a regional level Charron et al. (2014) develop the Quality of Governance (QoG) measure for the EU regions. This contains four pillars: control of corruption; rule of law; government effectiveness; and voice and accountability. The indicators utilized are drawn from many of the national-level sources such as the World Governance Indicators (WGI), but combine them with a citizen's survey to obtain regional-level variation. The citizen's survey covers education, healthcare, and law enforcement. The respondents were asked to rate these based on their own experience and perceptions in terms of quality, impartiality, and corruption (Charron et al., 2011). This allows the QoG measures to reflect differences in the provision and quality of services within countries, even where policy is consistent. Huggins and Thompson (2016) use the QoG measures and further adjust them to a more local level for an analysis of the UK, with the results summarized in Chapter 5. Others, however, have adopted a different approach by looking for historical measures that reflect the quality of institutions. Examples of this are Tabellini's (2010) measures for educational institutions reflected in historical literacy rates and historical measures of constraints on the executive (Acemoglu et al., 2005).

As with community culture, the literature seeking to measure institutions suffers from a lack of agreement about what they actually consist of, in addition to having a similar problem in terms of measuring them directly. Although some objective measures exist (Beck et al., 2001; Henisz and Zeiner, 2017), for regional-level analysis this may miss the point that rules, regulations, and checks may not be applied in a uniform fashion (Miörner et al., 2018). This means that more subjective measures are required based on stakeholder views (Charron et al., 2011). The danger with this is that measures begin to blur the different pillars to integrate cultural elements (Scott, 2007), and clearly for the behavioural model of regional development set out in Chapter 2 this is undesirable.

6.4   Relationships between Personality Psychology, Culture, and Institutions

When examining the culture and personality traits present within a locality or region, studies have frequently noted that the two are likely to be closely linked (Rentfrow et al., 2008). Rentfrow et al. (2009), in their study of voting patterns, suggest a bidirectional relationship between culture and the presence of particular personality traits. However, many studies still treat culture and personality traits as separate and either examine one or the other or assume in empirical analysis that they are independent. Rentfrow et al. (2008) show that the relationship is more complex, with traits influencing individual behaviours and—indirectly—the geographical representations of these traits and the behaviour they determine. However, these influences can also work in the opposite direction. While personality drives behaviour, the social norms created when particular forms of behaviour are common can influence the formation of personality traits. Likewise, these behavioural tendencies can be formalized as institutions that will constrain or promote other particular forms of behaviour. Finally, the social norms formed by the behaviour of some individuals can directly feed back and promote or discourage the behaviour of other individuals. Rentfrow et al. (2008) summarize five paths linking the prevalence of particular personality traits to behaviours and geographical representations where causality flows from one to the other two, making the impact of personality on regional development extremely strong. Due to the multiple linkages between personality traits, behaviours and geographical representations it is extremely difficult if not impossible to completely separate out individual flows between them or to fully understand how personality influences regional development.

Our view is that the overall combination of personality traits that are most common in a place and the community culture within this place are interdependent and will evolve together. We also understand that it is the final psychocultural behaviour profiles, rather than an individual trait or culture, which is likely to be important given the work on interactions between traits and contextual factors. In order to understand this co-evolution, it is necessary to examine the mechanisms that have been suggested by previous studies linking the development of one to the other. Although there are multiple

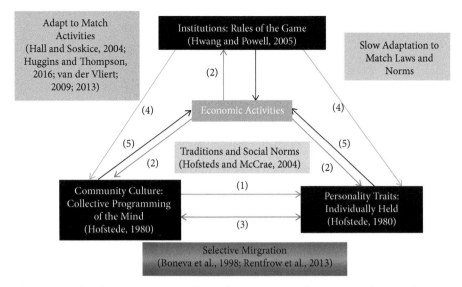

Figure 6.1 Links between personality and community culture at the urban and regional level.

routes, Figure 6.1 summarizes the main forces at work. The remainder of this section will first examine those links from culture to personality and then those running in the opposite direction.

It should be recognized that personality traits are usually found to be stable or slowly evolving at the individual level (Roberts et al., 2006; Cobb-Clark and Schurer, 2012). In this study we consider how average personality trait values may develop in a place over generations or through migration flows rather than being due to specific personal experiences or events (Boyce et al., 2015; Miller, 2016). As highlighted in Chapter 2, Rentfrow et al. (2015) highlight three routes that may result in differences in personality developing within countries or even regions. These three mechanisms act through traditions and social norms; physical environment; and selective migration.

In the first of these, traditions and customs that may be associated with the community cultures present generate particular social norms that act on individuals' attitudes and behaviours (Hofstede, 2001; Hofstede and McCrae, 2004). This is represented in Figure 6.1 by arrow (1) running from community culture to personality traits. For example, earlier studies on the psychological characteristics of individuals suggest that these characteristics are an outcome of child-rearing practices, but such practices are often influenced by the prevailing social norms (Adorno et al., 1950; Inkeles et al., 1958; Lewin, 1936). More broadly, it is suggested that personality can be influenced up to adolescence (Borghuis et al., 2017), although there is evidence that major life events after this can lead to changes (Bleidorn et al., 2018). This means that both informal and formal institutions may have an influence to a much later stage of development than childhood; for example, McCrae (1996) indicates that attendance at college has a positive effect on openness. Exposure to a more diverse population is also found to be positively associated with greater acceptance and openness (Pettigrew and Tropp, 2006). For instance, it might be expected that community cultures that display higher levels of femininity and caring activities generate a social norm of looking after and out for others in society. This may alter behaviours and expectations in such a manner that individuals within a locality become more agreeable. Studying attitudes towards alcohol consumption, Bourgeois and Bowen (2001) find students' own habits and perceptions of others are closely correlated with the drinking habits of those around them. Equally, where a strong importance is placed on adherence to social rules this may discourage rule-breaking, which can have implications associated with entrepreneurial activities later in life (Obschonka et al., 2013b).

Fritsch et al. (2019) note that role models play an important part in propagating the development of particular personality traits and they concentrate on the development of the entrepreneurial personality. They show that historic self-employment rates, particularly those in science-based industries, are positively associated with contemporary entrepreneurial personality levels. Furthermore, they also show that if the historical self-employment in science-based industries measure is replaced with one based on self-employment in agriculture, and those who are homeworkers, no such relationship is present. They attribute this to the particular and very specialized type of employment in agriculture and the over-reliance on a single large employer for homeworkers.

The second mechanism—physical climate—is more directly linked to the economic conditions that shape people's values and beliefs. As such, this mechanism could work on both personality traits (van der Vliert, 2009; 2013), but also on the community culture that is present (Huggins and Thompson, 2016). This is represented by the arrows (marked 2 in Figure 6.1) running from economic activities to community culture and personality, and a third arrow linking economic activities to institutions, as it is suggested by the varieties of capitalism literature that institutions adapt to the needs of the activities present (Hall and Soskice, 2001). From an occupational socialization perspective, the personality of workers is influenced by work conditions and experiences. This may mean, for example, that where employment involves more autonomy and complex tasks this may generate the types of personality associated with entrepreneurial activities (Kohn and Schooler, 1982; Roberts et al., 2003; Frese et al., 2007). Stuetzer et al. (2016) examine how entrepreneurial activity and an entrepreneurial culture develop depending on the types of industry that dominate the local economy. Using an instrumental variables approach, they indicate that entrepreneurial culture, as captured by personality traits (Obschonka et al. 2013b), is negatively associated with employment in large-scale industries, using distance from coalfields to instrument their presence. This might be explained by a limited demonstration and legitimation effect being present due to a lack of role models when large-scale employment dominates (Fornahl, 2003; Minniti, 2005; Wyrwich, 2015). This could also have an ongoing effect where the work experiences of adults generate a culture that dictates how they bring up their children (Luster et al., 1989; Crouter et al., 1999).

As discussed in Chapter 4, modernization and prosperity are generally expected to have an influence on cultural development. There are theories suggesting that there are universal patterns experienced, so that cultures become more tolerant, open, and less obedient to authority, with a greater emphasis placed on self-expression (Inglehart and Baker, 2000). It has also been suggested that this may lead to a convergence of values across modernized societies (Parsons, 1977). However, Eisenstadt (2004) introduces the theory of 'multiple modernities' whereby these global influences are adjusted according to the local traditions present, so that there is a degree of path dependency and persistence in cultures (Inglehart and Baker, 2000). In this case, there is an adjustment assumption about the development of culture (Hirschle and Kleiner, 2014). Urbanity is also a possible influence on cultural development, with research stemming from the work of Fischer (1975) suggesting that urban regions have the critical mass to allow subcultures to flourish. In the longer term, these can then influence and become absorbed into the mainstream (McCracken, 1990). Unlike modernization, Fischer's (1975) approach does not restrict the direction in which culture develops, leading to content freeness (Hirschle and Kleiner, 2014).

The third mechanism, selective migration, may also be linked to community culture. This is marked by arrow (3) in Figure 6.1. Jokelea (2009, 2013) finds that creative individuals are more likely to migrate along with those who are less friendly and agreeable than average (Boneva et al., 1998). In the US, Rentfrow et al. (2013) suggest that those with greater openness may seek out novelty, implying that states classed as relaxed and creative in their cluster analysis are the last to be settled by self-selecting individuals who were more adventurous. However, selective migration may not be directly associated with community culture, and an alternative view might have some similarities with Tiebout's (1956) hypothesis concerning public-sector economics. This work considered that individuals select locations based on a menu of taxation and public-service provision, but it is possible that individuals of different personalities seek out community cultures that provide a good psychocultural fit with their personality traits. Hirschle and Kleiner (2014) make a similar suggestion, indicating that certain types of regional culture will attract certain types of individual. This is consistent with studies that have examined the locational choices of particular groups of the population, such as the creative class who seek out more tolerant societies (Florida et al., 2008). Florida (2002) suggests that the correlation between bohemians and human capital and high-tech firms reflects a process whereby the culture created by bohemians attracts other skilled individuals, which makes a location attractive for firms requiring such skilled workforces. Consistent with this, Hirschle and Kleiner (2014) find that net in-migration is greater for those regions that display higher levels of hedonism, in other words the value placed on pleasure-seeking.

Rentfrow et al. (2013) suggest that the historical reason for the West Coast states of the US being relaxed and creative is the self-selecting original settlers, but they also suggest that the openness of these states attracts new creative individuals perpetuating the psychological profile of the states. Indeed, it would be understandable if individuals who have more agreeable natures and place a high importance on family links sought out communities with cultures that encourage the development of the type of social capital associated with close bonding ties rather than looser bridging ties. Rentfrow et al. (2013) further suggest that friendly and conventional states could retain their profile, as those with less compatible personalities move out. From data covering 119 NUTS2 regions in 14 European Union countries, Hirschle and Kleiner (2014) find that a region's social harmony, associated with less indifference towards others, has a negative impact on net migration to a region, and they suggest this is reflective of tight social bonds actually being off-putting as people fear feeling socially trapped and prefer 'quasi-anonymity' (Florida, 2003: 5).

Equally, those with higher levels of conscientiousness may be drawn to communities offering cultures that look for societal contributions through engagement with work and education, as well as more caring activities. This is consistent with the findings of studies that find a link between conscientiousness and conservative political views (Gosling et al., 2003; Roberts et al., 2007; Rentfrow et al., 2009). Individuals with such traits and views would be expected to be less likely to seek community cultures that promote and rely on a more collective approach. As noted above, studies such as

Obschonka et al. (2013a) find that rule-breaking in the earlier stages of life may have positive outcomes in terms of entrepreneurial activities in the future, but such individuals might feel pushed out of localities where a community culture of greater adherence to social rules is prominent.

The discussion above notes the manner in which community culture may influence the personalities of those residing in certain placed-based communities, but it is just as plausible that personality at an individual level will affect the development of community culture. Although a community culture may attract or deter the inward migration of certain personalities, once within a locality such personality traits may cause community cultures to evolve. This may be a slow process, but where, for instance, a less socially cohesive community culture may attract individuals of a more extravert nature, this could lead to a greater willingness to try out new ideas and create more bridging links rather than the bonding links in the networks already developed. However, an openness to individuals may not extend to an openness to new ideas, but the absorption of newcomers with such views could generate a community culture where adherence to pre-existing rules is weakened and experimentation encouraged.

As Hirschle and Kleiner (2014) note, the negative effect of social harmony on net inward migration discussed above may actually reflect a relationship in the opposite direction. They suggest that continual churn may not only attract those who are indifferent to others, who will continue to socially interact in this manner, but also make residents permanently adopt similar behaviours in terms of the limited development of relationships with an ever-changing population, especially neighbours or co-workers. Evidence of this kind of development is the difference across US states in terms of the tightness and looseness of how rules are enforced (Harrington and Gelfand, 2014). The potential for a reinforcing pattern to development is captured by studies such as those of Florida (2002), who, as already indicated, suggests that the presence of bohemians attracts other high-skilled individuals, presumably through the community culture that develops in part from the presence of those pursuing a bohemian lifestyle. At the other end of the spectrum, where agreeableness is higher it is suggested that outward migration is reduced and helps to generate social capital (Boneva et al., 1998; Jokela et al., 2008; Jokela, 2009). This tends to lead to a more socially cohesive society, potentially to such an extent that outsiders are excluded (Rodríguez-Pose and Storper, 2006). Figure 6.1 acknowledges this in terms of the double-headed nature of arrow (3).

To complete the analysis of the relationships between local personality and community culture, it is important to recognize the role played by formal institutions. It has been recognized by studies that collective community culture at an informal level is both an influence on endogenously formed formal institutions (Easterley et al., 2006) and can compensate where formal institutions are weaker (Farole et al., 2011; Gorodnichenko and Roland, 2017). Arrows marked (4) in Figure 6.1 reflect this and any similar influence on personality traits.

As discussed in Chapter 3, Huggins et al. (2018) investigate these relationships using the community culture dimensions drawn from Huggins and Thompson (2016) and the Big Five personality traits captured through the British Broadcasting Corporation's Lab UK website, as part of the BBC's and the University of Cambridge's Big Personality Test project (Rentfrow et al., 2015). Principal component analysis was used to identify the commonalities in the data as measured at the local authority district level in the UK. This was undertaken to investigate whether particular cultural dimensions and personality traits are found to develop in a complementary fashion, as theorized above. The direction of causality was not investigated but was presumed to be bidirectional, with selective migration and social norms playing a role. It was found that three psychocultural profiles emerged: *inclusive amenability*—high levels of agreeableness, conscientiousness, social cohesion, femininity and caring activities, and adherence to social rules, but low in openness; *individual commitment*—high in social cohesion, engagement with education and employment, conscientiousness, adherence to social rules, and low in collectiveness and openness; and *diverse extraversion*—high in extraversion and openness, but low in neuroticism and social cohesion. These psychocultural profiles, as discussed in Chapter 3 (Figure 3.1), have distinct spatial patterns within Great Britain and are found to be associated not just with economic development in general but with distinct patterns of growth during booms and recessions, which might be seen as relating not just to competitiveness but also the resilience of local economies (Martin, 2012; Martin and Sunley, 2017).

We now seek to understand the implications for the behavioural model of regional development from these specific combinations of personality and community culture in the form of different psychocultural profiles. In order to do this, we return to the point made in Section 6.3 that 'values' as such may not be appropriate measures of community culture, because, as demonstrated here and in Chapter 3, community culture and personality trait distributions are not independent. As such, we consider the values created as an outcome of the co-evolution of personality traits and community culture and seek to understand the distribution of such factors across Europe (Section 6.5), before attempting to capture the relationships with the types of psychocultural profiles already identified (Section 6.6).

6.5 The Distribution of Psychocultural Values across Europe

It is argued by Huggins and Thompson (2019) that the personality psychology and community culture present within a region, city, or locality will influence the values and norms created. As discussed above, the measures used by Welzel (2013) are sometimes described as reflecting the underlying culture but can also be recognized as the values stemming from the psychocultural profile of a place. Here we use data from the European Values Survey (EVS) to create measures of Emancipation and Secularization based on Welzel's (2013) approach, although in some places items have been substituted for those used in the original World Values Survey (WVS) data. The EVS data is used, as it can be utilized in combination with the European Social Survey (ESS) data, to create the measures of agency discussed in Chapter 7. The data is drawn from the fourth wave (2008/10) of the EVS. This is to produce measures that can be used to examine the impact that these values have on other factors a number of years later.

The emancipation index is designed to reflect a liberation orientation with an egalitarian qualification (Welzel, 2013). It includes four sub-indices: Autonomy, Choice, Equality, and Voice. When forming each of these, data is standardized to have the same range of values, but then simple averages are produced of the items in each sub-index. The first of these examines the emphasis placed on the need for autonomy and is captured by three items: qualities children can be encouraged to learn at home and considered to be important—imagination (0 not selected to 1 selected); qualities children can be encouraged to learn at home and considered to be important—independence (0 not selected to 1 selected); and reverse of qualities children can be encouraged to learn at home and considered to be important—obedience (0 not selected to 1 selected).

The second sub-index concerning choice originally reflects the valuing of freedom in reproductive choices. Unfortunately, the item relating to homosexuality was not available for Italy in the 2008 data. Rather than lose the Italian regions from the sample, we replace this item with a measure reflecting choices about life, but in terms of end-of-life choices. The three items used are: whether abortion can be justified or never justified (1 never to 10 always); whether suicide can be justified or never justified (1 never to 10 always); and whether divorce can be justified or never justified (1 never to 10 always).

The equality sub-index is designed to capture the emphasis on gender equality. We retain this focus but have to alter items that relate to education being more important for boys than girls, and men being perceived to be better political leaders. Replacing the education-based measure, we instead include an item reflecting expectations that men and women will both contribute to household income, and an item about equal responsibility for childcare. Unfortunately, neither captures perceptions of women in leadership roles, but the overall index does capture the extent to which women and men are expected to have equal standing and responsibilities in the main spheres of everyday life. It could be argued that these items do not necessarily reflect the full range of relationships in the modern world, and it would be preferable to have items that capture the diversity of the modern family, and also diversity and equality issues for other groups (Dwertmann et al., 2016). Nevertheless, the areas covered are: the reversed scale of when jobs are scarce men have more right to a job than women (1 disagree to 3 agree); men should take as much responsibility as women for the home and children (1 disagree to 3 agree); and both the husband and wife should contribute to household income (1 disagree to 3 agree).

The final sub-index, voice, considers the importance placed on being able to influence government decisions. It draws upon the same items used by Inglehart (1977) to generate his post-materialism index: protecting freedom of speech given first or second priority as an aim for the country (0 not selected to 1 selected); giving people more say in important government decisions as an aim for the country (0 not selected to 1 selected); important in a job that you have a say in significant decisions (0 not selected to 1 selected).

The four sub-indices are averaged to produce the overall emancipation index. The second index is the secularization index, which reflects the distance from four sources of power: religious authority (agnosticism); patrimonial authority (defiance); state authority (scepticism); and authority of conformity norms (relativism). As with the emancipation index, the secularization index produces a sub-index for each of the measures of distance from power and combines these into an overall index. The agnosticism index is based on three items outlined below. The second of these could be questioned as to whether it reflects values or actions, as it relates to church attendance. Given the lack of good alternatives, we retain the item as attendance which is likely to be a strong signal of accepting religious authority: 'Independent of whether you go to church or not, would you describe yourself as a religious person?' (1 a religious person to 3 a convinced atheist); 'Apart from weddings, funerals, and christenings, about how often do you attend religious services these days?' (1 more than once week to 7 never, practically never); and 'Children can learn the following qualities at home. Which if any do you consider to be especially important?'—religious faith (1 selected to 2 not selected).

The second sub-index of distance from patrimonial authority is captured by items relating to pride and respect for authority (defiance). The original item relating to parents originally reflected an emphasis on making parents proud, but this was missing from the 2008 EVS data. The item used to replace it is in some regards a better measure, as it reflects the distinction between always having to respect individuals such as parents or whether this should be earned: 'How proud are you to be a citizen of…[country]?' (1 very proud to 4 not proud at all); 'Which of the two statements do you tend to agree with? (a) Regardless of what the qualities and faults of one's parents are, one must always love and respect them; (b) One does not have the duty to respect and love parents who have not earned it by their behaviour and attitudes.' (1 tend to agree with statement (a) to 2 tend to agree with statement (b); 'Please tell me if the following were to happen whether you think it would be a good thing, a bad thing or don't you mind?'—greater respect for authority (1 good to 2 bad).

The sub-index of state authority considers confidence in state institutions (scepticism). Welzel (2013) argues that trust in institutions tends to be higher in authoritarian states, reflecting a true belief in authority. Given that this value reflects trust in formal institutions rather than the generalizable trust of others, there is a need to take care in interpreting this sub-index. How much confidence in armed forces? (1 a great deal to 4 none at all); how much confidence in the justice system? (1 a great deal to 4 none at all); and how much confidence in the police? (1 a great deal to 4 none at all).

The final sub-index of conformity norms concerns whether or not free-riding activities are seen as acceptable (relativism). Welzel (2013) argues that, since most people do not wish to admit to these deviant behaviours, the answer becomes dichotomous and if a respondent indicates even a slight willingness to condone such activities it is considered to reflect values associated with breaking norms. The behaviours considered are: 'Can the following always be justified, never justified, or something in between? Someone accepting a bribe in the course of their duties.' (1 never to 10 always); 'Can the following always be justified, never justified, or something in between? Cheating on tax if you have the chance.' (1 never to 10 always); and 'Can the following always be justified, never justified, or something in between? Avoiding a fare on public transport.' (1 never to 10 always).

Figure 6.2 presents the distribution of emancipation values across the European NUTS1 regions. Some care needs to be taken with German city regions, where there are smaller samples available. However, it does not appear that these regions are outliers compared to the other urbanized regions of northern and central Europe. It is clear that regions in Scandinavian countries display by far the highest levels of emancipation

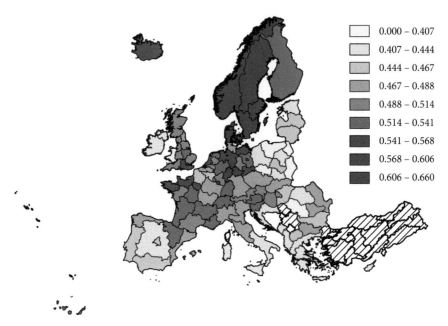

Figure 6.2 Distribution of emancipation values across European NUTS1 regions.

values on average. This is consistent with studies highlighting the progressive and equality-led desires of these countries. German and northern French regions also exhibit higher levels of emancipation. Interestingly, there is no obvious east–west divide between German regions. This runs contrary to studies such as Alesina and Fuchs-Schündeln (2007) and van Hoorn and Maseland (2010) that have found long-lasting differences between those regions previously located in communist-controlled East German regions and the West German regions. It should, however, be noted that other studies have found much less difference between the culture of former East and West Germany, relative to those differences between Germany as a whole and other countries (Rauch et al., 2000). Values and culture associated with particular behaviours, such as the employment of mothers, can lead to greater similarities between East and West German regions than with countries such as Belgium, even where institutional differences persist (Hummelsheim and Hirschle, 2010). In general, Polish, Romanian, and Bulgarian regions appear to display relatively low levels of emancipation values, which is also true of many Mediterranean regions.

Figure 6.3 presents the four sub-indices of emancipation. It is clear that, although there are general similarities between the sub-indices, there are also differences. Regions in the Scandinavian countries score highly for all four sub-indices, but in the case of both autonomy and voice there tends to

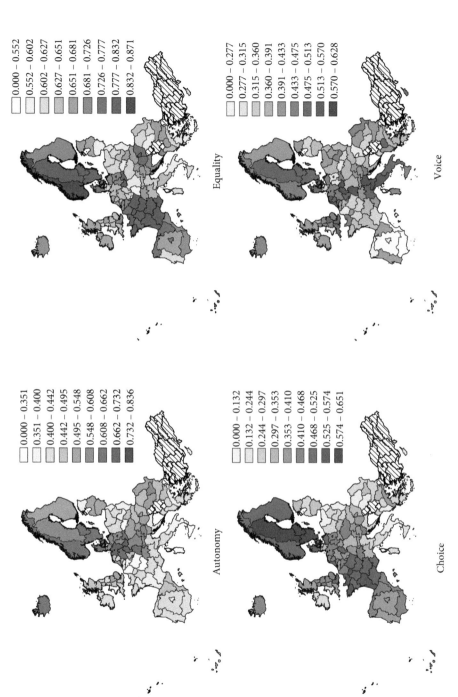

Figure 6.3 Distribution of emancipation sub-indices across European NUTS1 regions.

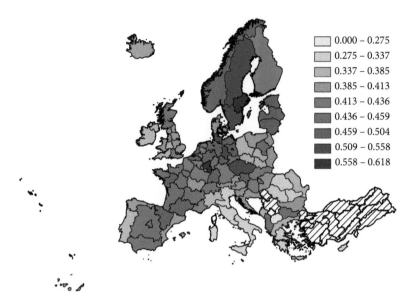

	0.000 – 0.275
	0.275 – 0.337
	0.337 – 0.385
	0.385 – 0.413
	0.413 – 0.436
	0.436 – 0.459
	0.459 – 0.504
	0.509 – 0.558
	0.558 – 0.618

Figure 6.4 Distribution of secular values across European NUTS1 regions.

be higher levels of these values in many German regions. For choice and equality, French regions tend to display higher levels. Equality stands out as the value where there are most obviously differences between East and West German regions, and values relating to equality appear to be relatively low across the regions of eastern Europe. With regard to secularization (see Figure 6.4), there is a pattern in which many north-western regions display higher levels than the south and east. However, an interesting exception is Great Britain and Ireland, where relatively low levels of secularization are present. Unlike the situation with emancipation, Spain also displays higher levels of secularization. As is the case with emancipation, the North East region of Spain reflects the fact that differences in values need not necessarily coincide with national boundaries, with the region having more in common with the southern French regions of Aquitaine-Limousin-Poitou-Charentes and Languedoc-Roussillon-Midi-Pyrénées.

As Figure 6.5 shows, the overall patterns relating to secularization hide to a great extent the different patterns evident in the sub-indices. These differences are much more striking than for the sub-indices of emancipation. Italy and much of eastern Europe is still greatly influenced by the power of the Church, with lower levels of agnosticism in these regions. Although there are exceptions such as Bavaria (in Germany), the Republic of Ireland, and Northern Ireland, agnosticism is generally quite high in north-west Europe. This compares to scepticism, where many of the regions displaying higher levels of this value are in the east of Europe. Welzel (2013) suggests that

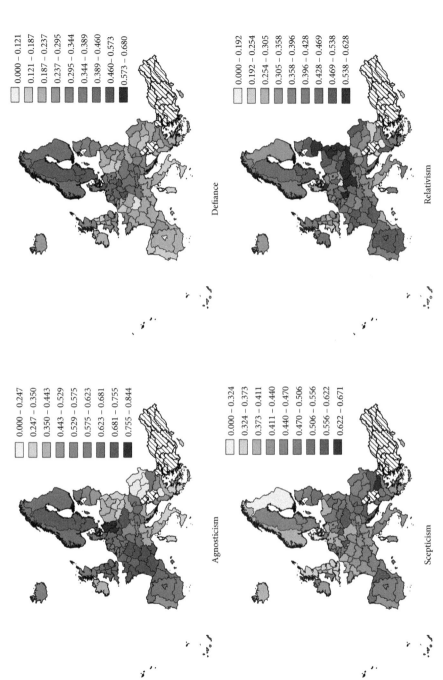

Figure 6.5 Distribution of secular sub-indices across European NUTS1 regions.

authoritarian states tend to see lower levels of this measure, but where such institutions have collapsed and power vacuums have been created, it appears that these values have actually advanced (Hibbing and Patterson, 1994; Závecz, 2017).

Higher levels of defiance are restricted to Scandinavian and more northern German regions. These regions, on average, have a greater presence of those people who do not necessarily seek recognition from important others, which may encourage greater human agency through values not based on pleasing others. Relativism helps explain why regions in countries such as Spain, which would be expected to have lower levels of secularism, actually display relatively high levels. With the exception of the East region of Spain, there appears to be much greater acceptance of breaking certain norms, and interestingly there are high levels of these values running through regions in the south of Germany, the Czech Republic, Slovakia, and into Poland. The lower levels of secularism in Great Britain and Ireland are driven by lower levels of defiance, scepticism and relativism.

6.6   Psychocultural Profiles and Values

Community culture and personality traits have been shown to co-evolve to produce particular combinations, which Chapter 3 and Section 6.4 described as psychocultural profiles (Huggins et al., 2018). According to the model presented in Chapter 2, and based on the work of Huggins and Thompson (2019), these combinations of personality traits and community culture are expected to lead to particular values being formed, such as those measured by Welzel (2013), which, as Section 6.5 showed, vary considerably across regions. These values can, then, be expected to influence the actions taken that determine the agency of individuals. What remains to be established is the extent to which the psychocultural profile of a region is linked to the underlying values present in that region. One difficulty in establishing whether or not this is the case is that different constructs are measured and held at different levels and, when held at the group level, often measured at different spatial levels. For example, as discussed in Section 6.3, personality is held at the individual level. However, studies such as Rentfrow et al. (2009), Rentfrow et al. (2013), Obschonka et al. (2015), Stuetzer et al. (2016), and Obschonka et al. (2018) have shown that 'regional personality' is often strongly associated with many behaviours, ranging from voting patterns and entrepreneurship, and outcomes such as economic development and well-being. Community culture is a group-level measure (van Maanen and

Schein, 1979), but it could be argued that the behaviour following it concerns the values formed by individuals. As individual datasets do not capture all of these simultaneously, it is not necessarily possible to identify all these influences at all relevant levels.

In order to tackle these issues, we conduct multilevel regressions of the values held at the individual level, using EVS data for the UK. These are regressed on the psychocultural profiles described in Section 6.4 measured at the local authority level. Unfortunately, the EVS does not contain Big Five personality measures at the individual level to examine whether a combination of group-level (psychocultural profile) and individual-level (personality traits) factors influence the values. Rentfrow et al.'s (2012) and Huggins et al.'s (2018) work on the holistic measurement of personality psychology and community culture suggests that it is better to consider the relationship using the psychocultural profile, but it is also possible that individual values will have stronger relationships with component community culture dimensions and personality traits. With these limitations in mind, we consider if a link can be found utilizing the following multilevel model:

$$Value_{ij} = \beta_0 + \beta_1 IncAmen_j + \beta_2 IndCom_j + \beta_3 DivExtra_j + \beta_3 Gender_{ij} \quad (6.1)$$
$$+ \beta_4 Age_{ij} + \beta_5 Age_{ij}^2 + \beta_6 Income_{ij} + u_{0j}$$

The regressions consider whether the values held by individual i in locality j ($Value_{ij}$) are associated with the prevailing community culture and personality trait distributions as captured by the psychocultural profile based on the inclusive amenability ($IncAmen_j$), individual commitment ($IndCom_j$), and diverse extraversion ($DivExtra_j$) present at the local level. The values considered here are those that can be easily extracted from the EVS dataset. These include the secular and emancipative values discussed in Section 6.5, along with the post-materialist measure (Inglehart and Abramson, 1999; Welzel, 2013). We examine both the overall indices and the sub-indices.

As Section 6.3 discussed, there are a large number of value measures used in empirical studies, and their operationalization is often determined by the availability of data captured in large datasets. This means that, although significant relationships between local psychocultural profiles and the values held by individuals in these localities would be consistent with the model presented in Chapter 2, it is not necessarily expected that all relationships will be significant. Data limitations in terms of the proxies used in the formation of psychocultural profiles and value measures may play a role. In addition, missing values or facets of personality and culture may mean key relationships are not actually tested, and these are themes returned to in Chapter 9 (Klotz and Neubaum, 2016).

As already indicated, there is a need to control for other individual characteristics that may influence values. As such, we control for gender ($Gender_{ij}$), as distinct differences have been found by studies between men and women (Beutel and Marini, 1995). Age (Age_{ij}) is included, given its significance in other studies, but whether this reflects changes over individual lifetimes or cohort differences, as argued by Welzel (2013), is unclear. We allow for a possible non-linear relationship by including centred terms and the quadratic (Age^2_{ij}). As action resources are found to be important influences on some values (Welzel, 2013), we include income ($Income_{ij}$). A relatively high number of non-responses with regard to income levels mean we run regressions both with and without this control.

Table 6.3 presents the regression estimations when considering the overall indices of emancipative values, secular values, and post-materialism. It is clear from the results that, when analysing values at the individual level across a single country, personal characteristics and resources have a strong influence. In particular, the secular and emancipative values fall for older respondents, although the negative quadratic term could also mean the

Table 6.3 Multilevel regression of aggregate values on psychocultural profiles

	Emancipative values		Secular values		Post-materialist values	
Inclusive amenability	−0.0110	−0.0020	0.0130	0.0120	−0.0890	−0.0780
	(0.067)	(0.739)	(0.031)	(0.087)	(0.000)	(0.009)
Individual commitment	0.0180	0.0050	−0.0090	−0.0080	0.0690	0.0540
	(0.000)	(0.405)	(0.072)	(0.183)	(0.001)	(0.038)
Diverse extraversion	0.0060	0.0090	0.0070	0.0130	−0.0020	0.0050
	(0.392)	(0.199)	(0.318)	(0.105)	(0.947)	(0.883)
Male	−0.0010	−0.0030	0.0370	0.0440	0.0810	0.0950
	(0.912)	(0.764)	(0.000)	(0.000)	(0.043)	(0.044)
Age	−0.1910	−0.1790	−0.2800	−0.2560	−0.1650	−0.1180
	(0.000)	(0.000)	(0.000)	(0.000)	(0.130)	(0.375)
Age^2	−0.8330	−0.8000	−0.3360	−0.3940	−1.8060	−1.7510
	(0.000)	(0.000)	(0.013)	(0.022)	(0.001)	(0.015)
Low income		−0.0290		0.0050		0.0250
		(0.016)		(0.721)		(0.661)
High income		0.2700		−0.0110		0.0160
		(0.000)		(0.432)		(0.790)
Constant	0.5250	0.5330	0.3850	0.3880	2.1040	2.0830
	(0.000)	(0.000)	(0.000)	(0.000)	(0.000)	(0.000)
N	923	675	923	675	923	675

Note: p-values in parentheses.

youngest respondents also display lower levels. In part, this may reflect the overall resources they have access to, and this is an explanation that may be particularly pertinent to emancipative values where income has a strong influence.

Reducing the sample size and controlling for income reduces the strength of some of the relationships, but in this case it is found that there are some significant relationships between inclusive amenability and individual commitment for all three overall value measures. Interestingly, living in places with higher inclusive amenability tends to be associated with lower emancipative values and post-materialism. At first it might be expected that social cohesion, preferences for collective activities, and agreeableness might be associated with objectives concerning broader well-being. However, if such a psychocultural profile develops, it may form part of a coping mechanism for addressing poor environmental conditions (Huggins et al., 2018). Likewise, stronger secularization might be expected where authority of different kinds has not necessarily been considered as supportive of the population. Individual commitment shows evidence of the opposing pattern to that found for inclusive amenability. In this case, social cohesion is supplemented with higher adherence to rules and strong engagement with education and employment. Such a climate may, therefore, be expected to generate values associated with the well-being derived from work rather than just the income obtained (Dow and Juster, 1985; Juster, 1985). The psychocultural profile dimension relating to diverse extraversion approaches a significant result with relation to secular values in the restricted sample where income is controlled for, but no significant relationship is found for the overall values indices. This potentially highlights that places with greater diverse extraversion may be subject to higher levels of migration, with those entering these places holding very particular values as a result of a range of different psychocultural backgrounds, bringing a mix of values into the host location.

Turning to the sub-indices for emancipative values (Table 6.4), there is again found to be no evidence that diverse extraversion is associated with these emancipative values, and for inclusive amenability the voice sub-index is lower. It is apparent that, unlike individual commitment, where there is evidence that such a psychocultural profile encourages individuals to desire a need to be heard and influence decisions, the more collective inclusive amenability psychocultural profile does not promote such values. This is consistent with a reliance on greater proxy agency, as discussed in Chapter 4 (Bandura, 2001). Before controlling for income, there is evidence that individual commitment is positively associated with the choice sub-index. Again,

Table 6.4 Multilevel regression of sub-indices of emancipative values on psychocultural profiles

	Autonomy		Choice		Equality	Voice	
Inclusive amenability	−0.0030 (0.803)	0.0160 (0.253)	−0.0010 (0.920)	0.0130 (0.279)	−0.0030 (0.708)	−0.0380 (0.001)	−0.0300 (0.013)
Individual commitment	0.0140 (0.162)	−0.0020 (0.878)	0.0240 (0.003)	0.0080 (0.424)	0.0080 (0.253)	0.0240 (0.008)	0.0130 (0.238)
Diverse extraversion	0.0050 (0.721)	0.0130 (0.445)	0.0190 (0.114)	0.0210 (0.107)	−0.0020 (0.824)	0.0010 (0.934)	0.0030 (0.830)
Male	−0.0210 (0.269)	−0.0290 (0.208)	−0.0400 (0.013)	−0.0400 (0.036)	0.0070 (0.590)	0.0500 (0.003)	0.0530 (0.008)
Age	−0.2410 (0.000)	−0.2400 (0.000)	−0.2490 (0.000)	−0.1980 (0.000)	−0.2020 (0.000)	−0.0760 (0.092)	−0.0570 (0.300)
Age^2	−1.4420 (0.000)	−1.4180 (0.000)	−0.9860 (0.000)	−0.7920 (0.005)	−0.2430 (0.173)	−0.6680 (0.005)	−0.6590 (0.027)
Low income		−0.0310 (0.269)		−0.0670 (0.002)			−0.0050 (0.835)
High income		0.0610 (0.036)		0.0190 (0.409)			0.0400 (0.110)
Constant	0.5220 (0.000)	0.5270 (0.000)	0.4760 (0.000)	0.4980 (0.000)	0.6450 (0.000)	0.4570 (0.000)	0.4440 (0.000)
N	923	675	923	675	923	923	675

Note: p-values in parentheses.

this is understandable in cases where people are exposed to a greater orientation towards taking responsibility.

The final set of regressions considers the relationship between the sub-indices for secular values and the psychocultural profiles (see Table 6.5). The psychocultural profiles are found to be significantly related to particular sub-indices of the secular values. It is understandable that the individual commitment psychocultural profile is positively associated with valuing self-expression rather than power distance. The one sub-index where there is a significant relationship found is for scepticism. Given the higher adherence to rules, respect and confidence in authority is understandable, but it is questionable whether such a measure truly reflects values in terms of trusting others. It could instead be regarded as a subjective measure of institutional quality. Given the result here, it might be expected that a negative relationship with relativism would also be found, but although the coefficients are negative, they are not significant.

Inclusive amenability is positively associated with agnosticism and scepticism, and it appears that such psychocultural profiles are linked to a strong

Table 6.5 Multilevel regression of sub-indices of secular values on psychocultural profiles

	Agnosticism		Defiance		Scepticism		Relativism	
Inclusive amenability	0.0170	0.0070	−0.0010	0.0060	0.0210	0.0190	0.0140	0.0150
	(0.089)	(0.525)	(0.912)	(0.586)	(0.009)	(0.035)	(0.318)	(0.378)
Individual commitment	−0.0040	−0.0040	−0.0090	−0.0070	−0.0140	−0.0100	−0.0090	−0.0120
	(0.617)	(0.689)	(0.199)	(0.437)	(0.020)	(0.212)	(0.453)	(0.424)
Diverse extraversion	−0.0040	−0.0030	0.0210	0.0270	0.0100	0.0260	−0.0010	0.0030
	(0.716)	(0.818)	(0.036)	(0.025)	(0.267)	(0.009)	(0.953)	(0.875)
Male	0.0580	0.0680	−0.0100	−0.0110	−0.0010	0.0280	0.1040	0.0910
	(0.000)	(0.000)	(0.475)	(0.518)	(0.934)	(0.046)	(0.000)	(0.001)
Age	−0.3390	−0.3450	−0.1720	−0.1460	−0.1140	−0.1760	−0.4910	−0.3540
	(0.000)	(0.000)	(0.000)	(0.002)	(0.001)	(0.000)	(0.000)	(0.000)
Age^2	−0.3410	−0.5030	−1.0710	−0.9630	−0.1540	−0.3370	0.2060	0.2140
	(0.111)	(0.067)	(0.000)	(0.000)	(0.368)	(0.114)	(0.511)	(0.596)
Low income		0.0440		−0.0250		0.0600		−0.0570
		(0.046)		(0.212)		(0.000)		(0.075)
High income		−0.0260		0.0060		−0.0220		0.0000
		(0.259)		(0.775)		(0.222)		(1.000)
Constant	0.6400	0.6350	0.2760	0.2900	0.3670	0.3370	0.2580	0.2910
	(0.000)	(0.000)	(0.000)	(0.000)	(0.000)	(0.000)	(0.000)	(0.000)
N	923	675	923	675	923	675	923	675

Note: p-values in parentheses.

community spirit, with less trust placed on broader institutions, be they religious or government-based. Diverse extraversion is not found to be associated with any of the overall values indices, and Table 6.5 provides an explanation for this in the case of secular values. Positive and significant results are found for the defiance and scepticism sub-indices, but the coefficients—while not significant—are negative for some of the estimates where agnosticism and relativism are the dependent variable. As noted above and examined in more detail below, the diverse open nature of places with higher diverse extraversion might mean that the influence of social norms on perpetuating this psychocultural profile may be less strong (Hofstede and McCrae, 2004; Rentfrow et al., 2008). Instead, the mechanism of selective migration may play a stronger role in cases where open and creative environments attract those who seek to innovate outside the control of regulatory authorities. Finally, the empirical analysis presented here has generally supported the model presented in Chapter 2, and there is evidence that psychocultural profiles are associated with individually held values, which can then be expected to drive different actions and lead to different kinds of agency.

6.7   Psychocultural Profiles and Migration

The preceding three sections of this chapter have outlined not only that there are differences in the distribution of personality traits and community culture across cities and regions but also that these traits and cultures are likely to co-evolve within these places to form differing psychocultural profiles (Huggins et al., 2018). It was also shown that these twin foundations of personality traits and community culture are associated with the development of different values. This section examines one of the sources of such a co-evolution in the form of selective migration (Rentfrow et al., 2008). To achieve this, we examine migration patterns across places of England and Wales with different psychocultural profiles. This data is drawn from the Office for National Statistics 'Internal Migration' datasets (Office for National Statistics, 2019). Migration patterns between local authorities are identified using the NHS Central Register (NHSCR) and General Practitioners (GP) patient registers. This information identifies not only when an individual enters a new area but also where they were previously registered, via their prior medical registration.

The data allows an examination of the extent to which particular psychocultural profiles attract inward migration, or experience larger outward migration patterns, and in combination can classify psychocultural profiles as promoting open populations with a higher turnover, or more stable populations. It is expected that places with higher levels of inclusive amenability and individual commitment will fall into the former, as social cohesion is higher within their psychocultural profile. However, it is also possible to examine whether or not those entering or leaving a locality with a high or low level of a particular psychocultural dimension are more likely to come from similar places or different ones. From Rentfrow et al.'s (2013) work, it is suggested that more open and extravert individuals would be expected to seek out similar areas and are more likely to migrate (Jokela, 2009). Although more agreeable individuals are perceived to be less likely to migrate (Jokela, 2009), it is interesting to examine whether or not they choose to leave places displaying a lower level of these personality traits to find places with a better fit. In both cases it is possible that this will provide a higher level of welfare (Jokela et al., 2015), as well as perpetuating the psychocultural profile of the host location (Rentfrow et al., 2008).

The psychocultural profiles developed by Huggins et al. (2018) are measured at the local authority district level for England and Wales, and to examine the relationship that these psychocultural profiles have with migration patterns we consider whether or not localities display above- or below-average levels of each psychocultural profile and their associated migration rate (persons per 1000 population). As local-level migration rates can display a degree of noise within the data, we take the average for the period 2012 to 2018. For the overall migration rates, we include all migrants entering or leaving the English and Welsh local authority areas from other areas of the UK (including Scotland and Northern Ireland as a whole). For the analysis of origins and destinations we only consider individuals moving between local authority districts of England and Wales, as we need to ascertain the psychocultural profile of both the origin and destination local authority areas, and for Northern Ireland and Scotland these are not disaggregated in this fashion.

When considering the origin and destination of migrants, we split the local authority areas into three equal groups for each psychocultural profile to reflect a low, medium, or high presence of each of the three profile types. This means that we can create a 3 × 3 matrix for all combinations of origin and destination for each psychocultural profile. Figure 6.6 shows the inward-migration rates for the localities split by whether or not they display above- or below-average presence of the three psychocultural profiles. It is clear from the data that a weak or strong presence of any psychocultural profile does not deter new entrants to the localities, as all types display inward-migration rates of more than 45 people per 1000 residents on average a year.

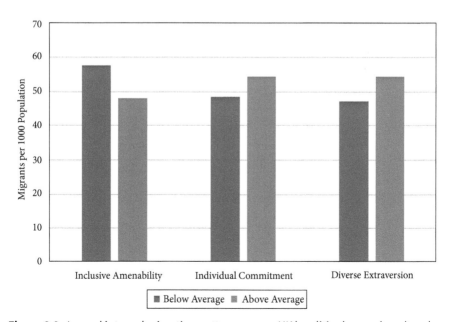

Figure 6.6 Inward internal migration patterns across UK localities by psychocultural profile.

Florida's (2003) and Hirschle and Kleiner's (2014) finding that socially harmonious places reduce inward migration, as outsiders may feel excluded, appears to be in evidence in our case with places having high levels of inclusive amenability being associated with lower in-migration. On average, 47.7 people per 1000 population enter localities with above-average inclusive amenability, while 57.5 people per 1000 population enter localities where inclusive amenability is below average. This difference is significant at the 1 per cent level (t statistic 5.960, d.f. [242], p-value = 0.000). Given the attraction of metropolitan areas such as London which display higher diverse extraversion (Lomax et al., 2014; Gordon, 2015), it is not a surprise that the opposite pattern is found, again in a statistically significant fashion (t statistic 6.732, d.f. [344], p-value = 0.000). Localities with high levels of individual commitment also display relatively high levels of inward migration, and such places are likely to support individual effort and achievement, and may attract entrepreneurial individuals (Casson, 1995).

The fact that localities with high inclusive amenability have lower inward migration, and those with higher diverse extraversion have higher inward migration, resonates with theories relating to the attraction of creative individuals such as Florida's (2002) creative class thesis. However, it is also of interest to note the source of internal migrants, and Figure 6.7 presents the localities split by displaying above- or below-average levels of each psychocultural profile and the outward migration rates. In localities with high

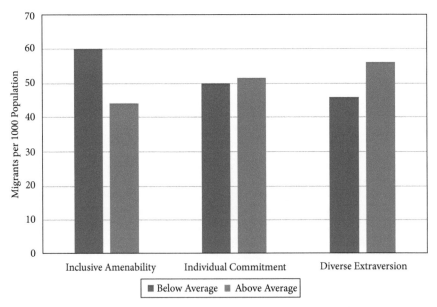

Figure 6.7 Outward internal migration patterns across UK localities by psychocultural profile.

levels of inclusive amenability, with their higher social cohesion and greater prevalence of agreeability, outward migration is lower. Those localities with higher levels of diverse extraversion have higher outward migration, and in general the higher presence of those displaying extraversion and openness is clearly associated with a greater propensity to migrate (Jokela, 2009). However, the fact that they are people who are migrating out of localities that would appear to be a good fit with the more commonly held personality traits is interesting. Jokela (2015) identifies that those individuals with a greater openness to new ideas display higher well-being in places that are generally open, and one potential explanation is that those with different personality traits—less open and more agreeable—may have lower levels of well-being. The analysis below helps to provide an insight into this by examining where these outward migrants from localities with higher diverse extraversion relocate. Although appearing to attract more inward migrants to those localities, individual commitment does not appear to have any effect on outward migration; on average 49.8 people per 1000 leave localities with below-average independent commitment compared to 51.5 people per 1000 in those with above-average levels, which is not a significant difference (t statistic 0.787, d.f. [176], p-value = 0.432).

Given that the patterns found for inward and outward migration tend to work in the same direction for the three psychocultural profiles, the overall effect on net migration (Figure 6.8) and gross migration (Figure 6.9) are relatively easy to predict. In terms of net migration, it is understandable that

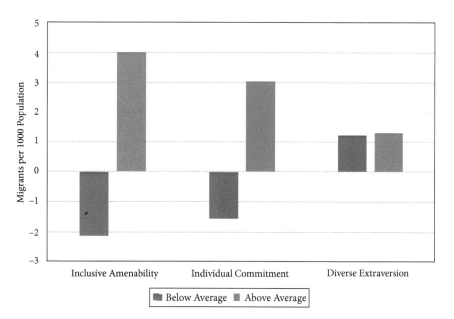

Figure 6.8 Net internal migration patterns across UK localities by psychocultural profile.

limited differences are found between those localities that are above and below the average level of each psychocultural profile. Where a psychocultural profile increases the number of individuals entering the locality, it also tends to increase the number leaving. However, it should be noted that the data we focus on is only for England and Wales, where it is disaggregated into local authority districts, but the data also includes those entering or leaving Northern Ireland and Scotland, so the totals do not have to sum to zero.

For both inclusive amenability (4.0 people per 1000 population) and individual commitment profiles (3.1 people per 1000 population), there is a positive net migration into localities with above-average levels, while it is negative for those places with below-average levels (inclusive amenability: −2.2 people per 1000 population; individual commitment: −1.6 people per 1000). Although these differences are small, they are significant (inclusive amenability t statistic 10.647, d.f. [239], p-value = 0.000; individual commitment t statistic 7.600, d.f. [272], p-value = 0.000). Therefore, these places with different perspectives on collective and individual actions both tend to attract more individuals than they lose, whereas places with potentially lower social capital tend to lose individuals overall. For diverse extraversion there is a small positive net inward migration of just over 1 person per 1000 population, regardless of whether the locality has above- or below-average levels of the psychocultural profile. The difference is not significant (t statistic 0.114, d.f. [346], p-value = 0.910).

The final stage of the migration analysis is to consider the differences or similarities in the types of psychocultural profiles of the localities that individuals firstly move from and then subsequently relocate to. We consider each of the psychocultural profiles in turn and examine the patterns of migration in terms of both origin and destination, starting with inclusive amenability (see Table 6.6). One expected pattern is that many more mobile open and extravert individuals will seek to move from places with high inclusive amenability to those areas that are more supportive of individual

Table 6.6 Origins and destinations of migrants across UK localities by inclusive amenability psychocultural profile

		Destination		
		Low	Medium	High
Origin	Low	63.3%	21.9%	14.8%
	Medium	50.1%	28.7%	21.2%
	High	40.3%	28.8%	30.8%

creativity (Jokela, 2009). This means that a higher proportion of those starting in high-inclusive amenability localities move to low- and medium-level areas. To some extent, this is the case with only 30.8 per cent of those coming from high-inclusive amenability places relocating to another locality with similar characteristics, with the largest percentage of individuals, 40.3 per cent, moving to places that have low levels of inclusive amenability. In total, only 14.8 per cent of those moving from low-inclusive amenability localities go to high-level areas, with nearly two-thirds of those moving from low-inclusive amenability localities moving to another place with a similar psychocultural profile.

Individual commitment provides a similar pattern of migration, but a little less marked (see Table 6.7). Of those leaving high individual commitment localities a majority do not go to another high-level place. The split of the remainder is roughly even between medium- and low-level localities, implying there is less desire to escape the socio-economic environment created by such a psychocultural profile, as was found for inclusive amenability. In terms of diverse extraversion, the opposite pattern may be expected, with more mobile individuals seeking out such places, as they are found to do in the case of Rentfrow et al.'s (2013) relaxed and creative states in the US. However, as Figure 6.7 indicates, outward migration is also higher in these localities, so it is interesting to examine where these individuals relocate. As already noted, some of those individuals leaving localities displaying higher levels of diverse extraversion have traits high in, for example, an agreeable temperament and therefore seek places with a better fit to their personality. Indeed, we find that one in five of those who move from a high diverse extra-vert places relocate to an area displaying a low level (see Table 6.8). However, this is the only psychocultural profile where a majority of those moving from a locality displaying high levels of diverse extraversion move to another similar locality. As such, approximately a half of the moves are potentially

Table 6.7 Origins and destinations of migrants across UK localities by individual commitment psychocultural profile

		Destination		
		Low	Medium	High
Origin	Low	56.9%	26.7%	16.4%
	Medium	40.7%	33.8%	25.5%
	High	28.3%	31.3%	40.4%

Table 6.8 Origins and destinations of migrants across UK localities by diverse extroversion psychocultural profile

		Destination		
		Low	Medium	High
Origin	Low	32.3%	38.5%	29.2%
	Medium	28.1%	35.7%	36.2%
	High	18.3%	30.6%	51.2%

creative, open, extravert individuals seeking new sources of ideas. This is likely to prove an important source of the interregional networks discussed in Chapter 5. It provides a first recognition of how the literature on networks and culture may intersect when considering the impact on urban and regional development.

6.8 Conclusion: Psychocultural Patterns and Geographical Differences

This chapter has built on the theoretical work primarily covered in Chapters 2 and 3. In particular, it has examined the extent to which empirical evidence exists to support propositions relating to the relationships between community culture, personality traits, and values. In order to achieve this, it was necessary to consider some of the conceptual issues concerning how the key constructs should be measured (Section 6.2) and how they are currently captured (Section 6.3). It is evident there is a growing literature that has sought to measure the key constructs (Beugelsdijk and Maseland, 2011), but what is less clear is the extent to which there is a consistent application of theory to distinguish between the constructs in empirical work. This reflects two often overlapping issues: (i) there is little agreement on the conceptual differences between culture, personality, values, and institutions; and (ii) often data that allows such distinctions to be made is not available.

In the case of the first issue, studies often claim to examine one construct, but the measures utilized may be more closely associated with another. In some cases, this is clear where, for example, regional measures of personality might be labelled as a measure of culture (Stuetzer et al., 2016). However, as discussed above, in many cases there is no clear distinction, as again, for example, less formalized institutions may be blended into measures of community culture (Scott, 2007; Huggins and Thompson, 2015a). In the case of the second issue, this can reflect the methods used to develop measures of the constructs, especially when they are data-driven rather than theoretically motivated (Hofstede, 2001; Welzel, 2013). It can also reflect the need to use data collected for other purposes in order to access sufficiently large datasets.

Section 6.4 indicates that the issues identified in the preceding two sections are likely to be amplified by the bidirectional relationships that lead to the co-evolution of personality and community culture. It is argued that the psychocultural profiles created (and previously discussed in Chapter 3) can be expected to yield particular values. Sections 6.5 and 6.6 explore the measurement of one set of values drawn and adapted from Welzel (2013), and they further consider their distribution across regions of Europe along with their association with psychocultural profiles within the UK. Evidence consistent with Huggins and Thompson's (2019) model that psychocultural profiles will generate particular values in the population is found, but an important result to reflect on is that the over-aggregation of values measures may not be appropriate as the patterns of values created are more diverse and subtle.

In part, the relationship between psychocultural profiles and the values formed appears to be influenced by mechanisms that lead to the perpetuation of the psychocultural profile (Renfrow et al., 2008). It is important to consider whether social norms or selective migration plays the stronger role. Evidence from Section 6.7 finds that migration patterns may reflect the 'sorting' of individuals, but for diverse extraversion, especially, movements between similar places may explain the advantages such cities and regions have in terms of networks (Chapter 5).

Finally, the chapter has shown the distinct geographical patterns associated with the foundations of the model presented in Chapter 2 in terms of personality, community culture, and the values they lead to. It would seem reasonable to assume that such differences can play a role in explaining the distinct and continuing development paths of cities and regions, both economically and socially. However, this will only be the case if personality, community culture, and values lead to particular deliberate and intentional actions in the form of human agency, as explored in Chapters 7 and 8.

7

The Nature and Sources of Agency

7.1 Introduction

The personality traits discussed in Chapter 6 are those considered to be passed on from parents and formed during adolescence and early adulthood (Roberts et al., 2008). Some studies refer to a number of other concepts as elements of personality, such as self-efficacy (Kerr et al., 2018), and this chapter sets out to argue that constructs such as self-efficacy and innovativeness are closely associated with agency. This refers to the ability of individuals to make changes to their environment. As discussed below, this is not just related to an individual's own abilities and skills but is also constrained by their power relations (Cumbers and McKinnon, 2011).

The different theoretical definitions of human agency cause some issues in terms of how to best capture it. For example, some refer to actions taken deliberately and purposively to change or reproduce previous actions (Bandura, 2001). However, Bandura (2006) also refers to such actions as the exercising of human agency, implying that the potential to undertake such actions is a form of agency itself, which may or may not be used. This means that agency could be captured both in terms of the potential capability to intentionally take actions to cause change or prevent change, or the actual actions themselves. Therefore, it may be best to think of the former as human agency potential (HAP) and the latter as manifestations of human agency, or human agency actualization (HAA), and this chapter will consider measures of both. Firstly, however, Section 7.2 looks back to Chapter 6 and seeks to establish the links from community culture and personality via values and norms to human agency. Section 7.3 expands on notions relating to HAP and HAA, and Section 7.4 empirically develops measures of HAP. The link between HAP/HAA and values is considered in Section 7.5, with links between the HAP and HAA in the form of a variety of change behaviours being examined in Section 7.6. Section 7.7 summarizes the chapter and looks ahead to Chapter 8, where the links between human agency and economic development are explored.

A Behavioural Theory of Economic Development: The Uneven Evolution of Cities and Regions. Robert Huggins and Piers Thompson, Oxford University Press (2021). © Robert Huggins and Piers Thompson.
DOI: 10.1093/oso/9780198832348.003.0007

7.2 Sources of Human Agency

Before examining the forms that human agency can take and how they can be measured, it is worth looking at the sources of this agency. As discussed in Chapters 2 and 3, human agency is originally influenced by culture and personality. It is these elements in combination, described as the psychocultural profile, that generate the values and behavioural intentions of individuals within a city or region. These behavioural intentions and values influence actualized behaviour that determines the extent to which individuals perceive and place themselves in a position to affect change (Chapter 4). As noted above, this might be referred to as human agency potential (HAP), which distinguishes it from manifestations of human agency or human agency actualization (HAA) whereby intentional deliberate actions are taken.

Clearly, measures used in behavioural studies may capture more than one of these constructs, or there may be dispute over the construct being captured. This is understandable as the data utilized to form the measures are often used for purposes beyond those its creators originally intended. The European Social Survey (ESS) provides one such example. Schwartz (2012) outlines how values relating to universalism, benevolence, conformity, tradition, security, power, achievement, hedonism, stimulation, and self-direction can be generated. Some studies have taken these and Schwartz's earlier measures of values (Schwartz, 1992) as measures of culture itself (Knox and Wolohan, 2014). However, it is also possible to examine constructs such as achievement motivation that are likely to promote or work with agency by providing a desire to take control of outcomes (Thomas, 1980). Taking the example of achievement, the items used to create this measure take the form of the importance of 'showing abilities and receiving admiration' and 'being successful and receiving recognition for achievements'. These reflect the outcomes of culture and personality in terms of reflecting the behaviours that individuals see as important and intend to pursue. They do not reflect any measure of the extent to which individuals feel positioned to be able to achieve these or make a change, as is the case with agency (Bandura, 1997, 2006). However, it would be understandable if such values create behavioural intentions that lead to behaviours that increase or decrease the likelihood of success (Welzel and Inglehart, 2010).

It would also be expected that economic and social conditions that can affect the evolution and persistence of both regional culture and personality play a role in determining agency through the institutional filter that is present (Boettke and Fink, 2011; Stiglitz, 2013; Piketty, 2014; Huggins and Thompson, 2019). In a broader sense this has been explored in work on the context-cognition nexus that seeks to examine how 'setting' shapes the behaviours, decision-making, and ultimately the human agency present in a place (Clark, 2018).

7.3 Measuring Human Agency

There is clearly more than one way of considering agency theoretically and, therefore, capturing it empirically. In some studies agency has been regarded as constituting all actions, an approach that has been criticized with intention seen as being a vital element in of the notion of such agency (Fuchs, 2001; Bandura, 2006; Castree, 2007). Others have suggested that agency is about the capability for willed voluntary action (Scott and Marshall, 1998; Biesta and Tedder, 2006). In the case of the latter, it is the potential to undertake intentional actions that will either perpetuate current behaviours or cause change, rather than the actual actions themselves. It has connections to Kant's (1992 [1784]) view of enlightenment as a reflection of the release from being unable to make use of understanding without direction from others. The potential to undertake voluntary action has similarities to those studies in psychology that have sought to understand the influences behind behaviour. For example, the social learning theory includes a measure of behaviour potential (Rotter, 1954, 1960). Behaviour potential (BP) is the likelihood of engaging in a particular behaviour (x) in a specific situation, for example m (s_m) (Rotter, 1954). It is assumed to be determined by the following formula:

$$BP_{x,s_m,Ra} = f\left(E_{n,s_m,R_a}, RV_{a,s_m}\right) \tag{7.1}$$

It is assumed from Equation 7.1 that the behaviour potential for x is a function of expectancy E, which is the subjective probability that a behaviour will lead to a particular outcome n. These outcomes are also referred to as reinforcement (R), as past experiences make particular behaviours more or less attractive. The expectancy is specific to the situation m which is present (s_m) where there are many different situations. Overall, it considers the ability to achieve the behaviour and the likelihood that the behaviour will yield a reinforcement a that is desired.

The other element influencing behaviour potential is the attractiveness or desirability of the outcome, with a reinforcement value a that it is hoped will be achieved (RV). Like expectancy, the reinforcement value is subjective and a number of different outcomes could be under consideration, each with a different value in different situations. Rotter (1960) argues that the behaviour potential is not necessarily best captured by simple independent or multiplicative functions of expectancy and reinforcement value.

In the theory of social learning it is suggested that behaviour with the highest potential in situation m will be chosen. It is clear to see that agency, when considered as the capability for willed voluntary action, has similarities to behaviour potential as self-efficacy will link closely to expectancy (Scott and Marshall, 1998; Biesta and Tedder, 2006). Given that actions are voluntary, expectancy has the goal of seeking outcomes that are desirable based on subjective values that will in part be driven by cultural and personality factors. However, where the two concepts diverge is that agency does not concern the ability to undertake a particular behaviour but utilizing a set of actions, often in combination, to achieve a particular aim over a period of time. It is also true that, unless a lack of action is regarded as one of the behaviours under consideration, this implies that all action to some extent is agency (Castree, 2007). This means that we are both focused on a narrower set of behaviours and actions in terms of those seeking to make a change and at the same time taking a wider perspective by not seeking to identify the capacity to undertake one specific action.

In this chapter we consider both wider definitions of human agency and the implications for measuring the capacity or capability to undertake actions, which building from the concept of behaviour potential, we describe as human agency potential (HAP), and the actions themselves, which we describe as manifestations of human agency, or human agency actualization (HAA). In terms of HAP, the capacity/potential to undertake agentic actions might be associated with regional competitiveness and resilience, as it broadens development paths that can be followed in a timely fashion (Huggins and Thompson, 2017a; Martin and Sunley, 2017). However, future situations may limit the extent to which broader HAP is converted into HAA, and to underpin the empirical work that follows we now outline the issues that need to be considered in generating measures of each of HAP and HAA.

In order to act as agents, individuals must possess the skills and capabilities to make changes. Whether or not individuals are completely aware of their true skills and capabilities is uncertain, but they will hold beliefs about these skills and capabilities. Self-efficacy is the perception of individuals in terms of their capability to pursue particular goals (Bandura, 1997). Clearly, this can relate to the confidence of the individual, but in terms of overconfidence it is also possible that particular individuals within the population may engage with particular risky or uncertain activities where their skills may not be appropriate (Åstebro et al., 2014). Also, the extent to which self-efficacy is converted into human agency can be influenced by the power relations that are present, and it may be possible for an agent to have confidence in the skills and capabilities to make an intentional change, but for others to have the power to prevent them (Coe and Jordhus-Lier, 2011; Coe, 2013). Given this, measures of HAP would ideally incorporate three elements: intention; self-efficacy; and power.

In the case of the first element, intention, it is hard to establish whether this is present or not. Values that identify the importance of particular outcomes or achievements have been noted as playing a role in determining behaviours that result in different levels and types of human agency (Welzel and Inglehart, 2010). However, such values do not necessarily capture the concrete intention to pursue a particular outcome. Studies relating to behavioural intentions in general (Armitage and Conner, 2001), and entrepreneurial activities in particular (Kwong and Thompson, 2016), have noted how the likelihood that intentions will become actual behaviour varies considerably depending on the degree of commitment required. As most data sources do not ask questions about the likelihood of undertaking particular actions (or why), and even when they are included they are very specific, it is hard to form such measures.

In terms of manifestations of human agency, there are again problems in capturing this as fully as would be desirable, particularly with regard to the notion of 'intention' (Bandura, 2001). It is possible to easily identify actions that could be seen as forms of human agency in different spheres of human life, but whether these actions are taken with an intention to alter or perpetuate particular institutions and behaviours is much harder to determine. For example, an entrepreneur may start a new business that introduces a disruptive innovation that alters how people interact, such as various forms of social media. This could either be intentional, if the individual sought to make a change, or the individual could feel forced into a form of necessity-driven entrepreneurship with no intention of influencing human behaviour or even starting a business (Pasteur, 1854; Austin, 1978; Bandura, 2001).

This means that we can examine change actions and behaviours that represent manifestations of human agency, but it is difficult to establish if they truly reflect HAA. However, by concentrating on behaviours that it is reasonable to assume would not be engaged in without some understanding and intention of the outcomes (or reinforcements) sought, HAA's relationship to HAP allows a better understanding of human agency as a whole. This means that the following sections will investigate the extent to which we can produce measures of HAP and examine if there is evidence that these become HAA.

7.4 Measuring Human Agency Potential (HAP) across Europe

In terms of HAP, it is important to capture the extent to which individuals perceive themselves to be in a position to influence outcomes (Bandura, 2000b; Welzel, 2013). The European Social Survey wave 8 from 2016 (ESS, 2019) provides a number of items that could be considered to capture the extent to which individuals consider they are able to influence different spheres of their lives. In particular: there are items that relate to influencing decisions taken by politicians either directly or indirectly, which we describe as political agency potential (Chang, 2013; Beer and Clower, 2014; Piketty, 2014); control over working patterns and influence on the work environment, described as labour/entrepreneurial agency potential (Coe and Jordhus-Lier, 2011), but also entrepreneurial agency in the wider sense (as it covers the potential for those working for others to explore entrepreneurial opportunities). We also consider the importance of sustainable-development issues relating to the extent to which individuals consider they can control changes to the environment, that is environmental agency potential (Brulle, 2000).

To establish items that are suitable for capturing each of these dimensions, an exploratory principal components analysis is undertaken. The items considered are those that are perceived to relate to each of the forms of HAP, but also items that can be considered to be manifestations of agentic behaviour. These are included in the initial principal components analysis to establish the extent to which HAP can be separated from the human agentic behaviours that it might be expected to yield, that is HAA. This is a list of items expanding on those used in studies such as Dalton et al. (2010), Welzel (2010), and Welzel (2013) and associated with peaceful civic protest or social movement activities (SMA).

As discussed in more detail below, and analysed in Chapter 8, there are expected to be differences in the levels of each form of agency across groups of individuals in each region. For example, with age and experience all forms of agency may increase; similarly, employment in certain occupations may increase specific types of agency. However, at the aggregate regional or local level many of these differences would be expected to be averaged out, unless, as predicted in Chapter 2, cultural or personality differences lead to persistently higher levels of particular types of agency. When testing for these it will also be important to control for economic and demographic differences, as this would be an alternative explanation.

The items considered are outlined below for each of the different forms of agency and behaviours.

Political Agency Potential
- How much would you say that the political system allows people like you to have an influence on politics?
- How much would you say the political system allows people like you to have a say in what the government does?
- How able do you think you are to take an active role in a group involved with political issues?
- How confident are you in your own ability to participate in politics?

Labour/Entrepreneurial Agency Potential
- How much does/did the management at your work allow you to decide how your own daily work is/was organized?
- How much does/did the management at your work allow you to influence policy decisions about the activities of the organization?

Environmental Agency Potential
- Overall, how confident are you that you could use less energy than you do now?
- To what extent do you feel a personal responsibility to try to reduce climate change?
- Imagine that large numbers of people limited their energy use. How likely do you think it is that this would reduce climate change?
- How likely do you think it is that limiting your own energy use would help reduce climate change?

Political, Environmental, Labour, and Change Behaviour—Human Agency Actualization (HAA)
- During the last 12 months, have you worked in a political party or action group?
- During the last 12 months, have you worked in another organization or association (to improve things in the country)?
- During the last 12 months, have you boycotted certain products (to improve things in your country)?
- During the last 12 months, have you worn or displayed a campaign badge or sticker?
- During the last 12 months, have you contacted a politician, government or local government official?

- During the last 12 months, have you signed a petition?
- During the last 12 months, have you taken part in a lawful demonstration?
- During the last 12 months, have you posted or shared anything about politics online, for example on blogs, via email or on social media such as Facebook or Twitter?
- In your daily life, how often do you do things to reduce your energy use?
- If you were to buy a large electrical appliance for your home, how likely is it that you would buy one of the most energy efficient ones?
- Did you vote in the last national elections?
- In your main job, do/did you have any responsibility for supervising the work of other employees?
- Are you or have you ever been a member of a trade union or similar organization?
- During the last twelve months, have you taken any course or attended any lecture or conference to improve your knowledge or skills for work?

In order to produce more distinct measures of agency and behaviour, the principal components analysis is conducted using a varimax rotation. A number of the variables, including supervisory responsibility and voting in national elections, did not load onto easily interpretable components and were therefore removed from the analysis. The analysis using the remaining variables yielded six components, as shown in Table 7.1.

The factors are relatively easy to interpret as Political Agency Potential (component 1), Environmental Agency Potential (component 2), Labour/ Entrepreneurial Agency Potential (component 4), two largely political-change behavioural measures (components 3 and 5), and an environmental-change behaviour measure (component 6). To produce clearer combined measures of the forms of agency and behaviour, those with large cross-loadings on more than one of the other components were removed from the analysis, yielding the results presented in Table 7.2.

One of the items drawn from the ESS is also used by Kaasa et al. (2013, 2014) for their measures of Power Distance. This is 'allowed to influence work directions', which loads onto labour agency. Hofstede's (1980, 2001) original conception of power distance was more about an acceptance of the hierarchical structure at the group level, while we argue that the 'ability to influence work directions' is more a reflection of the constraints perceived to be imposed on the individual, and therefore more reflective of their agency.

To create measures of agency, principal component analysis is run for each of the sets of items reflecting each of the types of agency. The first component

Table 7.1 Initial principal components analysis of human agency potential (HAP) and behavioural changes

	1	2	3	4	5	6	Commonalities
Political system allows influence on politics	0.827						0.722
Political system allows people to have a say	0.794						0.662
Able to take active role in political group	0.653		0.247		0.329		0.610
Confident in own ability to participate in politics	0.640		0.242		0.317		0.590
Limiting own energy use will reduce climate change		0.800					0.662
People limiting energy use will reduce climate change		0.770					0.596
Feel personal responsibility to reduce climate change		0.679	0.209			0.229	0.586
Confidence could use less energy than now		0.486	0.219				0.320
Signed petition about political cause			0.688		0.200		0.527
Boycotted particular goods			0.675				0.491
Posted material online about politics			0.630				0.440
Attended a course, training, etc. in last 12 months			0.522	0.892			0.354
Able to influence policy decisions of organization				0.888			0.822
Able to decide how daily work is organized					0.769		0.820
Worked for political party					0.769		0.600
Contacted a politician in last 12 months					0.689		0.513
Worked for another organization or association			0.299		0.513		0.382
How often do things to reduce energy use						0.802	0.655
Likelihood of buying most energy-efficient appliance						0.780	0.630
Percentage of variance explained	20.789	10.048	7.886	7.675	5.793	5.605	
Kaiser-Meyer-Olkin	0.774						
Bartlett's Test of Sphericity	139627.4	[171]	(0.000)				

Note: p-values in parentheses; degrees of freedom in square brackets.

Table 7.2 Reduced principal components analysis of human agency potential (HAP) and behavioural changes

	1	2	3	4	5	Commonalities
Political system allows influence on politics	0.838					0.729
Political system allows people to have a say	0.807					0.673
Able to take active role in political group	0.643		0.273		0.312	0.597
Confident in own ability to participate in politics	0.627		0.275		0.296	0.573
Limiting own energy use will reduce climate change		0.792				0.647
People limiting energy use will reduce climate change		0.761				0.582
Feel personal responsibility to reduce climate change		0.720	0.211			0.589
Confidence could use less energy than now		0.502				0.314
Boycotted particular goods			0.731			0.554
Signed petition about political cause			0.708			0.553
Dummy for posted material online about politics			0.648			0.456
Able to influence policy decisions of organization				0.896		0.827
Able to decide how daily work is organized				0.895		0.826
Worked for political party					0.769	0.599
Contacted a politician in last 12 months					0.701	0.525
Worked for another organization or association			0.252		0.546	0.394
Percentage of variance explained	23.5	11.3	9.1	8.6	6.5	
Kaiser-Meyer-Olkin	0.774					
Bartlett's Test of Sphericity	129429.4	[120]	(0.000)			

Note: p-values in parentheses; degrees of freedom in square brackets.

is taken to represent the agency measure following a similar technique to that used by Tabellini (2010) and Huggins and Thompson (2016) to create their measures of institutions and culture respectively. The scores for the measures are generated using the Anderson Rubin approach, which allows for non-correlated factor scores to be created if multiple components are generated (Tabacknick and Fidell, 2007). In each case, a single component is isolated from the items associated with the individual measures of agency.

The regional-level agency measures are taken as the mean average of the individual levels after applying design weights accounting for sample bias and non-responses (ESS, 2019). Although this is consistent with the approaches used by those examining patterns of the geography of personality (Obschonka et al., 2013a; Rentfrow et al., 2015; Lee, 2017), it should be recognized that this is not the only approach to developing measures of regional agency. For example, rather than requiring all members of the population to have a slightly higher level of agency, it may be a subset of the population, who are key change agents, that are important (Hall, 1998; Huggins and Thompson, 2019). In this case, the proportion of the population displaying agency over a particular level could be the key measure of such agency.

Figures 7.1, 7.2, and 7.3 show the distribution of Political, Environmental, and Labour Agency, respectively, across Europe. It is interesting to note that,

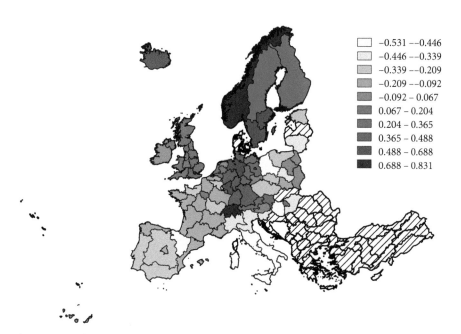

Figure 7.1 Political agency potential across European regions.
Source: Data from the European Social Survey Wave 8 (2016).

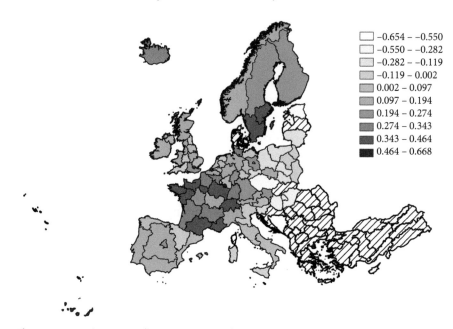

Figure 7.2   Environmental agency potential across European regions.
Source: Data from the European Social Survey Wave 8 (2016).

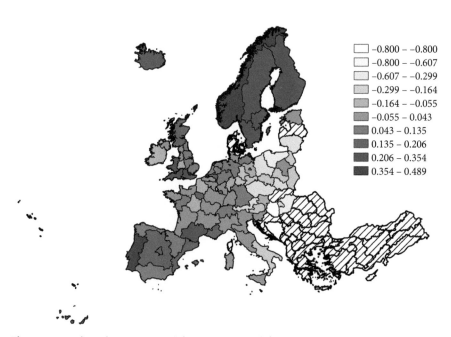

Figure 7.3   Labour/entrepreneurial agency potential across European regions.
Source: Data from the European Social Survey Wave 8 (2016).

although there are positive correlations between the agency measures at the individual level, there are also differences in the patterns found for the measures at the regional level.

In 2016 it appears that political agency is strongest in the northern countries of Europe, but this is not completely universal. The populations of Norway and Switzerland—interestingly both countries outside the European Union—perceive there to be greater political agency potential. This may reflect a perception of being closer and better able to influence those in authority, whereas the population of those countries inside a political and economic area such as the European Union may feel that their ability to influence politically and maintain a national identity is limited, given that some of the power resides further away in Brussels (Hooghe and Marks, 2005). However, there are also differences both between Northern European countries and within them. Firstly, at the national level, Scandinavian, Germanic, and Anglo-Saxon countries appear to possess more political agency potential, while Francophone and former Soviet countries display lower levels of political agency potential. In the case of the latter group of countries, this fits with formal institutions and culture having lasting effects that affect the perceived ability to make changes (Vachudova, 2005).

Moving to regional differences within nations, contrary to some studies, such as Reichert (2016) who examined voting patterns, there is no obvious difference between East and West Germany. More apparent, however, is the greater perceived political agency in regions that host parliaments such as London in the UK, Île-de-France in France, and Berlin in Germany. This is also apparent in countries that have much lower average levels of political agency such as Spain, where Madrid is an outlier. As well as being reflective of geographical proximity that facilitates more contact, networking, and the development of the social capital that is utilized when lobbying political agents (Coen, 2007), this is likely to be reinforced by the institutions and culture that forms (Stiglitz, 2013).

Turning to the regional distribution of environmental agency potential, at first there appears to be a division between the north-west of Europe and other areas, such as the Mediterranean regions and those in the former Soviet, East European nations. However, unlike political agency potential, which is the highest in countries such as Germany and the UK, for environmental agency potential the situation is reversed, with French regions displaying stronger perceptions of being able to make a difference through their actions. In general, there is no easily discernible pattern with regard to which regions have higher levels of environmental agency potential, and which have lower levels. For example, although capital regions are commonly more densely populated and have higher levels of environmental agency potential, some regions in densely populated countries such as the Netherlands display relatively low levels of environmental agency potential. In the UK, the more rural and peripheral region of Wales has a similar level of environmental agency potential as the more densely populated South East of England region.

When considering the distribution of labour/entrepreneurial agency potential, there are again commonalities with the other forms of HAP. As with both environmental and political agency potential, there is evidence of greater labour/entrepreneurial agency potential in Scandinavian countries and Iceland. It is also true that East European countries on the whole appear to display a lower level of labour/entrepreneurial agency potential. This might be expected where centrally organized, large-scale production approaches that were used in the past may have perpetuated particular personality traits, including higher levels of neuroticism and lower levels of conscientiousness, with these leading to reduced entrepreneurial activity (Glaeser et al., 2015; Stuetzer et al., 2016; 2018; Obschonka et al., 2017). This means that, despite the decline of centralized control and opening of markets in Eastern European nations and regions, it is no great surprise that HAP patterns will still be influenced. Given this direct socialization effect on activities relating to labour and entrepreneurship, it is understandable that the difference between regions in the former East and West Germany is more evident. This is consistent with Frese et al.'s (1996) study that effectively picks up measures of HAA, and it also fits with Fritsch et al.'s (2014) finding that, although self-employment rates in East and West Germany have equalized, there are still differences in the skills and motivation behind this entrepreneurship.

Unlike political and environmental agency potential patterns, there appears to be less evidence that labour/entrepreneurial agency potential has a north–south pattern across Europe. Portuguese and Spanish regions appear to have relatively high levels of labour/entrepreneurial agency potential, as do some regions in the south of France, while at the same time a number of UK regions including Wales, the South West of England, and the South East of England display higher levels of labour/entrepreneurial agency potential. It is interesting to note that, as with political and environmental agency potential, regions that are or contain national capitals tend to have higher levels of labour/entrepreneurial agency potential. This would be consistent with the arguments presented previously, with HAP in these regions being higher where residents consider themselves better positioned to influence policymakers and affect regulatory institutions (Kim and Law, 2016). As will be discussed in Chapter 8 in more detail, this raises the prospect that capital-city regions may benefit from factors that go beyond the centralization of resources (Mackay, 2001), the

Table 7.3 Correlation matrix for different forms of agency

	Political agency 2016	Environmental agency 2016
Environmental agency 2016	0.372 (0.000)	
Labour agency 2016	0.454 (0.000)	0.555 (0.000)

Note: p-values in parentheses.

attraction of diverse skilled employment due to clustering effects and agglomeration economies (Huggins and Izushi, 2011; Faggio et al., 2017), and cultural amenities (Florida, 2002; Mellander and Florida, 2011). In fact, the proximity to organizations associated with the evolution and maintenance of formal institutions increases HAP, and if such HAP has positive effects on changing behaviour beyond those targeted at changing institutions, such as those related to entrepreneurial and innovative endeavours, there may be additional social and economic benefits flowing from this.

Figures 7.1–7.3 show that there appears to be considerable overlap in the geographical distribution of the three forms of HAP explored here. Table 7.3 confirms this through the correlation coefficients. It is clear from the correlation coefficients that there are statistically significant links between the three forms of HAP. This suggests that culture and personality may generate the relevant conditions for HAP in general, but the institutional filter may determine the exact spheres in which they are applicable.

Changes in the questions asked by the ESS limit the extent to which political and environmental agency potential measures generated using the 2016 data can be replicated for earlier periods. In the case of environmental agency potential, the items are not included in any of the earlier waves, but for political agency potential the items are available for 2014. In terms of labour/entrepreneurial agency potential, the two items used are present through to the early stages of the Great Recession of 2008. In 2010, a third item associated with labour/entrepreneurial agency potential is also present in terms of the extent to which there is control over the pace of work. In order for the HAP measures generated above to be of value empirically, there is a requirement that the NUTS1 regional-level measures constructed from the micro-level data be relatively stable. Although culture, personality, institutions, and therefore the HAP they create are predicted to evolve over time, their evolution is expected to be relatively slow (North, 2005; Foreman-Peck and Zhou, 2013). This leads to the persistent differences found in economic activities such as entrepreneurship and innovation (explored in Chapter 8) and overall economic development (Freytag and Thurik, 2007).

Table 7.4 Correlation matrix for political and labour agency measures

	Political agency 2016	Political agency 2014	Labour agency 2016	Labour agency 2014	Labour agency 2012	Labour agency 2010
Political agency 2014	0.846 (0.000)					
Labour agency 2016	0.454 (0.000)	0.533 (0.000)				
Labour agency 2014	0.406 (0.000)	0.607 (0.000)	0.816 (0.000)			
Labour agency 2012	0.335 (0.002)	0.559 (0.000)	0.734 (0.000)	0.732 (0.000)		
Labour agency 2010	0.384 (0.001)	0.532 (0.000)	0.728 (0.000)	0.739 (0.000)	0.702 (0.000)	
Labour agency 2008	0.467 (0.000)	0.657 (0.000)	0.725 (0.000)	0.819 (0.000)	0.678 (0.000)	0.861 (0.000)

Note: p-values in parentheses.

Given that the ESS is a cross-sectional rather than panel survey, with each wave having a different sample of respondents, to be confident that the measures capture the different types of HAP at a regional level there needs to be a reasonable positive correlation over time. If the HAP measures are not correlated from one period to the next, there is a strong danger that any patterns found are reflective of the sampling process rather than underlying effects from the personality and culture of the region. Table 7.4 presents the correlation coefficients for the political and labour/entrepreneurial agency potential measures over time. It should be noted that the samples of countries in the ESS are not consistent through time. Although there are countries that are present in each wave, such as the UK and Germany, there are others such as Denmark and Italy which are not covered on a consistent basis, and therefore the correlations calculated are based on the common sub-samples of regions in each pair of years being compared.

The correlations confirm that the positive relationship between regional political and labour/entrepreneurial agency potential is applicable for more than one year. It also indicates that there is a strong relationship between the HAP measures in different time periods. For political agency potential, there is a correlation of 0.846 (p-value 0.000) between the measures in 2014 and 2016. The labour/entrepreneurial agency potential measures also display a strong correlation between the measure in different years, with the lowest correlation being 0.678 (p-value 0.000) between 2008 and 2012. Given the use of a completely different sample group in each period, and the quite different economic conditions experienced between 2008 towards the start of the Great

Recession and 2012, when the recovery was beginning to gain momentum, this is extremely promising with regard to providing an explanation for persistent differences between regions based on behavioural factors.

7.5 Sources of Human Agency Potential (HAP)

As outlined in Chapters 2 and 3 and revisited in Chapter 6, there is an expectation that community culture and personality will combine to create the values and norms of society. It is these values and norms that are expected to start to drive behavioural intentions and lead to HAA. Here, we consider the creation of the HAP that allows for agentic behaviour to take place. We consider the extent to which scholars such as Welzel and Inglehart (2010) and Huggins and Thompson (2019) are correct in their predictions that the values created by personality traits and community culture (psychocultural profile) are related to the patterns of HAP across Europe discussed in Section 7.4.

To represent values, the measures used are those discussed in Section 6.5, generated using the EVS from 2008/10. Although similar values could be generated from the ESS, there is a robustness check benefit in utilizing different data sources for each construct. We further seek to clarify the direction of influence by considering values in 2008/10 and the more recent measures of HAP considered above. It should be noted that this may weaken the associations between the measures, as values are expected to evolve over time (Inglehart, 1971) and may be influenced by exogenous events such as the Great Recession (Wink et al., 2017). However, the benefits of considering the relationship, by using two different points in time to reduce the likelihood of reverse causality, are deemed to form a worthy approach.

Initially we only consider the basic Pearson correlation coefficients, and the relationships between the main values index are considered along with the sub-indices that go into creating these. When interpreting these correlations care must be taken, as it is possible that a common factor may be influencing both the values present and the HAP. In terms of both of Inglehart's (1971) and Inglehart and Abramson's (1999) measures of post-materialism, a positive relationship is found for all three forms of HAP (see Table 7.5). This is the case regardless of whether post-materialism is measured as the percentage of the NUTS1 region's population who can be classified as post-materialists, or the average value from the scale is taken. Interestingly, the correlation is greater for political agency potential and weakest for environmental agency potential. Given that the environment is a clear example of values moving to consider choices beyond material possessions, this is an interesting result, but it must be remembered that the HAP measures reflect

Table 7.5 Correlation matrix for agency and values

	1. Political agency	2.	3.	4.	5.	6.	7.	8.	9.	10.	11.	12.	13.	14.
2. Environmental agency	0.372 (0.000)													
3. Labour/entrepreneurial agency	0.454 (0.000)	0.555 (0.000)												
4. Post-materialism index	0.487 (0.000)	0.262 (0.018)	0.363 (0.001)											
5. Post-materialism percentage	0.452 (0.000)	0.287 (0.009)	0.331 (0.002)	0.935 (0.000)										
6. Emancipation index	0.532 (0.000)	0.320 (0.003)	0.296 (0.007)	0.678 (0.000)	0.599 (0.000)									
7. Secularization index	0.416 (0.000)	0.116 (0.301)	0.094 (0.400)	0.343 (0.000)	0.283 (0.004)	0.597 (0.000)								
8. Autonomy sub-index	0.642 (0.000)	0.042 (0.706)	0.015 (0.893)	0.431 (0.000)	0.340 (0.000)	0.685 (0.000)	0.412 (0.000)							
9. Equality sub-index	-0.065 (0.564)	0.218 (0.049)	0.097 (0.388)	0.082 (0.407)	0.069 (0.485)	0.525 (0.000)	0.367 (0.000)	-0.022 (0.827)						
10. Choice sub-index	0.359 (0.001)	0.396 (0.000)	0.417 (0.000)	0.498 (0.000)	0.482 (0.000)	0.811 (0.000)	0.684 (0.000)	0.326 (0.001)	0.593 (0.000)					
11. Voice sub-index	0.338 (0.002)	0.074 (0.510)	0.209 (0.060)	0.711 (0.000)	0.637 (0.000)	0.475 (0.000)	-0.026 (0.795)	0.400 (0.000)	-0.177 (0.073)	0.081 (0.411)				
12. Agnostic sub-index	0.379 (0.000)	0.228 (0.039)	0.308 (0.005)	0.430 (0.000)	0.397 (0.000)	0.590 (0.000)	0.747 (0.000)	0.221 (0.024)	0.509 (0.000)	0.748 (0.000)	-0.047 (0.638)			
13. Defiance sub-index	0.631 (0.000)	0.037 (0.739)	0.058 (0.607)	0.465 (0.000)	0.411 (0.000)	0.624 (0.000)	0.701 (0.000)	0.724 (0.000)	0.058 (0.555)	0.445 (0.000)	0.347 (0.000)	0.367 (0.000)		
14. Scepticism sub-index	-0.258 (0.020)	-0.359 (0.001)	-0.400 (0.000)	-0.366 (0.000)	-0.399 (0.000)	-0.187 (0.057)	0.257 (0.008)	-0.063 (0.523)	0.105 (0.288)	-0.170 (0.084)	-0.281 (0.004)	-0.082 (0.405)	0.087 (0.379)	
15. Relativism sub-index	-0.020 (0.860)	0.112 (0.315)	0.006 (0.957)	0.008 (0.933)	0.032 (0.745)	0.074 (0.455)	0.461 (0.000)	0.066 (0.503)	-0.095 (0.339)	0.227 (0.021)	-0.138 (0.164)	0.083 (0.401)	0.178 (0.071)	-0.041 (0.680)

Note: p-values in parentheses.

the perception of being able to take action to cause a change, and although post-materialists may desire to take such action, and may undertake behaviour to increase their ability to do so, it is also possible that they become more informed about the difficulties in taking such effective action.

With regard to the overall emancipation index based on Welzel's (2013) measures, a similar pattern is found with all three measures of HAP being positively correlated with emancipation values. These correlations are all significant at the 1 per cent level. The strongest correlation is again between emancipation and political agency potential, with the correlation with the other two measures of HAP being smaller. It does, therefore, seem that results are consistent with the suggestion by Huggins and Thompson (2019) and Welzel and Inglehart (2010) that particular values encourage behaviours that position individuals to take intentional actions to make a change.

In some regards the sub-indices produce more interesting results, as not all are significantly related to all three measures of HAP. This gives a more detailed insight into the values that may encourage behaviours that develop the different forms of HAP. We examine each of the sub-indices in turn, and how they relate to each type of HAP. The autonomy sub-index is only significantly related to political agency potential. This is a surprise, as autonomy would be expected to be at the very least a key component of labour and entrepreneurial agency potential. However, it is consistent with the limited evidence found in Chapter 6 linking autonomy to the underlying psychocultural profile of a region.

The equality sub-index is positively associated with environmental agency potential, but not the other forms of HAP. This is understandable given that environmental issues are fundamentally related to issues of equality both across regions and groups within regions (Renger and Reese, 2017), but also between groups through time (Beckerman and Hepburn, 2007). Given the nature of labour/entrepreneurial agency potential, it may be surprising that control over decisions and work routines are not associated with equality, but this fits with the findings of Coe (2013), who highlights how changes in modern working that fragments labour have led to more uneven balances of power in labour relations. Political agency potential is easier to understand as it is not necessarily being driven by equality values (Carlsson and Johansson-Stenman, 2010).

The choice sub-index is positively related to all three measures of HAP, which is a natural outcome (Scott and Marshall, 1998), and for secularization, political agency potential has the strongest connection to the overall index. Compared with the sub-indices of emancipation, those for secularization are more interesting given that not all are positively associated with any of the HAP measures, and in some cases are negatively correlated. All three HAP measures are correlated with the agnosticism sub-index, but for environmental agency potential this is only at the 5 per cent level, while for the others it is at the 1 per cent level. This weaker relationship is understandable given the doctrine of many religious denominations of loving and respecting others. Therefore, it is consistent with the important role equality values play in encouraging behaviours that generate environmental agency potential. The weaker than expected result may reflect other findings indicating that religious participation both complements and substitutes for prosocial behaviour, leading to no overall effect (Tan, 2006).

The correlations with scepticism are perhaps the most surprising, as all three forms of HAP are significantly related to it, but negatively rather than positively. The relationship is strongest for labour/entrepreneurial agency potential and weakest for political agency potential. This is likely to reflect the nature of the values measure created. Unlike many of Welzel's (2013) and Schwartz's (1992) measures that reflect preferences for particular outcomes, the scepticism measure relates to trust in various institutions. Given the work on culture that has explored the importance of trust in aiding coordination (Rodríguez-Pose and Storper, 2006; Dasgupta, 2011), it is understandable that HAP would be negatively related to its absence. Welzel (2013) develops the measure on the expectation that unquestioning belief in these institutions is higher where there is less secularization, and therefore countries will start to question these institutions as they develop. However, the results presented here suggest that, while a lack of trust might increase a desire to make a change and exercise agency, the potential to exercise it will be limited without this trust, as individuals will feel unable to work within the system (Grix, 2000; Marien and Christensen, 2013). Therefore, agency must take more extreme forms and may be perceived by many to be outside their reach. The strength of the negative relationship with labour/entrepreneurial agency potential shows the importance of trust in the regulatory framework that allows change to take place (Hitt and Xu, 2016; Bosma et al., 2018). Finally, relativism is not significantly related to any of the forms of HAP. The coefficients estimated display a mix of signs, but given the lack of significance there is little point in trying to read too much into these results.

As noted above, although the correlation coefficients help to identify where values are associated with HAP years later, there is the possibility that both are being driven by a common factor. To try and confirm whether relationships are robust regarding this possibility, regressions are run with the three forms of HAP as the dependent variables. These are regressed on each of the values in turn, and controls are added for: the unemployment rate, the proportion of the population holding university-level qualifications, population density, employment in manufacturing, and employment in professional services. These controls reflect the economic conditions that may lead to personalities, cultures, and values that develop to cope with adversity (Steel et al., 2008; Jokela et al., 2015), employment that is more (manufacturing) or less (professional services) repetitive and affects autonomy (Stuetzer et al., 2016), and human capital acquisition that may move individuals up the hierarchy of needs (Maslow, 1943), but also drives enlightenment (Kant, 1992).

Population density is included to reflect that spatial proximity may lead to differing values and behaviours being created (Dye, 1975), but also differing interactions (Vernon, 1960; Patacchini et al., 2015). We also control for whether or not a region is from a former communist East European country in order to account for institutional changes that have occurred. This control takes two forms: in the first case we include a simple dummy for a region belonging to a former communist country; and in the second we run the regressions on a sub-sample of Western European regions to see if the relationships remain constant. With the exception of the East European dummy, all right-hand side variables are measured by natural logs, so that the coefficients are easier to compare in terms of magnitude. All these controls potentially could directly explain HAP, so their inclusion is to test the robustness of the results found from the simple correlations. With this in mind, and because the relationship is being examined at the regional level, which limits the number of observations, we consider any relationships significant at the 10 per cent level or better as worthy of discussion to avoid type-2 errors.

Table 7.6 presents the full regression results for examining the relationship between the post-materialism index and the three forms of HAP. This is used as an example of the full results, given that the large number of values measures (four indices and eight sub-indices) and forms of HAP (three measures) lead to thirty-six combinations for both the full sample and Western European samples. The regressions explain over half of the variance in regional HAP for political and labour/entrepreneurial agency potential, and nearly 40 per cent of the variance for environmental agency potential. Noting the caveats above concerning the impact of including controls in the regressions, it is notable that only political agency potential is significantly linked to post-materialism, whereas the basic correlations found a relationship for all three forms of HAP.

Economic conditions in terms of unemployment are only found to be significantly related to political agency potential. The lack of relationship with labour/entrepreneurial agency potential may reflect the measure becoming more closely associated with entrepreneurial agency rather than concentrating on traditional concerns about job security and pay specifically.

Table 7.6 Regressions of human agency potential (HAP) on post-materialism

	Political agency potential	Environmental agency potential	Labour/entrepreneurial agency potential
Post-materialism index	0.895 (0.017)	0.361 (0.266)	0.298 (0.203)
Unemployment rate	−0.283 (0.000)	0.002 (0.974)	0.052 (0.232)
University-educated	0.295 (0.009)	0.109 (0.264)	0.201 (0.005)
Population density	−0.022 (0.496)	0.028 (0.330)	−0.062 (0.004)
Manufacturing employment	−0.048 (0.549)	−0.056 (0.425)	−0.076 (0.136)
Professional services employment	0.157 (0.139)	−0.205 (0.029)	0.115 (0.088)
East Europe	0.007 (0.929)	−0.296 (0.000)	−0.348 (0.000)
Constant	−0.925 (0.099)	−0.104 (0.831)	−0.560 (0.113)
N	71	71	71
R^2	0.564	0.392	0.693
F-test	11.6 (0.000)	5.8 (0.000)	20.3 (0.000)

Note: p-values in parentheses.

As discussed above, there may also be a loss of traditional labour agency potential due to the fragmented nature of employment and production (Creed and Klisch, 2005; Coe, 2013).

Education, as emphasized by Kant (1992), would be expected to promote HAP by supplying the confidence and skills to affect change or promote the continuation of existing behaviours. Therefore, it is no surprise that the proportion of those with university degree-level qualifications in the population is positively associated with two of the three forms of HAP. Environmental agency potential is the exception, where no significant relationship is found, which is likely to be due to a lack of awareness (but which may rapidly move up personal agendas in coming years) (Eden et al., 2006). Labour/entrepreneurial agency potential, in general, might be expected to be promoted as the choice of education is selected with future careers in mind (Xie and Goyette, 2003; Eccles, 2011).

The strong links to political agency potential might be seen as surprising, given the lack of relationship with environmental agency potential, but is consistent with Hillygus (2005), who indicates that a social science curriculum may support such endeavours. In addition, in the case of political agency potential it may be that social networks interact with education to encourage engagement (McClurg, 2003). Berinsky and Lenz (2011) provide an alternative perspective by suggesting that those who are naturally more likely to be politically engaged are those who will also choose to stay in education. They suggest that when education was imposed by the Vietnam draft in the United States rather than being a free choice, no additional political engagement was observed.

Given existing research on clusters and knowledge spillovers, it is interesting that labour/entrepreneurial agency potential is not positively associated with population density (Vernon, 1960; Baker et al., 2005; Delgado et al., 2010). In fact, the opposite relationship is found. This relationship will need more investigation in the future, but one possible explanation is that suggested by Obschonka et al.'s (2018) work on the impact of large scale industry on the development of an entrepreneurial personality. As many of the large urban areas in Europe have developed around large scale industry that promoted repetitive activity, this may lead to particular migration patterns perpetuating the culture, personality traits, values generated, and outcomes achieved.

Levels of employment in professional services have opposing effects on environmental and labour/entrepreneurial agency potential. In the case of the former, more employment in these sectors reduces the expectation that individuals will be able to influence the environment (Elfenbein et al., 2010; Tvinnereim et al., 2017). Lastly, the differences between regions that have a longer history of free-market and democratic institutions present are apparent, but not necessarily for the measures of HAP that may be expected (Cerami and Stubbs, 2011).

Considering other values, Table 7.7 presents the coefficients for the values variables from the regressions of HAP. Political agency potential is significantly related to both the overall emancipation and secularization indices, although more strongly with the former. Of the emancipation sub-indices, autonomy appears to drive this where imagination and creativity is captured. As noted above, the desire to have the freedom to make changes would be expected to lead to behaviour creating the agency to do this. With regard to secularization, two sub-indices are significant at the 10 per cent level or better, that is defiance and scepticism. As with the basic correlations, defiance is positively associated with political agency potential, but scepticism has a negative relationship. This means, after controlling for other factors, there is still evidence that the willingness to challenge authority, and having less pride in a country, result in people positioning themselves to make a change as to how it is governed.

Environmental agency potential remains significantly related to emancipation, but none of the other overall values scales. The link to emancipation

Table 7.7 Regressions of human agency potential (HAP) on values (full European sample)

	Political agency potential	Environmental agency potential	Labour/entrepreneurial agency potential
Post-materialism index	0.895 (0.017)	0.361 (0.266)	0.298 (0.203)
Post-materialism percentage	0.105 (0.114)	0.070 (0.213)	0.039 (0.341)
Emancipation index	0.755 (0.004)	0.609 (0.007)	0.143 (0.389)
Secularization index	0.526 (0.028)	0.229 (0.266)	−0.104 (0.483)
Autonomy sub-index	0.860 (0.000)	0.252 (0.055)	0.028 (0.767)
Equality sub-index	−0.118 (0.650)	0.339 (0.119)	−0.093 (0.557)
Choice sub-index	0.026 (0.851)	0.233 (0.045)	0.049 (0.566)
Voice sub-index	0.157 (0.344)	0.057 (0.686)	0.155 (0.127)
Agnostic sub-index	0.217 (0.159)	−0.065 (0.620)	−0.022 (0.813)
Defiance sub-index	0.406 (0.000)	0.080 (0.286)	−0.031 (0.571)
Scepticism sub-index	−0.418 (0.070)	−0.205 (0.299)	−0.201 (0.158)
Relativism sub-index	−0.134 (0.211)	0.120 (0.186)	−0.023 (0.732)

Note: p-values in parentheses.

appears to come from the autonomy and choice sub-indices, which both remain significantly related to environmental agency potential at the 10 per cent level or better. For labour/entrepreneurial agency potential no significant results remain. This is likely to reflect the close association between this measure of HAP and the controls, which also will reflect the actions taken to increase labour/entrepreneurial agency potential. For example, investments in human capital are generally taken with career opportunities in mind, and migration to cities can also reflect entrepreneurial desires and ambitions (Casson, 1995).

We also undertake another regression model, not shown here, that indicates the results when concentrating on the Western European regions and excluding those that may have been affected by long-term institutional differences due to the communist era (Vachudova, 2005). The significant coefficients on particular values remain relatively similar, with a very small number of exceptions. For environmental agency potential, the secularization index becomes significant, as does the relativism sub-index, suggesting that breaking norms may be considered a valid approach to addressing sustainable-development issues (Almers and Wickenberg, 2008).

Labour/entrepreneurial agency potential for the Western European regions sees scepticism become significant at the 10 per cent level. As with the basic correlation results (Table 7.6), significant results for political agency potential are negative. These results may reflect a culture of trust and limited corruption that is present in economies with longer histories of free-markets, whereas the loss of authoritarian state control over the populations of Eastern European regions was followed, in many cases, by a transition with high levels of corruption and weaker formal institutions (Meyer and Peng, 2005; Batory, 2012). It is possible that in these regions cultural development compensates for the weaker formal institutions present in order to address the apparent corruption (Farole et al., 2011).

7.6   Human Agency: from Potential to Actualization

Although the preceding section indicates that the values associated with culture and personality are related to HAP, it is still not clear whether such HAP leads to human agency being actualized (HAA). It was reasoned in Chapter 2 and above that such HAP, if exercised as HAA, would lead to particular behavioural change that could directly impact upon social and economic development. It could also allow for institutions to be altered, enabling different development paths to be explored. However, it has yet to be determined whether HAP is connected to these realized agentic behaviours, and this will be explored in this section.

To achieve this, the ESS 2016 data is utilized to examine the relationship between HAP and change behaviours in the political, environmental, and work spheres reflecting HAA. Given that involvement in change behaviours is likely to be affected by a number of different factors beyond HAP, a multivariate analysis perspective is utilized. The majority of the variables examined are in the form of dichotomous variables reflecting where an action is taken or not taken. This makes ordinary least squares regressions inappropriate, and instead a binary logistic regression approach is adopted for those measures capturing the presence of a particular behaviour, or when the item reflects a degree of involvement or expected involvement, as captured by a Likert type scale, and ordered logits are used.

Initial expectations would be that each type of HAP will be most strongly connected with the change behaviours that reflect this type of agency being actualized. However, it should be noted that the model outlined in Chapter 2 reflects how agency works to alter the context through the evolution of institutions. In order to influence institutions that most strongly impact upon one sphere of activity, it may be necessary to engage with another sphere. For example, entrepreneurs seeking to exploit new opportunities may wish to influence regulatory institutions in their particular sector. Although direct engagement with regulatory bodies may be one method of adapting these institutions, an alternative may be to lobby in the political sphere. This could mean that entrepreneurs and entrepreneurial individuals who consider they have control and influence over their business activities may wish to further express their agentic activities in the political sphere. Equally, those with higher levels of political agency potential may engage with behavioural changes in other spheres as they have the confidence of having the relevant support and influence with important individuals.

The measures of political change behaviours covered are: voting in the last national elections; contacting politicians; wearing a political campaign badge; participating in a public demonstration; and working for a political party. It should be noted that, while these behaviours may represent activities reflecting a belief that an individual can intentionally change and influence the institutions present, there are considerable differences in the levels and nature of engagement. There is an extensive literature that has examined the rationale behind voting in elections (Downs, 1957; Dhillon and Peralta, 2002; Kaniovski, 2019). The likelihood of being the deciding vote in most elections is tiny, which makes the decision to vote irrational given the relative size of opportunity costs of voting against the expected return (Connolly and Munroe, 1999; Mueller, 2003; Hindricks and Myles, 2006). A wide range of explanations have been given including: risk aversion (Jones and Cullis, 1986); utility from the act of voting itself (Riker and Ordeshook, 1968); and explanations based around the regret that will be felt if the result is not as hoped for (Ferejohn and Fiorina, 1974; Blais et al., 2019).

Human agency, however, also provides an explanation for the belief that institutions can be changed through these mechanisms and will encourage such behaviour. This may be through proxy agency, whereby through voting an individual puts a proxy in a position to represent their values, as shaped by their culture and personality (Bandura, 2001). It should be noted that agency might be exerted and utility derived not through winning elections, but by registering preferences and identity (Fiorina, 1976; Brennan and Lomasky, 1993; Aldrich, 1997; Jones and Dawson, 2007; Hamlin and

Jennings, 2011, 2019; Taylor, 2015). For example, although the UK voted in 2016 to leave the European Union, some of the resistance along the lines of legal arguments to a no-deal Brexit from the House of Commons will have drawn upon the sizeable minority (48 per cent) that voted to remain (Ewing, 2017). Although many polls, forecasts, and predictions indicated an expectation that the UK would vote to remain, even in the last few days leading up to the referendum (Amador Diaz Lopez et al., 2017; Fisher and Shorrocks, 2018), the victory for leave may again have been in part because those voting to leave may not have believed they would win, but by engaging with the vote they could register their values and beliefs to influence the future relationship between the UK and the European Union and resist further integration (Goodwin and Heath, 2016).

Other behavioural changes may be more direct and involve direct contact or attempts to influence politicians, or collective agency such as through a petition or public demonstration in an organized collective manner (Bandura, 2001). The final change behaviour of working within a political party again is subtly different in that it reflects a deeper involvement with the political system from within, rather than an attempt to shape it from outside. The relationship between these measures of exercised agency and the HAP measures is likely to vary depending on the type of institutional change that is sought and within which sphere. An individual would need to consider their perceptions of being able to influence institutions through the political system (political agency potential), the extent to which the political sphere has influence over those institutions, and the relative (direct and opportunity) costs of engaging in such behaviours.

A limited number of measures are available that are identifiable as being directly associated with environmental change behaviours. It should be noted that many of the change behaviours associated with exercised political agency could be intended to alter institutions associated with the environment, such as demonstrations and the wearing of badges. However, within the environmental sphere of activity the change behaviour examined is the likelihood of buying the most energy-efficient appliance. Unfortunately, this is not a direct measure of whether or not the behaviour has been revealed, and although high levels of intention can be indicated, these may not be realized at the time when the higher upfront costs of more energy-efficient appliances are set against longer-run savings (Miller and Mannix, 2016). Differences in proposed and actual behaviour would be consistent with theories that apply hyperbolic discounting, rather than the more typically used exponential discounting (Ho et al., 2006). With hyperbolic discounting, discount rates vary depending on the time periods being considered. There is assumed to be a much greater discount rate between the present and the future compared with two time periods in the future. This is described as 'present bias', where any future pay-off, regardless of whether it is a long way in the future or just an hour or day ahead, will be valued much lower. The quasi-hyperbolic discount function $(D(t))$ is given as follows (Phelps and Pollak, 1968):

$$D(t) = \begin{matrix} 1 & if & t = 0 \\ \beta\delta^t & if & t > 0 \end{matrix} \quad 0 \leq \beta \leq 1 \quad and \quad 0 \leq \delta \leq 1 \qquad (7.2)$$

Where β reflects the present bias. If $\beta = 1$, no present bias is in existence as both the current period $(t = 0)$ and periods in the future $(t > 0)$ are discounted in the same manner. However, if β is less than 1, pay-offs will lose a portion of their value due to being in the future, regardless of how far in the future compared to the present. The δ^t term reflects the more standard discounting that reflects a constant proportion of value lost each period in the future. This means that the variable reflecting the likelihood of purchasing an energy-efficient appliance in the future should be approached with caution. However, it provides the best direct measure of agentic behaviour relating specifically to the environment in the ESS data. Its ordered nature means that ordered logits are utilized to examine it.

For the labour and entrepreneurial spheres of activity, the change behaviours considered are: membership of a trade union, both current and previous; engagement with courses and conferences to develop human capital; and having supervisory responsibility over others. In the past, labour agency might be reflected in membership of trade unions, where proxy and collective agency can be achieved (Bandura, 2001; Herod, 2001). Such behaviours may have supported resistance that directly challenge the prevailing power relations and benefit labour (Katz, 2004; Coe and Jordhus-Lier, 2011). However, changes in global production and labour markets have reduced the extent to which traditional collective bargaining is effective for many workers (Cumbers et al., 2008). Instead, a more direct proxy approach might be sought through the development of human capital as a form of resilience and obtaining positions of influence over others in organizations, which can be considered a form of reworking (Katz, 2004; King et al., 2005; Coe and Jordhus-Lier, 2011). Therefore, while resilience reflects those acts to get by when faced with everyday difficulties, reworking is related more to seeking to improve conditions from within the system as a means of recalibrating power relations (Coe and Jordhus-Lier, 2011).

We do not directly examine business ownership or self-employment here as a form of actualized entrepreneurial agency, because there is a strong expectation that reverse causality might be present. Those who are self-employed are likely to have influence over policy in their firm and an ability to control their work, as they are the owner-manager, or they will at least perceive this to be the case, although there are examples of many self-employed workers who are heavily reliant on a single or small number of clients (Román et al., 2011). In order to address this, Chapter 8 will return to the investigation of the links from HAP to entrepreneurship and innovation in more detail. In terms of trade union membership, a multinominal logit regression is applied, allowing for the possibility that past and present membership should be treated differently, but not necessarily in an ordered fashion. The other two measures are binary in nature, so a binary logistic regression approach is used. The correlation coefficients for the HAP variables and the independent variables used in the regressions do not show any obvious signs of collinearity problems. This is confirmed by the variance inflation factors of the regressions, which do not exceed the conventional threshold of 10. In all the regressions, controls are included for gender, migration status, ethnic-minority group membership, age, education, occupational status, household income, urban and rural nature of domicile, and size of business operated in. To account for any remaining unobserved heterogeneity at the regional levels, dummies are included for the NUTS1 regions.

All the binary logistic regressions can reject the null of constant probability at the 1 per cent level, and the Hosmer–Lemeshow test cannot reject the null of a good fit. The percentage of behaviours that are correctly predicted are all above 80 per cent, but this tends to reflect the uneven participation in these behaviours, with in most cases a relatively small percentage of the population engaging in them.

As might be expected, political agency potential is positively and significantly associated with all of the five change behaviours in the political sphere. Labour/entrepreneurial agency potential is also positively associated with four of the five behaviours. The exception is participating in public demonstrations. Environmental agency potential is positively associated with voting, wearing badges associated with causes and participating in demonstrations, but is not significantly related to working for a political party, and is negatively associated with contacting politicians. Therefore, environmental agency potential is more closely associated with behaviours that work from outside the political system to influence the institutions, rather than to engage directly with the existing system. Turning now to change behaviours that might be associated with sustainable regional development, we consider the adoption of the most energy-efficient household appliance. As would be expected, those who believe their actions will have an influence on the environment, and have the power to make them, are more likely to purchase the most energy-efficient appliances.

Within the labour/entrepreneurial sphere actions that are purposeful and intentional attempts to influence change could involve the development of relevant human and social capital through attendance at courses, conferences, or lectures to develop skills for work. Others include taking on supervisory roles where staff can be directly influenced. In both cases these can be seen as more direct agency (Bandura, 2001). The third example of exercising labour agency would be through membership of a trade union, which is more an example of collective and proxy agency. Table 7.8 presents the binary logistic regressions of the first two activities associated with human capital accumulation and supervisory roles. Around 30 per cent of the deviation relating to supervisory roles can be explained by the regression, and over 43 per cent for the engagement with sources of social and human capital. The null of a good fit to the data cannot be rejected by the Hosmer–Lemeshow test.

Both examples of labour/entrepreneurial agency actualization are positively associated with labour/entrepreneurial agency potential. As noted above, it is not possible to be entirely sure of the direction of causality, and theoretically it would be expected to flow in both directions, as such actions will both influence the institutions as desired and, in doing so, provide the agent with more power, thereby increasing their HAP in the future.

Political agency potential is similarly related in a positive fashion to the likelihood of engaging in courses, conferences, and lectures to build work-based skills. Education, in general, has been found to be positively associated with greater social participation and social capital (Huang et al., 2009). These activities, therefore, are often not just simply improving human capital but are also typically used as a source of social capital and a network opportunity (Tagliaventi and Mattarelli, 2006). They may have particular benefits for those seeking to progress entrepreneurial endeavours, whether within existing firms or as new venture creation (Lampel and Meyer, 2008). For those with greater political agency potential, it may be perceived to be an opportunity to influence others within their own and other organizations to affect institutional change (Lampel and Meyer, 2008). In terms of supervisory responsibility, there is a positive association with political agency potential, but the coefficient is much smaller than that found for labour/entrepreneurial agency. Without the social capital and networking element, this appears to be a direction of influence less desirable for those who possess political

Table 7.8 Logit regressions of human agency actualization for entrepreneurial/labour change behaviours

	Educational conference or course	Supervisory responsibility
Political agency potential	0.230 (0.000)	0.088 (0.000)
Environmental agency potential	0.087 (0.000)	−0.056 (0.001)
Labour agency potential	0.214 (0.000)	0.966 (0.000)
Male	−0.201 (0.000)	0.582 (0.000)
Immigrant	−0.241 (0.000)	0.081 (0.141)
Ethnic minority	−0.011 (0.882)	−0.056 (0.476)
Age	−0.022 (0.000)	0.007 (0.000)
Age^2	−0.050 (0.000)	−0.001 (0.856)
Education[i]		
Less than lower secondary	−0.619 (0.000)	−0.580 (0.000)
Lower secondary	−0.512 (0.000)	−0.401 (0.000)
Lower-tier upper secondary	−0.128 (0.023)	−0.015 (0.779)
Advanced vocational	0.361 (0.000)	0.248 (0.000)
Lower tertiary education	0.687 (0.000)	0.152 (0.006)
Higher tertiary education	0.912 (0.000)	0.195 (0.000)
Other education	−0.535 (0.218)	0.241 (0.472)
Occupational status[ii]		
Education	0.383 (0.000)	−0.449 (0.000)
Unemployed	−0.202 (0.018)	−0.060 (0.549)
Economically inactive	−0.822 (0.000)	0.055 (0.737)
Sick or disabled	−1.867 (0.000)	0.330 (0.001)
Retired	−1.980 (0.000)	0.380 (0.000)

Continued

Table 7.8 *Continued*

Homeworker	−1.306	0.055
	(0.000)	(0.457)
Community service	−0.620	0.023
	(0.000)	(0.892)
Household income[iii]		
Household income 1st decile	−0.186	−0.437
	(0.036)	(0.000)
Household income 2nd decile	−0.117	−0.305
	(0.133)	(0.000)
Household income 3rd decile	−0.143	−0.211
	(0.049)	(0.002)
Household income 4th decile	−0.015	−0.085
	(0.825)	(0.179)
Household income 6th decile	0.115	−0.026
	(0.078)	(0.681)
Household income 7th Decile	0.147	0.104
	(0.023)	(0.092)
Household income 8th decile	0.322	0.197
	(0.000)	(0.002)
Household income 9th decile	0.410	0.391
	(0.000)	(0.000)
Household income 10th decile	0.398	0.533
	(0.000)	(0.000)
Dependent children	0.050	0.030
	(0.182)	(0.396)
Live with partner	−0.183	−0.015
	(0.000)	(0.698)
Urban/rural location[iv]		
Big city	−0.077	−0.071
	(0.109)	(0.125)
Suburbs	−0.019	−0.022
	(0.728)	(0.658)
Country village	−0.040	−0.003
	(0.336)	(0.942)
Farm or hamlet	0.081	−0.166
	(0.227)	(0.009)
Employer size[v]		
Under 10 employees	−0.421	−0.570
	(0.000)	(0.000)
10 to 24 employees	−0.204	−0.062
	(0.000)	(0.192)
100 to 499 employees	0.120	0.136
	(0.018)	(0.005)
500 or more employees	0.297	0.315
	(0.000)	(0.000)
Constant	−0.499	−1.642
	(0.000)	(0.000)

N	27133	27208
LR-test	10321.8	6783.2
	[125]	[125]
	(0.000)	(0.000)
R^2	0.437	0.309
Hosmer–Lemeshow test	10.1	11.2
	[8]	[8]
	(0.260)	(0.193)
Percentage correct	77.5	74.7

Notes: p-values in parentheses; i. base category of upper secondary; ii. base category of in employment; iii. base category of 5th decile; iv. base category of town or small city; v. base category of 25 to 99 employees.

agency potential. Environmental agency potential is also positively associated with human capital acquisition activities. Again, this opportunity to influence others and gain skills to make change may be seen as a route to achieve more sustainable goals.

7.7 Conclusions

The central role of human agency in regional economic development has been discussed by a number of recent studies (Bristow and Healy, 2014; Wink et al., 2017; Huggins and Thompson, 2019). As this chapter has noted, it is important to address challenges with regard to difficulties in defining what is actually meant by agency. In some studies, the ability to purposefully take action to make changes, particularly those relating to the institutional context, has been the focus (Bristow and Healy, 2014). However, agency has often been recognized more in terms of the actions themselves (Castree, 2007). Theoretically, the need for this potential or actual action to be purposeful and intentional is crucial to operationalizing agency in a meaningful way (Bandura, 2001), and this can cause difficulties in terms of measuring forms of agency.

In addition, intention is exceptionally difficult to measure, and cognitive dissonance often means individuals will impose an intention on their actions after the event (Festinger, 1957). This means that even if respondents answer honestly, they may not be answering accurately with regard to their agency. In this chapter we suggest that a distinction needs to be made between human agency potential (HAP) and the realization of human agency—human agency actualization (HAA). In case of the former, the social learning theory of Rotter (1954, 1960) is built upon using the concept of behaviour potential while acknowledging the key differences. We argue that it is possible for considerable HAP to exist but not actually be exercised, as conditions do not necessarily encourage or necessitate it (Wink et al., 2017). At the same time, those with relatively low HAP could still exercise their human agency, so that there is evidence of HAA. In terms of regional development, we argue that HAP provides a city or region with the adaptability to create or modify different development paths; and HAA of course is also of ultimate importance in terms of realizing behavioural change.

This chapter has established three measures of HAP from the European Social Studies data covering political, labour/entrepreneurial, and environmental potential. There is clear evidence that these measures vary not only between countries but within countries as well. Although HAP in aggregate is stronger in some regions than others, the correlation between the three measures of HAP is not perfect and does evolve through time. This fits with the argument that human agency plays a key role in determining not just the level of regional development but also its nature. Its evolution through time is consistent with studies such as Welzel (2013), indicating that measures of culture and values evolve, and not always in a consistent pattern across countries.

The evidence of the link between culture and values with the HAP measures found here begins to provide further empirical results confirming the behavioural model of urban and regional development sketched in Chapter 2. These results further confirm that the link from culture and personality, through the values formed to generate HAP and through to HAA, opens up particular development paths more strongly than others. More generally, it is clear that human agency has an important role to play in urban and regional economic development. Although there are difficulties in truly capturing human agency, distinctions between potential human agency (HAP) and the exercising of this agency (HAA) can help provide some clarity, and the intra- and inter-country differences in the types of human agency found indicate that agency needs to be regarded within a multidimensional perspective.

8

Agency, Entrepreneurship, and Innovation

8.1 Introduction

The previous two chapters have considered how culture and personality can be measured and examined as a process of co-evolution, which underpins human agency potential (HAP). The expectation is that HAP reflects the capabilities of the individual, and at the urban and regional level the capacity of the population to engage in behavioural change reflects the actualization of this human agency (HAA), which catalyses regional social and economic development. In addition, the behaviour of key agents within a city or region will lead to institutional evolution that opens up different development paths.

Building upon this approach, the chapter examines evidence that links community culture, personality traits, and HAP to the types of behaviour that reflect the exercising of agency in a fashion associated with urban and regional economic development. Links to entrepreneurial and innovative behaviour are explored in order to ascertain the extent to which HAP can be linked to individual actions and regional-level development measures.

The chapter first explores whether community culture and personality traits are associated with entrepreneurial activities. It seeks to consider the importance of personality held at the individual level and culture held at the group level, as discussed in Chapter 6. This allows the connections between the foundations of the behavioural model of regional development—community culture and personality—and activities associated with the regional development to be explored. It further explores the extent to which HAP plays a role in determining the nature of entrepreneurial endeavours. This is examined by using the European Social Survey (ESS) data at the individual level and considers the relationship between HAP and job creation.

Following an examination of behavioural micro-relationships at the individual level, the analysis then moves on to examine evidence of the relationship between HAP and differing forms of regional development. It first focuses on traditional economic measures of development including GDP

A Behavioural Theory of Economic Development: The Uneven Evolution of Cities and Regions. Robert Huggins and Piers Thompson, Oxford University Press (2021). © Robert Huggins and Piers Thompson.
DOI: 10.1093/oso/9780198832348.003.0008

and unemployment, but also considers inputs and outputs from innovation and the entrepreneurial environment required to generate high-road regional competitiveness (Malecki, 2017). It should be borne in mind that throughout the analysis the model of behavioural urban and regional development should not be considered to consist of linear relationships between the key concepts, but self-reinforcing and iterative interactions that form the behavioural system of any city or region.

8.2 Behaviour, Entrepreneurship, and Innovation

There is a long history of exploring the personality of entrepreneurs and comparing it with the general public or those who are managers of companies (Kerr et al., 2018). Many of the personality traits captured by the Big Five dimensions of personality are assumed to be formed during adolescence and early adulthood (Roberts et al., 2003; Obschonka et al., 2018). Studies concentrating on entrepreneurship have shown the importance of self-efficacy, innovativeness, locus of control, and risk attitudes (Kerr et al., 2018). However, those factors particularly pertinent to human agency such as self-efficacy and achievement motivation are considered to be possible to adapt with the correct interventions (Rauch, 2014), and it is worth examining the evidence that links personality traits directly to entrepreneurship and innovation. It is understandable that entrepreneurial careers will be self-selecting, as work such as that of Weber (1930), McClelland (1961), and Uhlaner and Thurik (2007) have long illustrated that not all members of any population are as likely as others to become entrepreneurs. Even attempts to increase entrepreneurial engagement through enterprise education may have exaggerated effects, as it is often a voluntary choice to participate (Thompson and Kwong, 2016). For many scholars, this is a prime example of a choice that can be examined through the theory of planned behaviour (Ajzen, 1991), or similar approaches such as Shapero and Sokol's (1982) theory of the entrepreneurial event.

The key for much of the analysis that follows in this chapter is the argument that entrepreneurship is determined by a combination of perceived feasibility and perceived desirability. In the case, for example, of Evans and Jovanovic's (1989) model, much of this is simplified to the availability of capital (the constraints imposed on the prospective entrepreneur) and their latent ability, which can be linked to the personality factors noted above. This means that it is understandable that those with particular personality traits may be more likely to make particular work choices (Zhao and Seibert, 2006;

Rauch and Frese, 2007; Obschonka et al., 2013a). Here, we initially discuss how personality traits and community culture, individually, may influence engagement with entrepreneurship, as captured by self-employment, as well as considering how the two may combine. In particular, we will consider the two constructs at different levels of interest: the individual for personality traits; and the group (local/regional) level for community culture (Van Maanen and Schein, 1979). We will further consider work by scholars such as Jokela et al. (2015), who suggest that the 'fit' of personality with the prevailing contextual and environmental conditions may have a role to play. This can be related to two theories of entrepreneurship: that of the dissatisfied and/or frustrated entrepreneur (Noorderhaven et al., 2004); and that of the socially embedded entrepreneur (Davidsson and Honig, 2003).

Personality and entrepreneurship. A number of studies of entrepreneurship and self-employment have sought to identify the factors that individuals choose to start their own businesses, rather than working for others as employees or managers (Zhao and Seibert, 2006). Many studies utilizing broader personality traits, rather than traits specifically related to entrepreneurship, have drawn upon the Big Five personality traits to examine the relationship between personality and entrepreneurship (Zhao and Seibert, 2006; Obschonka et al., 2013a). This has been made easier by the wider availability of large personality psychology datasets such as those discussed in Chapter 6, which allow analyses at both the individual level and the relationship between personality traits and entrepreneurship at the spatial level (Obschonka et al., 2015). It is argued that entrepreneurs need to be emotionally stable while being able to retain their independence, so potentially have a low need for affiliation (Wainer and Rubin, 1969). Lower neuroticism and agreeableness will, therefore, be important to provide stability and independence. At the same time, they may need to be able to interact and network with others (Kirchler and Hoelzl, 2018), and this may suggest that extraversion should also have a positive impact (Zhao and Seibert, 2006).

In aggregate, the seeming importance of these traits has led to the development of the so-called entrepreneurial personality profile. Studies have sought to compare entrepreneurs with managers within companies, and they have generally found entrepreneurs to be more open and conscientious, but less agreeable and neurotic (Schmitt-Rodermund, 2004; Brandstätter, 2011). For those considering starting a business, higher conscientiousness, openness, and extraversion, along with a lower level of neuroticism, are found to be associated with entrepreneurial intentions (Brandstätter, 2011). Furthermore, those who start their own business have been found to be more likely to assert themselves and make decisions, as well as having greater emotional stability (lower neuroticism) compared to those inheriting or purchasing businesses from others (Brandstätter, 1997). Studies have also examined the longer-term consequences of personality on the success of businesses, and Ciavarella et al. (2004) find that the length of time a business has been operating is positively connected to conscientiousness. Interestingly, openness is found to potentially have a negative impact on longer-term survival when innovation and creativity may be less important.

Community culture and entrepreneurship. As well as personality psychology, cultural or institutional factors are also likely to determine rates of entrepreneurship (Grilo and Thurik, 2005), and studies such as those by Marcén (2014) examine the persistence of self-employment rates among second-generation immigrants to the US, based on self-employment rates in their ancestors' homelands. It is argued that second-generation individuals will be raised under the same laws and institutions, with the persistence in self-employment rates partly reflecting inherited culture. Many studies examining the role of culture have concentrated on the concept of social capital and the trust it creates (Stam et al., 2014). Results from these studies are often a little mixed, with some recognizing the fact that the resources and knowledge made available through networks help support new start-ups and small businesses by embedding them in the local culture (Davidsson and Honig, 2003). However, other studies have noted that if cultures are too cohesive it may restrict the flow of new ideas, hindering entrepreneurial activities and weakening existing small and medium sized enterprises (SMEs) (Westlund and Bolton, 2003).

A further stream of studies has argued that a broader conception of culture is needed, such as those discussed in Chapter 6, and this has included separating countries into cultural groupings based on secular-rational versus traditional, and survival versus self-expression (Hechavarria and Reynolds, 2009). Others have drawn upon Hofstede's (2001) dimensions of culture to make international comparisons (Hayton et al., 2002), and Liñán and Fernandez-Serrano (2014) build upon Schwartz's (2004) measures to concentrate on embeddedness versus autonomy, hierarchy versus egalitarianism, and mastery versus harmony. Drawing upon these previous studies, Huggins and Thompson (2016) find that less cohesive, less caring communities with less adherence to social rules and a preference for collective action generate more new businesses, but existing business activities are often protected by the opposite cultural conditions.

The interaction of personality and community culture. One explanation as to why inconsistent results have been found when considering the link between personality and business success is suggested to be the need to take moderating influences into account (Frese and Gielnik, 2014). Given the combination of factors that are likely to impact upon the establishment of human agency potential (HAP), it is highly probable that culture is one of the key moderating variables that influences the personality–entrepreneurship relationship. In order to examine this, it is worth considering Freytag and Thurik's (2007) suggestion that, in general, there are three routes through which culture can influence entrepreneurial activity, as well as considering how each of these mechanisms may interact with personality traits at the individual level.

The first is the 'aggregate trait' view, whereby particular cultures that promote the formation of entrepreneurial traits are likely to create more entrepreneurs (Uhlaner and Thurik, 2007). This perspective is likely to yield limited interaction between community culture and personality, as it is the entrepreneurial personalities themselves that are being created in greater numbers. Work such as that of Obschonka et al. (2013b) and Stuetzer et al. (2016) have examined how the underlying environment may generate or attract particular personality types that are more entrepreneurially prone.

The second perspective is that of the 'legitimation' or 'moral approval' approach, whereby culture promotes entrepreneurship by making the activity seem more acceptable and better rewarded (Anderson and Smith, 2007; Kibler et al., 2014). Compatibility or fit of individuals' personalities with those around them are found to raise well-being (Jokela et al., 2015), and group-level culture may be expected to have similar effects in terms of supporting the choices of those living within the community. This mechanism may have an important role to play in terms of encouraging more individuals with particular personality traits to engage in entrepreneurship. Although those most prone to entrepreneurial endeavours are more likely to engage regardless of the prevailing community culture, those with weaker entrepreneurial personalities are more likely to choose employment in the mainstream labour market unless the rewards, both financial and in terms of acceptance from the wider population, are greater. The social embeddedness approach may suggest that, among those with traits not traditionally associated with an entrepreneurial personality, a closer and more supportive community culture may encourage greater entrepreneurial activity (Davidsson and Honig, 2003).

The third approach is the 'push' theory, whereby entrepreneurs and non-entrepreneurs have different values and beliefs (Baum et al., 1993; Noorderhaven et al., 2004). It is expected that those with more entrepreneurial personality traits would be more likely to start businesses, for example, where social cohesion is high along with a strong adherence to rules, and therefore differing perspectives and outsiders may be excluded (Rodríguez-Pose and Storper, 2006; Obschonka et al., 2013b).

Summing up the above, Figure 8.1 outlines the routes through which personality and community culture may directly influence self-employment. It is also possible that community culture's influence could be mediated by the creation (or not) of individuals with entrepreneurial personalities (route 1 in Figure 8.1). It may also positively moderate the link between personality and self-employment through the second (legitimation) and third (push) routes. However, these work in quite different fashions, and through the legitimation or embedded route a more compatible community culture and personality are likely to increase entrepreneurial activities. With the push route, a disconnect between personality and community culture generates greater self-employment. Therefore, the same entrepreneurial personality could be promoted into greater self-employment by quite different community cultures. Finally, the direct link between community culture and entrepreneurship could disappear if it is fully mediated via personality.

Data and Methods—The main data used in this work was acquired through the British Broadcasting Corporation's (BBC) Lab UK website as part of the BBC's and University of Cambridge's Big Personality Test project. A total of 588,014 individuals completed the online survey. Respondents were required to sign up for a BBC ID to ensure that they did not complete the survey more than once. On completing the survey, respondents were given customized feedback about their personalities. The present sample uses a subset of 321,530 responses where all information required is available, including personal characteristics and information relating to respondents' location at the local authority district level. This data was used in Rentfrow et al. (2015) to map the distribution of personality in Great Britain, and the research provided a detailed examination of the Big Personality Test data and illustrates its representativeness at the local authority district level.

As will be examined in later sections of this chapter, entrepreneurship is a multifaceted concept with many different definitions appearing in the

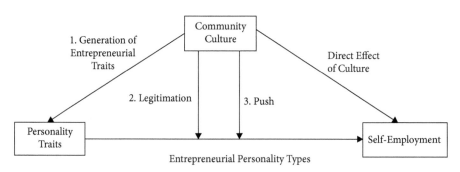

Figure 8.1 The influence of community culture on the personality–self-employment relationship.

literature, from those related to organizational characteristics (for example SMEs), behavioural theories, and those relating to performance (for example high growth and innovation) (Audretsch et al., 2015). Studies have frequently used the development and ownership of businesses as the ultimate manifestation of entrepreneurial behaviour (Audretsch and Keilbach, 2004). Other studies such as the Global Entrepreneurship Monitor (GEM) study have attempted to identify those starting and running businesses (Reynolds et al., 2005), but such measures are not always available and frequently self-employment has been used as a proxy (Kolvereid, 2016). In the case of the data used in this study, the employment situation of respondents is captured as being in employment for others, unemployed, or self-employed. Although not perfect, using self-employment as the measure of entrepreneurship allows us to identify those who are willing to take the risks of business ownership, even though they may not have started the business themselves (Bjuggren et al., 2012). Alongside the personality trait measures, for the community culture indicators we utilize the five dimensions outlined in previous chapters.

The choice to run a business, rather than work for others, is clearly influenced by a number of different factors, and to examine the influence of personality traits, culture, and the combination of the two it is necessary to adopt a multivariate approach. Furthermore, the collectively held nature of culture means that it cannot be entered into a normal regression approach as an independent variable. Overlooking this can have consequences for the efficiency of the regressions if separate terms are estimated for each locality, and the likelihood of the clustering of particular personality types within certain localities is ignored (Rasbash et al., 2017). This clustering will generally result in the underestimating of standard errors, which can lead to relationships being incorrectly identified as having a significant impact. As discussed above, and depicted in Figure 8.1, route 1 suggests that community culture facilitates the development of entrepreneurial traits and makes such clustering highly likely. This necessitates the use of a mixed-level regression approach, which also accommodates the fact that the choice to be self-employed is a discrete choice and the dependent variable takes the form of a dummy variable. For individual i in local authority area j this variable (*Self-Employed$_{ij}$*) will take the value 1 if they are self-employed and 0 otherwise. The regression, therefore, takes the following form:

$$p_{ij} = \Pr(Self-Employed_{ij} = 1 \mid Pers_{k,ij}, Cult_{m,j})$$
$$Logit(p_{ij}) = \beta_0 + \beta_1 Pers_{k,ij} + \beta_2 Cult_{m,j} + \beta_3 Pers_{k,ij} \cdot Cult_{m,j} + u_{0j} \qquad (8.1)$$
$$Var(u_{0j} \mid Pers_{k,ij}, Cult_{m,j}) = \sigma^2_{u_0 \mid Pers_k, Cult_m}$$

Where the probability of being self-employed (p_{ij}) is regressed on the personality traits of individual i in local authority area j ($Pers_{k,ij}$). For the purposes of simplicity and clarity, the personality traits are dealt with individually, and k represents the particular personality trait being studied (extraversion, agreeableness, conscientiousness, openness, and neuroticism). The contextual effect is captured by examining the individual dimensions of the community culture present in local authority area j ($Cult_{m',j}$), where m reflects the different dimensions of community culture (engagement with employment and education, social cohesion, feminine and caring attitudes, adherence to social rules, and collective actions). However, given the interest of this study in investigating the role played by the fit of the individual's personality with the prevailing local community culture in terms of the choices made by each individual, it is necessary to include the term $Pers_{ij} \cdot Cult_j$, where a significant coefficient β_3 will reflect an interaction between the individual and the contextual factors.

Initially, the regressions are run without the interaction term to ascertain which personality traits and community culture are associated with the decision to become self-employed. The interaction terms are then included for each of the twenty-five combinations of personality and community culture. Controls are included for those factors identified as affecting the likelihood of being self-employed in the existing literature. Although female entrepreneurship has increased considerably in many countries across the globe, studies consistently find a higher proportion of men in self-employment (Minniti and Naudé, 2010). This can relate to actual or perceived disadvantages in obtaining funding (Kwong et al., 2012; Carter et al., 2015) or the presence of gendered institutions, which constrain a woman's occupational choices (Lee et al., 2016). We therefore include a dummy for being male.

It is also important to control for age in a non-linear fashion, as individuals offset the requirement to acquire appropriate resources against the need for sufficient time to obtain a payoff (Lévesque and Minniti, 2006). We therefore include both age and a quadratic term to capture this compromise (Kim, 2007). Another resource that has been identified as important is the human capital present. We include dummies to represent different levels of qualifications obtained: no formal qualifications, vocational qualifications, GCSEs/O-levels (lower secondary school qualifications), A-levels (upper secondary school qualifications), undergraduate degree, and postgraduate degrees. This categorical form allows for particular qualifications that suit occupations where self-employment is more prevalent, and the fact the education may boost opportunity recognition (Arenius and De Clercq, 2005), but also increase the opportunity costs of self-employment (Le, 1999).

Studies in the UK have found evidence for both push and pull effects on those of ethnic-minority backgrounds (Thompson et al., 2010). Discrimination and disadvantage in the mainstream labour market may push individuals into starting their own businesses (Clark and Drinkwater, 2000). However, there is also the potential for those from an ethnic-minority background to be pulled into self-employment through the opportunity to serve their own communities (Wilson and Portes, 1980), or the majority population (McEvoy and Hafeez, 2007), with specialist goods. Although studies have found distinct differences between different ethnic groups, the data does not provide sufficiently large subsamples across all local authority areas to make such comparisons robust. Instead, a dummy for the majority white ethnic group is included.

Entrepreneurship, personality traits, and community culture. Table 8.1 presents the simple percentages of the population engaged in self-employment for each group based on whether or not they display levels of each personality trait that is above or below the sample average. The differences between the subsamples are compared using *t*-statistics. In all cases significant differences are found, but these vary considerably in size. A greater proportion of those individuals that are more extravert, conscientious, and open are found to be self-employed. Equally, a smaller proportion of those who are agreeable or neurotic are self-employed. More sizeable differences are present in the proportions of self-employed in groups that have above and below average levels of extraversion and openness. This fits with the discussion above concerning the benefits these bring as facilitators of the networking and innovation activities required for successful entrepreneurship (Kirchler and Hoelzl, 2018), and is consistent with the work on the entrepreneurial personality (Brandstätter, 2011).

Table 8.2 examines the proportions of those classed as self-employed based on whether the individual lives in a locality that displays above or below the British average levels for each community culture dimension. As with the personality traits at the individual level, the group-level community culture dimensions all display significant differences. A larger percentage of

Table 8.1 Proportion of self-employed by whether personality traits are above or below the mean

	Below average	Above average	chi-square	p-value
Extraversion	7.8%	10.0%	465.1	(0.000)
Agreeableness	9.4%	8.6%	60.1	(0.000)
Conscientiousness	8.8%	9.1%	5.7	(0.017)
Neuroticism	9.9%	8.1%	315.9	(0.000)
Openness	6.2%	11.5%	2837.6	(0.000)

Table 8.2 Proportion of self-employed by whether community culture dimensions are above or below the mean

	Below average	Above average	chi-square	p-value
Engagement with education and employment	8.4%	9.4%	84.8	(0.000)
Social cohesion	8.8%	9.1%	7.4	(0.007)
Feminine and caring activities	8.5%	9.5%	98.4	(0.000)
Adherence to social rules	8.1%	9.8%	296.4	(0.000)
Collective actions	9.8%	7.9%	355.6	(0.000)

the population is engaged in self-employment in those localities that have higher levels of: engagement with education and employment; social cohesion; feminine and caring activities; and adherence to social rules. Those localities with higher levels of collective actions have a lower proportion of the population in self-employment.

Some of the findings may at first appear a little surprising, such as the fact that a number of studies have conversely found social cohesion to be negatively associated with entrepreneurship (Levie, 2007). However, these differences are likely to be due to the types of entrepreneurship that are being analysed, such as new venture creation or the survival and existence of a small business culture, which are likely to differ in terms of the psychocultural profile that drives each (Huggins and Thompson, 2016; Lee, 2017; Davidsson and Honig, 2003). With regard to some of the other relationships, adherence to social rules may help to generate the trust required for coordination (Lorenzen, 2007), and feminine and caring activities may also aid survival where the community culture is more supportive rather than competitive and prioritizes other outcomes beyond financial success (Huggins and Thompson, 2015a).

In order to retain clarity, each pair of personality traits and community culture dimensions is investigated separately. Table 8.3 reports the results in full when using the mixed-level model to estimate self-employment when including the personality trait of extraversion and the community cultural dimension of 'engagement with education and employment'. These provide an example of the relationships found between the control variables and self-employment, which follow the theoretical relationships predicted and are consistent regardless of the pairs of personality traits and community culture considered (Clark, 2003; Kirchler and Hoelzl, 2018). Model 2 allows for an interaction between community culture and personality to be present. No

Table 8.3 Regressions of self-employment on Engagement with Education and Employment, and Extraversion

	Model 1	Model 2
Engagement with education and employment	0.0299	0.0295
	(0.000)	(0.000)
Extraversion	0.2523	0.2519
	(0.000)	(0.000)
Extraversion*Engagement with education and employment		0.0040
		(0.601)
Male	0.6954	0.6954
	(0.000)	(0.000)
White	−0.1243	−0.1243
	(0.000)	(0.000)
Educational attainment (base category GCSE)		
No formal	0.4852	0.0485
	(0.000)	(0.130)
Vocational	0.1621	0.1621
	(0.000)	(0.000)
A-Levels	0.0782	0.0782
	(0.000)	(0.000)
Undergraduate	0.1605	0.1605
	(0.000)	(0.000)
Postgraduate	0.0608	0.0608
	(0.002)	(0.002)
Age	0.0623	0.0623
	(0.000)	(0.000)
Age^2	−0.0023	−0.0023
	(0.000)	(0.000)
Constant	−2.5041	−0.2504
	(0.000)	(0.000)
N	321,530	321,530

Note: p-values in parentheses.

significant interaction is found in the case of extraversion and engagement with education and employment. This implies that, for some pairs of community culture and personality traits, both are able to independently influence the likelihood of being self-employed, one working at the individual level and the other at the group level.

We also generated the results covering all combinations of the dimensions of community culture and personality traits, and summarize some of the key results here. For the dimensions of community culture, engagement with education and employment and adherence to social rules are positively associated with self-employment. Collective action and social cohesion are negatively associated with self-employment. The first of these results is consistent with the expectation that self-employment thrives in environments where competition and individualism are encouraged (Casson, 1995). The negative relationship between self-employment and social cohesion is more consistent with those studies that find open and dynamic cultures to offer greater encouragement to entrepreneurship (Nathan and Lee, 2013).

With regard to personality, extraversion and openness are positively associated with self-employment, which is consistent with the entrepreneurial personality thesis (Brandstätter, 2011), while agreeableness and neuroticism have a negative relationship. Interestingly, conscientiousness is found to be negatively associated with self-employment. Again, the measure of entrepreneurship used here, self-employment, is important as it also captures those becoming self-employed for lifestyle rather than just wealth creation reasons (Marcketti et al., 2009). If a measure of entrepreneurship associated with growth and innovation is used, this may be reversed, with Lee (2017) finding that conscientiousness is one of the key factors behind the level of innovative behaviour present.

The major results we are interested in are the interaction terms between community culture and personality, as these provide evidence concerning which of the socially embedded or dissatisfied entrepreneur theories appear to dominate. They also provide insights into the model presented in Chapter 2 and discussed in more detail in Chapter 3 which suggests that community culture and personality traits will combine to ultimately determine the regional development paths followed, due to mechanisms such as entrepreneurship.

One personality trait that stands out as interacting with the different dimensions of culture is openness. A significantly negative interaction is found between openness to new ideas and all community culture dimensions, with the exception of preferences for collective action. This means that, although openness is positively associated with self-employment, this is suppressed when operating in community cultures that prize investment and self-sufficiency, social bonding, feminine and caring activities, and close adherence to rules. For the latter three dimensions of community culture, it appears that the socially embedded theory holds true to a greater extent. Those with a willingness to embrace new ideas are not further pushed into self-employment to exploit these opportunities where social rules constrain and fewer new ideas and individuals enter the community. Instead, without a culture that supports their willingness to explore novelty, these individuals are less likely to engage in self-employment. It is similarly found that extravert individuals are less likely to become self-employed where there is a community culture with a strong adherence to social rules and feminine and caring attitudes are valued. Conversely, individuals with agreeable personalities are significantly more likely to be self-employed in feminine and caring cultures. This suggests that less competitive individuals seek to run businesses in cultural environments with a more community-driven spirit. Community culture, therefore, provides a legitimizing force for particular types of self-employment.

In summary, this section has shown that community culture and personality traits are both sources of regional development, as they determine the likelihood that individuals will engage with entrepreneurship in the form of self-employment. Importantly, it is also shown that some combinations of community culture and personality traits combine to accelerate an engagement with entrepreneurial endeavours. These interactions are found to be more closely associated with the theory of the socially embedded entrepreneur (Davidsson and Honig, 2003), rather than the dissatisfied entrepreneur (Noorderhaven et al. 2004). This does not necessarily mean that regions with less entrepreneurially supportive community cultures are destined to be development deserts. Individuals possessing entrepreneurial personalities (Brandstätter, 2011) are still more likely to engage in entrepreneurship, but public sector interventions may need to assist in this process. In particular, policy can seek to encourage different types of entrepreneur that are 'less traditional', such as those associated with social enterprises; for example, community energy companies (Smith et al., 2016), which potentially offer a better fit with the prevailing community culture. This touches on the nature of entrepreneurship and the relationship with regional development (Pike et al., 2007; Shane, 2009; Mason and Brown, 2013), which are explored further in Chapter 9.

8.3 Agency and Entrepreneurship

This section considers whether or not different types of HAP are related to regional entrepreneurial development, which is important given that existing work has noted how entrepreneurial activity may have a U-shaped relationship with development (Wennekers et al., 2005). This may reflect different proportions of necessity- and opportunity-driven entrepreneurship, where the former tends to represent a larger proportion of entrepreneurship in less developed economies (Acs et al., 2008). As development increases, the need to start businesses to generate one's own employment falls, which leads to a decrease in overall entrepreneurial activity (Díaz Casero et al., 2013). However, higher levels of development create opportunities for more growth-orientated businesses to be voluntarily created, particularly when scale economies become less important (Carree et al., 2007), which eventually leads to an increase in entrepreneurial activity as a whole. It should be noted that Díaz Casero et al. (2013) suggest that this relationship can be best modelled by looking at the relationship between institutional quality and entrepreneurship, rather than economic development, and studies such as that by Wong et al. (2005) find that only high-growth-potential businesses looking to create twenty or more jobs in their first five years are significantly related to growth.

In order to investigate whether greater agency leads to entrepreneurial job creation, we consider a sub-sample of the respondents to the ESS in 2016, that is those who operated or had previously operated businesses. This subgroup was asked an additional question concerning their working arrangements in terms of the number of people employed in their business. It is expected that those with higher levels of agency will be better placed to undertake entrepreneurial endeavours with growth potential. However, there is an expectation that different forms of HAP will be more influential.

Given this, we explore whether or not individual-level political, environmental, and labour/entrepreneurial agency potential are associated with higher employment levels in entrepreneurial businesses. It may at first appear that those individuals displaying higher levels of labour/entrepreneurial agency potential would consider that they are more able to exploit opportunities to grow and take on more staff, as suggested by the literature relating to entrepreneurship and self-efficacy (Chen et al., 1998; Sweida and Reichard, 2013). However, given that all of this subgroup have had the confidence and belief to start their own businesses, levels of labour/entrepreneurial agency potential may be relatively high for all. It may, therefore, be that those who consider they are less constrained by the political and regulatory agencies are best placed to take advantage of opportunities to create employment (Estrin et al., 2013). This being the case, political agency potential may be more important.

Similarly, the extent to which environmental agency potential is positively or negatively related to growth is an interesting issue. One school of thought would suggest that more sustainable businesses may be able to utilize this as a competitive advantage and develop it to exploit a niche (Bryson and Lombardi, 2009). However, other studies have found that those individuals with values associated with sustainability may not necessarily see pecuniary and growth-related outcomes as the main objectives for their businesses (Swan and Morgan, 2016).

As with the change behaviours examined in Section 8.2, a large number of factors may influence the employment decisions of entrepreneurs, and multivariate analysis is therefore appropriate. However, an ordinary least squares regression approach is not appropriate, as the employment data reflects a count rather than a continuous variable. This makes it necessary to use an approach such as a Poisson regression. The Poisson regression fits the data to a Poisson distribution where the probability of the number of individuals employed (*Emp*) being k is given by:

$$\Pr(Emp_i = k_i \mid \mathbf{x}_i) = \frac{e^{-\lambda_i} \lambda_i^{k_i}}{k_i!} \tag{8.2}$$

Where λ is commonly assumed to take the form of a log-linear model:

$$\ln \lambda_i = \mathbf{x_i}'\boldsymbol{\beta} = \beta_0 + \beta_1 PolAgency_i + \beta_2 EnvAgency_i + \beta_3 LabAgency_i + \boldsymbol{\beta}_4 \mathbf{X}_{4,i} \tag{8.3}$$

In Equation 8.2 it is assumed that entrepreneurial employment is influenced by the level of political (*PolAgency*), environmental (*EnvAgency*), and labour/entrepreneurial (*LabAgency*) agency potential possessed by individual i alongside other personal characteristics as captured by matrix $\mathbf{X}_4$.

The negative binominal regression is also appropriate for count-based data and assumes that the data is distributed in a similar manner to the Poisson distribution. The negative binominal regression and Poisson regression differ to the extent that the former allows for data to be more widely dispersed than a true Poisson distribution, described as over-dispersion. In a Poisson distribution the expected number of events per period and variance are assumed to be given by:

$$E[k_i \mid \mathbf{x_i}] = Var[k_i \mid \mathbf{x_i}] = \lambda_i = e^{\mathbf{x_i}'\boldsymbol{\beta}} = e^{\beta_0 + \beta_1 PolAgency_i + \beta_2 EnvAgency_i + \beta_3 LabAgency_i + \boldsymbol{\beta}_4 \mathbf{X}_{4,i}} \tag{8.4}$$

Initial tests suggest that the distribution of entrepreneurial employment displays over-distribution. The negative binominal regression accommodates this by including an individual, unobserved effect (ε_i) in the conditional mean term:

$$\ln \mu_i = \ln \lambda_i + \ln u_i = \mathbf{x_i}'\mathbf{\beta} + \varepsilon_i = \beta_0 + \beta_1 PolAgency_i + \beta_2 EnvAgency_i$$
$$+ \beta_3 LabAgency_i + \mathbf{\beta_4 X}_{4,i} + \varepsilon_i \tag{8.5}$$

It is usually assumed that $u_i = e^{\varepsilon i}$ follows a gamma distribution normalized with an expected value of 1:

$$g(u_i) = \frac{\theta^\theta}{\Gamma(\theta)} e^{-\theta u_i} u_i^{\theta-1} \tag{8.6}$$

This means that the number of employees is assumed to be distributed with an expected value of λ_i as before, but a variance of $\lambda_i(1 + (1/\theta)\lambda_i)$. Where $\theta = 0$ the distribution becomes a Poisson distribution. Given the descriptive data, a negative binominal regression is adopted to estimate the relationship between the different types of HAP and entrepreneurial employment. Whether a simpler Poisson regression would have been appropriate can be established by using a likelihood ratio (LR) test to determine whether θ is significantly different from zero.

The controls included in the regression are similar to those utilized in the regressions of human agency actualization (HAA) in Chapter 7. It is, however, necessary to exclude a number of the individual and contextual characteristics included as they are likely to be endogenously related to the level of entrepreneurial employment. In terms of individual characteristics that are excluded, these include household income, as this is likely to be closely related to the size of the business. Occupational status is also excluded, as the regression is being run on a sub-sample of those who have their own business and will therefore class themselves as self-employed. One contextual variable is also excluded—the size of business that the individual works or worked in. Given that active business owners are being examined in this analysis, this figure will relate to the current business.

Table 8.4 presents the results of two specifications of the negative binominal regressions. In Model 1 the regression is run without the inclusion of regional dummies capturing unobserved regional influences, whereas in Model 2 these are included. The proportion of the variance in entrepreneurial employment explained increases from just under 6 per cent to closer to 10 per cent with the inclusion of the regional dummies. As noted above, the null of the entrepreneurial employment data following a Poisson distribution can be rejected at the 1 per cent significant level by the LR test for both specifications.

As discussed above, it can be expected that labour/entrepreneurial agency potential would have the biggest influence on the level of entrepreneurial employment achieved (Chen et al., 1998; Sweida and Reichard, 2013); however, it is only significant when not controlling for other unobserved regional effects (Model 1). This reflects the fact that we are examining a self-selecting subsample of the population, that is those who have chosen to be self-employed for potentially both opportunity- and necessity-driven reasons. Studies have suggested that such necessity-driven entrepreneurship is often less growth-orientated and may be seen by those involved as a short-term solution (Block and Sandner, 2009; Block and Wagner, 2010).

Unlike labour/entrepreneurial agency potential, the political agency potential coefficient is positive and significant regardless of the inclusion of regional dummies or otherwise. This is an important finding as it provides insights into why regions can have quite similar levels of entrepreneurship in terms of business ownership or self-employment but quite different levels of dynamism. In order to grow and establish a business to a substantial scale, entrepreneurs may have to move beyond perceiving their business as just part of a local market and seek to create a new market or influence institutions that help maintain the incumbent businesses (Schumpeter, 1934). To make such changes and to achieve this growth, individuals will have to engage not just with their customers and suppliers, but with wider society as a whole. Political agency comes into play here, and these individuals are likely to be the entrepreneurial agents discussed by authors such as Goss and Sadler-Smith (2018) and Sotarauta and Suvinen (2018). As such, they may be at least partly responsible for altering the development path of the region as a whole (Lippmann and Aldrich, 2016).

Finally, Model 1 indicates that environmental agency potential may play a role, with individuals having higher levels of this form of HAP being negatively related to entrepreneurial employment. In some cases this may reflect individuals operating businesses in a lifestyle fashion with an environmental focus (Swan and Morgan, 2016), which may mean that the business will have limited growth potential. However, in other cases the businesses started by these individuals could have high growth potential, but the entrepreneurs will not seek to grow at any cost, with the scale of development being slower, but with potentially significant influences on the regional economy, institutions, and culture (Swan and Morgan, 2016).

Table 8.4 Negative binominal regressions of entrepreneurial employment

	Model 1	Model 2
Political agency potential	0.4409	0.2329
	(0.000)	(0.000)
Environmental agency potential	−0.3647	−0.0681
	(0.000)	(0.110)
Labour agency potential	0.1666	0.0850
	(0.033)	(0.276)
Male	0.6840	0.6105
	(0.000)	(0.000)
Immigrant	0.8976	0.3641
	(0.000)	(0.024)
Ethnic minority	−0.2122	0.2736
	(0.373)	(0.258)
Age	0.0344	0.0286
	(0.000)	(0.000)
Age^2	−0.0221	−0.0210
	(0.200)	(0.184)
Education[i]		
Less than lower secondary	−0.7966	−0.6847
	(0.000)	(0.001)
Lower secondary	0.0119	−0.8041
	(0.943)	(0.000)
Lower-tier upper secondary	−0.5765	−0.6307
	(0.000)	(0.000)
Advanced vocational	−0.3141	−0.1907
	(0.031)	(0.179)
Lower tertiary education	0.6520	0.1372
	(0.000)	(0.374)
Higher tertiary education	0.0014	0.0389
	(0.992)	(0.783)
Urban/rural location[ii]		
Big city	−0.0587	−0.2771
	(0.658)	(0.036)
Suburbs	−0.2486	−0.4309
	(0.108)	(0.005)
Country village	−0.0083	−0.1543
	(0.942)	(0.160)
Farm or hamlet	−0.4720	−0.4279
	(0.001)	(0.005)
Constant	0.1229	0.1242
	(0.469)	(0.695)
Regional dummies	No	Yes
N	3,741	3,741

LR-test	836.1	1411.5
	[20]	[103]
	(0.000)	(0.000)
R^2	0.058	0.097
Overdispersion (θ)	5.733	4.417
LR test	1.40E+05	6.80E+04
$\theta = 0$	(0.000)	(0.000)
AIC	13695.7	13286.3
SIC	13832.7	13940.1

Notes: p-values in parentheses; i. base category of upper secondary; ii. base category of town or small city.

This section has shown that different forms of HAP are likely to influence the impact of business growth and subsequently regional development. More generally, the work covered in this section and the two preceding it have shown that entrepreneurial endeavours at the individual level are affected by culture, personality, and the HAP they generate. Building on this, the following sections explore evidence at the regional level of links between HAP and activities associated with regional economic growth and competitiveness.

8.4 Human Agency Potential (HAP), Development, and Innovation

Chapter 7 explored the potential for culture and personality differences across regions to have an important influence on the degree of HAP present. It was found that measures capturing different facets of HAP varied not only across regions in Europe but in a persistent manner over decades. In Chapters 2 and 4 it was hypothesized that the HAP created would not only directly influence entrepreneurial and innovative actions, and therefore regional development, but further influence such development by providing the mechanism to alter formal institutions. Exploring this relationship is tricky, as the model acknowledges that HAP and HAA are both a consequence and influence on formal institutions in the longer term. To address this, measures of labour agency allow the relationship with economic development to be explored over a longer period of time, as the ESS includes items allowing their estimation back to 2008. As not all countries are included in each year, to allow the coverage to be as wide as possible we create a measure of labour agency based on the 2010 data, but use the 2008 figures where no 2010 measures are available for regions within a particular country. As explored in Chapter 7, this should have little negative effect, as the labour agency measures were found to be highly stable over time.

The economic development and activity measures include GDP per capita; disposable income per capita; the unemployment rate for the 20–64 years age group; R&D personnel as a percentage of the population; R&D expenditure per capita; and patent applications per million population. We examine the latest available data for these measures to see if a positive association exists between labour agency potential and the economic development measures. The exact years of data used for the analysis depend on the availability of data, as some surveys are conducted on a biennial rather than an annual basis. Table 8.5 presents the correlation coefficients.

The correlations show that, with the exception of unemployment, labour/entrepreneurial agency potential in 2008/10 is positively related to all measures of economic development/activity levels. Therefore, there is a positive link between labour/entrepreneurial agency potential and high levels of economic development, and the activities that lead to high-road competitiveness based on knowledge intensive activities (Malecki, 2017). This is consistent with the theory outlined in Chapter 2, indicating that human agency is a key element in understanding the divergent success of regions with regard to economic development. Those regions displaying higher labour/entrepreneurial agency potential are not only those that have enjoyed greater success in terms of economic development but, given the links to innovative activities, are also those that are likely to display greater competitiveness in terms of being able to maintain the standard of living of their population and attract new resources (Huggins et al., 2014b; Huggins and Thompson, 2017a; Martin and Sunley, 2017). They are also the regions with the capability to adapt to shocks, and therefore are likely to have higher levels of resilience (Martin, 2012). Care, however, needs to be taken when interpreting these results, and while those regions with higher labour/entrepreneurial agency potential are also those with higher competitiveness and resilience, causality may not run from HAP to economic development.

As argued in Chapter 2, it is expected that the formal institutions formed as a consequence of rates and forms of economic development within a region are expected to feed back into behaviour and the agency present in this region. This is consistent with Rodríguez-Pose's (2013) observation that the literature is far from in agreement as to whether culture and institutions are a cause or consequence of economic development. The time period

Table 8.5 Correlation coefficients for labour/entrepreneurial agency potential and economic development/human agency actualization (HAA) measures

	1. Labour/ entrepreneurial agency potential 2008/10	2.	3.	4.	5.	6.
2. GDP per capita 2016	0.598 (0.000)					
3. Disposable income per capita 2016	0.632 (0.000)	0.907 (0.000)				
4. Unemployment rate 2018	0.091 (0.363)	−0.328 (0.000)	−0.228 (0.020)			
5. R & D personnel 2015	0.564 (0.000)	0.750 (0.000)	0.649 (0.000)	−0.308 (0.003)		
6. R & D expenditure per capita 2015	0.600 (0.000)	0.854 (0.000)	0.821 (0.000)	−0.367 (0.000)	0.930 (0.000)	
7. Patents per capita 2015	0.508 (0.000)	0.747 (0.000)	0.657 (0.000)	−0.385 (0.000)	0.692 (0.000)	0.808 (0.000)

Note: p-values in parentheses.

examined here helps assure that higher labour/entrepreneurial agency potential is associated with higher economic development measures in the future, but to establish the causal link a longer period of time would be beneficial, and ideally with a set of instruments related to agency and not economic development.

When considering the impact on regional economic outcomes, there is also the issue of convergence (Barro and Sala-i-Martin, 1991; Breinlich et al., 2014), with a small improvement in the factors affecting economic development for less developed regions allowing them to catch up and converge with more successful regions. In Europe, however, there have not been small changes in relevant institutions over the last thirty years but, rather, extremely large ones, with the fall of communism and embracement of market institutions (Ekiert and Hanson, 2003), and access to and membership of the European Union, plus the regulatory institutions this brings with it (Carmin and VanDeveer, 2005). The end result is that regions with consistently high levels of human agency may have achieved higher levels of wealth and technological development, and generated the institutions to maintain these, but regions moving towards this position have been able to grow much more quickly. This means that, when exploring the relationship between human agency and improvements in measures of economic outcomes and activities, it is necessary to control for the initial position of the region. As noted above, there is a danger of multicollinearity, as this initial position is also likely to be a consequence of the agency present. Keeping these caveats in mind, the strong association between HAP and economic development and innovation helps provide more detail in relation to the mechanisms that explain the results of studies linking culture and personality to economic development (Rentfrow et al., 2013; Huggins et al., 2018).

8.5 Human Agency Potential (HAP) and Regional Entrepreneurial Development

Obtaining consistent measures of entrepreneurship for regions is problematic, and the presence of businesses per capita can be misleading as higher rates do not necessarily reflect a dynamic regional economy. In some cases, higher business ownership can reflect the presence of smaller, less growth-orientated, and potentially lifestyle businesses operating with limited competition (Henrekson and Sanandaji, 2014). The Global Entrepreneurship Monitor (GEM) project provides measures of entrepreneurship that are more closely associated with new venture creation (Reynolds et al., 2005). Studies exist that have examined regional differences in both entrepreneurial values and entrepreneurship rates using the GEM data (Bosma and Schutjens, 2009). One such project that has combined these measures along with data on the institutions present and environment is the Regional Entrepreneurship and Development Index (REDI) (Szerb et al., 2013).

One of the potential weaknesses of using GEM data to capture regional entrepreneurship is that sample sizes are often small and require data for a number of years to be combined. This is also the case with the REDI data used in this section, where GEM data from 2007 to 2011 is utilized to create the 2013 index and from 2012 to 2015 for the 2017 index. This limits the extent to which causality can be determined, as the HAP measures are contemporaneous with or in some cases lag the REDI measure. Nevertheless, the large literature that links entrepreneurship to regional economic development, such as that associated with the knowledge spillover theory of entrepreneurship (Audretsch and Keilbach, 2004; Audretsch and Lehmann, 2005; Acs et al., 2013) and those associated with resilience, particularly when considering more adaptive forms of resilience (Martin, 2012; Huggins and Thompson, 2015b), make it a worthwhile project to examine this relationship. A positive relationship between the REDI index and the HAP measures would be consistent with the model proposed in Chapter 2, whereby HAP would lead to HAA in the form of entrepreneurship that positively affects regional development, as well as acknowledging that such activities are likely to also involve feedback loops.

For the analysis we concentrate on the correlation coefficients reflecting the relationship between the REDI index and the three different measures of HAP, with Table 8.6 presenting the Pearson correlation coefficients for the REDI and HAP measures. For the REDI measures data are examined for both the 2013 and 2017 indices, with the full score (relating to the individual decision-making behaviour, and an institutional component relating to the context) and the individual score based only on the individual decision-making behaviour. This makes it possible to examine any contemporaneous relationships between the labour/entrepreneurial agency potential measures generated using the 2008 and 2010 ESS with REDI indices from 2013, and to assess whether a relationship exists between the labour/entrepreneurial agency potential with the REDI 2017 indices. We also examine the labour/entrepreneurial agency potential measures from 2014 to see if in the later period the REDI 2017 indices are related to this agentic potential. As no early political agency potential measures exist, only the 2014 and 2014/16 combined measures are used for this variable.

From the correlation coefficients it is clear that both entrepreneurial and wider regional development are strongly related to the labour/entrepreneurial and political agency potential measures. This persists when considering the overall REDI scores from the 2017 index. When examining the REDI index based on the entrepreneurial data, and excluding institutions, the positive and significant relationships remain, although the coefficients are generally a little smaller. The one exception is the finding that the combined 2008/10 labour/entrepreneurial agency potential measure is not related to the REDI individual entrepreneurship measure in 2017. It appears, therefore, that the labour/entrepreneurial agency potential measure is better at picking up the potential to support wider regional development than measures more tightly associated with new venture creation specifically. This is understandable given the wider definition of entrepreneurship that has so far been applied in this book.

8.6 Conclusions

This chapter has examined the link from culture, personality, and agency to those activities associated with regional economic development. Theoretically, it is suggested that particular cultures and personalities will encourage

Table 8.6 Pearson correlation coefficients for the regional entrepreneurship and development index (REDI) and human agency potential (HAP)

	1. REDI 2013	2	3	4	5	6	7	8
2. REDI individual 2013	0.527 (0.000)							
3. REDI 2017	0.812 (0.000)	0.514 (0.000)						
4. REDI individual 2017	0.482 (0.000)	0.532 (0.000)	0.696 (0.000)					
5. Labour/entrepreneurial agency potential 2008/10	0.591 (0.000)	0.398 (0.000)	0.536 (0.000)	0.059 (0.587)				
6. Labour/entrepreneurial agency potential 2014	0.447 (0.000)	0.408 (0.000)	0.531 (0.000)	0.318 (0.005)	0.739 (0.000)			
7. Labour/entrepreneurial agency potential 2014/16	0.408 (0.000)	0.437 (0.000)	0.457 (0.000)	0.297 (0.006)	0.730 (0.000)	0.818 (0.000)		
8. Political agency potential 2014	0.582 (0.000)	0.288 (0.012)	0.747 (0.000)	0.394 (0.000)	0.532 (0.000)	0.607 (0.000)	0.538 (0.000)	
9. Political agency potential 2014/16	0.553 (0.000)	0.178 (0.107)	0.688 (0.000)	0.435 (0.000)	0.400 (0.000)	0.416 (0.000)	0.461 (0.000)	0.852 (0.000)

Note: p-values in parentheses.

behaviours that lead to human agency promoting entrepreneurship and innovation. These activities are seen as key factors for cities and regions to achieve high-road competitiveness (Malecki, 2017). This means that the results found in this chapter are pertinent not just to the UK localities and European regions examined here but also to regions across the globe, such as those in China which have moved from relying on supplies of cheap labour for their competitiveness towards being knowledge-based economies in their own right (Huggins et al., 2014a).

The chapter has added to the results of a number of studies that have found culture (Hayton et al., 2002; Freytag and Thurik, 2007; Uhlaner and Thurik, 2007; Huggins and Thompson, 2015a, 2015c) and personality traits (Obschonka et al., 2013a, 2015; Fritsch et al., 2019) to be linked to self-employment and entrepreneurship more broadly. However, it has also been shown that individuals can be more or less encouraged by the prevailing regional culture within which they are embedded. In general, those that tend to have a better fit with the community culture in terms of their personality will enjoy a positive interaction, making self-employment more likely. Furthermore, the nature and type of entrepreneurship will vary between regions as different types of individual are drawn to entrepreneurship either through opportunity or necessity. At a regional scale it is shown that human agency potential is positively linked to a variety of economic development measures including those associated with entrepreneurship in terms of innovation. A positive correlation between measures of regional entrepreneurship and development and the human agency measures relating to labour/entrepreneurship and politics is also evident.

The chapter has found empirical evidence to support the theoretical relationships set out in Chapter 2. However, more work is needed in the future to delve more deeply into these relationships and to establish the direction of causality at play. If, as predicted in this book, no linear relationship holds, there is a need for novel approaches such as the use of historical instruments to capture the key constructs. Perfect examples of such measures are unlikely to exist for all constructs and will in many cases have the potential to reflect more than one construct, rendering their ability to separate out the different causal links weak at best. Instead, future projects will be needed to capture data on a regular longitudinal basis, with items developed to specially reflect the key constructs and to further distinguish them and limit the overlap.

Finally, this chapter has sought to draw the links between culture and personality through to economic development, with a focus on activities that will help to generate urban and regional development. It helps to provide an understanding of why particular regions are more successful in terms of development, and why some regions with similar resources have emerged as new growth centres while others struggle. Less has been said, however, about issues concerning the well-being of the people living and working in cities and regions (Storper, 1997; Huggins, 2003; Aiginger, 2006; Aiginger and Firgo, 2017; Huggins and Thompson, 2017a). In order for a region to achieve high-road competitiveness, it is not simply enough for this to emerge through knowledge-intensive, innovative, and entrepreneurial activities (Pike et al., 2007). To be considered successful, economic growth and regional competitiveness should lead to higher levels of well-being for the population, and the following chapter will look at these factors in more detail.

9

An Extended Behavioural Model of Economic Development

9.1 Introduction

The previous three chapters have outlined relationships illustrating how culture, personality psychology, and human agency can lead to different development paths. This chapter seeks to bring these relationships together and assesses the extent to which they collectively allow a more extended and nuanced behavioural model of urban and regional economic development to be established. We first return to considering what 'development' actually means and how outcomes can be measured. This reflects a move away from depending solely on traditional measures of urban and regional development based on Gross Domestic Product. Instead, the first section of the chapter investigates the outcomes for individuals in terms of their economic positions and also measures of broader satisfaction.

To bring together the theoretical and empirical insights from the preceding chapters, we then turn to refining and unpacking the behavioural model of urban and regional development presented in Chapter 2, and propositions are developed from the insights gained throughout this book and incorporated into the model. At this stage, we also recognize some of the limitations of the empirical analysis undertaken and, as with many studies of culture and institutions, imperfect data is one of the primary factors holding back this analysis. Our work is no different in being held back by such data issues and therefore we consider the form these data limitations take, and how these might be addressed from both an ideal and more practical manner in the future. The chapter concludes by summarizing the findings in preparation for the practical and policy implications of the book analysed in Chapter 10.

A Behavioural Theory of Economic Development: The Uneven Evolution of Cities and Regions. Robert Huggins and Piers Thompson, Oxford University Press (2021). © Robert Huggins and Piers Thompson.
DOI: 10.1093/OSO/9780198832348.003.0009

9.2 Agency and Outcomes

In Chapter 8 it was shown that there is a strong positive relationship between particular forms of HAP and economic growth, as well as those entrepreneurial and innovative endeavours that allow for urban and regional development using high-road methods (Malecki, 2017). Up to this point, however, we have not examined whether or not those displaying higher levels of HAP are experiencing higher levels of overall well-being. Existing evidence suggests there is a relationship between economic and social development, and, for example, find that more competitive cities and regions in the UK are likely to display higher levels of well-being, as captured by a variety of different measures (Huggins and Thompson, 2012). Others such as Layard (2006) highlight the issue of relativity with regard to well-being, with individuals comparing themselves to others as a means of assessing such well-being. This is important and consistent with theories such as prospect theory that incorporate 'reference points' into the utility function, with individuals viewing their utility as not being determined by absolute wealth but relative to comparator groups (Kahneman and Tversky, 1979; Campbell, 2006). This is further influenced by adaptation and habitation whereby individuals alter behaviour to match their circumstances, which yields similar utility to those in previous times as changed circumstances become the norm and the new reference point (Clark et al., 2008).

In terms of entrepreneurial endeavours, Hangleberger and Merz (2015) suggest that improvements in well-being associated with self-employment can be explained as being similar to those from job changes, with apparent benefits disappearing over time through adaptation. This has led to suggestions that higher marginal tax rates should be imposed to dissuade self-defeating efforts linked to socially competitive consumption (Layard, 2005; Hirschauer et al., 2015). The implication of this is that those who feel a greater level of HAP may in fact display lower levels of subjective well-being as they strive to achieve more and acquire greater wealth. Instead, those who feel unable to make a difference and accept their position will compare themselves to a lower reference point, and therefore may enjoy a higher level of well-being. Clearly, this has multiple implications with regard to the development of cities and regions.

An alternative perspective is also available from the happiness and well-being literature, whereby this stream of work highlights the benefits of work itself and not just the financial rewards associated with it (Dow and Juster, 1985; Juster, 1985). This is consistent with findings indicating that while individual well-being appears to rapidly adjust to changes in life circumstances, such as divorce, bereavement, injury, and illness (Clark et al., 2008; Oswald and Powdthavee, 2008), unemployment appears to have a longer-run negative affect on the well-being of individuals (Clark and Oswald, 1994; Frey and Stutzer, 2000; Clark et al., 2008). In this respect, those with higher levels of HAP may feel they are better able to achieve higher levels in the hierarchy of needs (Maslow, 1943). Furthermore, being able to control their life, as well as their work, may lead to higher satisfaction with life or particular aspects of it.

In order to investigate this we use the 2016 data from the ESS to examine whether or not those with higher political, environmental, and labour/entre-preneurial agency potential display better self-reported outcomes. As noted above, outcomes could be financial as well as those associated with broader measures of well-being. We break these down into two groups: in the first group we consider financial position and satisfaction with different aspects of life; and in the second group measures of associated broader well-being and social relations. It should be noted that absolute household income levels will not necessarily provide an indication of financial satisfaction, as pros-pect theory suggests that the extent to which this is perceived to be a gain or loss depends on the reference point to which it is being compared (Kahneman and Tversky, 1979).

Reference points can be based on: past experience (Easterlin, 2005), out-comes for other individuals (Ferrer-i-Carbonell, 2005), outcomes for those with similar positions or backgrounds (van de Stadt et al., 1985; Senik, 2008), or individual expectations (Abeler et al., 2011). This reference point will differ for each individual, and so we measure financial outcomes using the following item: which of the descriptions on this card comes closest to how you feel about your household's income nowadays? Linked to this individual financial outcome, the second measure considered is based on an individual's satisfaction with the economy as a whole. Again, this is not an objective measure but subjective, and is based on the individual's perception of the economy from their perspective: on the whole how satisfied are you with the present state of the economy in your country? As outlined above, it is not clear whether or not HAP will be positively or negatively associated with these measures. The issue is that HAP could allow individuals to improve their financial position and exploit the opportunities available within the economy more successfully, but it may also raise the reference point with which outcomes are being compared.

Similar issues are frequently found when considering the impact of educa-tion. Outcomes are improved both in terms of pecuniary rewards and other factors such as job fit (Ilies et al., 2019), but so are aspirations (Clark et al., 2015). Well-being may only be improved when outcomes are better for an individual than others, described as the relative mechanism (Campbell, 2006). Our expectation is that labour/entrepreneurial agency potential will be most strongly related to these forms of outcomes, with there being an expectation that labour/entrepreneurial agency potential would position an individual to most effectively change their economic position. Environmental agency potential may have the weakest relationship with economic outcomes (Paço and Lavrador, 2017).

Moving beyond direct financial and economic items, we now consider related institutional issues concerning satisfaction with government and democracy, with two questions covered: now thinking about the [national] government, how satisfied are you with the way it is doing its job?; and on the whole, how satisfied are you with the way democracy works in [your country]? In general, it might be expected that those with more political agency potential will be more satisfied with the democratic system, as they may believe it operates in a manner that allows them to intentionally cause change. In some regards, it should not matter whether this is direct agency or proxy agency (Bandura, 2001), as both should be captured by the political agency potential measure.

As well as these measures of more specific outcomes, we also consider four measures that capture broader well-being. These are: (1) how often do you meet socially with friends, relatives or work colleagues?; (2) compared to other people of your age, how often would you say you take part in social activities?; (3) how is your health in general?; and (4) all things considered, how satisfied are you with your life as a whole nowadays? As these measures of economic, political and social satisfaction are likely to be affected by a wide range of factors beyond HAP, we adopt a multivariate analysis approach. Given the ordinal nature of the dependent variables, these are analysed using ordered logit regressions, and this allows the thresholds between categories to be unequal. Although the HAP measures are correlated, this is far from perfect, and there is also sufficient evidence from the factor analysis to observe that they are capturing distinct types of agency. Therefore, we allow all three measures of HAP to enter the regressions simultaneously.

We control for three sets of characteristics: personal and household; home and work environment; and regional. The first set of characteristics, relating to the individual's personal and household characteristics, includes controls for gender, minority-group membership (immigration status and ethnic minority membership), human capital (age and educational qualifications), socio-economic position (household income), and family composition (dependent children and living with partner).

Studies have regularly found that men and women value different outcomes, with men often placing a greater importance on financial success

(Schwartz and Rubel, 2005; Ferriman et al., 2009). There are also differences in the sources of support used (Strong et al., 2019). This may mean that men generally have lower satisfaction with financial and economic outcome measures, but this must be set against any discrimination (perceived or actual) that inhibits women's professional progression and leads to unequal pay (Buttrick et al., 2017; Batz and Tay, 2018). However, it should be noted that at the societal level some recent studies have suggested that inequality does not necessarily reduce well-being (Kelley and Evans, 2017). Similarly, those from an ethnic-minority or immigrant background may also face discrimination (Dion, 2002; Verkuyten, 2008; Thompson et al., 2010). Immigrants, in particular, may have quite different priorities and measures of success, especially when seeking to repatriate funds to family in their home country (Harris et al., 2013). Their well-being may also be affected by the host country's culture (Geeraert et al., 2019).

As noted above, education does not necessarily have a positive theoretical relationship with well-being (Desjardins, 2008). This is due to human capital offering better opportunities for employment raising rewards but also raising aspirations, with such effects tending to be the strongest for formal qualifications (Michalos, 2008). Previous studies suggest that education has a positive, but relatively small, influence on subjective well-being (Witter et al., 1984). Age is used to capture general experience, which may have a weaker influence of a kind similar to education. However, it also captures the balance between acquired experience, which can be 'invested in' over time, but also reduces the period in which to receive any return on the investment (Kim, 2007). This is reflected in the changing priorities and values of individuals throughout their lifetimes (Borg et al., 2017).

Financial prosperity is captured in terms of the household income decile of the respondent, and occupational status is included to reflect the potential for well-being measures being boosted by the act of working, as well as the income derived from it (Dow and Juster, 1985; Juster, 1985). This measure is expected to be positively related to all outcomes, but most strongly to financial or economic success. Family characteristics such as dependent children and living with a partner may be expected to boost well-being, but as discussed above, studies have often found adaptation and habituation effects lead to these often being relatively short-term (Clark et al., 2008; Doré and Bolger, 2018).

The second group of variables includes measures to capture the local area in terms of urbanity and the work environment. Respondents indicate which of the following best describe where they live: big city, suburbs of a large urban area, town or small city, country village, farm or home in the countryside. The controls account for the different cultural influences found from self-selecting migration (Rentfrow et al., 2008). The work environment is represented by the size of the business that respondents work or worked within, in terms of employees. This could have important implications for economic outcomes, whereby the balance between financial rewards and promotion, and the repetitive nature of activities and autonomy, are likely to vary considerably (Stuetzer et al., 2016; Obschonka et al., 2018). As noted above, there are also contestations concerning the impact of the autonomy of business ownership on overall well-being (Johansson Sevä et al., 2016; Patel et al., 2019; Wiklund et al., 2019), which may influence the institutional conditions present (Annink et al., 2016; Fritsch et al., 2019). It is also likely that employment in different-sized businesses and positions will affect the comparator group and ambitions (Fanta, 2015).

Analysing first the economic, financial, and democracy regressions, Table 9.1 shows that the deviation explained for each of the outcomes varies from 4.9 per cent for the satisfaction with government and democracy measures to 24.1 per cent for the relative perceptions of household income. All regressions outperform the null of constant probability at the 1 per cent level. Regardless of the outcome measure, the estimated coefficients for all three of the HAP measures are positive. These are mostly significant at the 1 per cent level, with the exception of environmental agency potential in the regressions for perceptions of household income, and labour/entrepreneurial agency potential for satisfaction with democracy. In the case of the former, it is understandable that for a purely financial/economic outcome, environmental agency potential cannot be expected to be related. It is interesting, however, that those with higher labour/entrepreneurial agency potential do not have higher levels of satisfaction with democracy, which suggests that these spheres of life and agency are relatively distinct.

In terms of perceptions of household income, labour/entrepreneurial agency has the strongest effect, and the marginal effects indicate that a 1 per cent change in labour/entrepreneurial agency potential is associated with a 0.002 per cent change in the latent perception of the household income variable compared to 0.001 per cent for political agency potential. This implies that those who consider they have more control over their work and working environment are those achieving a higher economic outcome. This indicates that, at a minimum, generating greater belief in being able to work in an autonomous and influential manner boosts financial well-being.

Interestingly, although labour/entrepreneurial agency potential remains a positive and significant influence on satisfaction with the economy, control over work does not necessarily have the greatest impact on satisfaction with the overall economy. The marginal effect of labour/entrepreneurial agency

Table 9.1 Ordered logit regressions of economic, financial, and political outcomes

	Perception of income	Satisfaction with economy	Satisfaction with democracy	Satisfaction with government
Political agency potential	0.1420 (0.000)	0.332 (0.000)	0.4256 (0.000)	0.421 (0.000)
Environmental agency potential	0.0248 (0.078)	0.175 (0.000)	0.1930 (0.000)	0.204 (0.000)
Labour/ entrepreneurial agency potential	0.1788 (0.000)	0.093 (0.000)	0.0082 (0.586)	0.064 (0.000)
Male	−0.0470 (0.077)	0.146 (0.000)	−0.0588 (0.023)	−0.020 (0.384)
Immigrant	−0.3027 (0.000)	0.372 (0.000)	0.3340 (0.000)	0.437 (0.000)
Ethnic minority	−0.3069 (0.000)	−0.192 (0.001)	−0.2679 (0.000)	−0.051 (0.353)
Age	0.0049 (0.000)	0.000 (0.924)	0.0009 (0.417)	0.003 (0.001)
Age^2	0.0697 (0.000)	0.037 (0.000)	0.0370 (0.000)	0.049 (0.000)
Education[i]				
Less than lower secondary	−0.4395 (0.000)	0.071 (0.175)	−0.0229 (0.690)	0.203 (0.000)
Lower secondary	−0.2994 (0.000)	−0.074 (0.063)	−0.0296 (0.502)	0.092 (0.021)
Lower–tier upper secondary	−0.1001 (0.027)	−0.040 (0.310)	−0.0272 (0.533)	0.046 (0.237)
Advanced vocational	−0.0596 (0.187)	−0.005 (0.904)	0.0189 (0.668)	0.008 (0.837)
Lower–tertiary education	0.1716 (0.000)	0.092 (0.024)	0.1124 (0.018)	0.032 (0.428)
Higher–tertiary education	0.3409 (0.000)	0.002 (0.963)	0.0877 (0.063)	−0.073 (0.071)
Occupational status[ii]				
Education	0.0179 (0.820)	0.013 (0.843)	0.1427 (0.067)	0.004 (0.954)
Unemployed	−1.3192 (0.000)	−0.427 (0.000)	−0.1761 (0.012)	−0.228 (0.000)
Economically inactive	−0.8491 (0.000)	−0.061 (0.556)	−0.2223 (0.049)	−0.160 (0.124)
Sick or disabled	−1.1398 (0.000)	−0.531 (0.000)	−0.4676 (0.000)	−0.394 (0.000)
Retired	−0.0878 (0.075)	0.073 (0.084)	0.0646 (0.177)	0.090 (0.033)

Continued

Table 9.1 *Continued*

	Perception of income	Satisfaction with economy	Satisfaction with democracy	Satisfaction with government
Homeworker	−0.2166 (0.000)	−0.052 (0.306)	−0.0314 (0.577)	0.004 (0.930)
Community service	−0.5238 (0.000)	−0.147 (0.229)	−0.3273 (0.019)	−0.140 (0.241)
Household income[iii]				
Household income 1st decile	−2.1995 (0.000)	−0.291 (0.000)	−0.2571 (0.000)	−0.216 (0.000)
Household income 2nd decile	−1.3185 (0.000)	−0.156 (0.002)	−0.0998 (0.070)	−0.048 (0.335)
Household income 3rd decile	−0.7228 (0.000)	−0.077 (0.104)	−0.0830 (0.117)	−0.047 (0.317)
Household income 4th decile	−0.3419 (0.000)	−0.071 (0.120)	−0.0589 (0.250)	−0.050 (0.268)
Household income 6th decile	0.3961 (0.000)	0.055 (0.227)	0.1559 (0.003)	0.012 (0.791)
Household income 7th decile	0.7577 (0.000)	0.160 (0.000)	0.1335 (0.011)	0.107 (0.019)
Household income 8th decile	1.1187 (0.000)	0.241 (0.000)	0.0937 (0.081)	0.076 (0.100)
Household income 9th decile	1.5803 (0.000)	0.314 (0.000)	0.2379 (0.000)	0.161 (0.001)
Household income 10th decile	2.3385 (0.000)	0.391 (0.000)	0.1837 (0.003)	0.196 (0.000)
Dependent children	−0.5978 (0.000)	−0.023 (0.369)	−0.0239 (0.421)	−0.003 (0.919)
Live with partner	−0.0269 (0.393)	0.048 (0.076)	0.0029 (0.923)	0.031 (0.254)
Urban/rural location[iv]				
Big city	−0.0842 (0.030)	−0.025 (0.445)	0.0198 (0.603)	−0.047 (0.154)
Suburbs	−0.0270 (0.552)	−0.044 (0.240)	0.0411 (0.348)	−0.012 (0.746)
Country village	0.0363 (0.273)	−0.008 (0.782)	−0.0167 (0.602)	0.031 (0.271)
Farm or hamlet	0.1261 (0.023)	−0.039 (0.398)	−0.0280 (0.605)	−0.056 (0.233)
Employer size[v]				
Under 10 employees	−0.0309 (0.394)	−0.090 (0.003)	−0.0255 (0.470)	−0.065 (0.035)
10 to 24 employees	0.0361 (0.356)	−0.027 (0.425)	−0.0006 (0.988)	−0.004 (0.898)
100 to 499 employees	−0.0164 (0.691)	0.001 (0.981)	−0.0159 (0.692)	−0.015 (0.657)

500 or more employees	0.1072 (0.024)	−0.053 (0.180)	−0.0421 (0.356)	−0.140 (0.000)
Threshold 1	−5.000	−3.871	−3.049	−2.571
Threshold 2	−2.810	−3.318	−2.483	−1.995
Threshold 3	0.425	−2.492	−1.740	−1.265
Threshold 4		−1.676	−1.014	−0.538
Threshold 5		−0.977	−0.383	0.066
Threshold 6		−0.104	0.566	0.894
Threshold 7		0.755	1.504	1.726
Threshold 8		1.971		2.856
Threshold 9		3.468		4.322
Threshold 10		4.600		5.416
N	27,150	26,994	20,985	26,886
LR-test	14559.8	9453.4	3986.6	5854.0
	[124]	[124]	[124]	[124]
	(0.000)	(0.000)	(0.000)	(0.000)
R^2	0.241	0.080	0.049	0.049

Notes: p-values in parentheses; i. base category of upper secondary; ii. base category of in employment; iii. base category of 5th decile; iv. base category of town or small city; v. base category of 25 to 99 employees.

potential indicates that a 1 per cent increase will boost satisfaction with the economy by 0.002 per cent, which is less than a third of the 0.008 per cent increase from political agency potential. This is consistent with arguments stating that only a very small minority of engineers, scientists, and entrepreneurs have sufficient agency to change the economy as a whole (Zucker et al., 1998; Moretti, 2012).

Satisfaction with democracy and government follows similar patterns in the sense that political agency potential is most strongly associated with positive outcomes. The marginal effects are similar, with a 1 per cent increase in political agency potential associated with a 0.02 per cent improvement in satisfaction with government and democracy. It appears that HAP has the larger effect when considering the outcomes associated with government and democracy than economic outcomes. In both cases environmental agency potential has the second largest effect, although less than half the size of that for political agency potential. One possible explanation is that in these spheres proxy and/or collective agency are more likely to be involved, which may make the expected change much larger (Bandura, 2001). For economic outcomes, direct agency or small-scale collective agency are likely to be the key levers of change (Coe and Jordhus-Lier, 2011; Coe, 2013).

With regard to controls, it appears that human capital, regardless of whether this is from experience or formal education, is positively associated with all outcomes. This means that although aspirations may rise, the opportunities available are increasing at a faster rate, producing an overall positive effect (Witter et al., 1984). Similarly, household income is positively associated with all outcomes. However, care should be taken as income is being measured in relative terms by being recorded as the percentile the individual is located in rather than the absolute level of income. Therefore, the positive results do not rule out the possibility that rising levels of income through time would have no impact on outcomes (Easterlin, 1974, 1995; Layard, 2006). Consistent with Juster (1985) and Dow and Juster's (1985) findings that employment brings its own reward beyond the income earned, better outcomes are found for those in employment than those in a majority of other occupational categories. The exception to this is for those in retirement, who show some evidence of being more satisfied with government. The presence of dependent children, although not significant for most regressions, tends to have a negative impact on outcomes. This becomes significant in the perception of household income regression, whereby dependent children will naturally increase strain.

Belonging to an ethnic minority reduces perceptions of household income, and satisfaction with the economy and democracy. Therefore, it seems possible that those belonging to these groups feel excluded from mainstream institutions and the benefits they bring (Simonsen, 2016). However, those who have entered the country as immigrants show a much more mixed relationship with the outcomes. Although household income perceptions are lower, immigrants are more satisfied with the economy, democracy, and government. This may reflect limited access to the labour market, holding back financial returns (Pitt et al., 2015), but satisfaction is higher due to comparisons with their home country (Bak-Klimek et al., 2015) or future hopes, especially those for their children (Pitt et al., 2015). Gender also produces inconsistent results, with a significantly positive effect from being male on satisfaction with the economy, but the opposite with regards to democracy. In the case of the former, this could reflect access to opportunities being more restricted or perceived to be more restricted for women, even the more highly educated (Manning and Swaffield, 2008; Kwong et al., 2012; Vuorinen-Lampila, 2016). There is no obvious explanation as to why men would be less satisfied with democracy than their female counterparts. In terms of the environmental controls, rural or urban nature of residence, and size of business, there is no clear pattern evident.

Turning to the wider measures of satisfaction with life (Table 9.2), the deviation explained varies from 3.4 per cent for the relative extent an individual meets friends and others socially to 12.4 per cent for subjective assessments

Table 9.2 Ordered logit regressions of social outcomes, health, and well-being

	Socially meet friends	Relative social activity	Subjective health	Life satisfaction
Political agency potential	0.1708 (0.000)	0.2550 (0.000)	0.1263 (0.000)	0.1316 (0.000)
Environmental agency potential	0.0307 (0.012)	0.0528 (0.000)	0.0341 (0.008)	0.1391 (0.000)
Labour/entrepreneurial agency potential	0.1134 (0.000)	0.1577 (0.000)	0.0665 (0.000)	0.1884 (0.000)
Male	−0.0984 (0.000)	−0.0909 (0.000)	0.0545 (0.025)	−0.1335 (0.000)
Immigrant	−0.1862 (0.000)	−0.1366 (0.002)	−0.0169 (0.701)	−0.0408 (0.325)
Ethnic minority	−0.0945 (0.089)	0.1058 (0.069)	−0.2074 (0.000)	−0.1987 (0.000)
Age	−0.0210 (0.000)	0.0000 (0.983)	−0.0340 (0.000)	−0.0044 (0.000)
Age^2	0.0316 (0.000)	0.0153 (0.001)	0.0163 (0.001)	0.0605 (0.000)
Education[i]				
Less than lower secondary	0.0405 (0.461)	−0.2817 (0.000)	−0.3794 (0.000)	−0.0310 (0.566)
Lower secondary	−0.0752 (0.065)	−0.1408 (0.001)	−0.2778 (0.000)	−0.0446 (0.266)
Lower−tier upper secondary	−0.0321 (0.415)	0.0089 (0.828)	−0.1455 (0.001)	0.0422 (0.282)
Advanced vocational	−0.0412 (0.293)	−0.0201 (0.626)	−0.0032 (0.939)	0.0214 (0.580)
Lower−tertiary education	−0.0256 (0.536)	0.0196 (0.653)	0.1850 (0.000)	0.0154 (0.704)
Higher−tertiary education	−0.1151 (0.005)	−0.0418 (0.331)	0.2254 (0.000)	−0.0210 (0.600)
Occupational status[ii]				
Education	0.3190 (0.000)	0.1720 (0.012)	−0.1730 (0.015)	−0.0781 (0.229)
Unemployed	−0.0291 (0.653)	−0.0796 (0.231)	−0.2867 (0.000)	−0.8066 (0.000)
Economically inactive	0.1358 (0.215)	−0.3622 (0.001)	−0.5955 (0.000)	−0.5419 (0.000)
Sick or disabled	−0.0995 (0.177)	−0.8228 (0.000)	−2.7966 (0.000)	−0.9509 (0.000)
Retired	0.1828 (0.000)	−0.0145 (0.749)	−0.3551 (0.000)	0.0833 (0.052)
Homeworker	0.0914 (0.078)	−0.2531 (0.000)	−0.1763 (0.001)	0.0619 (0.231)

Continued

Table 9.2 *Continued*

	Socially meet friends	Relative social activity	Subjective health	Life satisfaction
Community service	0.0625 (0.614)	0.1802 (0.166)	−0.4964 (0.000)	0.0027 (0.983)
Household income[iii]				
Household income 1st decile	−0.1673 (0.002)	−0.5115 (0.000)	−0.5302 (0.000)	−0.5500 (0.000)
Household income 2nd decile	−0.1029 (0.040)	−0.2546 (0.000)	−0.3400 (0.000)	−0.3016 (0.000)
Household income 3rd decile	−0.0766 (0.108)	−0.1792 (0.000)	−0.2299 (0.000)	−0.2278 (0.000)
Household income 4th decile	−0.0816 (0.076)	−0.2028 (0.000)	−0.0804 (0.099)	−0.0780 (0.091)
Household income 6th decile	0.0239 (0.604)	0.0052 (0.914)	0.0255 (0.602)	0.0899 (0.049)
Household income 7th decile	0.1078 (0.019)	0.0324 (0.502)	0.0982 (0.046)	0.2261 (0.000)
Household income 8th decile	0.0738 (0.116)	0.0525 (0.284)	0.1932 (0.000)	0.3080 (0.000)
Household income 9th decile	0.2345 (0.000)	0.1744 (0.001)	0.2557 (0.000)	0.4270 (0.000)
Household income 10th decile	0.3050 (0.000)	0.1844 (0.001)	0.3729 (0.000)	0.6111 (0.000)
Dependent children	−0.1684 (0.000)	−0.1947 (0.000)	−0.0965 (0.001)	−0.0479 (0.067)
Live with partner	−0.4403 (0.000)	−0.0401 (0.160)	0.0350 (0.226)	0.3347 (0.000)
Urban/rural location[iv]				
Big city	−0.1173 (0.000)	0.0130 (0.712)	−0.0138 (0.697)	−0.0664 (0.044)
Suburbs	−0.0906 (0.018)	0.0371 (0.356)	−0.0591 (0.149)	−0.0473 (0.211)
Country village	0.0217 (0.450)	0.0152 (0.611)	0.0651 (0.032)	0.0542 (0.056)
Farm or hamlet	−0.0030 (0.950)	−0.2031 (0.000)	0.1117 (0.026)	0.1869 (0.000)
Employer size[v]				
Under 10 employees	−0.0328 (0.296)	−0.1613 (0.000)	0.0311 (0.350)	−0.0747 (0.016)
10 to 24 employees	−0.0355 (0.295)	−0.0295 (0.403)	−0.0045 (0.899)	−0.0251 (0.452)
100 to 499 employees	−0.0389 (0.271)	−0.0534 (0.150)	0.0108 (0.774)	−0.0256 (0.464)

500 or more employees	−0.0625	−0.0619	0.0575	0.0910
	(0.116)	(0.137)	(0.176)	(0.021)
Threshold 1	−5.375	−3.119	−5.980	−5.527
Threshold 2	−3.140	−1.242	−3.909	−4.985
Threshold 3	−2.126	1.016	−1.587	−4.197
Threshold 4	−0.901	3.150	0.813	−3.406
Threshold 5	−0.009			−2.825
Threshold 6	1.727			−1.940
Threshold 7				−1.345
Threshold 8				−0.378
Threshold 9				0.999
Threshold 10				2.283
N	27,148	26,977	27,167	27,138
LR–test	6140.62	2361.83	8507.71	6242.2
	[124]	[124]	[124]	[124]
	(0.000)	(0.000)	(0.000)	(0.000)
R^2	0.065	0.034	0.124	0.058

Notes: p-values in parentheses; i. base category of upper secondary; ii. base category of in employment; iii. base category of 5th decile; iv. base category of town or small city; v. base category of 25 to 99 employees.

of general health. As before, the null of constant probability can be rejected for all the regressions at the 1 per cent level. As with the economic and democratic outcomes, the regressions indicate that HAP of all types is positively and significantly related to social and wider well-being outcomes, this time without exception. In cases where differences exist, it is in terms of the strength of the relationships. Across all outcomes, environmental agency potential is not the most influential measure, and while concerns about the environment and the future of the planet often appear in the press and media, the ability to make a difference is not as important as HAP in different areas. Clearly, pollution will have health impacts that affect overall well-being (Pearce et al., 2010), and our findings reflect the difficulties national and regional governments have in trying to encourage activities and promote policies to improve the environment (Chekima et al., 2016; Leonidou et al., 2016; Signoretta et al., 2019).

For both measures of social interaction and subjective health outcomes, political agency potential has the strongest association. The marginal effects indicate that a 1 per cent increase in political agency potential will raise social meetings by 0.001 per cent, relative social interaction by 0.02 per cent, and subjective health by 0.001 per cent. This indicates that the effects are relatively small, but in all cases the effect is twice that of labour/

entrepreneurial agency potential. This reflects the fact that, although labour/entrepreneurial agency potential provides flexibility within the work sphere, this is not always used to access wider social outcomes but, rather, to achieve the economic outcomes examined in Table 9.1 above.

The exception to the above results relates to satisfaction with life overall. Although social interaction may be aided by financial rewards from work and flexibility at work, the two spheres seem to be regarded in isolation. However, financial and professional success and esteem will be incorporated into the overall satisfaction for individuals. To an extent, this may result in a zero-sum game, with competitive consumption lowering the well-being of others, although with habituation this may be only temporary (Layard, 2005, 2006; Clark, 2017). It is also possible that freedom, influence, and autonomy at work or acting as entrepreneurs may raise overall well-being (Hausser et al., 2010; Stephan, 2018). Gains of this kind may also only be temporary (Hangleberger and Merz, 2015), but may still explain why labour/entrepreneurial agency potential has the largest impact on overall life satisfaction. The marginal effect sees a 1 per cent increase in labour/entrepreneurial agency potential raising overall well-being by 0.001 per cent; although small, this is half as large again as the effect of political agency potential.

In terms of the other variables, gender varies in terms of the direction of effect depending on the outcome under consideration. For most measures women achieve higher outcomes, the exception being health. Immigrants and those from ethnic minorities indicate that they socialize less than others, which may be partly explained by the financial constraints and deprivation that are associated with lower social acceptance (Zhang et al., 2019). This is consistent with higher household income raising all measures of well-being. Age displays a U-shaped relationship with some measures, indicating that both the young and the old (and particularly the retired) tend to have more time for socializing and achieving higher levels of overall life satisfaction. For those in middle age, work objectives may divert time and resources; similarly, this group will also experience the impact of dependent children. This group are also more likely to be married or live with their partner, which reduces socializing frequency but raises overall life satisfaction. As may be expected, the linear element of the age relationship for general health is larger and more negative. The other element of human capital, formal qualifications, does not display any clear association with well-being. This perhaps reflects the 'connoisseur effect', whereby higher levels of education can lead to lower satisfaction from knowledge (Michalos and Orlando, 2006).

9.3 Extending the Behavioural Model of Urban and Regional Development

Throughout this book the aim has been to understand how behavioural factors can be incorporated into models of urban and regional development in order to better understand how some cities and regions prosper while others continue to lag behind. Building on the work of others, we have developed a behavioural framework of urban and regional economic development, which was outlined in Chapter 2. This argues that community culture at the group level and personality traits at the individual level combine to create local psychocultural profiles, as presented in Chapter 3. These profiles are related to either encouraging or discouraging certain behaviour, so that particular spatial patterns of behavioural intentions form. Whether or not these intentions become actual behaviour will be influenced, at least in part, by urban and regional institutional filters, whereby some of these behaviours facilitate human agency impacting upon urban and regional development (Chapter 4).

The difficulty in testing the sequence of behavioural influences on development is related to feedbacks from such social and economic development to the institutional filter, the community culture, and personality traits present (Chapter 5). The empirical chapters of this book have provided evidence of the links at each stage but cannot confirm completely the model due to its endogenous nature and data limitations. In addition, and of importance for future work, the empirical analysis has indicated that, while the basic premise for the behavioural model of urban and regional development can be supported, there are further complexities that need to be taken into account, and we seek to address some of these below.

First, we have shown that, consistent with studies such as those by Rentfrow et al. (2013) and Huggins et al. (2018), community culture and personality are closely linked. This leads to the development of differing psychocultural profiles driven by a wide range of mechanisms examined in Rentfrow et al. (2008) and expanded in Chapter 6. Theoretically, all of the mechanisms presented appear plausible, and it would not be unreasonable to take all into account, but with regard to policy development it is rarely appropriate to simply establish those factors having an effect. Clearly, policymakers are constrained by limited resources and (should) target multiple outcomes (Pike et al., 2007), as will be discussed below. For effective policy to be developed, policymakers need to know where their policies can make a difference, the size of the difference caused by the intervention made, and the consequences of such a change. For example, in theory it would be possible to increase or decrease interregional migration through support in meeting resettlement costs or increasing taxes on housing associated with moves of this type. This could speed or slow down the process of psychocultural profile creation and reinforcement. However, this could have wider ramifications, such as pressures on services and rising costs for existing residents.

All of this may still be ineffectual if the social norms provided by the prevailing community culture lessen the impact of inward migration; and, for example, with regard to 'creative class' migrants it is hard to establish the direction of causality (Florida, 2002; Florida et al., 2010). This means that the extent to which the creative class can change a resistant community culture is harder to determine, which is important, as the retention of mobile individuals will be partly based on such characteristics (Mellander et al., 2011). In other studies it has been found that individuals with higher levels of openness and lower agreeability are more likely to migrate (Jokela, 2009), and in Chapter 6 we have shown that regions high in a particular psychocultural profile—diverse extraversion—display both the strongest patterns of inward and outward migration. It was also shown that migration tends to be greatest with regard to flows to other regions with similar psychocultural profiles. This is consistent with the findings of studies such as Jokela et al. (2015), which suggest that fit between individual and place-based personality characteristics are important for well-being.

More generally, such migration trends are likely to strengthen the global pipelines between such diverse and extravert regions, as indicated in Chapter 5 (Bathelt et al., 2004), but up to this point the behavioural model of urban and regional development has not explicitly recognized the role that interregional networks play, despite a considerable literature indicating the importance of such networks for both firms and individuals (Huggins and Prokop, 2017), and regions as a whole (Huggins and Thompson, 2014). This suggests the first proposition of an extended behavioural model:

Proposition 9.1
Intraregional migration will provide networks that connect regions in terms of knowledge, culture, and social outcomes.

This leads to further consideration of the role selective migration and psychocultural fit play in the evolution or perpetuation and reproduction of psychocultural profiles. Following the view of those claiming that personality is not necessarily fixed (Srivastava et al., 2003; Roberts and Mroczek, 2008; Wrzus and Roberts, 2017), and that the social norms of community culture can influence personality trait formation (Rentfrow et al., 2008), the confluence of these factors has potentially profound implications for regional psychocultural profiles. For example, if a relatively large group of individuals with particular personality traits are attracted to a particular city or region by incentives, the cultural change they could create would potentially have an immediate effect on wider regional society (Stoerring and Dalum, 2007; Thompson and Zang, 2018). Furthermore, empirical investigation has found significant links between psychocultural profiles and values, as derived from Welzel's (2013) work. The implication of this is that the formation of values should be added to the model as an outcome of the interaction of community culture and personality, which then influences behavioural intentions.

Proposition 9.2
Psychocultural profiles will promote or lessen the formation of particular values within regions.

Moving on from the psychocultural profile of a city or region, we have focused on the role of human agency within the model, which has been treated in different ways by different scholars. For some, there is the perspective that agency relates to the capability to take actions that will lead to change (Scott and Marshall, 1998; Biesta and Tedder, 2006); for others it is the intentional undertaking of these actions that constitutes agency (Castree, 2007). Within this study, we have acknowledged that both are important elements of the behavioural model of regional development. The capability we define as human agency potential (HAP) is developed from the psychological concept of behaviour potential (Rotter, 1954, 1960), reflecting the adaptive and dynamic potential of the economy. The extent to which HAP forms will depend on the actions taken by individuals to upgrade their skills, confidence, and broader self-efficacy. Whether or not such activities and ambitions are undertaken will depend upon the values promoted or constrained by the psychocultural profile in the region.

Proposition 9.3
Values and beliefs will promote or constrain the development of human agency potential (HAP).

The adaptation and flexibility created by HAP makes it highly significant for both the competitiveness and resilience of an urban or regional economy (Martin and Sunley, 2017). HAP is based on a perceived ability or self-efficacy to interact and ultimately undertake actions in an intentional fashion to achieve an individual's desired objectives. This opens up different directions for urban and regional development, economic or otherwise. It allows for the possibility that a relatively small number of key individuals within a city or region can drive its development. It also reflects the more day-to-day changes that a wider group of the population will make to reinforce and strengthen such moves.

Proposition 9.4
HAP provides the possibility of taking action in an intentional fashion to lead to change in order to achieve desired objectives.

Clearly, certain spheres of life and development paths that are opened up will not appear uniformly across all regions. In Chapters 4, 6, and 7 we argued that psychocultural profiles will not lead to all regions seeking development in the same fashion, and similarly the values created and actions taken to allow these to be fulfilled will not be identical. In Chapter 7 three separate measures of HAP were developed: political, environmental, and labour/entrepreneurial. Although it was shown that the geographical distribution of these measures of HAP is positively correlated, the correlation is far from perfect. This means that while HAP allows for a wider number of development paths to be followed, the precise set of development paths will depend on the nature of the HAP formed, which stems from the set of values found in a region.

Proposition 9.5
The forms taken by HAP will depend upon the values associated with the psychocultural profile of the region.

As noted above, both the capability and actual action taken are important, and we describe the latter as human agency actualization (HAA), which cannot take place without HAP, but does not necessarily occur if HAP is present. In this case, not all action is agency (Castree, 2007), and the same actions could take place and have the same impact; but, as Bandura (2001) indicates, for it to be HAA it has to be intentional. This requires the confidence of being able to take such action as manifested by HAP. The reason for HAP not always leading to HAA can reflect the impact of constraining institutions or external conditions that do not allow the opportunity or desire to make a specific change at a given moment in time (Wink et al., 2017). Therefore, the prevailing institutional constraints will influence HAP, but it may not be until individuals seek to take action that the true strength of these constraints becomes apparent. Also, the nature of HAP is important in determining the available options for HAA, but it would be unwise to assume that there is no crossover between particular spheres of life.

Proposition 9.6
HAP is a necessary condition for HAA, but not a guarantee of it occurring.

Proposition 9.7
The nature of HAP determines the forms which HAA is likely to take.

Work in recent years has begun to accept that the previous obsession with GDP as a measure of development is inappropriate, although it still dominates many of the policy choices made. As we have already indicated, development should be for the population of a city or region and take the form they wish (Pike et al., 2007). This is compatible with the notion of regional competitiveness but reflects Aiginger and Firgo's (2017) perspective that a broader set of goals should be included. With this in mind, it is necessary that the behavioural model of urban and regional development explicitly acknowledges that economic development will take many different forms, originally driven by the psychocultural profile present, and moved in this direction by the HAP and HAA this creates. This means taking into account a wider range of outcomes as the objectives of regional development, especially beyond those tightly associated with GDP.

Proposition 9.8
The nature of urban and regional development will be determined by the HAP and HAA present in these cities and regions.

Proposition 9.9
A broader set of measures is required to capture the outputs of urban and regional development than measures based on GDP.

The nine propositions outlined above have been incorporated in Figure 9.1. Overall it is clear that a more nuanced understanding of human agency and the forms that urban and regional development can take needs to be incorporated into theorizing. Furthermore, the figure indicates that agency and development flow from the foundations provided by the community culture and personality traits that generate the psychocultural profile of the region.

9.4 Future Empirical Analysis and Data Requirements

In order to more fully understand and refine the model illustrated in Figure 9.1 there are further areas of analysis that would be beneficial, but unfortunately some of the required data is not always available or collected over a

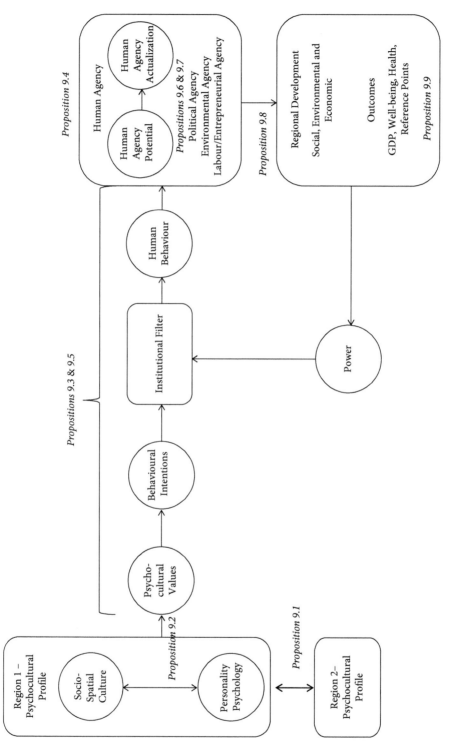

Figure 9.1 An extended behavioural model of urban and regional development.

sufficiently long period of time, as well as not being collected in a manner that is fine-grained enough to capture the detail of the model. Many studies have been produced that utilize novel and sophisticated methods for getting around these data limitations, and these all have helped to provide insights that have gone into developing the behavioural model of urban and regional development. However, their use of proxies and econometric techniques that control for endogeneity and bidirectional causality, rather than incorporate it fully, can lead to problems. Although the results may be consistent with the theories under investigation, their interpretation is rarely restricted to a single theory under consideration, but could support alternatives; or subtle changes to the analysis that could generate support for these alternatives, while providing less evidence for the focal theory.

Given these issues, this section outlines the analysis that is required and the data that would need to be collected to achieve further insights into the link between human behaviour and place-based development. First, an almost universal call throughout the empirical urban and regional development literature, and the social-science literature in general, is the need for more longitudinal data. The key difficulty faced by our behavioural model of urban and regional development is precisely that it is about development and evolution through time. The foundations of culture and personality are constantly influencing one another, interacting with the formal institutions present, and adapting to the economic and social activities present in a region or connected regions (Rentfrow et al., 2008; Nunn and Wantchekon, 2011; Huggins et al., 2018). All elements of the model are under a constant state of evolution. In the case of community culture and personality, these are often regarded as slowly evolving with a high degree of memory or persistence (Heydemann, 2008; Rentfrow et al., 2008; Welzel, 2013; Rentfrow et al., 2015; Lippmann and Aldrich, 2016), but nevertheless longitudinal data would allow changes in community culture, values, human agency, and economic development to be mapped.

Furthermore, the measurement of personality traits is an example of where longitudinal data would be useful, especially as personality traits at the regional level are assumed to alter through a number of different mechanisms. If personality traits remain relatively constant after adolescence (Obschonka et al., 2018), the main influences on regional patterns of personality traits will be driven by selective migration (Rentfrow et al., 2008), but if this is not the case, then the social norms effect becomes more important (Rentfrow et al., 2015). In this latter case, the influence of community culture on determining the psychocultural profiles of a region will be strengthened. By being able to track individuals through time using truly longitudinal data, it will be possible to provide greater insights into the migration patterns of different personality traits from one type of psychocultural profile region to another.

More broadly, longitudinal data reflecting the constructs in the model at the regional level would at least allow the causal direction to be more easily identified, along with any feedback loops. Without true longitudinal data at the individual level the mechanisms behind these relationships are clearly harder to determine. To address this, existing approaches have utilized historical instruments to represent key constructs—for example, culture analyses using literacy rates and political institutions (Tabellini, 2010), and industrial structure analyses using proximity to historical coalfields (Glaeser et al., 2015; Stuetzer et al., 2016). The difficulty with this approach is that, with such closely associated concepts, researchers have often used one to reflect another, and these instruments are likely to be valid for a number of elements. It also means that, while recognizing feedback loops, these are not explicitly factored into these analyses.

In terms of institutions, there are many national level measures available that are updated on an annual basis (Kaufmann et al., 2009; PRS Group, 2013; Schwab, 2018; Freedom House, 2019). Interestingly, many of these capture the effectiveness of institutions rather than their presence. This is preferable, although it necessitates measures being subjective, and there are questions about whose opinions should be given priority. Furthermore, the focus at the national level tends to ignore fluctuations across regions, especially with regard to how institutions operate due to differences in interpretation, monitoring, or interaction with the prevailing community culture (Scott, 2007; Miörner et al., 2018). Although some regional measures are produced, these are rarely on an annual basis (Charron et al., 2011; Charron et al., 2014), and this means there is a clear need for more systematic regional measures of institutions. However, perhaps the greatest challenge is to create measures that allow for differences in the implementation of institutions across regions, without conflating measures that capture community culture.

One set of data traditionally collected by governments is that relating to regional economic outcomes, but this chapter has shown that it is not necessarily appropriate to base analysis entirely on traditional economic measures (Costanza et al., 2014; Tomaney, 2015). Although there is a growing acknowledgement of capturing broader measures of well-being (Diener, 2006; Diener et al., 2015), there are disagreements as to what should be captured and how (Linton et al., 2016). To address this, a multidimensional measure such as the OECD Better Life Index seems appropriate

(Durand, 2015), but less data currently exists at the regional level, restricting the potential to use existing sources (Lawless and Lucas, 2011).

Finally, the data utilized in this book has concentrated on Europe, but perhaps the 'holy grail' for such analyses would be global coverage, allowing tests of the behavioural model of development without the danger of results being an artefact of European development. But the need to match data from a number of sources makes this difficult, if not impossible, using existing data sources. We are not blind to resource issues, however, and even improving the data for Europe would be a massive undertaking. Given costs, it is likely that compromises would need to be made, which then lead to questions over the depth versus breadth of regional coverage. In general, discussing the limitations imposed by data, we suggest that vast gaps in our knowledge still exist, but until these limitations are addressed much future work is likely to follow the approach of this book in utilizing more detailed data for particular nations either of a primary or secondary nature coupled with imperfect coverage from large international datasets with serviceable if imperfect proxies.

9.5   Summary and Conclusions

This chapter has built on the work of the preceding three empirical chapters. Here the focus has been on the links from HAP to development outcomes that include but go beyond traditional economic measures. This is an attempt to recognize that urban and regional development should be in the form preferred by the people who live and work in these places (Pike et al., 2007). This analysis, along with the results presented in previous chapters, is used to further develop and extend the behavioural model of urban and regional development set out in Chapter 2. Finally, the chapter has considered the limitations imposed by data restrictions on the analysis here and what data would ideally be required.

It has been found that human agency, in the form of HAP, is strongly related to a range of development outcomes. Political agency potential is found to have a particularly strong role to play for many of the measures of well-being, with labour/entrepreneurial agency potential often playing a secondary role for other outcomes. Environmental agency potential is frequently the weakest of the three HAP measures. This may reflect the fact that some choices are often seen as being an either/or choice between greater prosperity and sustainability.

Furthermore, the chapter has argued for an extended behavioural model of urban and regional development. For example, we have highlighted the need to consider interregional networks, with these links helping to shape the evolution of regional psychocultural profiles and the values that the model explicitly acknowledges as being promoted or constrained. Whereas the distinction between HAP and HAA requires the link from culture to be extended, this is also broadened to account for different types of agency. This is important, as these different measures of HAP are found to impact upon HAA, especially entrepreneurial and innovative activities, in different ways and not always in the manner that might be expected. It is also found that a requirement to account for the need to influence institutions at a regional and national level gives political agency potential a particularly important role. Finally, the extended model acknowledges the need to recognize that urban and regional development should incorporate not only traditional measures based on GDP but also wider measures of well-being.

We further note that, while the analysis undertaken in both theoretical and empirical terms has allowed the behavioural model to incorporate a fuller understanding of the constructs of importance, data limitations restrict confidence in being able to account for feedback loops, changes over time, and the 'true' appropriate measures policymakers should be using as their targets. In general four types of data limitation are identified: (1) a lack of longitudinal data to fully analyse issues of causality and feedback; (2) minimal microdata to truly investigate the mechanisms behind particular relationships; (3) an absence of items specifically designed to capture the constructs of interest in a manner that is appropriate and clearly distinguishes between them; and (4) issues of consistent regional coverage in terms of both the nations covered and the nature of the spatial boundaries.

Finally, throughout this chapter it has been established that a much broader perspective on urban and regional development should be taken by both scholarly research and policymaking. This fits naturally with the behavioural model of urban and regional development, and along with the findings from previous chapters highlights the need to extend the model. The next chapter will build on this chapter to consider the implications of the work here for policy. There are lessons to be learned from this work, but equally the issues relating to data availability uncovered here show that there is much to be done.

10

Addressing Unevenness

10.1 Introduction

The role of behavioural perspectives, encompassing culture, psychology, and agency, can provide new insights into the persistence of the long-term unevenness of development across cities and regions. A psychocultural theory of development builds upon person–environment theories that have previously sought to explain ecological behaviour across cities and regions rather than their economies (Aitken, 1991; Reid and Ellsworth-Krebs, 2019). In particular, it seeks to facilitate a better understanding of the connectivity between upstream and downstream explanations of urban and regional development, and indeed the extent to which such an 'upstream–downstream' dichotomy is valid. Such a perspective should further provide an indicator of how and why behaviour-based policy intervention may impact on urban and regional development outcomes. Indeed, it is also important to understand the motivations behind such policies, with governments potentially utilizing them to achieve the aims of a range of agendas, from shrinking the state to increasing their sphere of influence through the employment of 'psychocrats' who shape these policies (Whitehead et al., 2011).

Research in the field of urban and regional development highlights the need to consider who development is actually for, arguing that it should take into account a range of outcome factors including poverty, unemployment, inequality, justice, education, and the rights of citizenship (Storper, 2011; Pike et al., 2017). In general, people tend to care about issues of fairness and equity, but the level of care differs across places according to the underlying cultural conditions that mediate preferences regarding redistribution (Le Garrec, 2018). To this extent, cities and regions themselves determine the mix of development they desire, and this mix of motivations beyond the pure financial means that market intervention and incentives may be relatively weak in changing behaviours (Whitehead et al., 2011).

Furthermore, as Nisbett (2003) argues, those excluded for too long from the ability to exercise any significant power often consider that current power brokers are morally arrogant due to their inability or unwillingness to recognize

A Behavioural Theory of Economic Development: The Uneven Evolution of Cities and Regions. Robert Huggins and Piers Thompson, Oxford University Press (2021). © Robert Huggins and Piers Thompson.
DOI: 10.1093.OSO/9780198832348.003.0010

or assimilate cultural traits that differ from those of their own. Theoretically and empirically, this book has sought to tease out some of these challenges in terms of the connection between behaviour within cities and regions and their modes and rates of development. Psychocultural values relating to autonomy, voice, choice, equality, and power generally remain deeply embedded in the institutional frameworks of places, and these impact upon the nature of human agency in these places. This indicates significant challenges in formulating credible behavioural polices that can promote economic development in an environment that also considers broader issues of the well-being of citizens.

10.2 Behavioural Policies for Economic Development

Behavioural policies may come in the form of more endogenous interventions related to 'cultural engineering' through education systems and social-welfare policies, or more exogenous policy nudges related to the attraction, selection, migration, sorting, and matching of people and jobs. In terms of education, there is already evidence of such practices in the private sector, with Pykett and Enright (2016) highlighting the burgeoning industry of positive psychology educational courses. These provide workplace training aimed at increasing worker productivity, while also achieving the broader aims of allowing workers to develop their well-being. However, drawing upon the possession and exercise of power, attempts to adopt some elements of positive psychology for those on unemployment benefits have largely been unsuccessful (Pykett and Enright, 2016). This is potentially a result of negotiation and persuasion mechanisms becoming sidelined in favour of a more coercive approach (Cromby and Willis, 2014).

Other areas have focused on trying to enable individuals to think of the long-term consequences of actions through the extension of the decision-making moment into the future (Whitehead et al., 2011). Given the importance of the first decision that individuals make upon later decisions (imprinting), there is a need to consider the most relevant periods in people's lives to provide such education. The need to accelerate work in these areas is highlighted by the fact that private-sector provision and training-programme development are often running ahead of the research that supports them (Pykett, 2013). Indeed, an interesting issue for future analysis is the spatial variation in the provision and take-up of such support.

Relevant to this spatial variation is the suggestion that cities and regions that have evolved from a position of economic strength to long-term decline suffer from a case of 'social haunting', whereby there is a kind of 'ghosted' affective atmosphere that has endured long after the traditional industries associated with these places have disappeared (Gordon, 1997; Bright, 2016). Indeed, one of the questions left after considering the validity of a behavioural view on economic development is, to what extent can the psychocultures of economically less successful regions be realigned through policy interventions designed to emulate more dynamic and successful regions and cities (James, 2005, 2011)? Clearly, it is difficult to 'engineer prosperity' (Acemoglu and Robinson, 2012), and as Putnam (1995) has shown, intervention may actually impinge on development, with the American slum-clearance policy of the 1950s and 1960s renovating physical capital, but at a very high cost to existing social capital. Similarly, the findings stemming from this book represent a particular conundrum from the policymaking perspective; that is, would an underdeveloped region situated in an advanced nation benefit from a shaking off and changing its community cultural values to become a more atomistic, individualistic, and 'less caring' society, as perhaps typified by the more prosperous regions in that nation? This question can be asked regardless of whether or not such change is possible, and it suggests that policymakers pay heed to two key issues.

First is the issue of psychocultural evolution and the reasoning why it has developed its current traits. The analysis presented here logically suggests that the type of pyschoculture existing in a lagging post-industrial region may be a response to the long-term erosion of what was once clearly a 'work-oriented' economic culture. This suggests that the focus of policy should be the enhancement of economically relevant cultural dimensions (Guiso et al., 2006). Second, it is important to look beyond the macro-spatial and more toward the local to assess how policy intervention may be best utilized. Relatively deprived local communities in both developed and underdeveloped cities and regions are often more socially cohesive and produce high levels of trust. This suggests that social cohesion represents a potential strength, which policymakers can enhance as an economic development tool. Also, and as others indicate, policies and interventions that change personality can be used to address disadvantage and poverty (Almlund et al., 2011).

In reality, not only are lagging regions extremely unlikely to imitate the cultural traits of their more prosperous neighbours, but they should not actually seek to do so. A place-based approach to development, therefore, must clearly build on local values and a 'sense of community', while at the same time being open to values from outside (Sen, 2009; Barca et al., 2012; Weckroth and Kemppainen, 2016). The link between community and economic development has been increasingly recognized by policymakers, and numerous policies have sought to relate the need to improve social inclusion as a lever for facilitating wider economic development (Peet, 2000; Kockel, 2002; Keating et al., 2003; Storper, 2005; Tabellini, 2010). Given this, a mix of policies seeking to influence both behavioural and direct economic factors will be required to facilitate economic development, with interventions aimed at addressing industrial issues being compatible with the necessary changes in the underlying psychoculture. Also, community leaders attempting such a process must look at all outcomes of these changes, as captured by both economic and broader measures of well-being.

10.3 Addressing Psychocultural Behaviour

Overall, the findings outlined in this book indicate a significant challenge for policymaking in more peripheral cities and regions in terms of the extent to which they seek to evolve from socio-spatial psychocultures high in communal and collective values to cultural values that are more atomistic, as typified by many entrepreneurial places. As behavioural economics suggests, many cities and regions need to redesign their choice architecture, such as through nudge-type policies, to ensure more high-quality matches in terms of the individuals and firms they are able to attract (Banczyk et al., 2018). For such sorting policies to prove successful there is first a need to examine why a city or region has particular traits, which in the case of many of the weakest places may be a legacy of evolutionary factors such as post-industrialism. A mix of policies seeking to influence both socio-spatial culture and personality psychology is likely to be required to facilitate entrepreneurial and innovation-driven economic development, with a need for each form of intervention to be mutually compatible. Without such compatibility, success is likely to be limited.

With regard to psychoculturally related policies for promoting urban and regional economic development, engineering a particular psychocultural behavioural profile is clearly not something that policymakers can achieve overnight. As indicated above, however, the education system can be used to encourage the development of individuals more willing to express themselves, question rules, and be open to new ideas. Such programmes should be embedded within the citizenship and creativity elements of the curriculum, although there are debates concerning whether or not citizenship classes are already trying to achieve too wide a spectrum of results (Tonge et al., 2012). Studies on entrepreneurship education have often advocated the use of entrepreneurs to act as role models (Kwong et al., 2012).

More generally, the role of individual regional champions as agents who forge new institutions, networks, and catalyse the agency of others has been shown in many contexts to be instrumental in establishing the conditions for innovation and economic development (Feldman, 2014; Wyrwich et al., 2018). However, the evidence presented in this book suggests that such a role should focus on different aspects in different locations. For example, where the type of *diverse extravert* behaviour identified in Chapter 3 is more prevalent, there may be a requirement to focus on the importance of organization and work ethic, while in places of high *individual commitment* the creative and rule-breaking aspects may be the focus. Fundamentally, different psychocultural behavioural profiles are likely to encourage different forms of development, and policymaking should, as far as possible, account for both. Indeed, this study has shown that grand visions to reinvigorate large national economies such as the United Kingdom are unlikely to be successful if they are not tailored to account for the psychocultural behavioural profiles of local populations. It has also indicated that it is not necessarily individual personality traits or community culture components that are important, but the holistic psychocultural behavioural profile that stems from these components.

Like most studies that incorporate the geography of personality, this book has largely utilized the mean values for personality traits (Garretsen et al., 2019). However, the distribution of personality traits is also of importance (Mathieu et al., 2014), and studies should seek to explore the dispersion of personality traits. This aligns with research that has examined the impact of personality fit on well-being (Jokela et al., 2015; Götz et al., 2018). Person–city or person–region personality fit concerns the extent to which a personality fits in with the personalities of other people living and working in the same place (Bleidorn et al., 2016; Zhou et al., 2019). Therefore, cities and regions will possess either disruptive or compliant agents, which impacts upon the formation and breaking of the types of institutions and habits discussed not only by Schumpeter but also by others such Veblen and Bourdieu (Bögenhold et al., 2016). For example, given the importance of openness and diversity, there is an implication that cities and regions may not just benefit from having greater diverse extraversion per se, but in the way this diverse extraversion also allows the flourishing of other forms of behaviour through greater tolerance (Florida, 2002). As Stark (2009) suggests, a sense of what he terms 'dissonance' is likely to result in a diversity of value-frames that generate new combinations of resources.

For policy to be effective institutions have to take account of place-based psychocultures, with complementary institutions only likely to succeed through repeated interactions (Schröder and Voelzkow, 2014). The outcome of these interactions may limit or expand the directions in which a region or city can develop in the future. This hints at the need to set psychocultural–institutional analysis firmly within a spatio-temporal framework. More generally, the increasing acknowledgement of the evolutionary nature of regional and city economies (Boschma and Frenken, 2006; Glückler and Lenz, 2016) indicates the need for a fuller inclusion of the role of human behavioural factors in shaping their development trajectories. In particular, the role of cultural norms and values within regional and urban communities in facilitating or constraining the entrepreneurial and innovative capabilities of these places, as well as the means through which norms and capabilities are reproduced over time, should form a key locus of analysis within the emerging field of evolutionary economic geography.

10.4 Agency and Entrepreneurial Behaviour

Engineering behavioural change is a sensitive endeavour and is not something policymakers can easily achieve, and although it is undoubtedly impossible to replicate success stories, there are lessons that can be learned as to how to go about enhancing entrepreneurship and development. Importantly, there is a need to focus on establishing collective behaviour that catalyses social and knowledge networks between entrepreneurial agents (Fritsch and Kauffeld-Monz, 2008; Huggins and Thompson, 2017b; Fritsch et al., 2019). Before such networks can be established, however, there is a need to ensure a critical mass of entrepreneurial agents and, while boosterism has its critics, it does help to generate a strong mix of an appealing living and working environment—in cultural, physical, and business terms—as well as a cluster of stimulating people, businesses, and ideas across a broad cultural spectrum from the arts to high-technology economic activity. Such an environment has the potential to act as a factor in attracting and retaining key agents, with location decisions made by individuals being subject to creative lifestyle issues, which are not always given priority within the formulation of more traditional regional policy (Mellander et al., 2011). Research has indicated that high-quality living is seen by progressive regional policymakers to come in a wide range of forms and guises, including diversity, multicultural acceptance, low pollution, high levels of green space, and plentiful leisure activities—whether in the shape of night-time entertainment or historical and cultural attractions (Florida et al., 2011).

From the perspective of future policy research, this book shows a need for entrepreneurial agents to be more fully recognized in the regional development arena, especially to highlight the longer-term role and impact of behavioural factors stemming from the co-evolution of the underlying culture and institutions in regions (Alesina and Giuliano, 2015). Innovation and entrepreneurship do not just happen within cities and regions but are actually a force underlying the formation and evolution of these places (Florida et al., 2017). The attraction of entrepreneurial and innovative individuals represents a long-term factor in promoting economic development, and given that these agents tend to migrate to places that are conducive to their talents (Hall, 1998; Akcigit et al., 2017), there is obviously a role for sorting policies by ensuring that the hard and soft infrastructure required to attract and nurture such talent is made available. However, unexplored questions are: to what extent and how do entrepreneurial agents influence regional culture and institutions, and what are the factors that lead to the retention (or diminution) of entrepreneurial personalities and supportive cultures and institutions (Chell, 2008)? Similarly, an apparent fertile area of research concerns an exploration of the key entrepreneurial agents in regions, and their impact—both positive and potentially negative. Other questions concern whether these entrepreneurs are individual 'isolated' agents or operate through collective forms of agency, especially with political and other agents who create the right (or wrong) conditions for economic development, innovation, and transformation. This leads to further questions regarding the appropriate balance of 'power' to ensure long-term success and the wider behavioural life of entrepreneurs within their city or region.

The challenge is to harness the personal agency and intentions of, for example, entrepreneurially minded individuals in cities and regions with the joint commitments across the collection of agents in these places who are capable of impacting upon economic development. Similarly, the collective action of these agents should facilitate, rather than hinder, the intentions and personal agency of these individuals (Morgan, 2016). In leading cities and regions, there appears to be relatively strong alignment between personal and collective intentions and agency, at least with regard to economic development outcomes. In economically weaker cities and regions, the relationship between personal and collective agency and intentions is more likely to operate in counter directions that work against aggregate levels of development. Of crucial importance are the networks of relations, which are at a meso-level, and mediate the relationship between individual agency and wider psychocultural dimensions (Granovetter, 2017).

In this respect, dualisms such as the structure-agency formulation are somewhat limited as means of progressing policy due to the complex dynamics of economic and social life (Granovetter, 2017), with the emergence of joint commitment, shared agency, and shared values stemming from the more nuanced notion that aggregated and associational human behaviour results from 'fused egos' (Bratman, 1993; Gilbert, 2009, 2014). Such behavioural fusion is at the root of the collective intentionality that is a long-term predictor of economic development (Searle, 1995). Clearly, a lack of collective intentionality due to power tensions, especially between the state and civil society, hinders economic development (Jones et al. 2013; Acemoglu and Robinson, 2017), which is apparent not only across nations as a whole but within particular cities and regions. To this extent, research has indicated that connecting to power can be a significant means by which entrepreneurs and their firms can access the resources to innovate and subsequently stimulate economic development (Akcigit et al., 2017; Bussolo et al., 2018).

10.5   Economic Transformation and Renewal

Practically, and given the barriers facing many industrial mature regional and urban economies, there is an obvious need for these places to have access to public policies that give them the best opportunity to renew their economic base through innovation. Clearly, lagging regions and cities have been the targets of regeneration and development policies for many years, with some interventions achieving more success than others (Malecki, 2007; Wink et al., 2017). Although policies targeted at infrastructure development offer the allure of silver-bullet fixes, sustained renewal and transformation are only likely to emerge from an agency-based approach, that is, policies focused on people and their capacity to generate the types of regional ecosystems required to produce transformative change.

In the context of the discussion of Manchester and Glasgow in Chapter 4, it is notable that these cities, as well as many other mature urban and regional economies, have taken a number of positive steps to renew themselves (Dixon et al., 2011; Feliciotti et al., 2017). At the centre of many developments and policies has been the role of political agency in the form of strong intervention from key actors within local and regional government. A key role for political agents is to build the capacity of economic agents within cities and regions in order to realize their potential (Feldman et al., 2016). A useful concept for considering the extent to which human agency potential (HAP) is transferred to human agency actualization (HAA) is the notion of 'locus of control', in terms of the extent to which individuals consider that their own decisions control their lives—internal locus of control—or that they are in the hands of external factors relating to chance, fate, or the wider environment (Kerr et al., 2018). This locus of control is likely to be a psychoculturally dependent trait (Kerr et al., 2018), indicating that the actualization of potential agency may only be significantly mobilized if certain psychocultural conditions are in place. Whitehead et al. (2014) suggest that such conditions are related to the nature of the 'psychological capital' contained within a place, in the form of key personal attributes including confidence, optimism, perseverance, and resilience, coupled with a better sense of appreciation and understanding of the actions and agency of others.

As Beer and Clower (2014: 6) argue, putting these conditions in place requires effective political agents:

> ...effective leadership means that a city or region will take a strong role in setting a vision for the future and then move on to implement plans and processes that bring about change. Effective leadership, it is argued, will also monitor regional performance and adjust strategies and plans as necessary.... local leadership is a key driver of growth, as the quality of decisions made locally either adds or detracts from the region's growth potential. Put simply, places that make good decisions are more likely to grow; places that make poor choices are likely to squander their opportunities.

Many of these efforts have been positive in the sense that they have transformed physical environments, largely through policies focused on boosterism and consumption (Ferbrache and Knowles, 2017). Long-term economic renewal and transformation, however, will need a more production-focused approach to development, and this is most likely to come through entrepreneurial agency focused on innovation. Therefore, future policies should make central the requirement to nurture, attract, and retain such agents. Furthermore, top-level commitment and involvement by senior government officials and politicians are crucial factors for implementing new policy-thinking, and this reaffirms the importance of political agency (Huggins and Izushi, 2007).

Pragmatically, the most effective course of action for regions and cities is likely to be the promotion of agency that provides a balance of policies supporting the positive values of local community psychocultures as well as facilitating entrepreneurially driven local development. A key role for political leaders, therefore, is to act as boundary-spanning agents connecting valuable knowledge and their sources both within and outside their own city or region

(Beer et al., 2018). In particular, policymakers need to combine community resource strengths with strengths that emerge when new entrants—in the shape of individuals, entrepreneurs, and firms—enter a locality. In essence, high rates of local entrepreneurship and development will be fostered through the presence of community psychocultures that are open, but also allow local resources to be pooled and accessed for the greatest benefit of the population.

Although the above points to the role of policy in attracting, retaining, and supporting existing agents through nudges based on new policy incentives within the choice architecture, the key to long-term renewal and transformation is likely to lie with the nurturing of indigenous agents. To address this, perhaps the only route is through changes within local and regional education systems, especially those that seek to provide individuals with the personalities and mindsets to become the extravert entrepreneurial agents that are central to resilient regional ecosystems (Martin and Sunley, 2011, 2015b; Gorodnichenko and Roland, 2017). Equally, and as indicated above, it should be acknowledged that attempts to modify behaviour and culture through educational programmes may have unknown ramifications that will impact not only on entrepreneurial activity but also on the socio-economics of regional development as a whole (Huggins and Thompson, 2016). For example, some scholars have suggested that one route to renewal for mature regions is to focus on creating innovation and value in foundational sectors relating to universal basic services (Froud et al., 2018). To an extent, this is a plausible approach, with the potential capacity to trigger the renewal process, but it is likely to be limited in terms of achieving long-term and sustained renewal unless there are key entrepreneurial agents operating within these industries with the mindset, willingness, and power to disrupt existing economic systems and models.

10.6 Network Behaviour and Policy

The future of cities and regions will at least partly lie in the wealth of their networks and their ability to psychoculturally adapt to the radical transformations and behavioural changes in the way that humans interact (Benkler, 2006; Grillitsch, 2018). Cities, regions, and the networks that cut within and across these places are mutual constituents and intertwined dimensions of the socio-spatial relations mediating the nature of agency and the underpinning psychocultural features of a city or region (Jessop et al., 2008; Verdier and Zenou, 2017). The structure of networks is related to the agency of actors within these networks, and the nature of this agency is dependent on the personality of individual agents (Burt, 2012; Gulati and Srivastava, 2014; Jackson et al., 2016). Burt (2012) refers to this as a 'network-relevant personality', and the types of such network-related personalities within cities and regions will influence the nature and structure of the networks formed. For example, high-density urban locations tend to benefit from more efficient network structures due to a better quality of matching and clustering (Büchel and von Ehrlich, 2017). Furthermore, the psychocultural dimensions of cities and regions, both now and in the past, are key explanations as to how networks form, reproduce, and transform through differing modes of interpersonal relatedness (Emirbayer and Goodwin, 1994; Obschonka et al., 2018).

Chapter 5 suggests that urban and regional policymakers would be well-served by having access to more intelligence as to which agents in their city or region occupy the most central and prominent structural position within knowledge networks. The density of social connectedness is a good predictor of the role of networks in facilitating both economic and social interactions (Bailey et al., 2017). Therefore, better data and information would support the formulation of strategies that identify and utilize these actors as key network nodes in establishing more open urban and regional innovation ecosystems. The empirical results presented in Chapter 5 also indicate potential challenges and changes of direction for regional innovation policy in moving forward. Many policies have principally focused on the mobilization of entrepreneurial and start-up actors as a feature of network development policies, with the implicit assumption being that larger and more established firms can 'look after themselves' (Huggins and Thompson, 2015b; Stuetzer et al., 2016). Although this may be the case, it does lead to a situation in which the role of larger and often the most strategically important firms are overlooked by cluster and innovation ecosystem development policies and the like. Given the role of these firms as key bridging and boundary-spanning agents within and across networks, it can be argued that policymakers need to integrate the agency of these firms further into their strategies. Also, a bias towards local ties appears to be an indicator of relatively weak regional innovation performance. Therefore, urban and regional policymakers should not blindly pursue the notion that regionally based networks represent a desirable, or even an effective, means for matching the demand for and supply of knowledge for innovation.

Furthermore, the process of policy transfer from advanced to mature regions is now much maligned (Hospers, 2006) and, rather than seeking to replicate the components and ingredients of successful regions, a more fruitful approach for mature regions is to help agents connect with key actors in other regions. Saxenian (2006) suggests that diaspora can support policy-makers in defining strategy, transferring global 'best practice', connecting to partners, brokering technology or institutional adoption, and overcoming political opposition to reform. More generally, if entrepreneurs within a region are unable to assimilate knowledge from external sources, there is a potential role for intervention in the form of innovation policies that act as an 'emulsifier' allowing different types of knowledge to be more effectively combined. Similarly, policy should support entrepreneurs to ensure they are capable of accessing the most appropriate and suitable knowledge for their innovation needs (Kemeny et al., 2016). In particular, support should be made available for engagement within global communities of practice. Communities of practice are becoming ever more international in their dimensions, and to remain innovative, entrepreneurs must become better integrated into their respective global villages (Bathelt et al., 2004).

10.7 Urban and Regional Well-being

Given the level of interaction between the two phenomena of culture and psychology, which appear to be deeply interrelated, as well as the role of the economic cycle in mediating these relationships, behavioural economic development policies appropriate for one city or region may not be appropriate for another with a markedly different socio-spatial culture. In particular, the impact of any policy change is unlikely to be straightforward, since influences through changes in support mechanisms and formal institutions may have unknown impacts on the underlying socio-spatial culture. This link between education and socio-spatial culture is one that has become a very sensitive political issue in many nations, especially with regard to issues concerning social cohesion. Indeed, while policymakers are increasingly seeking to improve the economic development and competitiveness of the places for which they have responsibility (Huggins and Clifton, 2011; Malecki, 2007), perhaps the ultimate aim of place-based policymaking should be to increase such cohesion and the well-being of the population residing within these places (Easterlin, 1974).

It is not, however, always evident that policymaking related to achieving economic development improvements fully considers outcomes related to well-being. Although there is no definitive meaning of the term 'well-being', most research has taken a 'hedonistic approach', where happiness results from avoiding pain and seeking pleasure (Ballas and Tranmer, 2008; Bruni and Porta, 2005). An alternative approach is the 'eudaimonic view', which can be related to non-material pursuits and realizing one's potential or true nature (Ryan and Deci, 2000). In both approaches, the consumption of material goods associated with higher income is, at best, only one of a number of factors determining well-being (Conzo et al., 2017). This means that pursuing development and competitiveness gains may be no guarantee of maximizing well-being and may even have harmful long-term effects if relevant resources cannot be sustained.

Research on the moral economy suggests that capitalist market systems treat labour in an inappropriate manner due to the disregard of the social implications of work (Bolton and Laaser, 2013; Polanyi, 1957). The well-being of individuals is not just determined by the material resources they have access to, but also the social dimensions of life (Nussbaum, 2011). Therefore, some argue that capitalist market systems ignore the fact that work provides more than just wages and is a source of esteem for the skills held by the population (Bolton and Laaser, 2013). Palomera and Vetta (2016) argue that the moral economy and the market system are closely intertwined, with experiences within the workforce forming part of the consciousness of individuals, which is also informed by the norms and values of prevailing customs (Gramsci, 1971). This is associated with Thompson's (1993) perspective on the moral economy, whereby individuals are informed by the historical and intergenerational transfer of the customs of their communities. Therefore, sophisticated policymaking should consider the role of individuals in trying to achieve their own interests as well as those of their communities, and going beyond pure competitiveness concerns (Zijdeman, 2009; Sayer, 2011).

This suggests that the interaction between different forms of agency will lead to different development outcomes. For example, the environment may suffer where the development of heavy industry may initially boost competitiveness but subsequently result in places being unable to move to lower carbon-intensive outputs. From a policymaking perspective, therefore, it is crucial that future formulations pay more attention to the dynamic link between development and well-being at the city and regional level. Economic development, social cohesion, welfare, and environmental policies must become better integrated if they are to build sustainable local communities. The link between social and community development and economic development has been recognized for many years by progressive policymakers. In these cases, strategies at the regional level are formulated based on an understanding of the way in which policy initiatives related to improving social inclusion facilitate wider economic development, including community development.

10.8   A Summary of Policy Lessons

This section provides a short summary of the key policy lessons already discussed, including general issues of policy formulation as well as those more specifically related to achieving positive behavioural change that provides the basis for economically sustainable development in the urban and regional context. From a temporal perspective, urban and regional policymakers need to adopt a more long-term approach to the formulation of economic development policies and strategies. Positive and productive behavioural change requires patience, and policies should seek to avoid the vagaries of political expediency. From a policy mix perspective, economic development policies should be far more intertwined with strategies that seek to improve well-being and social development. A behavioural approach that focuses on the nature of people within cities and regions, rather than just firms and organizations, provides a basis for tackling both goals in tandem. The behavioural model outlined in this book begins to suggest an ontological shift in economic development thinking from the role of firms and organizations in cities and regions to the roles and agency of people within these places. For example, the inclusivity of citizens in the form of an appropriate balance of power across all agent types within a city or region is crucial for allowing broad access to the resources and the levers of change generating the forms of economic ecosystems that underpin transformation and renewal.

In terms of 'engineering' changes in the psychocultural dimensions of a city or region, the first task is to improve rates of human agency potential (HAP) that enable citizens to become better positioned to play a positive role in their city or region, that is to make improvements in psychological capital and self-efficacy. The next stage is to foster human agency actualization (HAA), and cities and regions possessing strong levels of social cohesion and collective thinking can positively use these traits to mobilize citizens to undertake new forms of agency. Community-based values and the spirit of entrepreneurship are far from mutually exclusive, and behavioural change triggering, for example, social entrepreneurship represents but one mode of economic and social development. Local and regional education policies can play a significant role in the development of a psychoculture embedded with significant self-efficacy and an awareness and openness concerning the roles and needs of others.

Given the above, the nurturing of indigenous agents with the psychological capital possessing an entrepreneurial mindset is central to establishing an economically sustainable innovation ecosystem within any city or region. As part of this process, new forms of entrepreneurial and innovative agency can be catalysed through the greater utilization of role models and champions who act as a nudge and stimulus for realizing particular forms of human agency potential. More generally, the nurturing, attraction, and retention of effective entrepreneurial agents will provide the behavioural life-blood for the future economic success of a city or region.

Behavioural change stemming from the attraction of new agents to a city or region will rely on the availability of access to high-quality hard and soft infrastructure. This represents a prerequisite feature of any economic development strategy that is likely to prove effective. Cities and regions should seek to accommodate and promote disruptive agents who work against the underlying accepted psychoculture if the dissonance they engender fosters the forms of innovation that spark economic development. Finally, positive and economically beneficial collective behaviour can be best established through the formation of social connectedness and networks that allow the diffusion of knowledge within and across cities and regions. Within this networked environment, political agents need to adopt an entrepreneurial mindset, especially in terms of their roles as network brokers and key bridging and boundary-spanning agents within and across networks.

10.9 Final Remarks

Social scientists with an interest in understanding the nature of uneven economic development across regions and cities have become increasingly focused on modes of analysis and theory-building based on explanations relating to the role of differences in socio-economic cultural context. This book has argued that psychocultural context in the form of human behavioural and institutional frameworks is an important explanatory factor underpinning the uneven development of cities and regions. This thesis echoes Schumpeter's (1934: 63) argument that:

> economic development is not a phenomenon to be explained economically, but that the economy, in itself without development, is dragged along by changes in the surrounding world, that the causes and hence the explanation of the development must be sought outside the group of facts which are described by economic theory.

These considerations of the impact of particular forms of human behaviour are coupled with more attention being paid to the evolutionary trajectories of urban and regional development and the way in which histories, especially cultural history, inform and impact upon contemporary economic development outcomes (Nunn, 2009; Schoenberger and Walker, 2016; Wadhwani and Lubinski, 2017; Molema and Svensson, 2019). Sociologists such as Granovetter (2017: 11) have similarly noted that: 'culture is not a once-for-all influence but an ongoing process, continuously constructed and reconstructed during interaction. It not only shapes its members but also is shaped by them, in part for their own strategic reasons.' This evolutionary-based approach resonates strongly with scholarly research addressing factors such as differences in rates and patterns of entrepreneurship and innovation, and the role of these in promoting urban and regional economic development. As Schumpeter himself acknowledged (1934: 58–9),

> it is not possible to explain *economic* change by previous economic conditions alone...just as describing the effects of the Counter Reformation upon Italian and Spanish painting always remains history of art, so describing the economic process remains economic history even where the true causation is largely non-economic.

This book hopefully goes some way to furthering and understanding this argument by proposing a human behavioural explanation of the process of economic development.

References

Abeler, J., Falk, A., Goette, L., and Huffman, D. (2011) 'Reference points and effort provision', *American Economic Review*, 101(2), 470–92.

Acemoglu, D. (2002). 'Technical change, inequality, and the labor market', *Journal of Economic Literature*, 40(1), 7–72.

Acemoglu, D., and Robinson, J. A. (2012) *Why Nations Fail? The Origins of Power, Prosperity and Poverty*, London and New York, NY: Profile Books and Crown.

Acemoglu, D., and Robinson, J. A. (2017) *The Emergence of Weak, Despotic and Inclusive States* (No. w23657), National Bureau of Economic Research.

Acemoglu, D., Johnson, S., and Robinson, J. (2005) 'The rise of Europe: Atlantic trade, institutional change, and economic growth', *American Economic Review*, 95(3), 546–79.

Acs, Z. J., Audretsch, D. B., and Lehmann, E. E. (2013) 'The knowledge spillover theory of entrepreneurship', *Small Business Economics*, 41(4), 757–74.

Acs, Z. J., Desai, S., and Hessels, J. (2008) 'Entrepreneurship, economic development and institutions', *Small Business Economics*, 31(3), 219–34.

Adler, P. S., and Kwon, S. W. (2002) 'Social capital: prospects for a new concept', *Academy of Management Review*, 27(1), 17–40.

Adorno, T. W., Frenkel-Brunswik, E., Levinson, D. J., and Sanford, R. N. (1950) *The Authoritarian Personality*, New York, NY: Harper.

Aghion, P., Alesina, A., and Trebbi, F. (2004) 'Endogenous Political Institutions', *Quarterly Journal of Economics*, 119(2), 565–612.

Agnew, J. (1989) 'The devaluation of place in social science', in Agnew, J., and Duncan, J. (eds.) *The Power of Place*, Boston, MA: Unwin Hyman, pp. 9–29.

Ahmetoglu, G., Leutner, F., and Chamorro-Premuic, T. (2011) 'EQ-Nomics: understanding the relationship between individual differences in trait emotional intelligence and entrepreneurship', *Journal of Personality and Individual Differences*, 51(8), 1028–33.

Ahuja, G. (2000) 'The duality of collaboration: Inducements and opportunities in the formation of interfirm linkages', *Strategic Management Journal*, 21(3), 317–43.

Ahuja, G., Soda, G., and Zaheer, A (2012) 'The genesis and dynamics of organizational networks'. *Organization Science*, 23(2), 434–48.

Aiginger, K. (2006) 'Competitiveness: from a dangerous obsession to a welfare creating ability with positive externalities', *Journal of Industry, Competition and Trade*, 6(2), 161–77.

Aiginger, K., and Firgo, M. (2017) 'Regional competitiveness: connecting an old concept with new goals', in Huggins, R., and Thompson, P. (eds.) *Handbook of Regions and Competitiveness: Contemporary Theories and Perspectives on Economic Development*, Cheltenham: Edward Elgar, pp. 155–91.

Aitken, S. (1991) 'Person-environment theories in contemporary perceptual and behavioural geography I: personality, attitudinal and spatial choice theories', *Progress in Human Geography*, 15(2), 179–93.

Ajzen, I. (1991) 'The theory of planned behaviour', *Organizational Behavior and Human Decision Processes*, 50(2), 179–211.

Ajzen, I. (2002) 'Perceived behavioral control, self-efficacy, locus of control, and the theory of planned behaviour', *Journal of Applied Social Psychology*, 32(4), 665–83.

Akcigit, U., Grigsby, J., and Nicholas, T. (2017) *The rise of American ingenuity: Innovation and inventors of the golden age* (No. w23047), National Bureau of Economic Research.

Aldrich, J. (1997) 'When is it rational to vote?', in D. C. Mueller (ed.), *Perspectives on Pubic Choice: A Handbook*, Cambridge: Cambridge University Press, pp. 379–90.

Alesina, A., and Angeletos, G. M. (2005) 'Fairness and redistribution', *American Economic Review*, 95(4), 960–80.

Alesina, A., and Fuchs-Schündeln, N. (2007) ,Good-bye Lenin (or not?): the effect of communism on people's preferences', *American Economic Review*, 97(4), 1507–28.

Alesina, A., and Giuliano, P. (2010) 'The power of the family', *Journal of Economic Growth*, 15(2), 93–125.

Alesina, A., and Giuliano, P. (2015) 'Culture and institutions', *Journal of Economic Literature*, 53(4), 898–944.

Alesina, A., and La Ferra, E. (2005) 'Preferences for redistribution in the land of opportunities', *Journal of Public Economics*, 89(5/6), 897–931.

Alfaki, I., and Ahmed, A. (2017) *From Oil to Knowledge: Transforming the United Arab Emirates into a Knowledge-Based Economy*. London: Routledge.

Alkire, S. (2005) 'Subjective quantitative studies of human agency', *Social Indicators Research*, 74(1), 217–60.

Allen, J. (2003) *Lost Geographies of Power*, Oxford: Blackwell.

Almers, E., and Wickenberg, P. (2008) 'Breaking and making norms', *Lund Studies of Sociology of Law*, 29(1), 227–45.

Almlund, M., Duckworth, A. L., Heckman, J. J., and Kautz, T. D. (2011) 'Personality psychology and economics', in Hanushek, E., Machin, S., and Woessman, L. (eds.) *Handbook of the Economics of Education*, Vol. 4, Amsterdam: Elsevier, pp. 1–181.

Alsop, R., Bertelsen, M., and Holland, J. (2006) *Empowerment in Practice from Analysis to Implementation*, Washington, DC: World Bank.

Amador Diaz Lopez, J. C., Collingnon-Delmar, S., Benoit, K., and Matsuo, A. (2017) 'Predicting the Brexit vote by tracking and classifying public opinion using twitter data', *Statistics, Politics and Policy*, 8(1), DOI: 10.1515/spp-2017–0006.

Amin, A., and Thrift, N. (eds.) (1994) *Globalization, Institutions and Regional Development in Europe*, Oxford: Oxford University Press.

Amin, A., and Thrift, N. (2017) *Seeing Like a City*, Cambridge: Polity Press.

Ananat, E. O., Gassman-Pines, A., Francis, D. V., and Gibson-Davis, C. M. (2017) 'Linking job loss, inequality, mental health, and education', *Science*, 356(6343), 1127–8.

Anderson A. R., and Smith R. (2007) 'The moral space in entrepreneurship: an exploration of ethical imperatives and the moral legitimacy of being enterprising', *Entrepreneurship and Regional Development*, 19(6), 479–97.

Annink, A., Gorgievski, M., and Dulk, L. D. (2016) 'Financial hardship and well-being: a cross-national comparison among the European self-employed', *European Journal of Work and Organizational Psychology*, 25(5), 645–57.

Arbia, G., Battisti, M., and Di Vaio, G. (2010) 'Institutions and geography: empirical test of spatial growth models for European regions', *Economic Modelling*, 27(1), 12–21.

Arenius, P., and De Clercq, D. (2005) 'Network-based approach on opportunity recognition', *Small Business Economics*, 24(3), 249–65.

Ariely, D. (2008) *Predictably Irrational: The Hidden Forces that Shape our Decisions*, New York, NY: Harper.

Armitage, C. J., and Conner, M. (2001) 'Efficacy of the theory of planned behaviour: a meta-analytic review', *British Journal of Social Psychology*, 40(4), 471–99.

Asendorpf, J. B., and van Aken, M. A. G. (1999) 'Resilient, overcontrolled, and undercontrolled personality prototypes in childhood: replicability predictive power, and the trait-type issue', *Journal of Personality and Social Psychology*, 77(4), 815–32.

Åstebro, T., Herz, H., Nanda, R., and Weber, R. A. (2014) 'Seeking the roots of entrepreneurship: insights from behavioural economics', *Journal of Economic Perspectives*, 28(3), 49–70.

Atkinson, R., and Kintrea, K. (2001) 'Disentangling area effects: evidence from deprived and non-deprived neighbourhoods', *Urban Studies*, 38(12), 2277–98.

Audretsch, D. B., and Fritsch, M. (2002) 'Growth regimes over time and space', *Regional Studies*, 36(2), 113–24.

Audretsch, D. B., and Keilbach, M. (2004) 'Entrepreneurship and regional growth: an evolutionary interpretation', *Journal of Evolutionary Economics*, 14(5), 605–16.

Audretsch, D. B., Keilbach, M., and Lehmann, E. E. (2006) *Entrepreneurship and economic growth*, Oxford: Oxford University Press.

Audretsch, D. B., Kuratko, D. F., and Link A. N. (2015) 'Making sense of the elusive paradigm of entrepreneurship', *Small Business Economics*, 45(4), 703–12.

Audretsch, D. B., and Lehmann, E. E. (2005) 'Does the knowledge spillover theory of entrepreneurship hold for regions?', *Research Policy*, 34(8), 1191–202.

Austin, J. H. (1978) *Chase, Chance, and Creativity: The Lucky Art of Novelty*, New York, NY: Columbia University Press.

Auty, R. M. (1993) *Sustaining Development in Mineral Economies: The Resource Curse Thesis*, London: Routledge.

Ayres, S. (2014) 'Place-based leadership: reflections on scale, agency and theory', *Regional Studies, Regional Science*, 1(1), 21–4.

Bailey, M., Cao, R. R., Kuchler, T., Stroebel, J., and Wong, A. (2017). *Measuring social connectedness* (No. w23608). National Bureau of Economic Research.

Baker, T., Gedajlovic, E., and Lubatkin, M. (2005) 'A framework for comparing entrepreneurship processes across nations', *Journal of International Business Studies*, 36(5), 492–504.

Bak-Klimek, A., Karatzias, T., Elliott, L., and Maclean, R. (2015) 'The determinants of well-being among international economic immigrants: a systematic literature review and meta-analysis', *Applied Research Quality Life*, 10(1), 161–88.

Ballas, D., and Tranmer, M. (2008) *Happy Places, Happy Households or Happy People? Building a Multi-Level Model of Happiness and Well-being*, Sheffield: Centre for Health and Wellbeing in Public Policy, University of Sheffield.

Banczyk, M., Laban, J., and Potts, J. (2018) 'Choosing cities: a behavioural economic approach', *The Annals of Regional Science*, 1–15.

Bandura, A. (1997) *Self-Efficacy: The Exercise of Control*, New York, NY: Freeman.

Bandura, A. (2000) 'Self-efficacy: the foundation of agency', in Perrig, W. J., and Grob, A. (eds.) *Control of Human Behavior, Mental Processes: Essays in Honor of the 60th Birthday of August Flammer*, Mahwah, NJ: Lawrence Erlbaum, pp. 16–30.

Bandura, A. (2001) 'Social cognitive theory: an agentic perspective', *Annual Review of Psychology*, 52(1), 1–26.

Bandura, A. (2006) 'Toward a psychology of human agency', *Perspectives on Psychological Science*, 1(2), 164–80.

Barca, F., McCann, P., and Rodrıguez-Pose, A. (2012) 'The case for regional development intervention: Place-based versus place-neutral approaches', *Journal of Regional Science*, 52(1), 134–52.

Barro, R. J., and Sala-i-Martin, X. (1991) 'Convergence across states and regions', *Brookings Papers on Economic Activities*, 1, 107–82.

Bathelt H., and Glückler, J. (2003) 'Toward a relational economic geography', *Journal of Economic Geography*, 3(2), 117–44.

Bathelt, H., Malmberg, A., and Maskell, P. (2004) 'Clusters and knowledge: local buzz, global pipelines and process of knowledge creation', *Progress in Human Geography*, 28(1), 31–56.

Batory, A. (2012) 'Why do anti-corruption laws fail in Central Eastern Europe? A target compliance perspective', *Regulation and Governance*, 6(1), 66–82.

Batz, C., and Tay, L. (2018) 'Gender differences in subjective well-being', in Diener, E., Oishi, S., and Tay, L. (eds.) *Handbook of Well-Being*, Salt Lake City, UT: DEF Publishers, pp. 382–96.

Baum, J. R., Olian J. D., Erez M., Schnell E. R., Smith K. G., Sims H. P., Scully J. S., and Smith K. A. (1993) 'Nationality and work role interactions: a cultural contrast of Israeli and U.S. entrepreneurs' versus managers' needs', *Journal of Business Venturing*, 8(6), 449–512.

Beck, T., Clarke, G., Groff, A., Keefer, P., and Walsh, P. (2001) 'New tools in comparative political economy: the database of political institutions', *World Bank Economic Review*, 15(1), 165–76.

Becker, S. O., and Woessmann, L. (2009) 'Was Weber wrong? A human capital theory of Protestant economic history', *Quarterly Journal of Economics*, 124(2), 531–96.

Beckerman, W., and Hepburn, C. (2007) 'Ethics of the discount rate in the Stern Review on the Economics of Climate Change', *World Economics*, 8(1), 187–210.

Bee, C., and Neubaum, D. O. (2014) 'The role of cognitive appraisal and motions of family members in the family business system', *Journal of Family Business Strategy*, 5(3), 323–33.

Beer, A., Ayres, S., Clower, T., Faller, F., Sancino, A., and Sotarauta, M. (2018) 'Place leadership and regional economic development: a framework for cross-regional analysis', *Regional Studies*, 1–12.

Beer, A., and Clower, T. (2014) 'Mobilizing leadership in cities and regions', *Regional Studies, Regional Science*, 1(1), 5–20.

Belussi, F., Sammarra, A., and Sedita, S. R. (2010) 'Learning at the boundaries in an "Open Regional Innovation System": A focus on firms' innovation strategies in the Emilia Romagna life science industry', *Research Policy*, 39(6), 710–21.

Benedict, R. (1946) *The Chrysanthemum and the Sword: Patterns of Japanese Culture*, Boston, MA: Houghton Mifflin.

Benkler, Y. (2006) *The Wealth of Networks How Social Production Transforms Markets and Freedom*, New Haven, CT, and London: Yale University Press.

Bennett, R., and Dann, S. (2000) 'The Changing Experience of Australian Female Entrepreneurs', *Gender, Work and Organization*, 7(2), 75–82.

Berinsky, A. J., and Lenz, G. S. (2011) 'Education and political participation: exploring the causal link', *Political Behaviour*, 33(3), 357–73.

Beugelsdijk, S., De Groot, H., and van Schaik, A. B. T. M. (2004) 'Trust and economic growth: a robustness analysis', *Oxford Economic Papers*, 56(1), 118–34.

Beugelsdijk, S., and Maseland, R. (2011) *Culture in Economics: History, Methodological Reflection*, Cambridge: Cambridge University Press.

Beugelsdijk, S., and Noorderhaven, N. (2004) 'Entrepreneurial attitude and economic growth: a cross-section of 54 regions', *Annals of Regional Science*, 38(2), 199–218.

Beugelsdijk, S., and Smulders, S. (2003) 'Bonding and bridging social capital: Which type is good for economic growth?', in Arts, W., Halman, L., and Hagenaars, J. (eds.) *The Cultural Diversity of European Unity: Findings, Explanations and Reflections from the European Values Study*, Boston, MA: Brill Leiden, pp.147–84.

Beugelsdijk, S., and van Schaik, T. (2005) 'Differences in social capital between 54 Western European regions', *Regional Studies*, 39(8), 1053–64.

Beutel, A. M., and Marini, M. M. (1995) 'Gender and values', *American Sociological Review*, 60(3), 436–48.

Bhabha, H. K. (1994) *The Location of Culture*, London and New York, NY: Routledge.

Biesta, G., and Tedder, M. (2006) 'How is agency possible? Towards an ecological understanding of agency-as-achievement', Learning Lives Working Paper No. 5.

Biscoe, A. (2001) 'European integration and the maintenance of regional cultural diversity: symbiosis or symbolism?', *Regional Studies*, 35(1), 57–64.

Bisin, A., and Verdier, T. (2008) 'Cultural transmission', in Durlauf, S. N., and Blume, L. N. (eds.) *The New Palgrave Dictionary of Economics*, Basingstoke: Palgrave Macmillan.

Bjørnskov, C. (2006) 'The multiple facets of social capital', *European Journal of Political Economy*, 22(1), 22–40.

Bjuggren, C. M., Johansson, D., and Stenkula, M. (2012) 'Using self-employment as proxy for entrepreneurship: some empirical caveats', *International Journal of Entrepreneurship and Small Business*, 17(3), 290–303.

Blais, A., Feitosa, F., and Sevi, S. (2019) 'Was my decision to vote (or abstain) the right one?', *Party Politics*, 25(3), 382–9.

Bleidorn, W., Hopwood, C. J., and Lucas, R. E. (2018) 'Life events and personality trait change', *Journal of Personality*, 86(1), 83–96.

Bleidorn, W., Schönbrodt, F., Gebauer, J. E., Rentfrow, P. E., Potter, J., and Gosling, S. D. (2016) 'To Live Among Like-Minded Others: Exploring the Links Between Person-City Personality Fit and Self-Esteem', *Psychological Science*, 27(3), 419–27.

Block, J., and Sandner, P. (2009) 'Necessity and opportunity entrepreneurs and their duration in self-employment: evidence from German micro data', *Journal of Industry Competition and Trade*, 9(2), 117–37.

Block, J. H., and Wagner, M. (2010) 'Necessity and opportunity entrepreneurs in Germany: characteristics and earnings differentials', *Schmalenbach Business Review*, 62(2), 154–74.

Boal, F. W., and Livingstone, D. N. (eds.) (1989) *The Behavioural Environment: Essays in Reflection, Application and Re-evaluation*, London: Routledge.

Boettke, P. J., Coyne, C. J., and Leeson, P. T. (2008) 'Institutional stickiness and the new development economics', *American Journal of Economics and Sociology*, 67(2), 331–58.

Boettke, P., and Fink, A. (2011) 'Institutions first', *Journal of Institutional Economics*, 7(4), 499–504.

Bögenhold, D., Michaelides, P. G., and Papageorgiou, T. (2016) 'Schumpeter, Veblen and Bourdieu on Institutions and the Formation of Habits', MPRA Paper 74585.

Bolton, S. C., and Laaser, K. (2013) 'Work, employment and society through the lens of moral economy', *Work, Employment and Society*, 27(3), 508–25.

Boneva, B. S., Frieze, I. H., Ferligoj, A., Jaršová, E., Pauknerová, D., and Orgocka, A. (1998) 'Achievement, power, and affiliation motives as clues to emigration desires: a four-countries comparison', *European Psychologist*, 3(4), 247–54.

Borg, I., Hertel, G., and Hermann, D. (2017) 'Age and personal values: similar value circles with shifting priorities', *Psychology and Aging*, 32(7), 636–41.

Borgatti, S. P., and Halgin, D. S. (2011) 'On network theory', *Organization Science*, 22(5), 1168–81.

Borghuis, J., Denissen, J. J. A., Oberski, D., Sijtsma, K., Meeus, W. H. J., Branje, S., Koot, H. M., and Bleidorn, W. (2017) 'Big five personality stability, change, and codevelopment across adolescence and early adulthood', *Journal of Personality and Social Psychology*, 113(4), 641–57.

Börzel, T. A. (1999) 'Towards convergence in Europe? Institutional adaptation to Europeanization in Germany and Spain', *Journal of Common Market Studies*, 37(4), 573–96.

Boschma, R., Balland, P. A., and de Vaan, M. (2014) 'The formation of economic networks: A proximity approach', in Torré, A., and Wallet, F. (eds.) *Regional Development and Proximity Relations*. Cheltenham: Edward Elgar, pp. 243–66.

Boschma, R., and Capone, G. (2015) 'Institutions and diversification: related versus unrelated diversification in a varieties of capitalism framework', *Research Policy*, 44(10), 1902–14.

Boschma, R. A., and Frenken, K. (2006) 'Why is economic geography not an evolutionary science? Towards an evolutionary economic geography', *Journal of Economic Geography*, 6(3), 273–302.

Boschma, R., and Martin, R. (2010) 'The aims and scope of evolutionary economic geography', in Boschma, R., and Martin, R. (eds.) *Handbook of Evolutionary Economic Geography*, Cheltenham and Northampton, MA: Edward Elgar Publishing, pp. 3–42.

Bosma, N., Content, J., Sanders, M., and Stam E. (2018) 'Institutions, entrepreneurship, and economic growth in Europe', *Small Business Economics*, 51(2), 483–99.

Bosma, N., and Schutjens, V. (2009) 'Mapping entrepreneurial activity and entrepreneurial attitudes in European regions', *International Journal of Entrepreneurship and Small Business*, 7(2), 191–213.

Bourdieu, P. (1986) 'The forms of capital', in Richardson, J. G. (ed.) *Handbook of Theory and Research for the Sociology of Education*, New York, NY: Greenwood, pp. 241–58.

Bourgeois, M. J., and Bowen, A. (2001) 'Self-organization of alcohol-related attitudes and beliefs in a campus housing complex: an initial investigation', *Health Psychology*, 20(6), 434–7.

Bowles, S., and Gintis, H. (2002) 'Social capital and community governance', *Economic Journal*, 112(483), 419–36.

Boyce, C. J., Wood, A. M., Daly, M., and Sedikides, C. (2015) 'Personality change following unemployment', *Journal of Applied Psychology*, 100(4), 991–1011.

Brandstätter, H. (1997) 'Becoming an entrepreneur – a question of personality structure?', *Journal of Economic Psychology*, 18(2/3), 157–77.

Brandstätter, H. (2011) 'Personality aspects of entrepreneurship: a look at five meta-analyses', *Personality and Individual Differences*, 51(3), 222–30.

Bratman, M. (1993) 'Shared intention', *Ethics*, 104, 97–113.

Breinlich, H., Ottaviano, G. I. P., and Temple, J. R. W. (2014) 'Regional growth and regional decline', in Aghion, P., and Durlauf, S. N. (eds.) *Handbook of Growth*, Vol. 2B, Oxford: Elsevier, pp. 683–779.

Brennan, A.., Rhodes, J., and Tyler, P. (2000) 'The nature of local area social exclusion in England and the role of the labour market', *Oxford Review of Economic Policy*, 16(1), 129–46.

Brennan, G., and Lomasky, L. (1993) *Democracy and Decision: The Pure Theory of Electoral Presences*, Cambridge: Cambridge University Press.

Brewer, P., and Venaik, S. (2010) 'GLOBE practices and values: a case of diminishing marginal utility?', *Journal of International Business Studies*, 41(8), 1316–24.

Bright, N.G. (2016) '"The lady is not returning!": educational precarity and a social haunting in the UK coalfields', *Ethnography and Education*, 11(2), 142–57.

Bristow, G., and Healy, A. (2014) 'Regional resilience: An agency perspective', *Regional Studies*, 48(5), 923–35.

Broekel, T., and Hartog, M. (2013) 'Explaining the structure of inter-organizational networks using exponential random graph models', *Industry and Innovation*, 20(3), 277–95.

Brulle, R. J. (2000) *Agency, Democracy, and Nature: The U.S. Environmental Movement from a Critical Theory Perspective*, Cambridge, MA: MIT Press.

Bruni, A., Gherardi, S., and Poggio, B. (2004) 'Doing gender, doing entrepreneurship: an ethnographic account of intertwined practices', *Gender, Work and Organization*, 11(4), 407–29.

Bruni, L., and Porta, P. L. (2005) *Economics and Happiness: Framing the Analysis*, Oxford: Oxford University Press.

Bryson, J. R., and Lombardi, R. (2009) 'Balancing product and process sustainability against business profitability: sustainability as a competitive strategy in the property development process', *Business Strategy and the Environment*, 18(2), 97–107.

Büchel, K., and von Ehrlich, M. (2017) *Cities and the structure of social interactions: Evidence from mobile phone data* (No. 6568), CESifo Working Paper.

Burt, R. S. (2005) *Brokerage and Closure: An Introduction to Social Capital*. Oxford: Oxford University Press.

Burt, R. S. (2012) 'Network-related personality and the agency question: multirole evidence from a virtual world', *American Journal of Sociology*, 118(3), 543–91.

Bussolo, M., Commander, S., and Poupakis, S. (2018) 'Political connections and firms: network dimensions', IZA DP No. 11498, IZA—Institute of Labor Economics, Bonn, Germany.

Callois, J. M., and Aubert, F. (2007) 'Towards indicators of social capital for regional development issues: The case of French rural areas', *Regional Studies*, 41(6), 809–21.

Camerer, C. F., and Loewenstein, G. (2004) 'Behavioral economics: past, present, future', in Camerer, C. F., Loewenstein, G., and Rabin, M. (eds.) *Advances in Behavioral Economics*, Woodstock and Princeton, NJ: Princeton University Press, pp. 3–52.

Campbell, D. E. (2006) 'What is education's impact on civic and social engagement?', in Desjardins, R., and Schuller, T. (eds.) *Measuring the Effects of Education on Health and Civic/Social Engagement*, Paris: OECD/CERI, pp. 25–126.

Camps, S., and Marques, P. (2014) 'Exploring how social capital facilitates innovation: the role of innovation enablers', *Technological Forecasting and Social Change*, 88, 325–48.

Cantillon R, (1931) *Essai sur la Nature du Commerce en Général*, London: Macmillan.

Capaldo, A. (2007) 'Network structure and innovation: the leveraging of a dual network as a distinctive relational capability', *Strategic Management Journal*, 28(6), 585–608.

Capello, R., and Camilla, L. (2013) 'Territorial patterns of innovation and economic growth in European Regions, *Growth and Change*, 44, 195–227.

Capello, R., and Nijkamp, P. (eds.) (2009) *Handbook of regional growth and development theories*, Cheltenham: Edward Elgar.

Carlsson, F., and Johansson-Stenman, O. (2010) 'Why do you vote and vote as you do?', *Kyklos*, 63(4), 495–516.

Carmin, J., and VanDeveer, S. D. (eds.) (2005) *EU Enlargement and the Environment: Institutional Change and the Environmental Policy in Central and Eastern Europe*, Abingdon: Routledge.

Carree, M., van Stel, A., Thurik, R., and Wennekers, S. (2002) 'Economic development and business ownership: an analysis using data of 23 OECD countries in the period 1976–1996', *Small Business Economics*, 19(3), 271–90.

Carree, M., van Stel, A., Thurik, R., and Wennekers, S. (2007) 'The relationship between economic development and business ownership revisited', *Entrepreneurship and Regional Development*, 19(3), 281–91.

Carter, S., Mwaura, S., Ram, M., Trehan, K., and Jones, T. (2015) 'Barriers to ethnic minority and women's enterprise: existing evidence, policy tensions and unsettled questions', *International Small Business Journal*, 33(1), 49–69.

Caspi, A. (2000) 'The child is father of the man: personality continuities from childhood to adulthood', *Journal of Personality and Social Psychology*, 78(1), 158–72.

Cassi, L., and Plunket, A. (2015) 'Research collaboration in co-inventor networks: Combining closure, bridging and proximities', *Regional Studies*, 49(6), 936–54.

Casson, M. (1993) 'Cultural determinants of economic performance', *Journal of Comparative Economics*, 17(2), 418–42.

Casson, M. (1995) *Entrepreneurship and Business Culture: Studies in the Economics of Trust Volume 1*, Aldershot: Edward Elgar.

Castree, N. (2007) 'Labour geography: a work in progress', *International Journal of Urban and Regional Research*, 31(4), 853–62.

Castree, N., Coe, N. M., Ward, K., and Samers, M. (2004) *Spaces of Work: Global Capitalism and the Geographies of Labour*, London: Sage.

Cattell, R. B. (1943) 'The description of personality: basic traits resolved into clusters', *Journal of Abnormal and Social Psychology*, 38(4), 476–506.

Cellini, R., Di Caro, P., and Torrisi, G. (2017) 'Regional resilience in Italy: do employment and income tell the same story?', in Huggins, R., and Thompson, P. (eds.) *Handbook of Regions and Competitiveness: Contemporary Theories and Perspectives on Economic Development*, Cheltenham: Edward Elgar, pp. 308–31.

Cerami, A., and Stubbs, P. (2011) 'Post-communist welfare capitalisms: bringing institutions and political agency back in', EIZ Working Papers No. EIZ-WP-1103.

Chang, H. J. (2011) 'Institutions and economic development: theory, policy and history', *Journal of Institutional Economics*, 7(4), 473–98.

Chang, H. J. (2013) 'Hamlet without the Prince of Denmark: how development has disappeared from today's "development" discourse', in Held, D., and Roger, C. (eds.) *Global Governance at Risk*, Cambridge: Polity Press, pp. 129–48.

Chapman, B. P., and Goldberg, L. R. (2011) 'Replicability and 40 year predictive power if childhood ARC types', *Journal of Personality and Social Psychology*, 101(3), 593–606.

Charron, N., Dijkstra, L., and Lapuente, V. (2014) 'Regional governance matters: quality of government within European Union member states', *Regional Studies*, 48(1), 68–90.

Charron, N., Lapuente, V., and Rothstein, B. (2011) *Measuring Quality of Government and Sub-National Variation*, Brussels: European Commission Directorate-General Regional Policy Directorate Policy Development.

Chekima, B., Chekima, S., Wafa, S. A. W. S. K., Igau, O. A., and Sondoh Jr., S. L. (2016) 'Sustainable consumption: the effects of knowledge, cultural values, environmental advertising, and demographics', *International Journal of Sustainable Development and World Ecology*, 23(2), 210–20.

Chell, E. (2008) *The Entrepreneurial Personality: A Social Construction*, Hove and New York, NY: Routledge.

Chen, C. C., Greene, P. G., and Crick, A. (1998) 'Does entrepreneurial self-efficacy distinguish entrepreneurs from managers?', *Journal of Business Venturing*, 13(4), 295–316.

Ciavarella, M. A., Buchholtz, A. K., Riordan, C. M., Gatewood, R. D., and Stokes, G. S. (2004) 'The big five and venture survival: is there a linkage?', *Journal of Business Venturing*, 19(4), 465–83.

Clark, A. E. (2003) 'Unemployment as a social norm: psychological evidence from panel data', *Journal of Labor Economics*, 21(2), 323–51.

Clark, A. E. (2017) 'Happiness, income and poverty', *International Review of Economics*, 64(2), 145–58.

Clark, A. E., Diener, E., Georgellis, Y., and Lucas, R. E. (2008) 'Lags and leads in life satisfaction: a test of the baseline hypothesis', *Economic Journal*, 118(529), F222–43.

Clark, A. E., Kamesaka, A., and Tamura, T. (2015) 'Rising aspirations dampen satisfaction', *Education Economics*, 23(5), 515–31.

Clark, A. E., and Oswald, A. J. (1994) 'Unhappiness and unemployment', *Economic Journal*, 104(424), 648–59.

Clark, C. (2018) 'Explaining behaviour in economic geography: the cognition-context nexus online' Centre for Employment Work and Finance (CEWF) Working Papers No. WPG 18–05.

Clark, G., and Cummins, N. (2014) 'Inequality and social mobility in the era of the industrial revolution', in Floud, R., Humphries, J., and Johnson, P. (eds.) *The Cambridge Economic History of Modern Britain Volume 1 1700–1870*, Cambridge: Cambridge University Press, pp. 211–36.

Clark, K., and Drinkwater, S. (2010) 'Recent trends in minority ethnic entrepreneurship in Britain', *International Small Business Journal*, 28(2), 136–46.

Cobb-Clark, D. A., and Schurer, S. (2012) 'The stability of big-five personality traits', *Economic Letters*, 115(1), 11–15.

Coe, N. (2013) 'Geographies of production: making space for labour', *Progress in Human Geography*, 37(2), 271–84.

Coe, N. M., Johns, J. L., and Ward, K. (2009) 'Agents of casualisation? The temporary staffing industry and labour market restructuring in Australia', *Journal of Economic Geography*, 9(1), 55–84.

Coe, N. M., and Jordhus-Lier, D. C. (2011) 'Constrained agency? Re-evaluating the geographies of labour', *Progress in Human Geography*, 35(2), 211–33.

Coe, N. M., and Kelly, P. F. (2002) 'Languages of labour: representational strategies in Singapore's labour control regimes', *Political Geography*, 21(3), 341–71.

Coen, D. (2007) 'Empirical and theoretical studies in EU lobbying', *Journal of European Public Policy*, 14(3), 333–45.

Coleman, J. (1988) 'Social capital in the creation of human capital', *American Journal of Sociology*, 94(Suppl.), S95–120.

Connolly, S., and Munroe, A. (1999) *Economics of the Public Sector*, London: Prentice Hall.

Conzo, P., Aassve, A., Fuochi, G., and Mencarini, L. (2017) 'The cultural foundations of happiness', *Journal of Economic Psychology*, 62, 268–83.

Cooke, P. (2004) 'Regional innovation systems: an evolutionary approach', in Cooke, P., Heidenreich, M., and Braczyk, H. (eds.) *Regional Innovation Systems: The Role of Governance in a Globalised World*, London: Routledge, pp. 1–18.

Cooke, P., Asheim, B., Boschma, R., Martin, R., Schwartz, D., and Tödtling F. (eds.) (2011) *Handbook of Regional Innovation and Growth*, Cheltenham and Northampton, MA: Edward Elgar Publishing.

Cooke, P., Clifton, N., and Oleaga, M. (2005) 'Social capital, firm embeddedness and regional development', *Regional Studies*, 39(8), 1065–77.

Costa Jr., P. T., and McCrae, R. R. (1992) *Revised NEO personality inventory (NEO-PI-R) and NEO five-factor inventory (NEO-FFI) professional manual*, Odessa, FL: Psychological Assessment Resources.

Costanza, R., Kubiszewski, I., Giovannini, E., Lovins, H., McHlade, J., Pickett, K. E., Ragnarsdóttir, K. V., Oberts, D., De Vogli, R., and Wilkinson, R. (2014) 'Time to leave GDP behind', *Nature*, 505, 283–5.

Couttenier, M., and Sangier, M. (2015) 'Living in the Garden of Eden: mineral resources and preferences for redistribution', *Journal of Comparative Economics*, 43(2), 243–56.

Crafts, N. (2004) 'Regional GDP in Britain, 1871-1911: some estimates', London School of Economics Working Paper No. 03/04, London: London School of Economics, Dept of Economic History.

Credé, M., Harms, P., Niehorster, S., and Gaye-Valentine, A. (2012) 'An evaluation of the consequences of using short measures of the Big Five personality traits', *Journal of Personality and Social Psychology*, 102(4), 874–88.

Creed, P. A., and Klisch, J. (2005) 'Future outlook and financial strain: testing the personal agency and latent deprivation models of unemployment and well-being', *Journal of Occupational Health Psychology*, 10(3), 251–60.

Crespo J., Suire R., and Vicente J. (2014) 'Lock-in or lock-out? How structural properties of knowledge networks affect regional resilience', *Journal of Economic Geography*, 14, 199–219.

Cromby, J., and Willis, M. E. (2014) 'Nudging into subjectification: governmentality and psychometrics', *Critical Social Policy*, 34(2), 241–59.

Crouch, C., Schröder, M., and Voelzkow, H. (2009) 'Regional and sectoral varieties of capitalism', *Economy and Society*, 38(4), 654–78.

Crouter, A. C., Bumpus, M. F., Maguire, M. C., and McHale, S. M. (1999) 'Linking parents' work pressure to adolescents' well-being: insights into dynamics in dual earner families', *Developmental Psychology*, 35(6), 1453–61.

Cumbers, A., Featherstone, D., MacKinnon, D., Ince, A., and Strauss, K. (2016) 'Intervening in globalization: the spatial possibilities and institutional barriers to labour's collective agency', *Journal of Economic Geography*, 16(1), 93–108.

Cumbers, A., and MacKinnon, D. (2011) 'Putting "the political" back into the region: power, agency and a reconstituted regional political economy', in Pike, A., Rodríguez-Pose, A., and Tomaney, J. (eds.) *Handbook of Local and Regional Development*, Abingdon: Routledge, pp. 249–58.

Cumbers, A., MacKinnon, D., and McMaster, R. (2003) 'Institutions, power and space: assessing the limits to institutionalism in economic geography', *European Urban and Regional Studies*, 10(4), 325–42.

Cumbers, A., Nativel, C., and Routledge, P. (2008) 'Labour agency and union positionalities in global production networks', *Journal of Economic Geography*, 8(3), 369–87.

Dahl, R. A. (1957) 'The concept of power', *Systems Research and Behavioral Science*, 2(3), 201–15.

Dalton, R. J., van Sickle, A., and Weldon, S. (2010) 'The individual-institutional nexus of protest behaviour', *British Journal of Political Science*, 40(1), 51–73.

Dasgupta, P. (2011) 'A matter of trust: social capital and economic development', in Lin, J. Y., and Pleskovic, B. (eds.) *Annual Bank Conference on Development Economics (ABCDE)— Global 2010: Lessons from East Asia and the Global Financial Crisis*, Washington, DC: World Bank, pp. 119–55.

Datta, K., McIlwaine, C., Evans, Y., Herbert, J., May, J., and Wills, J. (2007) 'From coping strategies to tactics: London's low-pay economy and migrant labour', *British Journal of Industrial Relations*, 45(2), 404–32.

Davidsson, P., and Honig, B. (2003) 'The role of social and human capital among nascent entrepreneurs', *Journal of Business Venturing*, 18(3), 301–31.

Davidsson, P., and Wiklund, J. (1997) 'Values, beliefs and regional variations in new firm formation rates', *Journal of Economic Psychology*, 18(2/3), 179–99.

Delgado, M., Porter, M. E., and Stern, S. (2010) 'Clusters and entrepreneurship', *Journal of Economic Geography*, 10(4), 495–518.

Deshpande, S. P., and Fiorito, J. (1989) 'Specific and general beliefs in union voting models', *Academy of Management Journal*, 32(4), 883–97.

Desjardins, R. (2008) 'Researching the links between education and well-being', *European Journal of Education*, 43(1), 23–35.

Dhillon, A., and Peralta, S. (2002) 'Economic theories of voter turnout', *Economic Journal*, 112(480), F332–52.

Diamond, J. (2006) *Collapse: How Societies Choose to Fail or Succeed*, London: Penguin.

Díaz Casero, J. C., Almodóvar Gonzálex, M., de la Cruz Sánchez Escobedo, M., Coduras Martínez, A., and Hernández Mogollón, R. (2013) 'Institutional variables, entrepreneurial activity and Economic development', *Management Decision*, 51(2), 281–305.

Diener, E. (2006) 'Guidelines for national indicators of subjective well-being and ill-being', *Applied Research in Quality of Life*, 1(2), 151–7.

Diener, E., Oishi, S., and Lucas, R. E. (2015) 'National accounts of subjective well-being', *American Psychologist*, 70(3), 234–42.

DiMaggio, P. J., and Powell, W. W. (1983) 'The iron cage revisited: institutional isomorphism and collective rationality in organizational fields', *American Sociological Review*, 48(2), 147–60.

DiMaggio, P. J., and Powell, W. W. (1991) 'Introduction', in Powell, W. W., and DiMaggio, P. J. (eds.) *The New Institutional Analysis*, Chicago, IL: University of Chicago Press, pp. 1–38.

Dimitrova, D. D., and Dzhambov, A. M. (2017) 'Perceived access to recreational/green areas as an effect modifier of the relationship between health and neighbourhood noice/air quality: results from the 3rd European Quality of Life Survey (EQLS, 2011-2012)', *Urban Forestry and Urban Greening*, 23, 54–60.

DiNisi, A. S. (2015) 'Some further thoughts on the entrepreneurial personality', *Entrepreneurship Theory and Practice*, 39(5), 997–1003.

Dion, K. L. (2002) 'The social psychology of perceived prejudice and discrimination', *Canadian Psychology/Psychologie Canadienne*, 43(1), 1–10.

Di Tella, R., Dubra, J., and MacCulloch, R. (2010) 'A resource belief-curse? Oil and individualism', in Hogan, W., and Stursenegger, F. (eds.) *The Natural Resources Trap: Private Investment without Public Commitment*, Cambridge, MA: MIT Press, pp. 119–54.

Dixon, T., Otsuka, N., and Abe, H. (2011) 'Critical success factors in urban brownfield regeneration: an analysis of "hardcore" sites in Manchester and Osaka during the economic recession (2009–10)', *Environment and Planning A*, 43(4), 961–80.

Dolan, S. L., Díez-Piñol, M., Fernández-Alles, M., Martín-Pruis, A., and Martínez-Fierro, S. (2004) 'Exploratory study of within-country differences in work and life values: the case of Spanish business students', *International Journal of Cross Cultural Management*, 4(2), 157–80.

Dopfer, K., Foster, J., and Potts, J. (2004) 'Micro–meso–macro', *Journal of Evolutionary Economics*, 14(3), 263–279.

Dopfer, K., and Potts, J. (2004) 'Evolutionary realism: a new ontology for economics', *Journal of Economic Methodology*, 11(2), 195–212.

Doran, J., Jordan, D., and O'Leary, E. (2012) 'The effects of the frequency of spatially proximate and distant interaction on innovation by Irish SMEs', *Entrepreneurship and Regional Development*, 24(7/8), 705–27.

Doré, B., and Bolger, N. (2018) 'Population- and individual-level changes in life satisfaction surrounding major life stressors', *Social Psychological and Personality Science*, 9(7), 875–84.

Douty, H. M. (1960) 'Collective bargaining coverage in factory employment, 1958', *Monthly Labour Market Review*, 83, 345–9.

Dow, G. K., and Juster, F. T. (1985) 'Goods, time, and well-being: the joint dependence problem', in Juster, F. T., and Stafford, F. P. (eds.) *Time, Goods, and Well-being*, Ann Arbor, MI: Institute for Social Research, pp. 397–413.

Downs, A. (1957) *An Economic Theory of Democracy*, New York, NY: Harper & Row.

Drakopoulou Dodd, S., and Anderson, A. R. (2007) 'Mumpsimus and the mything of the individualistic entrepreneur', *International Small Business Journal*, 25(4), 341–60.

Durand, M. (2015) 'The OECD better life initiative: how's life? and the measurement of well-being', *Review of Income and Wealth*, 61(1), 4–17.

Durkheim, E. (1893) *The Division of Labour in Society*, New York, NY: Macmillan.

Durlauf, S.N., and Fafchamps, M. (2003) 'Empirical Studies of Social Capital: A Critical Survey. Wisconsin Madison', Social Systems Working Paper Series, Paper No. 12, Madison, WI: University of Wisconsin/Social Systems Research Institute.

Dwertmann, D. J. G., Nishii, L. H., and van Knippenberg, D. (2016) 'Disentangling the fairness and discrimination and synergy perspectives on diversity climate: moving the field forward', *Journal of Management*, 42(5), 1136–68.

Dye, T. R. (1975) 'Population density and social pathology', *Urban Affairs Quarterly*, 11(2), 265–75.

Easterlin, R. A. (1974) 'Does economic growth improve the human lot? Some empirical evidence', in David, P. A., and Reder, M. W. (eds.) *Nations and Households in Economic Growth: Essays in Honor of Moses Abramovitz*, New York, NY: Academic Press, pp. 89–125.

Easterlin, R. A. (1995) 'Will raising the incomes of all increase the happiness of all?', *Journal of Economic Behavior and Organization*, 27(1), 35–47.

Easterlin, R. A. (2005) 'A puzzle for adaptive theory', *Journal of Economic Behavior and Organization*, 56(4), 513–21.

Easterly, W., and Levine R. (1997) 'Africa's growth tragedy: politics and ethnic divisions', *Quarterly Journal of Economics*, 112(4), 1203–50.

Easterly, W., Ritzen, J., and Woolcock, M. (2006) 'Social cohesion, institutions, and growth', *Economics and Politics*, 18(2), 103–20.

Eccles, J. (2011) 'Gendered educational and occupational choices: applying the Eccles et al. model of achievement-related choices', *International Journal of Behavioral Development*, 35(3), 195–201.

Eden, S., Donaldson, A., and Walker, G. (2006) 'Green groups and grey areas: scientific boundary-work, nongovernmental organisations, and environmental knowledge', *Environment and Planning A*, 38(6), 1061–76.

Eisenstadt, S. N. (2004) 'Social evolution and modernity: some observations on Parson's comparative and evolutionary analysis: Parson's analysis from the perspective of multiple modernities', *American Sociologist*, 35(4), 5–24.

Ekiert, G., and Hanson, S. E. (2003) 'Time, space, and institutional change in Central and Eastern Europe', in Ekiert, G., and Hanson, S. E. (eds.) *Capitalism and Democracy in Central and Eastern Europe*, Cambridge: Cambridge University Press, pp. 15–48.

Elfenbein, D. W., Hamilton, B. H., and Zenger, T. R. (2010) 'The small firm effect and the entrepreneurial spawning of scientists and engineers', *Management Science*, 56(4), 659–81.

Emirbayer, M., and Goodwin, J. (1994) 'Network Analysis, Culture, and the Problem of Agency', *American Journal of Sociology*, 99(6), 1411–54.

Emirbayer, M., and Mische, A. (1998) 'What is agency?', *American Journal of Sociology*, 103(4), 962–1023.

Erdem, T., and Keane, M. P. (1996) 'Decision-making under uncertainty: capturing dynamic brand choices processes in turbulent consumer goods markets', *Marketing Science*, 15(1), 1–20.

Erikson, R., and Goldthorpe, J. H. (1992) *The Constant Flux: A Study of Class Mobility in Industrial Societies*, Oxford: Oxford University Press. ESS (2019) ESS8-2016, ed. 2.2—Multilevel Data: Study Documentation, London: ESS-ERIC.

Estrin, S., Korostevleva, J., and Mickiewicz, T. (2013) 'Which institutions encourage entrepreneurial growth aspirations?', *Journal of Business Venturing*, 28(4), 564–80.

Ettlinger, N. (2003) 'Cultural economic geography and a relational and microspace approach to trusts, rationalities, networks, and change in collaborative workplaces', *Journal of Economic Geography*, 3(2), 1–28.

Evans, D. S., and Jovanovic, B. (1989) 'An estimated model of entrepreneurial choice under liquidity constraints', *Journal of Political Economy*, 97(4), 808–27.

Ewing, K. (2017) 'Brexit and parliamentary sovereignty', *Modern Law Review*, 80(4), 711–26.

Faggio, G., Silva, O., and Strange, W. C. (2017) 'Heterogeneous agglomeration', *Review of Economics and Statistics*, 99(1), 80–94.

Fanta, A. B. (2015) 'Exploring the economic significance of small and medium enterprises', *Journal of Governance and Regulation*, 4(1), 27–34.

Farole, T., Rodríguez-Pose, A., and Storper, M. (2011) 'Human geography and the institutions that underlie economic growth', *Progress in Human Geography*, 35(1), 58–80.

Fayolle, A. Basso, O., and Bouchard, V. (2010) 'Three levels of culture and firms' entrepreneurial orientation: a research agenda', *Entrepreneurship and Regional Development*, 22(7/8), 707–30.

Feinstein, C. H. (1998) 'Pessimism perpetuated: real wages and the standard of living in Britain during and after the industrial revolution', *Journal of Economic History*, 58(3), 625–58.

Feldman, M. (2014) 'The character of innovative places: entrepreneurial strategy, economic development, and prosperity', *Small Business Economics*, 43(1), 9–20.

Feldman, M., Hadjimichael, T., Lanahan, L., and Kemeny, T. (2016) 'The logic of economic development: a definition and model for investment', *Environment and Planning C: Government and Policy*, 34, 5–21.

Feliciotti, A., Romice, O., and Porta, S. (2017) 'Urban regeneration, masterplans and resilience: the case of the Gorbals in Glasgow', *Urban Morphology*, 21(1), 61–79.

Felps, W., Mitchell, T. R., and Byington, E. (2006) 'How, when, and why bad applies spoil the barrel: negative group members and dysfunctional groups', *Research in Organizational Behavior*, 27, 174–222.

Ferbrache, F., and Knowles, R. D. (2017) 'City boosterism and place-making with light rail transit: a critical review of light rail impacts on city image and quality', *Geoforum*, 80, 103–13.

Ferejohn, J. A., and Fiorina, M. P. (1974) 'The paradox of not voting: a decision theoretic analysis', *American Political Science Review*, 68(2), 525–36.

Fernández, R., Fogli, A., and Olivetti, C. (2004) 'Mothers and sons: preference formation and female labor force dynamics', *Quarterly Journal of Economics*, 119(4), 1249–99.

Ferrer-i-Carbonell, A. (2005) 'Income and well-being: an empirical analysis of the comparison income effect', *Journal of Public Economics*, 89(5/6), 997–1019.

Ferriman, K., Lubinski, D., and Benbow, C. P. (2009) 'Work preferences, life values, and personal views of top math/science graduate students and the profoundly gifted: developmental changes and gender differences during emerging adulthood and parenthood', *Journal of Personality and Social Psychology*, 97(3), 517–32.

Festinger, L. (1957) *A Theory of Cognitive Dissonance*, Stanford, CA: Stanford University Press.

Fiorina, M. P. (1976) 'The voting decision: instrumental and expressive aspects', *Journal of Politics*, 38(2), 390–413.

Fischer, C. S. (1975) 'Toward a subculture theory of urbanism', *American Journal of Sociology*, 80(6), 1319–41.

Fischer, C.S. (ed.) (1977) *Networks and Places: Social Relations in the Urban Setting*, New York, NY: Free Press.

Fisher, S. D., and Shorrocks, R. (2018) 'Collective failure? Lessons from combining forecasts for the UK's referendum on EU membership', *Journal of Elections, Public Opinion and Parties*, 28(1), 59–77.

Flanagan, S. C. (1982) 'Changing values in advanced industrial societies: Inglehart's silent revolution from the perspective of Japanese findings', *Comparative Political Studies*, 14(4), 403–44.

Fleming, L., King, C., and Juda, A. I. (2007) 'Small worlds and regional innovation', *Organization Science*, 18(6), 938–54.

Flora, C., and Flora, J. (1993) 'Entrepreneurial social infrastructure: a necessary ingredient', *Annals of the American Academy of Political and Social Science*, 529(1), 48–58.

Florida, R. (2002) *The Rise of the Creative Class*, New York, NY: Basic Books.

Florida, R. (2003) 'Cities and the creative class', *City and Community*, 2(1), 3–19.

Florida, R. (2017) *The New Urban Crisis: How Our Cities Are Increasing Inequality, Deepening Segregation, and Failing the Middle Class and What We Can Do About It*, New York, NY: Basic Books.

Florida, R., Adler, P., and Mellander, C. (2017) 'The city as innovation machine', *Regional Studies*, 51(1), 86–96.

Florida, R., Mellander, C., and Stolarick, K. (2008) 'Inside the black box of regional development–human capital, the creative class and tolerance', *Journal of Economic Geography*, 8(5), 615–59.

Florida, R., Mellander, C., and Stolarick, K. M. (2010) 'Talent, technology and tolerance in Canadian regional development', *The Canadian Geographer/Le Géographe Canadien*, 54(3), 277–304.

Florida, R., Mellander, C., and Stolarick, K. (2011) 'Beautiful places: the role of perceived aesthetic beauty in community satisfaction', *Regional Studies*, 45(1), 33–48.

Foreman-Peck, J., and Zhou, P. (2013) 'The strength and persistence of entrepreneurial cultures', *Journal of Evolutionary Economics*, 23(1), 163–87.

Fornahl, D. (2003) 'Entrepreneurial activities in a regional context', in Fornahl, D., and Brenner, T. (eds.) *Cooperation, Networks, and Institutions in Regional Innovation Systems*. Cheltenham: Edward Elgar, pp. 38–57.

Fratesi, U., and Rodríguez-Pose, A. (2016) 'The crisis and regional employment in Europe: what role for sheltered economies?', *Cambridge Journal of Regions, Economy and Society*, 9(1), 33–57.

Frederking, L. C. (2002) 'Is there an endogenous relationship between culture and economic development?', *Journal of Economic Behavior and Organization*, 48(2), 105–26.

Freedom House (2019) *Democracy in Retreat: Freedom in the World 2019*, Washington, DC: Freedom House.

Freeman, R. B., and Medoff, J. L. (1984) *What Do Unions Do?*, New York, NY: Basic Books.

Frese, M., Garst, H., and Fay, D. (2007) 'Making things happen: reciprocal relationship between work characteristics and personal initiative in a four-wave longitudinal structural equation model', *Journal of Applied Psychology*, 92(4), 1084–102.

Frese, M., and Gielnik, M. M. (2014) 'The psychology of entrepreneurship', *Annual Review of Organizational Psychology and Organizational Behavior*, 1, 413–38.

Frese, M., Kring, W., Soose, A., and Zempel, J. (1996) 'Personal initiative at work: differences between East and West Germany', *Academy of Management Journal*, 39(1), 37–63.

Frey, B. S., and Stutzer, A. (2000) 'Happiness, economy and institutions', *Economic Journal*, 110(466), 918–38.

Freytag, A., and Thurik, R. (2007) 'Entrepreneurship and its determinants in a cross country setting', *Journal of Evolutionary Economics*, 23(1), 163–87.

Fritsch, M., Bublitz, E., Sorgner, A., and Wyrwich, M. (2014) 'How much of a socialist legacy? The re-emergence of entrepreneurship in East German transformation to a market economy', *Small Business Economics*, 43(2), 427–46.

Fritsch, M., and Kauffeld-Monz, M. (2008) 'The impact of network structure on knowledge transfer: an application of social network analysis in the context of regional innovation networks', *Annals of Regional Science*, 44(1), 21–38.

Fritsch, M., Obschonka, M., and Wyrwich, M. (2019) 'Historical roots of entrepreneurship-facilitating culture and innovation activity – an analysis for German regions', *Regional Studies*, 53(9). DOI: 10.1080/00343404.2019.1580357

Fritsch, M., Sorgner, A., and Wyrwich, M. (2019) 'Self-employment and well-being across institutional contexts', *Journal of Business Venturing*, 34(6), DOI: 10.1016/j.jbusvent.2019.105946

Fritsch, M., and Wyrwich, M. (2014) 'The long persistence of regional levels of entrepreneurship: Germany, 1925-2005', *Regional Studies*, 48(6), 955–73.

Fritsch, M., and Wyrwich, M. (2015) 'Does Persistence in Start-Up Activity Reflect Persistence in Social Capital?', Research Paper No. 2015–009, Jena: Friedrich-Schiller-University, Max-Planck Institute of Economics.

Froud, J., Johal, S., Moran, M., Salento, A., and Williams, K. (2018) *Foundational Economy: The Infrastructure of Everyday Life*, Manchester: Manchester University Press.

Fryer, D. M. (1986) 'Employment deprivation and personal agency during unemployment: a critical discussion of Jahoda's explanation of the psychological effects of unemployment', *Social Behaviour*, 1(1), 3–23.

Fuchs, S. (2001) 'Beyond agency', *Sociological Theory*, 19(1), 24–40.

Fukumoto, I. K., and Grusky, D. B (1993) 'Social mobility and class structure in early-industrial France', in Miles, A., and Vincent, D. (eds.) *Building European Society: Occupational Change and Social Mobility in Europe, 1840–1940*, Manchester: Manchester University Press, pp. 40–67.

Fukuyama, F. (1995) *Trust: The Social Virtues and the Creation of Prosperity*, London: Hamish Hamilton.

Fukuyama, F. (2001) 'Social capital and civil society and development', *Third World Quarterly*, 22(1), 7–20.

Fullagar, C. J. A., Gallagher, D. G., Gordon, M. E., and Clark, P. F. (1995) 'Impact of early socialization on union commitment and participation: a longitudinal study', *Journal of Applied Psychology*, 80(1), 147–57.

Galassi, J. P., Delo, J. S., Galassi, M. D., and Bastien, S. (1974) 'The college self-expression scale: a measure of assertiveness', *Behavior Therapy*, 5(2), 165–71.

Gallo, L. C., and Matthews, K. A. (2003) 'Understanding the association between socioeconomic status and physical health: do negative emotions play a role?', *Psychological Bulletin*, 129(1), 10–51.

Galor, O., and Moav, O. (2004) 'From physical to human capital accumulation: Inequality and the process of development', *The Review of Economic Studies*, 71(4), 1001–26.

Garcilazo, E. (2011) 'The evolution of place-based policies and the resurgence of geography in the process of economic development', *Local Economy*, 26(6/7), 459–66.

Garretsen, H., Stoker, J. I., Soudis, D., Martin, R., and Rentfrow, J. (2019) 'The relevance of personality traits for urban economic growth: making space for psychological factors', *Journal of Economic Geography*, 19(3), 541–65.

Geeraert, N., Li R., Ward, C., Gelfand, M., and Demes, K. A. (2019) 'A tight spot: how personality moderate the impact of social norms on sojourner adaptation', *Psychological Science*, 30(3), 333–42.

Gelb, A., Knight, J. B., and Sabot, R. H. (1991) 'Public sector employment, rent seeking and economic growth', *Economic Journal*, 101(408), 1186–99.

Gerhards, J. (2010) 'Non-discrimination towards homosexuality: the European Union's policy and citizens' attitudes towards homosexuality in 27 European countries', *International Sociology* 25(1), 5–28.

Gerson, K. C., Stueve, A., and Fischer, C. (1977) 'Attachment to place', in Fischer, C. (eds.) *Networks and Places: Social Relations in the Urban Setting*, New York, NY: Free Press, pp. 139–61.

Gertler, M. S. (1997) 'The invention of regional culture', in Lee, R., and Wills, J. (eds.) *Geographies of Economies*, London: Arnold, pp. 47–58.

Giavazzi, F., Petkov, I., and Schiantarelli, F. (2014) 'Culture: persistence and evolution', Working Paper No. 20174, Cambridge, MA: National Bureau of Economic Research.

Giddens, A. (1984) *The Constitution of Society: Outline of the Theory of Structuration*, Berkeley, CA: University of California Press.

Gilbert, M. (2009) 'Shared intention and personal intentions', *Philosophical Studies*, 144(1), 167–87.

Gilbert, M. (2014) *Joint Commitment: How We Make the Social World*. Oxford: Oxford University Press.

Gill, I. (2010) 'Regional Development Policies: Place-Based or People-Centred?', Paris: OECD Regional Development Policy Division.

Giuliani, E. (2007) 'Networks and heterogeneous performance of cluster firms', in Frenken, K. (ed.) *Applied Evolutionary Economics and Economic Geography*. Cheltenham: Edward Elgar, pp. 161–79.

Glaeser, E. L. (2002) 'Learning in cities', *Journal of Urban Economics*, 46, 254–77.

Glaeser, E. L. (2011) *Triumph of the City: How Our Greatest Invention Makes us Richer, Smarter, Greener, Healthier and Happier*, London: Macmillan.

Glaeser, E. L., Kallal, H. D., Scheinkman, J. A., and Shleifer, A. (1992) 'Growth in cities', *Journal of Political Economy*, 100(6), 1126–52.

Glaeser, E. L., Kerr, S. P., and Kerr, W. R. (2015) 'Entrepreneurship and urban growth: an empirical assessment with historical mines', *Review of Economics and Statistics*, 97(2), 498–520.

Glaeser, E. L., La Porta, R., Lopez-De-Silanes, F., and Shleifer, A. (2004) 'Do institutions cause growth?', *Journal of Economic Growth*, 9(3), 271–303.

Glückler, J. (2013) 'Knowledge, networks and space: Connectivity and the problem of non-interactive learning', *Regional Studies*, 47, 6, 880–94.

Glücker, J., and Lenz, R. (2016) 'How institutions moderate the effectiveness of regional policy: A framework and research agenda', *Investigaciones Regionales*, 36, 255–77.

Goldberg, L. R. (1992) 'The development of markers for the Big-Five factor structure', *Psychological Assessment*, 4(1), 26–42.

Goodwin, M. J., and Heath, O. (2016) 'The 2016 referendum, Brexit and the left behind: an aggregate-level analysis of the result', *Political Quarterly*, 87(3), 323–32.

Gordon, A. (1997) *Ghostly Matters: Haunting and the Sociological Imagination*, Minneapolis, MN: University of Minnesota Press.

Gordon, I. R. (2015) 'Ambition, human capital acquisition and the metropolitan escalator', *Regional Studies*, 49(6), 1042–55.

Gordon, I. R., and McCann, P. (2005) 'Innovation, agglomeration, and regional development', *Journal of Economic Geography*, 5(5), 523–43.

Gordon, P. (2013) 'Thinking about economic growth: cities, networks, creativity and supply chains for ideas', *Annals of Regional Science*, 50(3), 667–84.

Gorodnichenko, Y., and Roland, G. (2017) 'Culture, institutions and the wealth of nations', *Review of Economics and Statistics*, 99(3), 402–16.

Gosling, S. D., Rentfrow, P. J., and Swann Jr., W. B. (2003) 'A very brief measure of the Big Five personality domains', *Journal of Research in Personality*, 37(6), 504–28.

Goss, D., and Sadler-Smith, E. (2018) 'Opportunity creation: entrepreneurial agency, interaction, and affect', *Strategic Entrepreneurship Journal*, 12(2), 219–36.

Götz, F.M. 1, Ebert, T., and Rentfrow, P.J. (2018) 'Regional cultures and the psychological geography of Switzerland: Person–Environment–Fit in personality predicts subjective wellbeing', *Frontiers in Psychology*, 9:517, DOI: 10.3389/fpsyg.2018.00517.

Gradstein, M., and Justman, M. (2000) 'Human capital, social capital, and public schooling', *European Economic Review*, 44(4/6), 879–89.

Gramsci, A. (1971). *Selections from the Prison Notebooks*, London: Lawrence and Wishart.

Granovetter, M. (1973) 'The strength of weak ties', *American Journal of Sociology*, 78(6), 1360–80.

Granovetter, M. (1985) 'Economic action and social structure: the problem of embeddedness', *American Journal of Sociology*, 91(3), 481–510.

Granovetter, M. (2017) *Society and Economy: Framework and Principles*, Cambridge, MA: Belknap.

Gregson, N. (2005) 'Agency, structure', in Cloke, P., and Johnston, R. (eds.) *Spaces of Geographical Thought*, London: Sage, pp. 21–41.

Greif, A. (1994) 'Cultural beliefs and the organization of society: a historical and theoretical reflection on collectivist and individualist societies', *Journal of Political Economy*, 102(5), 912–50.

Grillitsch, M. (2018) 'Following or breaking regional development paths: on the role and capability of the innovative entrepreneur', *European Planning Studies*, 26(8), 1638–62.

Grix, J. (2000) 'East German political attitudes: socialist legacies v. situational factors a false antithesis', *German Politics*, 9(2), 109–24.

Guiso, L., Sapienza, P., and Zingales, L. (2004) 'The role of social capital in financial development', *American Economic Review*, 94(3), 526–56.

Guiso, L., Sapienza, P., and Zingales, L. (2006) 'Does culture affect economic outcomes?', *Journal of Economic Perspectives*, 20(2), 23–49.

Guiso, L., Sapienza, P., and Zingales, L. (2008) 'Long term persistence', NBER Working Paper No. 14278.

Gulati, R., and Srivastava, S. B. (2014) 'Bringing agency back into network research: Constrained agency and network action', *Research in the Sociology of Organizations*, 40, 73–93.

Gulati, R., Sytch, M., and Tatarynowicz, A. (2012) 'The rise and fall of small worlds: Exploring the dynamics of social structure', *Organization Science*, 23(2), 449–71.

Gupta, A., and Ferguson, J. (eds.) (1997) *Culture, Power, Place: Explorations in Critical Anthropology*, London: Duke University Press.

Gylfason, T. (2001) 'Natural resources, education, and economic development', *European Economic Review*, 45(4/6), 847–59.

Habermas, J. (1989) *The Condition of Postmodernity*, Cambridge, MA: Basil Blackwell.

Hall, P. (1998) *Cities in Civilization*, New York, NY: Pantheon Books.

Hall, P. A., and Soskice, D. (2001) 'An introduction to varieties of capitalism', in Hall, P. A., and Soskice, D. (eds.) *Varieties of Capitalism: The Institutional Foundations of Comparative Advantage*, Oxford: Oxford University Press, pp. 1–68.

Hall, S. (1993) 'Culture, community, nation', *Cultural Studies*, 7(3), 349–63.

Hall, S. G., and Ahmad, M. (2012) 'Institutions-growth spatial dependence: an empirical test', *Procedia—Social and Behavioural Sciences*, 65, 925–30.

Hamlin, A., and Jennings, C. (2011) 'Expressive political behaviour: foundations, scope and implications', *British Journal of Political Science*, 41(3), 645–70.

Hamlin, A., and Jennings, C. (2019) 'Expressive voting', in Congleton, R. D., Grofman, B., and Voigt, S. (eds.) *Oxford Handbook of Public Choice Volume 1*, Oxford: Oxford University Press, pp. 333–51.

Hampden-Turner, C., and Trompenaars, F. (1994) *The Seven Cultures of Capitalism*, London: Piatkus.

Hanglberger, D., and Merz, J. (2015) 'Does self-employment really raise job satisfaction? Adaptation and anticipation effects on self-employment and general job changes', *Journal of Labour Market Research*, 48(4), 287–303.

Harrington, J. R., and Gelfand, M. J. (2014) 'Tightness-looseness across the 50 United States', *Proceedings of the National Academy of Science*, 111(22), 7990–5.

Harris, C., Moran, D., and Bryson, J. R. (2013) 'EU accession migration: national insurance number allocations and the geographies of Polish labour immigration to the UK', *Tijdschrift voor Economishe en Social Geografie*, 103(2), 209–21.

Harrison, L. E., and Huntington, S. P. (eds.) (2000) *Culture Matters: How Values Shape Human Progress*, New York, NY: Basic Books.

Harrison, R. T., Cooper, S. Y., and Mason, C. M. (2004) 'Entrepreneurial activity and the dynamics of technology-based cluster development: The case of Ottawa', *Urban Studies*, 41(5/6), 1045–70.

Hart, D., Atkins, R., and Fegley, S. (2003) 'Personality and development in childhood: A person centred approach', *Monographs of the Society for Research in Child Development*, 68(1), 1–122.

Harvey, D. (2001) Spaces of Capital: Towards a Critical Geography, Edinburgh: Edinburgh University Press.

Harvey, D. (2003) *The New Imperialism*, Oxford: Oxford University Press.

Hassink, R., and Klaerding, C. (2012) 'The end of the learning region as we knew it; towards learning in space', *Regional Studies*, 46(8), 1055–66.

Hauser, C., Tappeiner, G., and Walde, J. (2007) 'The learning region: The impact of social capital and weak ties on innovation', *Regional Studies*, 41(1), 75–88.

Hausser, J. A., Mojzisch, A., Niesel, M., and Schulz-Hardt, S. (2010) 'Ten years on: a review of recent research on the job demand-control (-support) model and psychological well-being', *Work and Stress*, 24(1), 1–35.

Hayton, J. C., and Cacciotti, G. (2013) 'Is there an entrepreneurial culture? A review of empirical research', *Entrepreneurship and Regional Development*, 25 (9/10), 708–31.

Hayton, J. C., George, G., and Zahra, S. A. (2002) 'National culture and entrepreneurship: a review of behavioural research', *Entrepreneurship Theory and Practice*, 26(4), 33–55.

Heberle, R. (1948) 'Social consequences of the industrialization of southern cities', *Social Forces*, 27(1), 29–37.

Hechavarria, D. M., and Reynolds, P. D. (2009) 'Cultural norms and business start-ups: the impact of national values on opportunity and necessity entrepreneurs', *International Entrepreneurship and Management Journal*, 5(4), 417–37.

Henisz, W. J., and Zelner, B. A. (2017) *Measures of Political Risk*, Philadelphia, PA: Wharton School, University of Pennsylvania.

Henn, S. (2015) 'Knowledge generation and field reproduction in temporary clusters and the role of business conferences', *Geoforum*, 58, 104–13.

Henrekson, M., and Sanandaji, T. (2011) 'The interaction of entrepreneurship and institutions', *Journal of Institutional Economics*, 7(1), 47–75.

Henrekson, M., and Sanandaji, T. (2014) 'Small business activity does not measure entrepreneurship', *Proceedings of the National Academy of Sciences of the United States of America*, 111(5), 1760–5.

Herod, A. (2001) *Labor Geographies: Workers and the Landscapes of Capitalism*, New York, NY: Guildford Press.

Hester, L. K., and Fuller Jr., J. B. (2001) 'Building union commitment: the impact of parental attitudes and participation', *Labor Studies Journal*, 26(2), 17–30.

Heydemann, S. (2008) 'Institutions and economic performance: the use and abuse of culture in new institutional economics', *Studies in Comparative and International Development*, 43(1), 27–52.

Hibbing, J. R., and Patterson, S. C. (1994) 'Public trust in the new parliaments of central and eastern Europe', *Political Studies*, 42(4), 570–92.

Hillygus, D. S. (2005) 'The missing link: exploring the relationship between higher education and political engagement', *Political Behavior*, 27(1), 25–47.

Hindricks, J., and Myles, G. D. (2006) *Intermediate Public Economics*, Cambridge, MA: MIT Press.

Hirsch, F. (1977) *Social limits to growth*, London: Routledge & Kegan Paul.

Hirschauer, N., Lehberger, M., and Musshoff, O. (2015) 'Happiness and utility in economic thought-or: what can we learn from happiness research for public policy analysis and public policy making', *Social Indicators Research*, 121(3), 647–74.

Hirschle, J., and Kleiner, T-M. (2014) 'Regional cultures attracting interregional migrants', *Urban Studies*, 51(16), 3348–64.

Hirschman, A.O. (1965) 'Obstacles to development: a classification and a quasi-vanishing act', *Economic Development and Cultural Change*, 13(4), 385–93.

Hitt, M. A., and Xu, K. (2016) 'The transformation of China: effects of the institutional environment on business actions', *Long Range Planning*, 49(5), 589–93.

Ho, T. H., Lim, N., and Camerer, C. F. (2006) 'Modeling the psychology of consumer and firm behaviour with behavioural economics', *Journal of Marketing Research*, 43(3), 307–31.

Hodgson, G. M. (2006) 'What are institutions?', *Journal of Economic Issues*, 40(1), 1–25.

Hodgson, G. M. (2007) 'Meanings of methodological individualism', *Journal of Economic Methodology*, 14(2), 211–26.

Hodson, G., and Sorrentino, R. M. (1999) 'Uncertainty orientation and the Big Five personality structure', *Journal of Research in Personality*, 33(2), 253–61.

Hofstede, G. (1980) *Culture's Consequences: International Differences in Work-Related Values* (1st edn), Beverly Hills, CA: Sage.

Hofstede, G. (1991) *Cultures and Organizations: Software of the Mind*, London: McGraw-Hill.

Hofstede, G. (2001) *Culture's Consequences: Comparing Values, Behaviors, Institutions, and Organizations Across Nations* (2nd edn), Thousand Oaks, CA: Sage.

Hofstede, G., and Bond, M. H. (1988) 'The Confucius connection: from cultural roots to economic growth', *Organizational Dynamics*, 16(4), 4–21.

Hofstede, G., De Hilal, A. V. G., Malvezzi, S., Tanure, B., and Vinken, H. (2010) 'Comparing regional cultures within a country: lessons from Brazil', *Journal of Cross-Cultural Psychology*, 41(3), 336–52.

Hofstede, G., and McCrae, R. R. (2004) 'Personality and culture revisited: linking traits and dimensions of culture', *Cross-Cultural Research*, 38(1), 52–88.

Hollanders, H., Es-Sadki, N., and Buligescu, B., et al. (2014) *Regional Innovation Scoreboard 2014*, Brussels: European Commission.

Holmes, T. J. (2006) 'Geographic spillover of unionism', National Bureau of Economic Research Working Paper No. 12025.

Hooghe, L., and Marks, G. (2005) 'Calculation, community and cues: public opinion on European integration', *European Union Politics*, 6(4), 419–43.

Hooghe, L., Marks, G. N., and Schakel, A. H. (2010) *The Rise of Regional Authority: A Comparative Study of 42 Democracies*, London: Routledge.

Hopkins, E. (2000) *Industrialisation and Society: A Social History, 1830–1951*, Abingdon: Routledge.

Hospers, G.-J. (2006) 'Silicon somewhere? Assessing the usefulness of best practices in regional policy', *Policy Studies*, 27(1), 1–15.

House, R. J., Hanges, P. J., Javidan, M., Dorfman, P. W., and Gupta, V. (2004) *Culture, Leadership and Organizations: The GLOBE Study of 62 Societies*, Thousand Oaks, CA: Sage.

Hoyman, M., McCall, J., Paarlberg, L., and Brennan, J. (2016) 'Considering the role of social capital for economic development outcomes in US counties', *Economic Development Quarterly*, 30(4), 342–57.

Huang, J., van den Brink, H. M., and Groot, W. (2009) 'A meta-analysis of the effect of education on social capital', *Economics of Education Review*, 28(4), 454–64.

Hudson, R. (2001) *Producing Places*, London: Guilford Press.

Huggins, R. (2003) 'Creating a UK competitiveness index: regional and local benchmarking', *Regional Studies*, 37(1), 89–96.

Huggins, R. (2008) 'The evolution of knowledge clusters progress and policy', *Economic Development Quarterly*, 22, 277–89.

Huggins, R. (2016) 'Capital, institutions and urban growth systems', *Cambridge Journal of Regions, Economy and Society*, 9(2), 443–63.

Huggins, R., and Clifton, N. (2011) 'Competitiveness, creativity, and place-based development', *Environment and Planning A*, 43(6), 1341–62.

Huggins, R., and Izushi, H. (2007) *Competing for Knowledge: Creating, Connecting and Growing*, London: Routledge.

Huggins, R., and Izushi, H. (eds.) (2011) *Competition, Competitive Advantage and Clusters: The Ideas of Michael Porter*, Oxford: Oxford University Press.

Huggins, R., Izushi, H., Prokop, D., and Thompson, P. (2014b) *The Global Competitiveness of Regions*, Abingdon: Routledge.

Huggins, R., and Johnston, A. (2010) 'Knowledge flow and inter-firm networks: The influence of network resources, spatial proximity, and firm size', *Entrepreneurship and Regional Development*, 22(5), 457–84.

Huggins, R., Luo, S., and Thompson, P. (2014a) 'The competitiveness of China's leading regions: benchmarking their knowledge-based economies', *Tijdschrift voor Economishe en Sociale Geografie*, 105(3), 241–67.

Huggins, R., and Prokop, D. (2017) Network structure and regional innovation: A study of university–industry ties, *Urban Studies*, 54(4) 931–52.

Huggins, R., and Thompson, P. (2012) 'Well-being and competitiveness: are the two linked at a place-based level?', *Cambridge Journal of Regions, Economy and Society*, 5(1), 45–60.

Huggins, R., and Thompson, P. (2014) 'A network-based view of regional growth', *Journal of Economic Geography*, 14 (3), 511–45.

Huggins, R., and Thompson, P. (2015a) 'Culture and place-based development: a socio-economic analysis', *Regional Studies*, 49(1), 130–59.

Huggins, R., and Thompson, P. (2015b) 'Entrepreneurship, innovation and regional growth: a network theory', *Small Business Economics*, 45(1), 103–28.

Huggins, R., and Thompson, P. (2015c) 'Local entrepreneurial resilience and culture: the role of social values in fostering economic recovery', *Cambridge Journal of Regions, Economy and Society*, 8(2), 313–30.

Huggins, R., and Thompson, P. (2016) 'Socio-spatial culture and entrepreneurship: some theoretical and empirical observations', *Economic Geography*, 92(3), 269–300.

Huggins, R., and Thompson, P. (2017a) 'Introducing regional competitiveness and development: contemporary theories and perspectives', in Huggins, R., and Thompson, P. (eds.) *Handbook of Regions and Competitiveness: Contemporary Theories and Perspectives on Economic Development*, Cheltenham: Edward Elgar, pp. 1–31.

Huggins, R., and Thompson, P. (2017b) 'Networks and regional economic growth: a spatial analysis of knowledge ties', *Environment and Planning A*, 49(6), 1247–65.

Huggins, R., and Thompson, P. (2019) 'The behavioural foundations of urban and regional development: culture, psychology and agency', *Journal of Economic Geography*, 19(1), 121–46.

Huggins, R., Thompson, P., and Obschonka, M. (2018) 'Human behaviour and economic growth: a psychocultural perspective on local and regional development', *Environment and Planning A*, 50(6), 1269–89.

Huggins, R., and Williams, N. (2011) 'Entrepreneurship and regional competitiveness: The role and progression of policy', *Entrepreneurship and Regional Development*, 23(9/10), 907–32.

Huggins, R., and Williams, N. (2012) 'Entrepreneurship and economic development', in Carter, S., and Jones-Evans, D. (eds.) *Enterprise and Small Business: Principles, Practice and Policy* (3rd Edn), London: Prentice Hall, pp. 27–45.

Hülsbeck, M., and Pickavé, E. N. (2014) 'Regional knowledge production as determinant of high-technology entrepreneurship: empirical evidence for Germany', *International Entrepreneurship and Management Journal*, 10(1), 121–38.

Hummelsheim, D., and Hirschle, J. (2010) 'Mother's employment: cultural imprint or institutional governance?', *European Societies*, 12(3), 339–66.

Humphrey, S. E., Nahrgang, J. D., and Morgeson, F. P. (2007) 'Integrating motivational, social, and contextual work design features: a meta-analytic summary and theoretical extension of the work design literature', *Journal of Applied Psychology*, 92(5), 1332–56.

Hundley, G. (2001) 'What and when are the self-employed more satisfied with their work?', *Industrial Relations*, 40(2), 293–316.

Hurtz, G. M., and Donovan, J. J. (2000) 'Personality and job performance: the big five revisited', *Journal of Applied Psychology*, 85(6), 869–79.

Hwang, H., and Powell, W. W. (2005) 'Institutions and entrepreneurship', in Alvarez, S. A., Agarwal, R., and Sorenson, O. (eds.) *Handbook of Entrepreneurship Research: Interdisciplinary Perspectives*, New York, NY: Springer, pp. 201–32.

Ilies, R., Scott, B. A., and Judge, T. A. (2006) 'A multilevel analysis of the effects of positive personal traits, positive experienced states and their interactions on intraindividual patterns of citizenship behaviour at work', *Academy of Management Journal*, 49(3), 561–75.

Ilies, R., Yao, J., Curseu, P. L., and Liang, A. X. (2019) 'Educated and happy: a four-year study explaining the links between education, job fit, and life satisfaction', *Applied Psychology*, 68(1), 150–76.

Ince, A., Featherstone, D., Cumbers, A., MacKinnon, D., and Strauss, K. (2015) 'British jobs for British workers? Negotiating work, nation, and globalisation through the Lindsey Oil Refinery disputes', *Antipode*, 47(1), 139–57.

Inglehart, R. (1971) 'The silent revolution in Europe: intergenerational change in six countries', *American Political Science Review*, 65(4), 991–1017.

Inglehart, R., and Abramson, P. R. (1999) 'Measuring postmaterialism', *American Political Science Review*, 93(3), 665–77.

Inglehart, R., and Baker, W. E. (2000) 'Modernization, cultural change, and the persistence of traditional values', *American Sociological Review*, 65(1), 19–51.

Inglehart, R., and Welzel, C. (2010) 'Changing mass priorities: the link between modernization and democracy', *Perspectives on Politics*, 8(2), 551–67.

Inkeles, A., Hanfmann, E., and Beier, H. (1958) 'Modal personality and the adjustment to the Soviet socio-political system', *Human Relations*, 11(1), 3–22.

Inkeles, A., and Levinson, D. J. (1969) 'National character: the study of modal personality and sociocultural systems', in Lindzey, G., and Aronson, E. (eds.) *The Handbook of Social Psychology: Volume IV, Group Psychology and the Phenomenon of Interaction*, New York, NY: McGraw-Hill, pp. 418–506.

Jackson, M. O., Rogers, B., and Zenou, Y. (2016) 'Networks: An Economic Perspective', CEPR Discussion Paper Series No. DP11452.

Jackson, P. (1991) 'Mapping meanings: a cultural critique of locality studies', *Environment and Planning A*, 23(2), 215–28.

Jackson, T. (2017) *Prosperity Without Growth: Foundations for the Economy of Tomorrow*, London: Routledge.

Jacobs, J. (1961) *The Death and Life of Great American Cities*, New York, NY: Modern Library.

Jacobs, J. (1969) *The Economy of Cities*, New York, NY: Random House.

Jaffe, A. B., Trajtenberg, M., and Henderson, R. (1993) 'Geographic localization of knowledge spillovers as evidenced by patent citations', *Quarterly Journal of Economics*, 108(3), 577–98.

James, A. (2005) 'Demystifying the role of culture in innovative regional economies', *Regional Studies*, 39(9), 1197–216.

James, A. (2011) 'Regional cultural economy: evolution and innovation', in Cooke, P., Asheim, B., Boschma, R., Martin, R., Schwartz, D., and Tödtling, F. (eds.) *Handbook of Regional Innovation and Growth*, Cheltenham: Edward Elgar, pp. 246–64.

Jejeebhoy, S., Acharya, R., Alexander, M., Garda, A., and Kanade, S. (2010) 'Measuring agency among unmarried young women and men', *Economic and Political Weekly*, 45(30), 24–30.

Jessop, B., Fairclough, N., and Wodak, R. (2008) *Education and the Knowledge-Based Economy in Europe*, Rotterdam: Sense Publishers.

Johansson Sevä, I., Larsson, D., and Strandh, M. (2016) 'The prevalence, characteristics and well-being of "necessity" self-employed and 'latent' entrepreneurs: findings from Sweden', *International Journal of Entrepreneurship and Small Business*, 28(1), 58–77.

John, O. P., Naumann, L. P., and Soto, C. J. (2008) 'Paradigm shift to the integrative Big Five taxonomy: history, measurement and conceptual issues', in John, O. P., Robins, R. W., and Pervin, L. A. (eds.) *Handbook of Personality: Theory and Research*, New York, NY: Guilford Press, pp. 114–58.

John, O. P., and Srivastava, S. (1999) 'The big five trait taxonomy: history, measurement, and theoretical perspectives', in John, O. P., and Pervin, L. A. (eds.) *Handbook of Personality: Theory and Research,* New York, NY: Guilford Press, pp. 102–38.

Johnstone, H., and Lionais, D. (2004) 'Depleted communities and community business entrepreneurship: revaluing space though place', *Entrepreneurship and Regional Development*, 16(3), 217–33.

Jokela, M. (2009) 'Personality predictions migration within and between US states', *Journal of Research in Personality*, 43(1), 79–83.

Jokela, M. (2013) 'Personality and the realization of migration desires', in Rentfrow, P. J. (ed.) *Geographical Psychology: Exploring the Interaction of Environment and Behaviour*, Washington, DC: American Psychological Association, pp. 71–87.

Jokela, M., Bleidorn, W., Lamb, M. E., Gosling, S. D., and Rentfrow, P. J. (2015) 'Geographically varying associations between personality and life satisfaction in the London metropolitan area', *Proceedings of the National Academy of Sciences of United States of America*, 112(3), 725–30.

Jokela, M., Elovainio, M., Kivimäki, M., and Keltikangas-Järtvinen, L. (2008) 'Temperament and migration patterns in Finland', *Psychological Science*, 19(9), 831–7.

Jones, P., and Dawson, P. (2007) '"Choice" in collective decision-making processes: instrumental or expressive approval?', *Journal of Socio-Economics*, 36(1), 102–17.

Jones, P. R., and Cullis, J. G. (1986) 'Is democracy regressive? A comment on political participation', *Public Choice*, 51(1), 101–7.

Jones, R. (2012) 'State encounters', *Environment and Planning D: Society and Space*, 30(5), 805–21.

Jones, R., Pykett, J., and Whitehead, M. (2013) 'Behaviour change policies in the UK: an anthropological perspective', *Geoform*, 48, 33–41.

Judge, T. A., Higgins, C. A., Thoresen, C. J., and Barrick, M. R. (1999) 'The big five personality traits, general mental ability, and career success across the life span', *Personnel Psychology*, 52(3), 621–52.

Juster, F. T. (1985) 'Preferences for work and leisure', in Juster, F. T., and Stafford, F. P. (eds.) *Time, Goods, and Well-being*, Ann Arbor, MI: Institute for Social Research, pp. 333–51.

Justman, M., and Gradstein, M. (1999) 'The industrial revolution, political transition, and the subsequent decline in inequality in 19th-century Britain', *Explorations in Economic History*, 36(2), 109–27.

Kaasa, A., Vadi, M., and Varblane, U. (2013) 'European Social Survey as a source of new cultural dimensions estimates for regions', *International Journal of Cross Cultural Management*, 13(2), 137–57.

Kaasa, A., Vadi, M., and Varblane, U. (2014) 'Regional cultural differences within European countries: evidence from multi-country surveys', *Management International Review*, 54(6), 825–52.

Kahneman, D. (2003) 'Maps of bounded rationality: Psychology for behavioral economics', *American Economic Review*, 93(5), 1449–75.

Kahneman, D., and Tversky, A. (1979) 'Prospect theory: an analysis of decision under risk', *Econometrica*, 47(2), 263–91.

Kaniovski, S. (2019) 'Turnout: why do voters vote?', in Congleton, R. D., Grofman, B., and Voigt, S. (eds.) *Oxford Handbook of Public Choice Volume 1*, Oxford: Oxford University Press, pp. 310–32.

Kant, I. (1992) [1784] 'An answer to the question: what is enlightenment?', in P. Waugh (ed.), *Postmodernism: A Reader*, London: Edward Arnold, pp. 89–95.

Katz, C. (2004) *Growing Up Global: Economic Restructuring and Children's Everyday Lives*, Minneapolis, MN: University of Minnesota Press.

Kaufmann, D., Kraay, A., and Mastruzzi, M. (2009) 'Governance matters VIII: aggregate and individual governance indicators for 1996–2008', World Bank Policy Research Working Paper No. 4978.

Kearns, A., and Forrest, R. (2000) 'Social cohesion and multilevel urban governance', *Urban Studies*, 37(5/6), 995–1017.

Keating, M., Loughlin, J., and Deschouwer, K. (2003) *Culture, Institutions and Economic Development: A Study of Eight European Regions*, Cheltenham: Edward Elgar.

Kelley, J., and Evans, M. D. R. (2017) 'Societal inequality and individual subjective well-being: results from 68 societies and over 200,000 individuals, 1981-2008', *Social Science Research*, 62, 1–23.

Kemeny, T., Feldman, M., Ethridge, F., and Zoller, T. (2016) 'The economic value of local social networks', *Journal of Economic Geography*, 16(5), 1101–22.

Kerr, S. P., Kerr, W. R., and Xu, T. (2018) 'Personality traits of entrepreneurs: a review of recent literature', *Foundations and Trends® in Entrepreneurship*, 14(3), 279–356.

Khandwalla, P. (1977) *The Design of Organizations*, New York, NY: Harcourt Brace Jovanovich.

Kibler, E., Kautonen, T., and Fink, M. (2014) 'Regional social legitimacy of entrepreneurship: implications for entrepreneurial intention and start-up behaviour', *Regional Studies*, 48(6), 995–1015.

Kim, G. (2007) 'The analysis of self-employment levels over the life-cycle', *Quarterly Review of Economics and Finance*, 47(3), 397–410.

Kim, S., and Law, M. T. (2016) 'Political centralization, federalism, and urban development: evidence from US and Canadian capital cities', *Social Science History*, 40(1), 121–46.

King, Z., Burke, S., and Pemberton, J. (2005) 'The bounded career: an empirical study of human capital, career mobility and employment outcomes in a mediated labour market', *Human Relations*, 58(8), 981–1007.

Kirchler, E., and Hoelzl, E. (2018) *Economic Psychology: An Introduction*, Cambridge: Cambridge University Press.

Kirkman, B. L., Lowe, K. B., and Gibson, C. B. (2006) 'A quarter century of "Culture's Consequences": a review of empirical research incorporating Hofstede's cultural values framework', *Journal of International Business Studies*, 37(3), 285–320.

Kirzner, I. M. (1973) *Competition and Entrepreneurship*, Chicago, IL: University of Chicago.

Kitson, M., Martin, R., and Tyler, P. (2004) 'Regional competitiveness: An elusive yet key concept?', *Regional Studies*, 38(9), 991–9.

Klotz, A. C., and Neubaum, D. O. (2016) 'Research on the dark side of personality traits in entrepreneurship: observations from an organizational behavior perspective', *Entrepreneurship Theory and Practice*, 40(1), 7–17.

Klyver, K., and Foley, D. (2012) 'Networking and culture in entrepreneurship', *Entrepreneurship and Regional Development*, 24(7/8), 561–88.

Knack, S., and Keefer, P. (1997) 'Does social capital have an economic impact? A cross-country payoff', *Quarterly Journal of Economics*, 112(4), 1251–88.

Knight, F. (1921) *Risk, Uncertainty and Profit*, New York, NY: Houghton Mifflin.

Knight, G. A. (1997) 'Cross-cultural reliability and validity of a scale to measure firm entrepreneurial orientation', *Journal of Business Venturing*, 12(3), 213–25.

Knoke, D., and Kuklinski, J. (1982) *Network Analysis*. Beverley Hills, CA: Sage.

Knott, D., Muers, S., and Aldridge, S. (2008) 'Achieving cultural change: a policy framework', Strategy Unit Discussion Paper, London: Cabinet Office.

Kockel, U. (2002) *Regional Culture and Economic Development: Explorations in European Ethnology*, Aldershot: Ashgate.

Kohn, M. L., and Schooler, C. (1982) 'Job conditions and personality: a longitudinal assessment of their reciprocal effects', *American Journal of Sociology*, 87(6), 1257–86.

Kohn, M. L., and Schooler, C. (1983) *Work and Personality: An Inquiry into the Impact of Social Stratification*, Norwood, NJ: Ablex.

Kolvereid, L. (2016) 'Preference for self-employment: prediction of new business start-up intentions and efforts', *International Journal of Entrepreneurship and Innovation*, 17(2), 100–9.

Kolvin, I., Charles, G., Nicholson, R., Fleeting, M., and Fundudis, T. (1990) 'Factors in prevention in inner-city deprivation', in Goldberg, D., and Tantam, D. (eds.) *The Public Health Impact of Mental Disorder*, Lewiston, NY: Hogrefe & Huber, pp. 115–23.

Komlos, J. (1998) 'Shrinking in a growing economy? The mystery of physical stature during the Industrial Revolution', *Journal of Economic History*, 58(3), 779–802.

Kramer, J.-P., Marinelli, E., Iammarino, S., and Revilla Diez, J. (2011) 'Intangible assets as drivers of innovation: Empirical evidence on multinational enterprises in German and UK regional systems of innovation', *Technovation*, 31(9), 447–58.

Kramer, J.-P., and Revilla Diez, J. (2012) 'Catching the local buzz by embedding? Empirical insights on the regional embeddedness of multinational enterprises in Germany and the UK', *Regional Studies*, 46(10), 1303–17.

Krugman, P. (2005) 'Second winds for industrial regions?', in Coyle D., Alexander, W., and Ashcroft, B. (eds.) *New Wealth for Old Nations: Scotland's Economic Prospects*, Princeton, NJ: Princeton University Press, pp. 35–47.

Kwon, S. W., and Adler, P. S. (2014) 'Social capital: Maturation of a field of research', *Academy of Management Review*, 39(4), 412–22.

Kwong, C., Jones-Evans, D., and Thompson, P. (2012) 'Differences in perceptions of access to finance between potential male and female entrepreneurs: evidence from the UK', *Internal Journal of Entrepreneurial Behaviour and Research*, 18(1), 75–97.

Kwong, C., and Thompson, P. (2016) 'The when and why: student entrepreneurial aspirations', *Journal of Small Business Management*, 54(1), 299–318.

Lampel, J., and Meyer, A. D. (2008) 'Field-configuring events as structuring mechanisms: how conferences, ceremonies, and trade shows constitute new technologies, industries, and markets', *Journal of Management Studies*, 45(6), 1025–35.

Landes, D. (1953) 'Social attitudes, entrepreneurship and economic development: a comment', *Explorations in Entrepreneurial History*, 6(4), 245–72.

Lavoie, D. (1991) 'The discovery and interpretation of profit opportunities: culture and the Kirznerian entrepreneur', in Berger, B. (ed.) *The Culture of Entrepreneurship*, San Francisco, CA: ICS Press, pp. 33–51.

Lawless, N. M., and Lucas, R. E. (2011) 'Predictors of regional well-being: a county level analysis', *Social Indicators Research*, 101(3), 341–57.

Lawton Smith, H., Romeo, S., and Virahsawmy, M. (2012) 'Business and professional networks: Scope and outcomes in Oxfordshire', *Environment and Planning A*, 44(8), 1801–18.

Layard, R. (2005) 'Rethinking public economics: the implications of rivalry and habit', in Bruni, L., and Porta, P. L. (eds.) *Economics and Happiness: Framing the Analysis*, Oxford: Oxford University Press, pp. 147–70.

Layard, R. (2006) *Happiness: Lessons from a New Science* (2nd edn), London: Penguin.

Laybourn, K. (1992) *A History of British Trade Unionism c.1770–1990*. Sutton Publishing Ltd.

Le, A. (1999) 'Empirical studies of self-employment', *Journal of Economic Surveys*, 13(4), 381–416.

Lee I. H., Paik Y., and Uygur, U. (2016) 'Does gender matter in the export performance of international new ventures? Mediation effects of firm-specific and country specific advantages', *Journal of International Management*, 22(4), 365–79.

Lee, N. D. (2017) 'Psychology and the geography of innovation', *Economic Geography*, 93(2), 106–30.

Lee, R. (1989) 'Social relations and the geography of material life', in Gregory, D., and Walford, R. (eds.) *Horizons in Human Geography*, London, and New York, NY: Macmillan, pp. 152–69.

Lee, S. M., and Peterson, S. J. (2000) 'Culture, entrepreneurial orientation, and global competitiveness', *Journal of World Business*, 35(4), 401–16.

Le Garrec, G. (2018). 'Fairness, social norms and the cultural demand for redistribution'. *Social Choice and Welfare*, 50(2), 191–212.

Lenartowicz, T., Johnson, J. P., and White, C. T. (2003) 'The neglect of intracountry cultural variation in international management research', *Journal of Business Research*, 56(12), 999–1008.

Leonidou, L. C., Christodoulides, P., and Thwaites, D. (2016) 'External determinants and financial outcomes of an eco-friendly orientation in smaller manufacturing firms', *Journal of Small Business Management*, 54(1), 5–25.

Lerner, D. (1958) *The Passing of Traditional Society: Modernising the Middle East*, New York, NY: Free Press.

Leutner, F., Ahmetoglu, G., Akhtar, R., and Chamorro-Premuzic, T. (2014) 'The relationship between the entrepreneurial personality and the Big Five personality traits', *Personality and Individual Differences*, 63(1), 58–63.

Lévesque, M., and Minniti, M. (2006) 'The effect of aging on entrepreneurial behaviour', *Journal of Business Venturing*, 21(2), 177–94.

Levie, J. (2007) 'Immigration, in-migration, ethnicity and entrepreneurship in the United Kingdom', *Small Business Economics*, 28(2/3), 143–69.

Le Vine, R. A. (2001) 'Culture and personality studies, 1918-1960: myth and history', *Journal of Personality*, 69(6), 803–18.

Lewin, K. (1936) 'Some social psychological differences between the United States and Germany', *Journal of Personality*, 4(4), 265–93.

Lewis, H. G. (1963) *Unionism and Relative Wages in the United States: An Empirical Inquiry*, Chicago, IL: University of Chicago Press.

Licht, A.N., Goldschmidt, C., and Schwarz, S.H. (2007) 'Culture rules: the foundations of the rule of law and other norms of governance', *Journal of Comparative Economics*, 35(4), 659–88.

Lier, D. C. (2009) *The Practice of Neoliberalism: Responses to Public Sector Restructuring Across the Labour-Community Divide in Cape Town. NIBR Report 2009*, Oslo: Norwegian Institute for Urban and Regional Research.

Liñán, F., and Fernandez-Serrano, J. (2014) 'National culture, entrepreneurship and economic development: different patterns across the European Union', *Small Business Economics*, 42(4), 685–701.

Linton, M.-J., Dieppe, P., and Medina,-Lara, A. (2016) 'Review of 99 self-report measures for assessing well-being in adults: exploring dimensions of well-being and developments over time', *BMJ Open*, 6, e010641. DOI: 10.1136/bmjopen-2015-010641.

Lippmann, S., and Aldrich, H. (2016) 'A rolling stone gathers momentum: generational units, collective memory, and entrepreneurship', *Academy of Management Review*, 41(4), 658–75.

Lipset, S. M. (1992) 'The work ethic, then and now', *Journal of Labor Research*, 13(1), 45–54.

Lomax, N., Stillwell, J., Norman, P., and Rees, P. (2014) 'Internal migration in the United Kingdom: analysis of an estimated inter-district time series, 2001-2011', *Applied Spatial Analysis*, 7(1), 25–45.

Longhurst, B. (1991) 'Raymond Williams and local cultures', *Environment and Planning A*, 23(2), 229–38.

Lorenzen, M. (2007) 'Social capital and localised learning: proximity and place in technological and institutional dynamics', *Urban Studies*, 44(4), 799–817.

Lowndes, V., and McCaughie, K. (2013) 'Weathering the perfect storm? Austerity and institutional resilience in local government', *Policy and Politics*, 41(4), 533–49.

Lowndes, V., and Roberts, M. (2013) *Why Institutions Matter: The New Institutionalism in Political Science*, London: Palgrave Macmillan.

Lundberg, U., Granqvist, M., Hansson, T., Magnusson, M., and Wallin, L. (1989) 'Psychological and physiological stress responses during repetitive work at an assembly line', *Work and Stress*, 3(2), 143–53.

Luster, T., Rhoades, K., and Haas, B. (1989) 'The relation between parental values and parenting behaviour: a test of the Kohn hypothesis', *Journal of Marriage and the Family*, 51(1), 139–47.

Luttmer, E. F. P., and Singhal, M. (2011) 'Culture, context, and the taste for redistribution', *American Economic Journal: Economic Policy*, 3(1), 157–79.

Lynch, J. W., Kaplan, G. A., and Shema, S. J. (1997) 'Cumulative impact of sustained economic hardship on physical, cognitive, psychological, and social functioning', *New England Journal of Medicine*, 337(26), 1889–95.

McCann, P., and Ortega-Argilés, R. (2015) 'Smart specialization, regional growth and applications to European Union cohesion policy', *Regional Studies*, 49(8), 1291–302.

McClelland, D. C. (1961) *The Achieving Society*, Princeton, NJ: Van Nostrand.

McClurg, S. D. (2003) 'Social networks and political participation: the role of social interaction in explaining political participation', *Political Research Quarterly*, 56(4), 449–64.

McCracken, G. (1990) *Culture and Consumption: New Approaches to the Symbolic Character of Consumer Goods and Activities*, Bloomington, IN: Indiana University Press.

McCrae, R. R. (1996) 'Social consequences of experiential openness', *Psychological Bulletin*, 120(3), 323–37.

McCrae, R.R., and Terracciano, A. (2005) 'Personality profiles of cultures: aggregate personality traits', *Journal of Personality and Social Psychology*, 89(3), 407–25.

McDowell, L. (2009) *Working Bodies: Interactive Service Employment and Workplace Identities*, Oxford: Wiley-Blackwell.

McEvoy, D., and Hafeez, K. (2007) 'Dispersal and diversity in ethnic minority enterprise in England and Wales', Paper presented at the 1st International Colloquium on Ethnic Entrepreneurship and Management, 22–23 March 2007, Bradford, UK.

Macfarlane, A. (1978) *The Origins of English Individualism*, Oxford: Oxford University Press.

Mackay, R. R. (2001) 'Regional taxing and spending: the search for balance', *Regional Studies*, 35(6), 563–75.

MacKinnon, D. (2017) 'Labour branching, redundancy and livelihoods: towards a more socialised conception of adaptation in evolutionary economic geography', *Geoforum*, 79, 70–80.

MacKinnon, D., Cumbers, A., and Chapman, K., (2002) 'Learning, innovation and regional development: a critical appraisal of recent debates', *Progress in Human Geography*, 26(3), 293–311.

MacKinnon, D., Cumbers, A., Pike, A., Birch, K., McMaster, R. (2009) 'Evolution in economic geography: institutions, political economy, and adaptation', *Economic Geography*, 85(2), 129–50.

Malecki, E. J. (2007) 'Cities and regions competing in the global economy: knowledge and local development policies', *Environment and Planning C: Government and Policy*, 25(5), 638–54.

Malecki, E. J. (2017) 'Economic competitiveness and regional development dynamics', in Huggins, R., and Thompson, P. (eds.) *Handbook of Regions and Competitiveness: Contemporary Theories and Perspectives on Economic Development*, Cheltenham: Edward Elgar, pp. 136–52.

Manning, A., and Swaffield, J. (2008) 'The gender pay gap in early-career wage growth', *Economic Journal*, 113(530), 983–1024.

Manski, C. F. (2000) 'Economic analysis of social interactions', *Journal of Economic Perspectives*, 14(3), 115–36.

Marcén, M. (2014) 'The role of culture on self-employment', *Economic Modelling*, 44 (S1), S20–32.

Marcketti, S. B., Niehm, L. S., and Fuloria, R. (2009) 'An exploratory study of lifestyle entrepreneurship and its relationship to life quality', *Family and Consumer Science*, 34(3), 241–59.

Marien, S., and Christensen, H. S. (2013) 'Trust and openness: prerequisites for democratic engagement?', in Demetriou, K. (ed.) *Democracy in Transition*, Berlin: Springer, pp. 109–34.

Marshall, F. R. (1967) *Labor in the South*, Cambridge, MA: Harvard University Press.

Martin, R. (2000) 'Institutional approaches in economic geography', in E. Sheppard and T. J. Barnes (eds.) *A Companion to Economic Geography*, 77–94. Oxford: Blackwell.

Martin, R. (2012) 'Regional economic resilience, hysteresis and recessionary shocks', *Journal of Economic Geography*, 12(1), 1–32.

Martin, R., Gardiner, B., and Tyler, P. (2014) '*The evolving economic performance of UK cities: city growth patterns 1981–2011*', Future of cities: working paper, London: Foresight, Government Office for Science.

Martin, R., and Sunley, P. (2003) 'Deconstructing clusters: chaotic concept of policy panacea?', *Journal of Economic Geography*, 3(1), 5–35.

Martin, R., and Sunley, P. (2006) 'Path dependence and regional economic evolution', *Journal of Economic Geography*, 6(4), 395–437.

Martin, R., and Sunley, P. (2011) 'Conceptualizing cluster evolution: beyond the life cycle model?', *Regional Studies*, 45(10), 1299–318.

Martin, R., and Sunley, P. (2015a) 'Towards a developmental turn in evolutionary economic geography?', *Regional Studies*, 49(5), 712–32.

Martin, R., and Sunley, P. (2015b) 'On the Notion of Regional Economic Resilience: Conceptualization and Explanation', *Journal of Economic Geography*, 15 (1): 1–42.

Martin, R., and Sunley, P. (2017) 'Competitiveness and regional economic resilience', in Huggins, R., and Thompson, P. (eds.) *Handbook of Regions and Competitiveness: Contemporary Theories and Perspectives on Economic Development*, Cheltenham: Edward Elgar, pp. 287–307.

Marx, K. (1859. [1979]) *A Contribution to the Critique of Political Economy*, New York, NY: International Publishers.

Maseland, R., and van Hoorn, A. (2010) 'Values and marginal preferences in international business', *Journal of International Business Studies*, 41(8), 1425–9.

Maslow, A. (1970) *Motivation and Personality*, New York, NY: Harper & Row.

Maslow, A. H. (1943) 'A theory of human motivation', *Psychological Review*, 50(4), 370–96.

Mason, C., and Brown, R. (2013) 'Creating good public policy to support high-growth firms', *Small Business Economics*, 40(2), 211–25.

Massey, D. (1984) *Spatial Divisions of Labour: Social Structures and the Geography of Production*, London: Macmillan.

Massey, D. (2001) 'Geography on the agenda', *Progress in Human Geography*, 25(1), 5–17.

Massey, D. (2004) 'The responsibilities of place', *Local Economy*, 19(2), 97–101.

Mathieu, J. E., Tannenbaum, S. I., Donbach, J. S., and Alliger, G.M. (2014) 'A review and integration of team composition models: moving toward a dynamic and temporal framework', *Journal of Management*, 40(1), 130–60.

Matthews, K. A., and Gallo, L. C. (2011) 'Psychological perspectives on pathways linking socioeconomic status and physical health', *Annual Review of Psychology*, 62, 501–30.

Mauss, M. (1925/1990) *The Gift: The Form and Reason for Exchange in Archaic Societies*, trans. Halls, D. W., New York, NY: W.W. Norton.

Mead, M. (1951) *Soviet Attitudes Toward Authority: An Interdisciplinary Approach to Problems of Soviet Character*, New York, NY: McGraw-Hill.

Mellander, C., and Florida, R. (2011) 'Creativity, talent, and regional wages in Sweden', *Annual of Regional Science*, 46(3), 637–60.

Mellander, C., Florida, R., and Stolarick, K. (2011) 'Here to stay – the effects of community satisfaction on the decision to stay', *Spatial Economic Analysis*, 6(1), 5–24.

Meltzer, A. H., and Richard, S. F. (1981) 'A rational theory of the size of government', *Journal of Political Economy*, 89(5), 914–27.

Meyer, K. E., and Peng, M. W. (2005) 'Probing theoretically into Central and Eastern Europe: transactions, resources, and institutions', *Journal of International Business Studies*, 36(6), 600–21.

Michalos, A. C. (2008) 'Education, happiness and wellbeing', *Social Indicators Research*, 87(3), 347–66.

Michalos, A. C., and Orlando, J. A. (2006) 'A note on student quality of life', *Social Indicators Research*, 79(1), 51–9.

Milkis, S., and Baldino, T. (1978) 'The future of the silent revolution: a re-examination of intergenerational change in Western Europe', Paper presented at the annual meeting of the Mid-West Political Science Association, 21 April 1978, Chicago.

Miller, B. (1992) 'Collective action and rational choice: place, community, and the limits to individual self-interest', *Economic Geography*, 68(1), 22–42.

Miller, D. (2014) 'A downside to the entrepreneurial personality', *Entrepreneurship Theory and Practice*, 39(1), 1–8.

Miller, D. (2016) 'Response to "Research on the dark side of personality traits in entrepreneurship: observations from an organizational behaviour perspective"', *Entrepreneurship Theory and Practice*, 40(1), 19–24.

Miller, D., and Friesen, P. (1978) 'Archetypes of strategy formulation', *Management Science*, 24(9), 921–33.

Miller, S. E., and Mannix, B. F. (2016) 'One standard to rule them all: the disparate impact of energy efficient regulations', in Abdukadirov, S. (ed.) *Nudge Theory in Action: Behavioral Design in Policy and Markets*, Basingstoke: Palgrave Macmillan, pp. 251–88.

Minniti, M. (2005) 'Entrepreneurship and network externalities', *Journal of Economic Behavior and Organization*, 57(1), 1–27.

Minniti, M., and Naudé, W. (2010) 'What do we know about the patterns and determinants of female entrepreneurship across countries?', *European Journal of Development Research*, 22(3), 277–93.

Miörner, J., Zukauskaite, E., Trippl, M., and Moodysson, J. (2018) 'Creating institutional preconditions for knowledge flows in cross-border regions', *Environmental and Planning C*, 36(2), 201–18.

Mizruchi, M., and Galaskiewicz, J. (1994) 'Networks of interorganizational relations', in Wasserman S., and Galaskiewicz, J. (eds.) *Advances in Social Network Analysis*, London: Sage, pp. 230–53.

Mokyr, J. (2015) 'Intellectuals and the rise of the modern economy', *Science*, 349(6244), 141–2.

Mokyr, J. (2017) *A Culture of Growth: The Origins of the Modern Economy*, Princeton, NJ: Princeton University Press.

Molema, M., and Svensson, S. (eds.) (2019) *Regional Economic Development and History*, Abingdon: Routledge.

Moos, A. I., and Dear, M. J. (1986) 'Structuration theory in urban analysis: 1. Theoretical exegesis', *Environment and Planning A*, 18(2), 231–52.

Moretti, E. (2012) *The New Geography of Jobs*, New York, NY: Houghton Mifflin & Harcourt.

Morgan, K. (1997) 'The learning region: institutions, innovation and regional renewal', *Regional Studies*, 31, 491–504.

Morgan, K. (2016) 'Collective entrepreneurship: the Basque model of innovation', *European Planning Studies*, 24(8), 1544–60.

Moulaert, F., and Nussbaumer, J. (2005) 'The social region: beyond the territorial dynamics of the learning economy', *European Urban and Regional Studies*, 12(1), 45–64.

Mueller, D. C. (2003) *Public Choice III*, Cambridge: Cambridge University Press.

Mueller, P. (2006) 'Entrepreneurship in the region: breeding ground for nascent entrepreneurs', *Small Business Economics*, 27(1), 41–58.

Mueller, S. L., and Thomas, A. S. (2001) 'Culture and entrepreneurial potential: a nine country study of locus of control and innovativeness', *Journal of Business Venturing*, 16(1), 51–75.

Murphy, K., Shleifer, A., and Vishny, R. (1993) 'Why is rent seeking so costly to growth?', *American Economic Review*, 83(2), 409–14.

Murphy, L., Huggins, R., and Thompson, P. (2016) 'Social capital and innovation: A comparative analysis of regional policies', *Environment and Planning C: Government and Policy*, 34(6), 1025–57.

Myrdal, G. (1957) *Economic Theory and Underdeveloped Regions*, London: Methuen.

Myrdal, G. (1968) *Asian Drama: An Inquiry into the Poverty of Nations*, London: Allen Lane.

Nathan, M., and Lee, N. (2013) 'Cultural diversity, innovation and entrepreneurship: firm-level evidence from London', *Economic Geography*, 89(4), 367–94.

Nelson, R. R., and Winter, S. G. (1982*) An evolutionary theory of economic change*, Cambridge MA: Belknap Press.

Nisbett, R. E. (2003) *The Geography of Thought: How Asians And Westerners Think Differently…and Why*, New York, NY: The Free Press.

Noorderhaven, N., Thurik, R., Wennekers, S., and van Stel, A. (2004) 'The role of dissatisfaction and per capita income in explaining self-employment across 15 European countries', *Entrepreneurship Theory and Practice*, 28(5), 447–66.

North, D. C. (1990) *Institutions, institutional change and economic performance*, Cambridge: Cambridge University Press.

North, D. C. (2005) *Understanding the Process of Economic Change*, Princeton, NJ: Princeton University Press.

Nowak, P. (2015) 'The past and future of trade unionism', *Employee Relations*, 37(6), 683–91.

Nunn, N. (2008) 'The long-term effects of Africa's slave trades', *Quarterly Journal of Economics*, 123(1), 139–75.

Nunn, N. (2009) 'The importance of history for economic development', *Annual Review of Economics*, 1(1), 65–92.

Nunn, N., and Wantchekon, L. (2011) 'The slave trade and the origins of mistrust in Africa', *American Economic Review*, 101(7), 3221–52.

Obschonka, M., Schmitt-Rodermund, E., Silbereisen, R. K., Gosling, S. D., and Potter, J. (2013a) 'The regional distribution and correlates of an entrepreneurship-prone personality profile in the United States, Germany, and the United Kingdom: a socioecological perspective', *Journal of Personality and Social Psychology*, 105(1), 104–22.

Obschonka, M., Andersson, H., Silbereisen, R. K., and Sverke, M. (2013b) 'Rule-breaking, crime, and entrepreneurship: a replication and extension study with 37-year longitudinal data', *Journal of Vocational Behavior*, 83(3), 386–96.

Obschonka, M., Stuetzer, M., Audretsch, D. B., Rentfrow, P. J., Potter, J., and Gosling, S. D. (2016) 'Macropsychological factors predict regional economic resilience during a major economic crisis', *Social Psychological and Personality Science*, 7(2), 95–104.

Obschonka, M., Stuetzer, M., Gosling, S. D., Rentfrow, P. J., Lamb, M. E., Potter, J., and Audretsch, D. B. (2015) 'Entrepreneurial regions: do macro-psychological cultural characteristics of regions help solve the "knowledge paradox" of economics?', *PLoS ONE*, 10(6), e0129332. DOI: 10.1371/journal.pone.0129332.

Obschonka, M., Stuetzer, M., Rentfrow, P. J., Potter, J., and Gosling, S. D. (2017) 'Did Strategic Bombing in the Second World War Lead to "German Angst"? A Large-scale Empirical Test Across 89 German Cities', *European Journal of Personality*, 31(3), 234–57.

Obschonka, M., Stuetzer, M., Rentfrow, P. J., Shaw-Taylor, L., Satchell, M., Silbereisen, R. K., Potter, J., and Gosling, S. D. (2018) 'In the shadow of coal: how large-scale industries contributed to present-day regional differences in personality and well-being', *Journal of Personality and Social Psychology*, 115(5), 903–27.

Office for National Statistics (2016) *Travel to work area analysis in Great Britain: 2016*, Newport: Office for National Statistics.

Office for National Statistics (2019) *Local Area Migration Indicators Suite QMI*, Fareham: Office for National Statistics.

Olson, M. (1965) *The Logic of Collective Action*, Cambridge, MA: Harvard University Press.

Olson, M. (1982) *Rise and Decline of Nations*, New Haven, CT: Yale University Press.

Oswald, A. J., and Powdthavee, N. (2008) 'Does happiness adapt? A longitudinal study of disability with implications for economists and judges', *Journal of Public Economics*, 92(5/6), 1061–77.

Ozer, E. M., and Bandura, A. (1990) 'Mechanisms governing empowerment effects: a self-efficacy analysis', *Journal of Personality and Social Psychology*, 58(3), 472–86.

Paço, A., and Lavrador, T. (2017) 'Environmental knowledge and attitudes and behaviours towards energy consumption', *Journal of Environmental Management*, 197, 384–92.

Palomera, J., and Vetta, T. (2016) 'Moral economy: Rethinking a radical concept', *Anthropological Theory*, 16(4), 413–32.

Parasuraman, S., Purohit, Y. S., Godshalk, V. M., and Beutell, N. J. (1996) 'Work and family variables, entrepreneurial career success, and psychological well-being', *Journal of Vocational Behavior*, 48(3), 275–300.

Parker, S. C. (2004) *The Economics of Self-Employment and Entrepreneurship*, Cambridge: Cambridge University Press.

Parks-Leduc, L., Feldman, G., and Bardi, A. (2015) 'Personality traits and personal values: a meta-analysis', *Personality and Social Psychology Review*, 19(1), 3–29.

Parsons, T. (1977) *The Evolution of Societies*, Englewood-Cliffs, NJ: Prentice-Hall.

Pasteur, L. (1854) *Inaugural Lecture*, Lille: University of Lille.

Patacchini, E., Picard, P. M., and Zenou, Y. (2015) 'Urban social structure, social capital and spatial proximity', CERP Discussion Paper No. DP10501.

Patel, P. C., Wolfe, M. T., and Williams, T. A. (2019) 'Self-employment and allostatic load', *Journal of Business Venturing*, 34(4), 731–51.

Peabody, D. (1988) *National Characteristics*, Cambridge: Cambridge University Press and Maison des Sciences de l'Homme.

Pearce, J. R., Richardson, E. A., Mitchell, R. J., and Shortt, N. K. (2010) 'Environmental justice and health: the implications of the socio-spatial distribution of multiple environmental deprivation for health inequalities in the United Kingdom', *Transactions of the Institute of British Geographers*, 35(4), 522–39.

Peck, J. (2001) *Workforce States*, New York, NY: Guilford Press.

Peck, J., and Zhang, J. (2013) 'A variety of capitalism…with Chinese characteristics?', *Journal of Economic Geography*, 13(3), 357–96.

Peet, R. (1997) 'The cultural production of economic forms', in Lee, R., and Wills, J. (eds.) *Geographies of Economies*, London: Arnold, pp. 37–46.

Peet, R. (2000) 'Culture, image, and rationality in regional economic development', *Environment and Planning A*, 32(7), 1215–34.

Perdue, C., Dovideo. J., Gurtman, M., and Tyler R. (1990) 'Us and them: Social categorization and the process of intergroup bias', *Journal of Personality and Social Psychology*, 59(3), 475–86.

Persson, T., and Tabellini, G. (2000) *Political Economics: Explaining Economic Policy*, London: MIT Press.

Peterson, G. (2000) 'Political ecology and ecological resilience: an integration of human and ecological dynamics', *Ecological Economics*, 35(3), 323–36.

Pettigrew, T. F., and Tropp, L. R. (2006) 'A meta-analytical test of intergroup contact theory', *Journal of Personality and Social Psychology*, 90(5), 751–83.

Phelps, E. S., and Pollak, R. A. (1968) 'On second-best national saving and game-equilibrium growth', *Review of Economic Studies*, 35(2), 185–99.

Philo, C. (1989) 'Thoughts, words, and 'creative locational acts', in Boal, F. W., and Livingstone, D. N. (eds.) *The Behavioural Environment: Essays in Reflection, Application and Re-evaluation*, London: Routledge, pp. 205–34.

Pike, A. (2007) 'Contesting closures: the limits and prospects of social agency', in Cumbers, A., and Whittingham, G. (eds.) *Reclaiming the Economy: Alternatives to Market Fundamentalism in Scotland and Beyond*, Glasgow: Scottish Left Review Press, pp. 64–78.

Pike, A., Birch, K., Cumbers, A., MacKinnon, D., and McMaster, R. (2009) 'A geographical political economy of evolution in economic geography', *Economic Geography*, 85(2), 175–82.

Pike, A., MacKinnon, D., and Cumbers, A. (2015) 'Doing evolution in economic geography', *Economic Geography*, 92(2), 123–44.

Pike, A., Rodríguez-Pose, A., and Tomaney, J. (2007) 'What kind of local and regional development and for whom?', *Regional Studies*, 41(9), 1253–69.

Pike, A., Rodríguez-Pose, A., and Tomaney, J. (2017) 'Shifting horizons in local and regional development', *Regional Studies*, 51(1), 46–57.

Piketty, T. (1995) 'Social mobility and redistributive politics', *Quarterly Journal of Economics*, 110(3), 551–84.

Piketty, T. (2014) *Capital in the Twenty-First Century*, Cambridge, MA: The Belknap Press of Harvard University Press.

Pitt, R. S., Sherman, J., and Macdonald, M. E. (2015) 'Low-income working immigrant families in Quebec: exploring their challenges to well-being', *Canadian Journal of Public Health/Revue Canadienne de Santé Publique*, 106(8), e539–45.

Polanyi, K. (1957) *The Great Transformation*, New York, NY: Rhinehart.

Porter, M. E. (1981) 'The contributions of industrial organization to strategic management', *Academy of Management Review*, 6(4), 609–20.

Portes A., and Landolt P. (1996) 'The downside of social capital', *American Prospect*, 26, 18–21.

Portes A., and Landolt P. (2000) 'Social capital: promise and pitfalls of its role in development', *Journal of Latin American Studies*, 32(2), 529–47.

Powell, W. W., Koput, K. W., and Smith-Doerr, L. (1996) 'Interorganizational collaboration and the locus of innovation: Networks of learning in biotechnology', *Administrative Science Quarterly*, 41(1), 116–45.

Power, A., Plöger, J., and Winkler, A. (2010) *Phoenix Cities: The Fall and Rise of Great Industrial Cities*, Bristol: Policy Press.

Prager, J.-C., and Thisse, J.-F. (2012) *Economic Geography and the Unequal Development of Regions*, London: Routledge.

Pred, A. (1967) *Behavior and Location. Foundations for a Geographic and Dynamic Location Theory*, Lund: C.W.K Gleerup.

Prewett, M. S., Brown, M. I., Goswami, A., and Christiansen, N. D. (2018) 'Effects of team personality composition on member performance: a multilevel perspective', *Group and Organization Management*, 43(2), 316–48.

Price, R. (1971) 'The working men's club movement and Victorian social reform ideology', *Victorian Studies,* 15(2), 117–47.

PRS Group (2013) *ICRG Methodology*, East Syracuse, NY: PRS Group.

Puntscher, S., Hauser, C., Walde, J., and Tappeiner, G. (2015) 'The impact of social capital on subjective well-being: a regional perspective', *Journal of Happiness Studies*, 16(5), 1231–46.

Putnam, R. (1995) 'Bowling alone: America's declining social capital', *Journal of Democracy*, 6(1), 65–78.

Putnam, R. (2000) *Bowling Alone: The Collapse and Revival of American Community*, New York, NY: Simon & Schuster.

Putnam, R. D., Leonardi, R., and Nanetti, R. Y. (1993) *Making Democracy Work: Civic Traditions in Modern Italy*, Princeton, NJ: Princeton University Press.

Pykett, J. (2013) 'Neurocapitalism and the new neuros: using neuroeconomics, behavioural economics and picoeconomics for public policy', *Journal of Economic Geography*, 13(5), 845–69.

Pykett, J., and Enright, B. (2016) 'Geographies of brain culture: Optimism and optimisation in workplace training programmes', Cultural Geographies, 23(1), 51–68.

Raco, M. (2007) 'Securing sustainable communities: citizenship, safety and sustainability in the new urban planning', *European Urban and Regional Studies*, 14(4), 305–20.

Radcliffe, S. (ed.) (2006) *Culture and Development in a Globalising World: Geographies, Actors and Paradigms*, London: Routledge.

Rae, D. (2010) 'Universities and enterprise education: responding to the challenges of the new era', *Journal of Small Business and Enterprise Development*, 17(4), 591–606.

Rafiqui, P.S. (2009) 'Evolving economic landscapes: Why new institutional economics matters for economic geography', *Journal of Economic Geography*, 9(3), 329–53.

Rasbash, J., Steele, F., Browne, W. J., and Goldstein, H. (2017) *A User's Guide to MLwinN: Version 3.01*, Bristol: University of Bristol.

Rattsø, J., and Stokke, H. (2014) 'Regional convergence of income and education: investigation of distribution dynamics', *Urban Studies*, 51(8), 1672–85.

Rauch, A. (2014) 'Predictions of entrepreneurial behaviour: a personality approach', in Chell, E., and Karatas-Ozkan, M. (eds.) *Handbook of Research on Small Business and Entrepreneurship*, London: Edward Elgar, pp. 165–83.

Rauch, A., Frese, M., and Sonnentag, S. (2000) 'Cultural differences in planning/success relationships: a comparison of small enterprises in Ireland, West Germany, and East Germany', *Journal of Small Business Management*, 38(4), 28–41.

Rauch, A., Frese, M., Wang, Z.-M., Unger, J., Lozada, M., Kupcha, V., and Spirina, T. (2013) 'National Culture and Cultural Orientations of Owners Affecting the Innovation–Growth Relationship in Five Countries', *Entrepreneurship and Regional Development*, 25(9/10), 732–55.

Redford, A., and Chaloner, W. H. (eds.) (1976) *Labour Migration in England, 1800–1850*, Manchester: Manchester University Press.

Reichert, F. (2016) 'How internal political efficacy translates political knowledge into political participation: evidence from Germany', *Europe's Journal of Psychology*, 12(2), 221–41.

Reid, L., and Ellsworth-Krebs, K. (2019) 'Nudge(ography) and practice theories: Contemporary sites of behavioural science and post-structuralist approaches in geography?', *Progress in Human Geography*, 43(2), 295–313.

Reinert, E. S., Ghosh, J., and Kattel, R. (eds.) (2016) *Handbook of Alternative Theories of Economic Development*, Cheltenham: Edward Elgar.

Renger, D., and Reese, G. (2017) 'From equality-based respect to environmental activism: antecedents and consequences of global identity', *Political Psychology*, 38(5), 867–79.

Rentfrow, P. J. (2010) 'Statewide differences in personality: Toward a psychological geography of the United States', *American Psychologist*, 65(6), 548–58.

Rentfrow, P. J., Gosling, S. D., and Potter, J. (2008) 'A theory of the emergence, persistence, and expression of geographical variation in psychological characteristics', *Perspectives on Psychological Science*, 3(5), 339–69.

Rentfrow, P. J., Gosling, S. D., Jokela, M., Stillwell, D. J., Kosinski, M., and Potter, J. (2013) 'Divided we stand: three psychological regions of the United States and their political, economic, social and health correlates', *Journal of Personality and Social Psychology*, 105(6), 996–1012.

Rentfrow, P. J., Jokela, M., and Lamb, M. E. (2015) 'Regional personality differences in Great Britain', *PLoS ONE*, 10(3). DOI: 10.1371/journal.pone.0122245.

Rentfrow, P. J., Jost, J. T., Gosling, S. D., and Potter, J. (2009) 'Statewide differences in personality predict voting patterns in 1996–2004 U.S. presidential elections', in Jost, J. T., Kay, A. C., and Thorisdottir, H. (eds.) *Social and Psychological Bases of Ideology and System Justification*, Oxford: Oxford University Press, pp. 314–50.

Reynolds, P. D., Bosma, N., Autio, E., Hunt, S., De Bono, D., Servais, I., Lopez-Garcia, L., and Chin, N. (2005) 'Global Entrepreneurship Monitor: data collection design and implementation 1998-2003', *Small Business Economics*, 24(3), 205–31.

Riker, W. H., and Ordeshook, P. C. (1968) 'A theory of the calculus of voting', *American Political Science Review*, 62(1), 25–42.

Roberts, B. W., Caspi, A., and Moffitt, T. E. (2003) 'Work experiences and personality development in young adulthood', *Journal of Personality and Social Psychology*, 84(3), 582–93.

Roberts, B. W., Kuncel, N. R., Shiner, R., Caspi, A., and Goldberg, L. R. (2007) 'The power of personality: the comparative predictive validity of personality traits, SES, and cognitive ability for important life outcomes', *Perspective on Psychological Science*, 2(4), 313–45.

Roberts, B. W., and Mroczek, D. (2008) 'Personality trait change in adulthood', *Current Directions Psychological Science*, 17(1), 31–5.

Roberts, B. W., Walton, K. E., and Viechtbauer, W. (2006) 'Patterns of mean-level change in personality traits across the life course: a meta-analysis of longitudinal studies', *Psychological Bulletin*, 132(1), 1–25.

Robinson, D. (2007) 'The search for community cohesion: key themes and dominant concepts of the public policy Agenda', *Urban Studies*, 42(8), 1411–27.

Robinson, J. A. (2013) 'Measuring institutions in the Trobriand Islands: a comment on Voigt's paper', *Journal of Institutional Economics*, 9(1), 27–9.

Rodríguez-Pose, A. (2001) 'Local production systems and economic performance in Britain, France, Germany, and Italy', in Crouch, C., Le Galès, P., Trigilia, C, and Voelzkow, H. (eds.) *Local Production Systems in Europe. Rise or Demise?*, Oxford: Oxford University Press, pp. 25–45.

Rodríguez-Pose, A. (2013) 'Do institutions matter for regional development?', *Regional Studies*, 47(7), 1034–47.

Rodríguez-Pose, A., and Hardy, D. (2015) 'Cultural diversity and entrepreneurship in England and Wales', *Environment and Planning A*, 47(2), 392–411.

Rodríguez-Pose, A., and Storper, M. (2006) 'Better rules or stronger communities? On the social foundations of institutional change and its economic effects', *Economic Geography*, 52(1), 1–25.

Román, C., Congregado, E., and Millán, J. M. (2011) 'Dependent self-employment as a way to evade employment protection legislation', *Small Business Economics*, 37(3), 363–92.

Romer, T. (1975) 'Individual welfare, majority voting, and the properties of a linear income tax', *Journal of Public Economics*, 4(2), 163–85.

Rothbard, N. P., and Wilk, S. L. (2011) 'Waking up on the right or wrong side of bed: start-of-workday mood, work events, employee affect, and performance', *Academy of Management Journal*, 54(5), 959–80.

Rotter, J. B. (1954) *Social Learning and Clinical Psychology*, New York, NY: Prentice Hall.

Rotter, J. B. (1960) 'Some implications of a social learning theory for the prediction of goal directed behaviour from testing procedures', *Psychological Review*, 67(5), 301–16.

Rutherford, T., and Holmes, J. (2007) ' "We simply have to do that stuff for our survival": labour, firm innovation and cluster governance in the Canadian automotive parts industry', *Antipode*, 39(1), 194–221.

Rutten, R., and Boekema, F. (2007) 'Regional social capital: Embeddedness, innovation networks and regional economic development', *Technological Forecasting and Social Change*, 74(9), 1834–46.

Rutten, R., and Boekema, F. (2012) 'From learning region to learning in a socio-spatial context', *Regional Studies*, 46(8), 981–92.

Rutten, R., and Geilssen, J. (2010) 'Social values and the economic development of regions', *European Planning Studies*, 18, 921–39.

Ryan, R. M., and Deci, E. L. (2000) 'Self-determination theory and the facilitation of intrinsic motivation, social development, and well-being', *American Psychologist*, 55(1), 68–78.

Sachs, J. (2000) 'Notes on a new sociology of economic development', in Harrison, L. E., and Huntington, S. P. (eds.) *Culture Matters: How Values Shape Human Progress*, New York, NY: Basic Books, pp. 29–43.

Sammarra, A., and Biggiero, L. (2008) 'Heterogeneity and specificity of inter-firm knowledge flows in innovation networks', *Journal of Management Studies*, 45(4), 800–29.

Sanderson, M. (1972) 'Literacy and social mobility in the industrial revolution in England', *Past and Present*, 56, 75–104.

Sauer, C. (1941) 'Forward to Historical Geography', *Annals of the Association of American Geographers*, 31(1), 1–24.

Sautet, F., and Kirzner, I. (2006) 'The Nature and Role of Entrepreneurship in Markets: Implications for Policy', Policy Primer No. 4, Mercatus Policy Series, Fairfax, VA: George Mason University.

Saxenian, A. (1994) *Regional Advantage: Culture and Competition in Silicon Valley and Route 128*, Cambridge, MA: Harvard University Press.

Saxenian, A. (2006) *The New Argonauts: Regional advantage in a global economy*, Cambridge, MA: Harvard University Press.

Saxenian, A., and Sabel, C. (2008) 'Roepke lecture in economic geography: Venture capital in the "periphery": the new argonauts, global search, and local institution building', *Economic Geography*, 84(4), 379–94.

Say J. B. (1880) *A Treatise on Political Economy*, Philadelphia, PA: Claxton, Remsen & Hoffelfinger.

Sayer, A. (2011). *Why Things Matter to People: Social Science, Values and Ethical Life*. Cambridge: Cambridge University Press.

Schilling, M. A., and Phelps, C. C. (2007) 'Interfirm collaboration networks: The impact of large-scale network structure on firm innovation', *Management Science*, 53(7), 1113–26.

Schjoedt, L. (2009) 'Entrepreneurial job characteristics: an examination of their effect on entrepreneurial satisfaction', *Entrepreneurship Theory and Practice*, 33(3), 619–44.

Schmitt, D. P., Allik, J., McCrae, R. R., and Benet-Martínez, V. (2007) 'The geographical distribution of big five personality traits: Patterns and profiles of human self-description across 56 nations', *Journal of Cross-Cultural Psychology*, 38(2), 173–212.

Schmitt-Rodermund, E. (2004) 'Pathways to successful entrepreneurship: parenting, personality, early entrepreneurial competence, and interests', *Journal of Vocational Behavior*, 65(3), 498–518.

Schneider, G., Plumper, T., and Baumann, S. (2000) 'Bringing Putnam to the European regions: on the relevance of social capital for economic growth', *European Urban and Regional Studies*, 7(4), 307–17.

Schröder, M., and Voelzkow, H. (2014) 'Varieties of regulation: how to combine sectoral, regional and national levels', *Regional Studies*, 50(1), 7–19.

Schumpeter, J. A. (1934) [2007] *The Theory of Economic Development: An Inquiry into Profits, Capital, Credit, Interest, and the Business Cycle*, New Brunswick, NJ: Transaction Publishers.

Schwab, K. (2018) *The Global Competitiveness Report 2018*, Geneva: World Economic Forum.

Schwartz, S. H. (1992) 'Universals in the content and structure of values: theoretical advances and empirical tests in 20 countries', *Advances in Experimental Social Psychology*, 25(1), 1–65.

Schwartz, S. H. (1999) 'A theory of cultural values and some implications for work', *Applied Psychology: an International Review*, 48(1), 23–47.

Schwartz, S. H. (2006) 'A theory of cultural value orientations: explication and applications', *Comparative Sociology*, 5(2/3), 137–82.

Schwartz, S. H. (2012) 'An overview of the Schwartz theory of basic values', *Online Readings in Psychology and Culture*, 2(1), DOI: 10.9707/2307-0919.1116.

Schwartz, S. H., and Rubel, T. (2005) 'Sex differences in value priorities: cross-cultural and multimethod studies', *Journal of Personality and Social Psychology*, 89(6), 1010–28.

Scott, A., and Storper, M. (2003) 'Regions, globalization, development', *Regional Studies*, 37(6/7), 549–78.

Scott, J., and Marshall, G. (1998) *Oxford Dictionary of Sociology* (2nd edn), Oxford: Oxford University Press.

Scott, W. R. (2005) 'Institutional theory: contributing to a theoretical research program', in Smith, K. G., and Hitt, M. A. (eds.) *Great Minds in Management: The Process of Theory Development*, Oxford: Oxford University Press, pp. 460–84.

Scott, W. R. (2007) *Institutions and Organizations: Ideas and Interests*, Thousand Oaks, CA: Sage.

Searle, J. R., (1995) *The Construction of Social Reality*, London: Simon & Schuster.

Sebestyén, T., and Varga, A. (2013) 'Research productivity and the quality of interregional knowledge networks', *Annals of Regional Science*, 51(1), 155–89.

Sen, A. (2009) *The Idea of Justice*, London: Allen Lane.

Sen, A. K. (1985) 'Well-being agency and freedom: the Dewey Lectures 1984', *Journal of Philosophy*, 82(4), 169–221.

Sen, A. K. (1999) *Development as Freedom*, Oxford and New York, NY: Oxford University Press.

Senik, C. (2008) 'Ambition and jealousy: income and interactions in the "old" Europe versus the "new" Europe and the United States', *Econometrica*, 75(299), 495–513.

Shane, S. (1993) 'Cultural influences on national rates of innovation', *Journal of Business Venturing*, 8(1), 59–73.

Shapero, A., and Sokol, L. (1982) 'Social dimensions of entrepreneurship', in Kent, C., Sexton, D., and Vesper, K. (eds.) *The Encyclopedia of Entrepreneurship*, Englewood Cliffs, NJ: Prentice Hall, pp. 72–90.

Shearmur, R., Carrincazeaux, C., and Doloreux, D. (2016) 'The geographies of innovations: beyond one size-fits-all', in Shearmur, R., Carrincazeaux, C., and Doloreux, D. (eds.) *Handbook on the Geographies of Innovation*, Cheltenham and Northampton, MA: Edward Elgar Publishing, pp. 1–21.

Shields, R. (1999) 'Culture and the economy of cities', *European Urban and Regional Studies*, 6(4), 303–11.

Shihadeh, E. S., and Ousey, G. C. (1998) 'Industrial restructuring and violence: the link between entry-level jobs, economic deprivation, and Black and White homicide', *Social Forces*, 77(1), 185–206.

Shneor, R., Metin Camgöz, S., and Bayhan Karapinar, P. (2013) 'The interaction between culture and sex in the formation of entrepreneurial intentions', *Entrepreneurship and Regional Development*, 25(9/10), 781–803.

Signoretta, P. E., Buffel, V., and Bracke, P. (2019) 'Mental wellbeing, air pollution and the ecological state', *Health and Place*, 57, 82–91.

Silvey, R. (2003) 'Spaces of protest: gendered migration, social networks, and labor activism in West Java, Indonesia', *Political Geography*, 22(2), 129–55.

Simmie, J., and Martin, R. (2010) 'The economic resilience of regions: towards an evolutionary approach', *Cambridge Journal of Regions, Economy and Society*, 3(1), 27–43.

Simon, H. A. (1982) *Models of Bounded Rationality: Empirically Grounded Economic Reason*, London and Cambridge, MA: MIT Press.

Simonsen, K. B. (2016) 'How the host nation's boundary drawing affects immigrants' belonging', *Journal of Ethnic and Migration Studies*, 42(7), 1153–76.

Smith, A. (1776) *The Wealth of Nations*, London: Harriman House.

Smith, A., Hargreaves, T., Hielscher, S., Martiskainen, M., and Seyfang, G. (2016) 'Making the most of community energies: three perspectives on grassroots innovation', *Environment and Planning A*, 48(2), 407–32.

Smith, D. M. (1999) 'Geography, community, and morality', *Environment and Planning A*, 31(1), 19–35.

Smith, N. (1984) *Uneven Development: Nature, Capital and the Production of Space*, Oxford: Blackwell.

Sotarauta, M., and Suvinen, N. (2018) 'Institutional agency and path creation: intentional path from industrial to knowledge city', in Isaksen, A., Martin, R., and Trippl, M. (eds.) *New Avenues for Regional Innovation Systems—Theoretical Advances, Empirical Cases and Policy Lessons*, Cham: Springer, pp. 85–104.

Spence, J. T., and Helmreich, R. L. (1978) *Masculinity and Femininity: Theory Psychological Dimensions, Correlates, and Antecedents*, Austin, TX: University of Texas Press.

Spigel, B. (2017) 'The relational organization of entrepreneurial ecosystems', *Entrepreneurship Theory and Practice*, 41 (1), 49–72.

Srivastava, S., John, O. P., Gosling, S. D., and Potter, J. (2003) 'Development of personality in early and middle adulthood: set like plaster or persistent change?', *Journal of Personality and Social Psychology*, 84(5), 1041–53.

Stam, E. (2013) 'Knowledge and entrepreneurial employees: a country-level analysis', *Small Business Economics*, 41(4), 887–98.

Stam, W., Arzlanian, S., and Elfring, T. (2014) 'Social capital of entrepreneurs and small firm performance: a meta-analysis of contextual and methodological moderators', *Journal of Business Venturing*, 29(1), 152–73.

Stark, D. (2009) *The sense of dissonance: Accounts of worth in economic life*, Princeton, NJ, and Woodstock: Princeton University Press.

Steel, P., Schmidt, J., and Shultz, J. (2008) 'Refining the relationship between personality and subjective well-being', *Psychological Bulletin*, 134(1), 138–61.

Steenkamp, J.-B. E. M. (2001) 'The role of national culture in international marketing research', *International Marketing Review*, 18(1), 30–44.

Stephan, U. (2018) 'Entrepreneurs' mental health and well-being: a review and research agenda', *Academy of Management Perspectives*, 32(3), 290–322.

Stephan, U., and Uhlaner, L. M. (2010) 'Performance-based vs. socially supportive culture: a cross-national study of descriptive norms and entrepreneurship', *Journal of International Business Studies*, 41(8), 1347–64.

Stephan, U., Uhlaner, L. M., and Stride, C. (2015) 'Institutions and social entrepreneurship: the role of institutional voids, institutional support, and institutional configurations', *Journal of International Business Studies*, 46(3), 308–31.

Stiglitz, J. E. (2013) *The Price of Inequality*, London: Penguin.

Stimson, R., Stough, R. R., and Nijkamp, P. (eds.) (2011), *Endogenous Regional Development: Perspectives, Measurement and Empirical Investigation*, Cheltenham and Northampton, MA: Edward Elgar Publishing.

Stimson, R., Stough, R., and Salazar, M. (2009) *Leadership and Institutions in Regional Endogenous Development*, Cheltenham: Edward Elgar.

Stoerring, D., and Dalum, B. (2007) 'Cluster emergence: a comparative study of two cases in North Jutland, Denmark', in Cooke, P., and Schwartz, D. (eds.) *Creative Regions: Technology, Culture and Knowledge Entrepreneurship*, Abingdon: Routledge, pp. 127–47.

Storper, M. (1997) *The Regional World: Territorial Development in a Global Economy*, London: Guilford.

Storper, M. (2005) 'Society, community and economic development', *Studies in Comparative International Development*, 39(4), 30–57.

Storper, M. (2008) 'Community and economics', in Amin, A., and Roberts, J. (eds.) *Community, Economic Creativity, and Organization*, New York, NY: Oxford University Press, pp. 37–68.

Storper, M. (2010) 'Why does a city grow? Specialisation, human capital or institutions?', *Urban Studies*, 47(10), 2027–50.

Storper, M. (2011) 'Justice, efficiency and economic geography: should places help one another to develop?', *European Urban and Regional Studies*, 18(1), 3–21.

Storper, M. (2013) *Keys to the City: How Economics, Institutions, Social Interaction and Politics Shape Development*, Oxford and Princeton, NJ: Princeton University Press.

Storper, M. Lavinas, L., and Mercado-Célis, A. (2007) 'Society, community, and development: a tale of two regions', in Polenske, K. (ed.) *The Economic Geography of Innovation*, Cambridge: Cambridge University Press, pp. 310–39.

Strauss, K. (2008) 'Re-engaging with rationality in economic geography: behavioural approaches and the importance of context in decision-making', *Journal of Economic Geography*, 8(2), 137–56.

Streeck, W. (1992) *Social Institutions and Economic Performance: Studies of Industrial Relations in Advanced Capitalist Economies*, London: Sage.

Strong, S., Overall, N. C., and Sibley, C. G. (2019) 'Gender differences in the associations between relationship status, social support, and wellbeing', *Journal of Family Psychology*, 33(7), DOI: 10.1037/fam0000540.

Stuetzer, M., Audretsch, D. B., Obschonka, M., Gosling, S. D., Rentfrow, P. J., and Potter, J. (2018) 'Entrepreneurship culture, knowledge spillovers, and the growth of regions', *Regional Studies*, 52(5), 608–18.

Stuetzer, M., Obschonka, M., Audretsch, D. B., Wyrwich, M., Rentfrow, P. J., Coombes, M., Shaw-Taylor, L., and Satchell, M. (2016) 'Industry structure, entrepreneurship, and culture: an empirical analysis using historical coalfields', *European Economic Review*, 86(1), 52–72.

Sturgis, P., Brunton-Smith, I., Kuha, J., and Jackson, J. (2014) 'Ethnic diversity, segregation, and the social cohesion of neighborhoods in London', *Ethnic and Racial Studies*, 37(8), 1286–309.

Sunley, P. (2008) 'Relational economic geography: A partial understanding or a new paradigm?', *Economic Geography*, 84(1), 1–26.

Swan, C. D., and Morgan, D. (2016) 'Who wants to be an eco-entrepreneur? Identifying entrepreneurial types and practices in ecotourism businesses', *International Journal of Entrepreneurship and Innovation*, 17(2), 120–32.

Sweida, G. L., and Reichard, R. J. (2013) 'Gender stereotyping effects on entrepreneurial self-efficacy and high-growth entrepreneurial intention', *Journal of Small Business and Enterprise Development*, 20(2), 296–313.

Syssner, J. (2009) 'Conceptualizations of culture and identity in regional policy', *Regional and Federal Studies*, 19(3), 437–58.

Szerb, L., Acs, Z. J., Autio, E., Ortega-Argilés, R., and Komlósi, É. (2013) *REDI: The Regional Entrepreneurship and Development Index—Measuring Regional Entrepreneurship Final Report*, Brussels: European Commission, Directorate-General for Regional and Urban Policy.

Tabacknick, B. G., and Fidell, L. S. (2007) *Using Multivariate Statistics*, Boston: Allyn & Bacon.

Tabellini, G. (2010) 'Culture and institutions: economic development in the regions of Europe', *Journal of the European Economic Association*, 8(4), 677–716.

Tagliaventi, M. R., and Mattarelli, E. (2006) 'The role of networks of practice, value sharing, and operational proximity in knowledge flows between professional groups', *Human Relations*, 59(3), 291–319.

Tan, J. H. W. (2006) 'Religion and social preferences: an experimental study', *Economics Letters*, 90(1), 60–7.

Taylor, B. (2015) 'Strategic and expressive voting', *Constitutional Political Economy*, 26(2), 159–70.

Tenner, E. (2018) *The Efficiency Paradox: What Big Data Can't Do*, New York: Alfred A Knopf.

Ter Wal, A., and Boschma, R. (2011) 'Co-evolution of firms, industries and networks in space', *Regional Studies*, 45(7), 919–33.

Thaler, R. H., and Sunstein, C. R. (2008) *Nudge: Improving Decisions About Health, Wealth and Happiness*, London: Yale University Press.

Thomas A. S., and Mueller S. L. (2000) 'A case for comparative entrepreneurship: assessing the relevance of culture', *Journal of International Business Studies*, 31(2), 287–301.

Thomas, J. W. (1980) 'Agency and achievement: self-management and self-regard', *Review of Educational Research*, 50(2), 213–40.

Thompson, E. P. (1993) *Customs in Common*, London: Penguin.

Thompson, F. M. L. (1981) 'Social control in Victorian Britain', *Economic History Review*, 34(2), 189–208.

Thompson, P., and Huggins, R. (2018) 'Self-employment and the relationship between personality and culture', Paper presented at the ISBE conference, November 7–8, Birmingham, UK.

Thompson, P., Jones-Evans, D., and Kwong, C. C. Y. (2010) 'Education and entrepreneurial activity: a comparison of White and South Asian men', *International Small Business Journal*, 28(2), 147–62.

Thompson, P., and Kwong, C. (2016) 'Compulsory school-based enterprise education as a gateway to an entrepreneurial career', *International Small Business Journal*, 34(6), 838–69.

Thompson, P., and Zang, W. (2018) 'The foreign business and domestic enterprise relationship: its implications for local entrepreneurial resilience', *Local Economy*, 33(1), 10–37.

Thompson, S. (2008) 'From paternalism to industrial welfare: The evolution of industrial welfare capitalism in the South Wales coalfield', Paper presented at Annual Conference of the Economic History Society, University of Nottingham, March 30, 2008.

Thornton, P. H. (1999) 'The sociology of entrepreneurship', *Annual Review of Sociology*, 25, 19–46.

Thrift, N. (2000) 'Pandora's Box? Cultural geographies of economies', in Clark, G. L., Feldman, M. P., and Gertler, M. S. (eds.) *The Oxford Handbook of Economic Geography*, pp. 689–704, Oxford: Oxford University Press.

Tiebout, C. M. (1956) 'A pure theory of local expenditures', *Journal of Political Economy*, 64(5), 416–24.

Tödtling, F., and Kaufman, A. (2001) 'The role of the region for innovation activities of SMEs', *European Urban and Regional Studies*, 8(3), 203–15.

Tomaney, J. (2014) 'Region and place I: Institutions', *Progress in Human Geography*, 38(1), 131–40.

Tomaney, J. (2015) 'Region and place III: well-being', *Progress in Human Geography*, 41(1), 99–107.

Tonge, J., Mycock, A., and Jeffery, B. (2012) 'Does citizenship education make young people better engaged citizens?', *Political Studies*, 60(3), 578–602.

Tönnies, F. (1957) *Community and Society*, New York, NY: Harper & Row.

Torre, A. (2008) 'On the role played by temporary geographical proximity in knowledge transmission', *Regional Studies*, 42(6), 869–89.

Tranter, N. (1988) *Sport, Economy and Society in Britain 1750–1914*. Cambridge: Cambridge University Press.

Trigilia, C. (1992) 'Italian industrial districts: neither myth nor interlude', in Pyke, F., and Sengenberger, W. (eds.) *Industrial Districts and Local Economic Regeneration*, Geneva: International Labour Organization, pp. 33–47.

Tupes, E. C., and Christal, R. E. (1961) *Recurrent personality factors based on trait ratings, Technical Report ASD-TR-61-97*, Lackland, TX: Personnel Laboratory Aeronautical Systems Division Air Force Systems Command, Lackland Air Force Base.

Turok, I. (2004) 'Cities, regions and competitiveness', *Regional Studies*, 38(9), 1069–83.

Tvinnereim, E., Liu, X., and Jamelske, E. M. (2017) 'Public perceptions of air pollution and climate change: different manifestations, similar causes, and concerns', *Climate Change*, 140, 399–412.

Tylor, E. B. (1871) *Primitive Culture*, Vol. 2. New York, NY: Brentano's.

Uhlaner, L., and Thurik, R. (2007) 'Postmaterialism influencing total entrepreneurial activity across nations', *Journal of Evolutionary Economics*, 17(2), 161–85.

Uzzi, B., and Spiro, J. (2005) 'Collaboration and creativity: the small world problem', *American Journal of Sociology*, 111, 447–504.

Vachundova, M. A. (2005) *Europe Undivided: Democracy, Leverage, and Integration After Communism*, Oxford: Oxford University Press.

Van den Bergh, J. C., and Stagl, S. (2003) 'Coevolution of economic behaviour and institutions: towards a theory of institutional change', *Journal of Evolutionary Economics*, 13(3), 289–317.

Van de Stadt, H., Kapteyn, A., and van de Geer, S. (1985) 'The relativity of utility: evidence from panel data', *Review of Economics and Statistics*, 67(2), 179–87.

Van de Vliert, E. (2009) *Climate, Affluence, and Culture*. Cambridge: Cambridge University Press.

Van de Vliert, E. (2013) 'Climato-economic habitats support patters of human needs, stresses, and freedoms', *Behavioral and Brain Sciences*, 36(5), 465–80.

van Hoorn, A., and Maseland, R. (2010) 'Cultural differences between East and West Germany after 1991: communist values versus economic performance?', *Journal of Economic Behavior and Organization*, 76(3), 791–804.

Van Leeuwen, M. H. D., and Maas, I. (2010) 'Historical studies of social mobility and stratification', *Annual Review of Sociology*, 36, 429–51.

Van Maanen, J., and Schein, E. H. (1979) 'Toward a theory of organizational socialization', *Research in Organizational Behavior*, 1(1), 209–64.

van Wijik, R., Jansen, J. J. P., and Lyles, M. A. (2008) 'Inter- and intra-organizational knowledge transfer: a meta-analytic review and assessment of its antecedents and consequences', *Journal of Management Studies*, 45(4), 830–53.

Vasilev, A. (2013) 'On The Cost Of Rent-Seeking By Government Bureaucrats In A Real-Business Cycle Framework', SIRE Discussion Paper, SIRE-DP-2013–84, Edinburgh: Scottish Institute for Research in Economics.

Verdier, T., and Zenou, Y. (2017) 'The role of social networks in cultural assimilation', *Journal of Urban Economics*, 97, 15–39.

Verkuyten, M. (2008) 'Life satisfaction among ethnic minorities: the role of discrimination and group identification', *Social Indicators Research*, 89(3), 391–404.

Vernon, R. (1960) *Metropolis 1985: Interpretation of the Findings of the New York Metropolitan Region Study*, Cambridge, MA: Harvard University Press.

Voigt, S. (2013) 'How (not) to measure institutions', *Journal of Institutional Economics*, 9(1), 1–26.

Vuorinen-Lampila, P. (2016) 'Gender segregation in the employment of higher education graduates', *Journal of Education and Work*, 29(3), 284–308.

Wade, R. (1987) 'The management of common property resources: finding a cooperative solution', *World Bank Research Observer*, 2(2), 219–34.

Wadhwani, R.D., and Lubinski, C. (2017) 'Reinventing entrepreneurial history', *Business History Review*, 91, 767–99.

Wainer, H. A., and Rubin, I. M. (1969) 'Motivation of research and development entrepreneurs: determinants of company success', *Journal of Applied Psychology*, 53(3), 178–84.

Watts, D. J. (1999) *Small Worlds: The Dynamics of Networks Between Order and Randomness*. Princeton: Princeton University Press.

Watts D. J., and Strogatz, S. H. (1998) 'Collective dynamics of "Small-World" networks', *Nature*, 393, 440–2.

Weber, M. (1930) *The Protestant Ethic and the Spirit of Capitalism*, London: Routledge.

Weber, M. (1947) *The Theory of Social and Economic Organization*, New York, NY: Oxford University Press.

Webster, E., Lambert, R., and Bezuidenhout, A. (2008) *Grounding Globalization: Labour in the Age of Insecurity*, Malden, MA: Blackwell.

Weckroth, M., and Kemppainen, T. (2016) 'Human capital, cultural values and economic performance in European regions', *Regional Studies, Regional Science*, 3(1), 239–57.

Wei, Y. H. D., and Ye, X. (2009) 'Beyond convergence: Space, scale, and regional equality in China', *Tijdschrift voor Economische en Sociale Geografie*, 100, 58–90.

Weiner, M. (ed.) (1966) *Modernization: The Dynamics of Growth*, New York, NY: Basic Books.

Welzel, C. (2010) 'How selfish are self-expression values? A civicness test', *Journal of Cross-Cultural Psychology*, 41(2), 152–74.

Welzel, C. (2013) *Freedom Rising: Human Empowerment and the Quest for Emancipation*, Cambridge: Cambridge University Press.

Welzel, C., and Inglehart, R. (2010) 'Agency, values, and well-being: a human development model', *Social Indicators Research*, 97(1), 43–63.

Wennberg, K., Pathak, S., and Autio, E. (2013) 'How culture moulds the effects of self-efficacy and fear of failure on entrepreneurship', *Entrepreneurship and Regional Development*, 25(9/10), 756–80.

Wennekers, S., and Thurik, R. (1999) 'Linking entrepreneurship and economic growth', *Small Business Economics*, 13(1), 27–56.

Wennekers, S., van Stel, A., Thurik, R., and Reynolds, P. (2005) 'Nascent entrepreneurship and the level of economic development', *Small Business Economics*, 24(3), 293–309.

Westlund, H., and Bolton, R. (2003) 'Local social capital and entrepreneurship', *Small Business Economics*, 21(2), 77–113.

Whitehead, M., Jones, R., Howell, R., Lilley, R., and Pykett, J. (2014) 'Nudging all over the world', ESRC Report, Swindon and Edinburgh: Economic and Social Research Council.

Whitehead, M., Jones, R., and Pykett, J. (2011) 'Governing irrationality, or a more than rational government? Reflections on the rescientisation of decision making in British public policy', *Environment and Planning A*, 43(12), 2819–37.

Whittington, K. B., Owen-Smith, J., and Powell, W. W. (2009) 'Networks, propinquity, and innovation in knowledge-intensive industries', *Administrative Science Quarterly*, 54, 90–122.

Wiklund, J., Nikolaev, B., Shir, N., Foo, M.-D., and Bradley, S. (2019) 'Entrepreneurship and well-being: past, present, and future', *Journal of Business Venturing*, 34(4), 579–88.

Williams, N., Huggins, R., and Thompson, P. (2017) 'Social capital and entrepreneurship: does the relationship hold in deprived urban neighbourhoods', *Growth and Change*, 48(4), 719–43.

Williams, R. (1958) *Culture and society, 1780–1950*, New York, NY: Columbia University Press.

Williams, R. (1989) *What I Came to Say*, London: Radius.

Williamson, O. E. (2000) 'The new institutional economics: taking stock, looking ahead', *Journal of Economic Literature*, 38(3), 595–613.

Wilson, K. L., and Portes, A. (1980) 'Immigrant enclaves: an analysis of the labour market experience of Cubans in Miami', *American Journal of Sociology*, 86(2), 295–319.

Wink, R., Kirchner, L., Koch, F., and Speda, D. (2017) 'Agency and forms of path development along transformation processes in German cities', *Cambridge Journal of Regions, Economy and Society*, 10(3), 471–90.

Witt, L. A., Burke, L. A., Barrick, M. A., and Mount, M. K. (2002) 'The interactive effects of conscientiousness and agreeableness on job performance', *Journal of Applied Psychology*, 87(1), 164–9.

Witter, R. A., Okun, M. A., Stock, W. A., and Haring, M. J. (1984) 'Education and subjective well-being: a meta-analysis', *Educational Evaluation and Policy Analysis*, 6(2), 165–73.

Wolfe, D. A. (2017) 'Innovation and creativity in city-regions', in Shearmur, R. Carrincazeaux, C., and Doloreux, D. (eds.) *Handbook on the Geographies of Innovation*, Cheltenham: Edward Elgar, pp. 174–86.

Wong, P. K., Ho, Y. P., and Autio, E. (2005) 'Entrepreneurship, innovation and economic growth: evidence from GEM data', *Small Business Economics*, 24(3), 335–50.

Woolcock, M. (1998) 'Social capital and economic development: Toward a theoretical synthesis and policy framework', *Theory and Society*, 27(2), 151–208.

Wrzus, C., and Roberts, B. W. (2017) 'Processes of personality development in adulthood: the TESSERA framework', *Personality and Social Psychology Review*, 21(3), 253–77.

Wyrwich, M. (2015) 'Entrepreneurship and intergenerational transmission of values', *Small Business Economics*, 45(1), 191–213.

Wyrwich, M., Sternberg, R., and Stuetzer, M. (2018) 'Failing role models and the formation of fear of entrepreneurial failure: a study of regional peer effects in German regions', *Journal of Economic Geography*, 19(3), https://doi.org/10.1093/jeg/lby023.

Xie, Y., and Goyette, K. (2003) 'Social mobility and the education choices of Asian Americans', *Social Science Research*, 32(3), 467–98.

Zaheer, A., and Bell, G. (2005) 'Benefiting from network position: Firm capabilities, structural holes, and performance', *Strategic Management Journal*, 26(9), 809–25.

Zaheer, A., Gözübüyük, R., and Milanov, H. (2010) 'It's the connections: The network perspective in interorganizational research', *Academy of Management Perspectives*, 24(1), 62–77.

Zaheer, A., and Soda, G. (2009) 'Network evolution: The origins of structural holes', *Administrative Science Quarterly*, 54, 1–31.

Zak, P., and Knack, S. (2001) 'Trust and growth', *Economic Journal*, 111(470), 295–321.

Závecz, G. (2017) 'Post-communist societies of Central and Eastern Europe', in Zmerli, S., and van der Meer, T. W. G. (eds.) *Handbook on Political Trust*, Cheltenham: Edward Elgar, pp. 440–60.

Zhang, J., and Peck, J. (2016) 'Variegated capitalism, Chinese style: Regional models, multi-scalar constructions', *Regional Studies*, 50(1), 52–78.

Zhang, Y., Wong, H., Chen, J.-K., and Tang, V. M. Y. (2019) 'Comparing income poverty gap and deprivation on social acceptance: a mediation model with interpersonal communication and social support', *Social Policy and Administration*, https://doi.org/10.1111/spol.12536.

Zhao, H., and Seibert, S. E. (2006) 'The big five personality dimensions and entrepreneurial status: a meta-analytical review', *Journal of Applied Psychology*, 91(2), 259–71.

Zhao, H., Seibert, S. E., and Lumpkin, G. T. (2010) 'The relationship of personality to entrepreneurial intentions and performance: a meta-analytic review', *Journal of Management*, 36(2), 381–404.

Zhao, S.X., and Tong, S.P. (2001) 'Unequal economic development in China: spatial disparity and regional policy: 1985–95', *Regional Studies*, 34(6), 549–61.

Zhou, M., Zhou, Y., Zhang, J., Obschonka, M., and Silbereisen, R. K. (2019) 'Person–city personality fit and entrepreneurial success: An explorative study in China', *International Journal of Psychology*, 54(2), 155–63.

Zijdeman, R. L. (2009) 'Like my father before me: intergenerational occupational status transfer during industrialization (Zeeland, 1811–1915)', *Continuity and Change*, 24(3), 455–86.

Zucker, L. G., Darby, M. R., and Armstrong, J. (1998) 'Geographically localized knowledge: spillovers or markets?', *Economic Inquiry*, 36(1), 65–86.

Index